# LEARNING TO WIN

THE FRED W. MORRISON
SERIES IN SOUTHERN STUDIES

# Learning to Win

Sports, Education,
and Social Change
in Twentieth-Century
North Carolina

**PAMELA GRUNDY**

The University of
North Carolina Press

Chapel Hill & London

The paper in this book meets the guidelines for perma-
nence and durability of the Committee on Production
Guidelines for Book Longevity of the Council on Library
Resources.

Library of Congress Cataloging-in-Publication Data
Grundy, Pamela.  Learning to win: sports, education, and
social change in twentieth-century North Carolina /
by Pamela Grundy.
p. cm.—(Fred W. Morrison series in Southern studies)
Includes bibliographical references and index.
ISBN 0-8078-2619-7 (cloth: alk. paper)
ISBN 0-8078-4934-0 (pbk.: alk. paper)
1. Sports—North Carolina—History—20th century.
2. College sports—North Carolina—History—20th
century.  3. School sports—North Carolina—History—
20th century.  4. Educational change—North Carolina—
History—20th century.  5. Social change—North
Carolina.  I. Title.  II. Series.
GV584.N8 G78 2001    796'.09756'0904—dc21    00-048928

Portions of this work have been published previously, in
somewhat different form, as "From Amazons to Glamazons: The Rise and Fall of North Carolina Women's Basketball, 1920–1960," *Journal of American History* 87 (June
2000): 112–46, and are reprinted with permission of the
publisher.

05  04  03  02  01    5  4  3  2  1

**To my father, Scott M. Grundy**
for whom a high school state
championship was only a beginning

# CONTENTS

# ILLUSTRATIONS

# LEARNING TO WIN

I n a dusty yard far down a rural road, a young man aims at a battered hoop that once served as a bicycle tire rim but which has been transformed into a basketball goal. As the light begins to fade, and the buzz of rural evening builds up from the ground, he lofts the ball again and again, sending the rim clattering, savoring the joy of motion and the pleasure of accomplishment. "The thing about basketball—even if there's nobody else around you can always practice on your own," David Thompson explained, years after his solitary workouts in the small black community of Boiling Springs, North Carolina, helped build him into one of the greatest basketball players the world had ever seen. "I did a lot of that. Just the satisfaction of seeing the ball go through the basket was the thing that kept me going."[1]

But for David Thompson, as for many of his peers, basketball quickly became far more than play. Between 1891, when a young man named James Naismith drew up basketball's first thirteen rules, and the mid-1950s, when Thompson first picked up a worn, brown ball, competitive athletics had grown into one of this nation's most significant cultural institutions, offering talented players countless opportunities to profit from their skills. And so David Thompson embarked on a journey that had become a cornerstone of American mythology. He left Boiling Springs, traveling first to Crest High School in the nearby town of Shelby and then to North Carolina State University, where his great leaping ability and deft sense of the game propelled the Wolfpack to the 1974 National Collegiate Athletic Association title and made him national player of the year.[2]

Thompson thus joined a pantheon of sporting heroes—Choo-Choo Justice, Wallace Wade, Sam Jones, Dean Smith, Mia Hamm, Michael Jordan—whose exploits have sunk deep into the hearts of North Carolina residents, reaching beyond the boundaries of court or field to touch the pulse of daily life. The day

Opposite: Katie Lee Griffith coached women's basketball at rural Dixie High School in the 1910s. Courtesy of Betty Berryhill McCall.

that Thompson suffered a terrifying fall during the 1974 national tournament, tumbling from above the basket and landing squarely, stunningly, on his head, the sight of his unmoving body lying on the court brought his humanity so powerfully home to one white North Carolina woman that she began to pray, promising that if Thompson's life were spared, she would never be prejudiced again. A decade after Thompson's exploits, when another North Carolina State team won an improbable national title, Charlotte resident Titus Ivory drew lessons that went well beyond the game. "Everybody had just said that N.C. State had no chance of winning that national championship," he explained. "Nobody ever gave N.C. State a chance. And when N.C. State won that game, I just threw my hands up and I said, 'Hey, anybody can win, if they just put their minds to it. And that to me just reminds me that you can't give up. You just have to play and play as if this is the last game you're going to play, and you've got to win it.'"3

Still, for all the power such celebrated exploits wield, athletics' greatest significance can be found elsewhere, in the more modest fields, courts, and gymnasiums that have become part of the landscape of American life. After the Civil War, as interest in organized sports began to spread across the country, athletics wove into the fabric of existence in myriad American communities. On small-town ball grounds, in industrial leagues, in high schools large and small, athletic contests drew a wide range of citizens to the regular rituals of football in the fall, basketball in the winter, and baseball in the spring and summer, embedding the structures and rhythms of competition—the rounds of victory and loss, of strategy and teamwork, of fortitude and failure—deeply into national life. More than almost any institution that would grace U.S. culture in the ensuing century, athletics brought communities into its orbit, ringing young and old, men and women—people of all colors and social standings—around athletic fields. The dramas that ensued would be etched into collective memories, recounted time and again in front-porch family exchanges, in Saturday morning barbershop convocations, at school reunions, in newspaper columns, and around the smoking stoves of country crossroads stores.

In this work I attempt to trace some meanings of these games, delving into the athletic history of a single state to consider what its citizens made of the many ways they played. It is a complex task. Athletic contests have proved so enthralling in part because they engage so much of human potential, demanding and displaying physical agility, mental skill, individual achievement, collective effort, and—supporters claim—great moral fortitude. At the same time, the apparent parallels between organized team competition, the clashes of democratic politics, and the developing structures of industrial capitalism transformed American athletics into a multifaceted metaphor for American society, its strengths, and its failings. The athletic clashes enacted throughout North Carolina, from the hardscrabble fields of the poorest rural communities to the palatial gymnasiums of its most lavishly endowed universities, thus embodied complex cultural dramas, testing a rich range of ingenuity and courage while providing an arena where communities engaged the tensions, possibilities, and contradictions of the world around them.[4]

The games in which North Carolina citizens would invest such emotional force formed part of a new world that took shape within the state after the Civil War. In the last decades of the nineteenth century, the Tar Heel State fell beneath the sway of the economic forces that were transforming life throughout the nation, building a world that moved not to the seasonal rhythms of agricultural endeavor but to the more rapid beat of industrial production and commercial exchange, in which success or failure depended less on the weather than on the forces of supply, demand, and competition. As growing numbers of North Carolinians began to study law and business, to trade plows and mules for the spindles and looms that drove a rapidly expanding textile industry, or to essay the treacherous waters of commercial agriculture, many also labored to remake themselves. Like their predecessors in other regions of the country, who had responded to the challenge of intricate machinery, market-driven competition, and ever larger business enterprise by schooling themselves in disciplines such as punctuality, self-restraint, hard work, and attention to detail, North Carolina's most ambitious citizens began to discard old ways of life in favor of this new vision.[5]

Nowhere did these efforts wield greater force than in the state's public schools. Schooling was taking on new significance around the country, as a wide range of citizens began to look to formal education as much as to custom or tradition to give children the skills to make their way within a rapidly changing world. Educators would also expand their goals, seeking not simply to offer academic lessons but also to promote the habits of thought and action suited to a society in which "not birth but worth" was seen to determine social position. Memorization gave way to experiment; recitation, to more active reasoning. Student performance was judged according to a set of fixed criteria, a "single standard of honor." Written examinations, numeric grades, and elaborate award ceremonies were all designed to foster application and ambition, preparing students for a world in which, one reformer argued, each citizen must "win for himself his place, and must show himself worthy of [that] place by winning it anew each day."[6]

Competitive athletics meshed neatly with many of these goals. As the games of the antebellum era—largely straightforward tests of strength and skill—gave way to contests governed by more complex rules and strategies as well as more exacting measures of success, advocates of school athletics claimed their new games taught young people many of the qualities they would need to make their way in a challenging, competitive world. Not only did sports such as football and basketball inculcate the Victorian-tinged virtues of self-discipline and steady effort, supporters argued; they also nurtured a heightened sense of competitive self-assertion that echoed the Darwinian tenor of late-nineteenth-century society. The structure of athletics, within which teams and individuals rose or fell according to their own talents and efforts, embodied the philosophy that guided graded schooling and the society whose demands it sought to meet. Although school officials did not always wholeheartedly embrace athletics, the power of these associations helped promoters of school sports make steady progress, building athletic programs into integral components of school life.[7]

For thousands of eager participants, athletics also held other attractions, offering a means to negotiate the fluid identities of an emerging modern era. The array of transformations that swept over postbellum North Carolina forced state residents to redefine identities, communities, and ideals, drawing not simply on custom and tradition but also on shifting social and economic opportunities, on reconfiguring political debates, and on the tantalizing images found in the broadening realm of market-driven popular culture. Athletic challenges that included discipline, physical self-mastery, team cohesion, and public performance created arenas in which young people could grapple with such varied influences in both body and mind, exploring their connections to the communities around them while delving into the contested realms of manhood, womanhood, and race.[8]

The powerful effects athletics worked on individuals and communities thus gave sports yet another function, as an arena for contesting the inequalities that became as integral a part of North Carolina as tobacco or sweet tea. The social order taking shape within the state was not the level playing field of patriotic rhetoric or sporting legend. Rather, it comprised an intricately patterned hierarchy of law, custom, and belief, an order most visibly embodied in the Jim Crow laws that governed racial interaction but that also divided men from women, industrialists from farmers and workers, rural from urban dwellers, South from North. Such divisions lent athletic contests added layers of significance. When teams from the state's white colleges took to the field or court, the compelling vision of vigorous, dramatic competition could seem a confirmation of the superior social position such young men enjoyed, as well as the system that had placed them at the top of state society. Conversely, the equally compelling games played at African American schools, among the state's young women, or on the dusty fields abutting textile mills mounted symbolic challenges to such ideas, demonstrating that qualities such as discipline, determination, and competitive zeal were hardly the exclusive province of a white male elite and implicitly critiquing a society built around that assumption.[9]

Athletics thus sat at the center of cross-cutting cultural currents, becoming an arena in which individuals and communities negotiated aspects of their own identities as well as their position in the state's new social order. Sports remained in part a realm of play, where participants reached into themselves to discover strength, self-confidence, and creative joy. But even as they played, athletes became inextricably entangled in the world around them. Assessments of strategy and character segued easily into discussions that ranged from business ethics to racial difference to community honor, as residents disputed or defended the shape their society had assumed and the place they occupied within it. The wide variety of uses to which athletic contests could be put offer one key to their widespread popularity; in the multifaceted society of twentieth-century America, the most successful cultural institutions have been those that can support multiple meanings, be put to many ends. Yet they also complicate efforts at interpretation. Athletic contests, like paintings, plays, or dreams, compress multiple ideas and images into singular, compelling events that can be profoundly moving but which resist easy reading, drawing aspiring interpreters in numerous directions all at once.[10]

In this work I explore this murky realm, seeking to illuminate some of these cultural currents and to understand what North Carolinians made of the many games they played. I examine dialogues that unfolded in newspaper articles, school publications, academic writings, public discussions, and private correspondence, attempting to discern the larger assumptions and debates that informed such conversations as well as the ways athletic metaphor and experience shaped approaches to the world beyond the field. I also draw extensively on oral history interviews. The stories related by coaches, fans, and athletes capture a range of experiences far broader than those fixed in the spotlight that has shone so brightly on the state's major college teams. At the same time, the memories that individuals and communities so often hold so dear offer myriad insights into the understandings these many citizens took away from their experiences, the ideas, myths, narratives, and habits of thought on which they would draw as they faced the challenges and dilemmas of their lives.[11] I build chapters from collections of these overlapping stories, seeking less to construct explicit arguments than to throw athletic narratives and events into relief, linking them to larger patterns of historical change and to insights culled from the array of works in history, folklore, and culture on which this study rests. I pursue a narrative style, with liberal use of direct quotation, in an attempt to bring varying voices and perspectives into this dialogue as fully and effectively as possible, as well as to convey at least some of the creativity and passion with which North Carolinians approached their sporting endeavors.[12]

I emphasize, of necessity, selected themes, institutions, and periods of history, concentrating on moments and places that seemed to offer especially telling insights both into sports and into the changing society they reflect and influence. I focus more on public than on private institutions because public schools reached out to the greatest share of the state's population; more on basketball and football than on baseball because baseball achieved less prominence in educational settings; more on times of conflict than on periods of calm because conflict forces participants to articulate ideas with especial clarity and force. While most of the chapters center on games that took place within a specific context—women's colleges, African American high schools, the integrating institutions of the 1960s—their themes slip through those bounds, weaving in and out of narratives much as arrays of ideas, traditions, images, and beliefs have filtered across the state's diverse communities, assuming different forms in different times and places. The choices I have made emphasize some connections and downplay others. But the result, I hope, depicts worlds both separate and connected, a broad canvas of activity across which themes and individuals diverge and intersect, somewhat as they do in the grand confusion of daily life.[13]

Through these efforts I have worked to fashion a portrait that reaches beyond the state to touch on a more broadly American history. While the South is often seen as a distinctive region of the United States, southerners were also Americans, profoundly influenced by nationwide transformations such as war, industrialization, a growing federal government, and the spreading reach of national popular culture. Within many of the South's own diverse cultures, athletics became an institution with especially close ties to this national realm. The dilemmas that North Carolinians encountered—of race, of manhood and womanhood, of the meanings of competition and the measures of success—resonated around the country, touching Americans from myriad walks of life. At the same time, the process by which North Carolinians fashioned and drew meaning from their sporting institutions, the ways they mixed local circumstance with national developments, mirrored similar processes of transformation taking place in countless other American communities. Examining the shapes that sports assumed at such profoundly local levels—how, for example, the intersecting issues of race, fairness, and the desire to win took concrete form in a white coach's decision about how many black players he would start—thus sheds light not only on the ways that national ideas take shape in local institutions but also on the process by which a culture's most profound assumptions are embodied or contested through the smallest rituals of daily life.[14]

North Carolina games also illuminate aspects of U.S. culture as a whole. One of the most powerful themes of American sporting history involves the ways that immigrants have found in sports a means not only to grasp central tenets of American life but to become American themselves. The story of North Carolina sports emphasizes that native-born citizens themselves have also had to tread this path, becoming Americans not simply by birth or inheritance but, rather, through a lifetime of engaging the circumstances and challenges of living in this country. For them as well, athletics has frequently played a major role in such endeavors. In few other countries has athletic competition been woven so completely into institution, ideology, and everyday life, encompassing, for good or ill, many key components of what passes for a common national culture. These connections have turned athletics into a particularly potent realm for discussing or debating some of the fundamental tensions that beset U.S. society. The compelling dramas that unfold on court and field have also lent emotional and intellectual force to one of this country's most powerful ideals, the vision of a free and fair society in which individuals enter the competitive fray of political, social, and economic life and rise and fall on their own merits.[15]

The ways that North Carolinians contended with these many issues, the lively force they brought to both play and debate, underscore the energy and creativity with which a wide range of Americans have approached their lives, using the materials at hand to bring meaning to the times in which they live, as well as to transform themselves and their world. In the stories told by these many individuals, tales encompassing joy and struggle, dreams and disappointments, lie many of the enduring meanings of American athletics, the challenges it has helped people meet, and the points where it has let them down. Within the confines of a modest southern state, on grassy fields, dirt courts, and hardwood floors, North Carolinians have wrestled with, bowed to, and triumphed over some of the central dilemmas of American society, issues that involve men and women, black and white, force and restraint, fairness and victory. Today, when adulation of athletic competition has reached unprecedented heights, and when the dilemmas of sportsmanship, fair play, and competitive strife confront us with particular urgency, contemplating the process by which our predecessors learned to win, as well as the many battles they waged around such thorny issues, offers insights not only into their worlds, but into ours as well.

## CHAPTER ONE

# The Fire of Rivalry

## Men's College Athletics, 1880–1901

I n the spring of 1891 the student magazine at a small African American college in Salisbury, North Carolina, set in type a curious complaint. "I don't know by whose authority, but the base ball grounds given to us by the President through the consent of the Faculty, has been trespassed upon by some person or persons taking it upon themselves to plough it up," the author fumed. "Turnips are good things in their places; the same is true of the other members of the vegetable kingdom; but nobody will say that their proper place is on a base ball field in a college where young men are during the months of April and May."[1]

With this circumspect and yet insistent plea, students at Livingstone College defended their right to play sports while at school. At Livingstone in the spring of 1891, someone had apparently concluded that the direct benefits of vegetable cultivation outweighed any advantage to be gained from hitting, throwing, or chasing small, white balls. The students' protest cast the dispute as a conflict in authority, arguing that college president J. C. Price had specifically designated the piece of ground as an athletic field and implying that the instigator of "this false step in agricultural pursuits" disagreed with that decision. But beneath the issue of who controlled school property ran the implication that the action also voiced a broader protest, declaring that Livingstone's students should not take time from their studies for the frivolity of games. The complaint's anonymous author certainly suspected some such message was intended, observing, "It's rather strange to me that out of fifty acres of land, the base ball diamond should be the best acre on which to grow turnips, cabbage, water melons etc."[2]

Livingstone College records do not reveal whether the students carried out a threat to retrieve their field by means of "a mighty big turnip pulling." Still, their cause was on the rise. Like basketball, football, and other "modern" sports that took shape in the last half of the nineteenth century, baseball was far more than just a game. The sport retained a rural air—its grassy field, the absence of a

Livingstone College in 1910. While sports met with initial resistance at the school, they soon became an established institution. Note the baseball field at left. From *An Appeal for the Girls' New Building*; photograph courtesy of the North Carolina Collection, University of North Carolina Library, Chapel Hill.

clock. But its play was governed less by custom or tradition than by a set of written rules applicable across social and geographical divides. It also called for a blend of precise action, team coordination, and increasingly elaborate strategy that tied it tightly to the rhythms and demands of the new society beginning to emerge within North Carolina's borders. The Livingstone dispute thus augured a wholesale transformation in the way North Carolinians approached their daily lives, one that would raise athletic contests to unprecedented significance in educational affairs.[3]

Before the Civil War, most North Carolinians lived in largely self-sufficient isolation between the mountains that rose at one end of the state and the treacherous coastline that lay along the other. A small number of planters and a few middle-class professionals dominated the realms of commerce and state government, and the bulk of the state's residents, its small-scale farmers and enslaved African Americans, focused on agricultural production and on small communities of family and friends. Plantations operated as worlds unto themselves. Family farmers pursued seasonal rounds of planting and harvest punctuated by occasional community gatherings and by worship in small religious congregations. Even the inhabitants of the hundreds of trading towns scattered throughout the state kept largely to themselves. In Charlotte, with an antebellum population that barely topped 2,000 inhabitants, connections to the wider world could seem so insignificant that a resident would later recall, "Mail was not of much importance, as few expected to get any."[4]

After the cataclysm of the Civil War, however, North Carolinians were pulled with alarming speed into a very different world. The hills and rushing streams that rolled through the middle portion of the state had been unsuited to plantation agriculture, but they proved ideal for water-powered industry. As regional boosters began to preach the gospel of the New South, eager entrepreneurs began building dozens of "manufactories"—mostly textile mills—throughout the Piedmont region. As production grew and railroad-building spread, towns that had once been little more than crossroads and trading posts began to hum with commerce, becoming home to dry goods stores, pharmacies, railroad depots, livery stables, cotton warehouses, wagon-building establishments, grocers, tailors, booksellers, gun merchants, and a whole host of other businesses. North Carolinians who had once tended plows or homes found themselves divining the intricate mechanisms of textile looms, elbowing through packs of strangers on newly laid city streets, or standing behind store counters, ringing up cash sales, keeping an eye on competitors' prices, and placing orders for whatever goods had lately come into fashion.[5]

Such wrenching change nurtured both great hope and great concern. The havoc the Civil War had wreaked on the state's old social order held out new opportunities for citizens once at the margins of state life—newly freed African Americans and whites who lacked the benefits of family wealth or position. The expansion of voting rights gave many residents a new voice in state affairs. But the resulting scramble to reshape state society also fostered deep anxiety. As growing numbers of state residents ventured into the heady realms of commerce, and as the deferential politics of the antebellum era gave way to a more energetically contested democracy, metaphors of competition gained new prominence, particularly among the members of the state's expanding middle class, which was coming to dominate public affairs. Proclaimed in newspaper editorials, in college lecture halls, and in political speeches, these visions wove tightly into public discourse, depicting a world that frequently seemed to mirror the Darwinian struggles that were capturing the imagination of many of the nation's social thinkers.

"This is a practical age, one in which each individual or corporation is striving to outstrip every other in the attainment of the supremacy; whether in the accumulation of property, the winning of fame, the monopolizing of industries or the aggrandizement of public patronage," African American political activist Annie Blackwell cautioned a Charlotte Young Men's Christian Association (YMCA) audience in 1897. "Every one is pushing ahead trying to be foremost in the race." An alumnus of white Davidson College echoed these words in the school's student magazine, warning students that "to win success amid these conditions involves not alone resolute purpose and unresting effort, but a keen eye to the economy of time and energy, that not an hour be lost or ill-employed—not an impulse of energy be misapplied or wasted." Livingstone College alumnus William Fonvielle veered into near-apocalyptic prose as he urged the school's new graduates to gird themselves for the challenges that lay ahead. "A great battle is raging out here," he wrote. "If you come out prepared—if you are competent, there is plenty of room. If you are not prepared, it is very doubtful whether or not you can find a place on which to stand. The lists of incompetents are already crowded; and every month, every day, yea, every hour records the undoing of some one, some incompetent borne to the rear; forced to the wall; unhorsed, unmitred, unfrocked; beaten down by a stronger antago-nist—suffocated by the great army of the unprepared."[6]

In the midst of such wide-ranging transformations, North Carolina's male collegians made their first forays into organized athletics. Sports caught the spirit of the new age. The contests on the field seemed to mirror the competitive conditions prevailing in the society at large, and the discipline, self-assertion and reasoned strategy that sports were credited with teaching meshed neatly with the qualities required for business and political success. But newly popular athletic games would also become a focus for debate. The economic, political, and cultural struggles that marked the last decades of the nineteenth century reached to the very heart of North Carolina society, disputing the direction of economic growth, the coutours of manhood and womanhood, the lessons of history, and the meanings of race. Athletics, which would become so closely tied to male identity, would throw many of these issues into relief, as the often bitter struggles over athletic programs mirrored the national rise of a new vision of manly prowess and played into the state's increasingly polarized racial politics. The young men who loped across the state's fields and gridirons were thus engaged in larger cultural endeavors, with stakes far higher than the final score.

As North Carolinians labored to remake themselves in a new image, the task took on especial urgency in North Carolina colleges, which were charged with the daunting work of preparing the state's youth to take their places in a chang-ing world. Before the Civil War the University of North Carolina and the state's handful of denominational schools had catered largely to the sons of the south-ern slaveholding elite. Secure in the assumption that such privilege would assure their future, many of that era's students had taken their studies lightly, spending the bulk of their time developing rhetorical skills, forging social connections, devising ingenious pranks, and defending personal honor. But after the war, the number of colleges and the stakes for success grew rapidly. New institutions sprang up around the state, among them church-funded schools for African Americans, newly ambitious women's colleges, and state-sponsored institutions for agriculture and teacher training. Within the walls of all these schools, a new generation of faculty members focused on teaching a wide range of students the skills required to negotiate the era's new opportunities.[7]

Both faculty and students approached their labors with a sense of mission, working to build what many called a New South. Frequently attributing the South's military defeat to its lack of industrial might, North Carolinians at established institutions labored to remake themselves along more modern lines, seeking to "keep step with the century in its march of knowledge, invention and discovery." At newer schools, women and African Americans seized on higher learning not simply as a means toward regional prosperity but also as a way to carve out spaces for themselves within North Carolina society. "In no way can the real manhood of the Race be more forcibly demonstrated than in the realm of the intellect," Livingstone president Joseph Price argued in 1893, echoing the faith so many African Americans were placing in education as an avenue toward racial advancement. "For in the intellect is discerned the chief mark of difference between human beings and the lower order of animals. In fact, it is the intellect that exalts and dignifies the animal in human beings. It ennobles every phase of human life."[8]

The energy that North Carolina's educators poured into their tasks showed particularly clearly in the efforts of John Franklin Crowell, who became president of Trinity College in 1887. The Pennsylvania-born educator had come to North Carolina while still in his twenties, determined to remake southern higher education in the image of northeastern schools, most notably his alma mater, Yale. He threw himself into the work with a vengeance. When he arrived, Trinity College was a rural, Methodist school with limited enrollment, focused largely on producing candidates for the ministry. Crowell entertained far grander visions. He raised money to consolidate and expand the library. He encouraged scientific research, hired new faculty members with specialized training, and helped shift the curriculum away from textbook recitations, emphasizing instead lectures and experiments. He fought for the faculty's right to express political opinions without fear of censure. Perhaps most significantly, he engineered a move from the Randolph County countryside into the growing town of Durham and secured the assistance of some of the region's prominent industrialists, most notably tobacco magnate Washington Duke, for whom the school would eventually be renamed.[9]

The students arriving at college gates throughout the state were equally determined. Colleges were inundated with requests for admittance, frequently from young people with exceedingly modest backgrounds. At Livingstone College, W. F. Fonvielle recounted, "a young man, possessing more zeal than money, called upon the President one night, and when he had left off speaking it was made known that he lived where the tides ebb and flow, and that he had walked two hundred fifty-five miles of the two hundred ninety. It is needless to say that this young man had nothing, save himself and a great desire to drink from the fountain of knowledge, to recommend him. He had but one shirt. . . . For a time this young man went to school in the daytime and at night washed his clothes and dried them by the heat of the stove."[10]

Walter Lingle, who entered Davidson College in the fall of 1888, recounted a similar experience. Presbyterian-funded Davidson, founded in 1836, was far from an imposing institution. Although the school's buildings boasted neoclassical facades, they had no electricity, no running water, and no indoor plumbing. The dormitory had no furniture; the classrooms, no desks. The adjoining town had no paved roads, although Lingle recalled that town leaders "took a great step forward, in my student days, in making a sidewalk on the west side of Main Street, by laying two planks, about a foot wide, in parallel lines for several hundred yards." But Lingle, a farmer's son who had recently lost his father, counted himself highly fortunate to be at school and was determined to succeed. His classmates were similarly situated. "Many of them were from the country and had very little money and less polish, but they meant business."[11]

Students such as Fonvielle and Lingle approached their educations with a mixture of excitement and trepidation, anticipating the rewards that lay ahead but concerned about their chances for success in an increasingly competitive world. As well as imbibing the new curriculum their professors offered, students sought to shape their character to meet the challenges they expected to confront. Just as their northeastern counterparts had responded to the demands of a complex, commerce-based world by focusing on hard work and sober self-control, North Carolinians filled their student writings with odes to Victorian-tinged character development. A banner at Livingstone College encouraged students to be "Prudent, Resolute, Industrious, Courteous, Economical." At schools throughout the state, students exhorted one another to work harder, to be more punctual, to develop greater discipline, to read more widely, and to study the lives of successful individuals. The world they planned to enter was nothing like the one their parents knew, and they saw their education not as a rite of passage but as a crucial period of transformation.[12]

"Life at college is intense," wrote a Davidson College student in 1897. "Influences here are perhaps stronger than anywhere else." A year later a young woman at Greensboro's Normal and Industrial College urged her fellow scholars to take full advantage of the opportunities the institution offered. "There is probably no other period in our lives during which our lives and our characters receive a more decided impetus for good or bad," she wrote, warning that "if we are content to drift with the tide through these years, we will find ourselves helpless to battle with the great waves of after life." Horace Williams, who had arrived at the University of North Carolina from the small, rural community of Holly Ridge, marked the break even more sharply, writing in his autobiography that "entering the University of North Carolina was a birthday for me."[13]

Such transformations ranged well beyond intellectual development. As students worked to shape themselves to a new way of life, their writings frequently touched on physical well-being, advocating efforts to fit body as well as mind to new demands. An 1896 article in the *Davidson Monthly* that bore the economically apt title "Marginal Hours" argued for the value of physical exertion by placing it squarely within a worldview that focused on rational calculation and long-term planning. The essay began with a typically alarming portrait of the world, stating that "competition is growing thicker and fiercer, contesting every step, the standards of efficiency are daily becoming more severely exacting, and the significance of superior training is being more sharply emphasized." Within these Darwinian conditions, the author argued, success depended on taking extraordinary measures, on putting every waking moment to productive use, even though "there are some who will say that if the price of success involves the application of definite planning and purpose to even one's spare or 'free' time, then it is too much to expect, and they refuse to accept the conditions." Rather than suggest that a young person's extra time be put to extra work, the author recommended that spare moments be spent exercising: "Knowing that continuous hard study tends steadily to overthrow the equilibrium between mind and body unless the body also is exercised continuously the student cannot do better than devote his marginal time to a compensating development of the body."[14]

In the antebellum era, student athletic efforts had been linked to rebellion. The most popular endeavor at many schools was "bandy" or "shimmy," a contact sport that involved few rules and frequent injuries, and whose exuberantly chaotic violence represented, in the words of one Chapel Hill graduate, a "ceaseless, tremendous, vigorous kick by the entire student body against every regulation of the Faculty." Postwar athletics would at times serve similar purposes, as young men found the joy of movement and the rushing emotion of competitive games a welcome alternative to increasing academic demands. But this new generation of athletics would be cast in far more serious terms, as supporters began to turn the pleasures of physical activity to more productive ends, describing organized sports as useful outlets for youthful energies and beginning to link the traits of character developed on the playing field to those they sought to nurture in other college endeavors.[15]

"A sound mind plus a sound body equals a good man," a Livingstone student wrote in the fall of 1890. "Let everyone heed this. To cultivate the mental and neglect physical training hazards our possibilities for future usefulness." Horace Williams, writing from his lofty position as chairman of the University of North Carolina philosophy department, waxed even more enthusiastic, arguing in 1893 that "athletics is as necessary to the success of an institution and as legitimate a part of our life as my own department." He then continued:

> I wish you could see the transformation that has taken place in the life of our students since the introduction of athletics three years ago. Then the picture was this: In the afternoon boys gather slowly in a room. First jokes, then cigarettes, then cards, then dirtier jokes. Supper, more cigarettes, more jokes. Nine o'clock p.m.—the boy's blood is up, nothing but wine and women will suffice. . . . Now the picture is this: About four p.m., boys begin to gather on the field. Lazy play and guying, good play and applause. Tons of fresh air taken in, muscles strained, mind refreshed and quickened, then a bath, then supper, then the boy feels at peace with himself and the world, his blood is cool, his head clear, his muscles are weary. Nine p.m., and his eyes are so heavy that he can't stand it; he tumbles into bed and sleeps the child's sleep. . . . Next morning in the class room, there is a man to lecture to. He braces everything about him. Pile on the work; he smiles. No burden makes him sick. His heart is stout.[16]

A year later, when the university inaugurated an *Alumni Quarterly* designed to keep its growing numbers of alumni interested in school activities, athletics received even more fulsome praise. In one article no less a figure than President George Tayloe Winston compared the existing program to the unchecked energies of earlier years, contrasting the discipline of athletics with the older era of schoolboy pranks. "Animal exuberance abounds, but overflows into new and healthful channels of energy," Winston wrote.

> No power has been repressed. The energy that formerly spent itself in riotous living, nocturnal revels or vociferous rowdyism is now happily and enthusiastically and healthfully employed on the athletic grounds. The college Hercules of to-day scorns to carry off city gates or to lug bullocks into third-story recitation rooms. His glory is on the ball ground; his prowess is in manly conflict with his peers; his preparation is in carefully regulated diet, in self-sworn abstinence from late hours, lust and liquor, and in daily drinking deep drafts of pure air into lungs expanding responsive to manly exercise and enthusiasm. His physical exuberance is not slept off, nor eaten off, nor drunk off. It is worked down, and converted into healthful energy. He weighs himself on the athletic scales, goes on the ball-grounds and in ninety minutes

works off from two to eight pounds of vice, idleness and corruption com-
monly known as fat.

The article concluded with a statement that echoed Horace Williams's enthusiasm, asserting, "It would be dishonest not to say that the greatest force in the
life of the University to-day contributing to sobriety, manliness, healthfulness
and morality generally is athletics."[17]

Students at North Carolina schools pursued a variety of activities. They
played baseball, ran track, and even tried their hands at the brand-new game of
basketball, invented in 1891. But these efforts were overshadowed by the game
that would become indelibly linked with colleges around the country: the
recently created sport of football. The first football rules had been hammered
out among Ivy League schools during the 1870s. The new game spread quickly
throughout the country, and by the 1890s dozens of schools were taking part.
The first southern game was played in 1877, and a decade later, in 1888, Trinity
College met the University of North Carolina in a game described as the first
example of "scientific" football in the state ("scientific" meant the game was
played according to official rules). African American colleges picked up the
trend as well. In the winter of 1892, a year and a half after Livingstone students
defended their right to a baseball field, a Livingstone football team played
Charlotte-based Biddle University in the nation's first football game between
black schools.[18]

During the 1890s football would ascend from such modest beginnings to a
major campus event—and a major source of strife. The 1890s would prove a decade of extraordinary conflict in North Carolina—and throughout the nation—
as a wide range of Americans struggled for control over social and economic
changes that were refashioning the country in innumerable ways. Such conflicts
would reverberate to the deepest levels of North Carolina society, engaging,
among other issues, what it meant to be a man. Football, with its blend of
strategy and force, would become a potent symbol for the debates that resulted.
Even as the sport's advocates lauded "animal exuberance" and "manly conflict,"
dedicated critics cast it as a "source of evil" and an unruly "craze." But by the
end of the decade, as one group of North Carolinians emerged triumphant
from the state's political fray, football, too, would have vanquished its opponents, becoming a celebrated model for a new kind of manhood and firmly
establishing a long-term influence over state and national culture.[19]


As football spread into North Carolina, its proponents touted not only its
physical benefits but also the way it shaped the character of its participants.

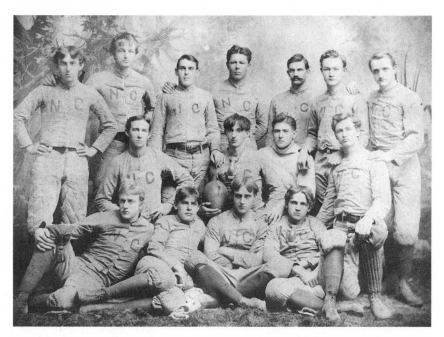

One of the University of North Carolina's first football teams, 1890s. Note the nose guards and makeshift, somewhat tattered uniforms. Courtesy of the North Carolina Collection, University of North Carolina Library, Chapel Hill.

Yale's Walter Camp, a football pioneer and clock manufacturing executive, eloquently described the way that football encouraged "team work, strategy and tactics," later claiming that the sport had "come to be recognized as the best school for instilling into the young man those attributes which business desires and demands." Southern supporters seized on such language, using metaphors that combined traits of character with those of industrial production. John Franklin Crowell saw football as a "new educational force." University of North Carolina professor (and future president) F. P. Venable went even farther. "No half-way work will answer," he wrote in 1894. "A player must bring out every power, must develop to the utmost every faculty, must learn thorough self-control, must work for the team and not for himself, must make himself part of a perfectly working machine, must be full of nerve and pluck and strategy."[20]

The demands of athletics, Venable contended a few years later, could prove even more significant than classroom work, particularly for graduates who chose careers in the expanding realms of commerce: "To the average college graduate, who finds his life-work in the busy mart, the facts, so painfully gathered in his college days, are soon lost in a haze of forgetfulness, but the power of sharp analysis, of logical thought, of concentration of mind, in fact of general mental control and self-mastery is never lost until old age dims all faculties; and these are the gifts which make him successful and useful."[21]

This new sporting zeal, however, represented more than a growing interest in self-discipline and efficient use of time. It also focused on the supposedly exalting power of intense competition, particularly in matches between schools. In the view of Horace Williams, it was precisely such heated encounters, where honor and reputation were at stake, that inspired young men to draw forth their greatest efforts and achieve their most splendid results. "Just as you cannot educate a boy at home, but must throw him into competition with boys from other homes, so the athlete needs the fire of rivalry with another spirit to win him to his fullest powers," Williams wrote. The crowds that began to attend intercollegiate matches and the excitement that the contests generated on many campuses testified to the popularity of this new vision of school sports.[22]

Still, even as students picked school colors and eager spectators began their pilgrimages to college football fields, these new activities sparked considerable conflict, illuminating several of the cleavages that marked North Carolina's emerging society. While young educators such as Horace Williams and John Franklin Crowell linked school sports with the vigorous spirit required to approach late-nineteenth-century challenges, other North Carolinians were more skeptical—often with good reason. Even as the greater effort and emotion invested in heated competition offered the possibility of greater rewards, they also held greater dangers. Athletics has always had the power to call forth strong emotions, giving the clash of rivals an attraction that often seems to transcend rationality. College sports in the 1890s were thus enticing and foreboding, suggesting forces that could easily get out of hand. The fire of rivalry might spur students on to better efforts. But it might also jump its confines, threatening the fragile order in the world that lay beyond the field. In the midst of one of the most turbulent decades in state and national history, many North Carolinians worried that students would lose sense of who they were, would be swept by a tide of emotion beyond the cherished edge of rational control.

While many critics painted a still-familiar portrait of college sports as unproductive distractions from the real goals of education, suggesting that institutions engage in "battles of brains instead of useless trials of muscle" and noting that young men could be "taught to play football at a much less price than $300 a year," a key element of the nineteenth-century sports debate focused on broader issues of self-control. Football's sudden popularity was frequently referred to as a "craze," suggesting a movement out of kilter. Although writing with tongue in cheek, Davidson students caught both the energy and the flavor of irrationality in the game's rapid spread, remarking, "We fear ere long it in company with its devotees, will be thrust back into the dark regions of oblivion

A scene from the first Alabama-Auburn football contest, 1892. Limited padding and often chaotic play made early football a dangerous endeavor. Courtesy of Duke University Archives.

with no sound issuing forth save the sad and bitter wail, 'What fools we mortals be, who were so strangely led astray by the foot-ball craze.' "[23]

The realities of nineteenth-century athletics lent such concerns considerable credence. Even as supporters of athletics lauded qualities such as discipline, teamwork, and character building, the raw violence that infused many sports often made such words ring hollow. Walter Lingle, who eventually became president of Davidson College, described intramural football at his school in words that said little about the game's educational potential. "The forward pass had not yet been introduced," Lingle wrote in his memoirs. "A player could run on a fumbled ball if he was lucky enough to get it. There was no referee with a whistle to blow a signal to down the ball. The player who had the ball could crawl with it after he had been tackled, and the whole opposing team would pile on him until he cried, 'Down!' If he did not have enough breath left in him to give that signal it was just too bad."[24]

Football's advocates spent much of the late nineteenth century constructing bulwarks of "scientific" rules, trying to erect a structure that encouraged the intensity of conflict while keeping it within accepted bounds. Their efforts, however, did not necessarily reduce violence. Success in football rested on forceful forward motion, and students of the game eventually reasoned that the most foolproof way to move down the field was to form a solid mass of players around the man holding the ball—a formation known as the flying wedge—and batter through an equally massed defense. The frequent injuries and periodic deaths produced by such a strategy only heightened criticisms of the sport. And even the most careful planning seems to have provided only a partial shield against the powerful emotions football games called forth. In developments that proved much more disturbing than a few afternoons of missed classwork, the fire of rivalry threatened to escape the carefully drawn lines around the field and enter a society already fraught with emotions far more troubling than Frank Venable's nerve and pluck.[25]

Descriptions of early games suggest that organizers sometimes struggled to maintain strict bounds around the contests, preventing the conflict from spilling beyond the field. The accounts of college contests that began to appear in North Carolina newspapers typically mentioned good feelings after games, suggesting that despite the intensity of the actions on the ground, the players were engaged in the common endeavor of preparing themselves and their opponents for future leadership. A newspaper account of Trinity's 1888 victory over the University of North Carolina described the game in such fraternal terms: "The very finest of feeling prevailed between the two teams . . . and at the close of the game the University gave three cheers for Trinity, which were returned with a will." Such glowing words, however, could mask the intensity of emotion that sports inspired. John Franklin Crowell later recalled that the game in question sparked an event that failed to reach newspaper readers: an argument between two of the players that ended with a challenge to a duel. The two players had already chosen seconds and were about to set a time for their encounter when Crowell intervened, attempting to redraw the boundary between the contest and the world outside by explaining "that I believed that in the intensity of football playing such misunderstanding were perfectly natural; as a rule, however, no insulting intent inhered in things said or done on the field of contest."[26]

The presence of alcohol at games contributed to concerns about disorder. Drinking quickly became an institution both on and off the field, and in a region where the hotly contested politics of temperance underlined larger concerns about modern self-control, such indulgence became a thorny issue. "In behalf of all lovers of pure athletics, we wish to enter an urgent protest against the custom of using intoxicants on the foot-ball field," the *Davidson College Magazine* reported in 1899. "In two of the games played this year, whiskey was openly administered to players when they were hurt or winded. To do this, in the presence of ladies, and under the authority of the management of the team is certainly degrading, and tends to arouse public sentiment against the game. It is a sad thing to see young men use intoxicants, but to see them openly encouraged in doing so is shameful."[27]

Spectator actions, often under alcoholic inspiration, provoked even greater concerns. Sports-related riots did not become as much of an institution in North Carolina as they did in some northern cities, where football games regularly sent hordes of students rampaging through city streets. Still, the possibility of violence remained quite real. Walter Lingle described one such outbreak when a group of Davidson students turned out to watch a black baseball team from nearby Concord play a black team from the town of Davidson on the college field. "The game went beautifully for a while, but unfortunately a Negro spectator from Concord got in front of a hot-tempered student from the town of Davidson," Lingle recalled.

> The student ordered him to get out of his line of vision. As he didn't move promptly the student cut him with a riding whip. He got out of the way and said nothing, but another Negro took it up and used some abusive language to the student and made as if he was ready to fight. The student drew his pistol. The Negro ducked into the crowd with the student right after him with drawn pistol. He did have sense enough not to shoot into the crowd. As the Negro emerged from the crowd he was right under the window where I sat, with the student a few paces behind. When the student was immediately under my window he fired at the Negro, who was running in the direction of the Richardson athletic field.[28]

Back on the field, Lingle continued, "pandemonium reigned supreme. Some students got hold of the baseball bats and were swinging them right and left. The field was soon cleared and nobody was really hurt. Later the Concord team sent a friendly Davidson Negro to the students asking if they might have their bats and sweaters. The request was speedily granted and the incident was closed. But it might have been terrible, and all on account of a hot temper."[29]

The uncertain dynamics of emotion and restraint made college football a precarious undertaking in the late nineteenth century, circumstances reflected in the varying support North Carolina institutions offered varsity teams. Despite the objections of some faculty, including President Kemp Plummer Battle (who called the sport "an incitement to drinking and rowdyism"), the University of North Carolina played regularly after 1888. Although the faculty of Davidson College held out against student pleas for intercollegiate games until 1898, after that the school competed on a regular basis. By the mid-1890s, however, several schools had taken a different path, choosing to stop the sport entirely. Shortly after the 1892 Livingstone-Biddle contest, Biddle faculty banned football from the school. Wake Forest College eliminated the game in 1895. And in a particularly dramatic confrontation, one that highlighted a growing split between diverging views of manly character within the state, Trinity College's Methodist trustees ordered ardent football supporter John Franklin Crowell to purge the game from his program.[30]

In Crowell's mind, football had undergirded all his efforts to transform Trinity into a thriving, modern institution. In his memoirs he described football in glowing terms, speaking of its "value in developing prowess, preventing softness of life in student communities, and sustaining prolonged self-sacrifice for team practice and team efficiency," as well as the sport's encouragement of "virility, self-control and daring courage." Football enthusiasts did run certain risks, he admitted, describing the "danger of exaggerating the athletic over the intellectual, of substituting a physical for a mental enthusiasm." He remained, however, firmly convinced that football had played a major role in the goal that he and his white peers pursued with such zeal: training young white southern men to meet the challenges of raising their region from the wreckage of the Civil War into the modern, industrial world. Football's "tendency to excesses," Crowell later explained, paled "when set over against the one great asset of the larger, more virile, and victorious sense of young manhood as the dominant note in the Southern youth's new outlook upon life."[31]

Trinity College trustees were less sanguine about the sport's significance. The many transformations Crowell worked upon the college produced considerable concern among trustees, who still viewed the world around them according to older visions of moral order, and who defined manhood not by physical dominance but by a superior capacity for reason and self-control. Throughout the first part of the nineteenth century, this religion-tinged vision of self-development had dominated college instruction and middle-class ideals, calling on young men to build character by mastering themselves through individual battles with vices such as anger or dissipation. Within this worldview, athletic metaphors had invoked the foot races or wrestling matches described in the Bible, contests that were generally viewed in terms of obstacles to spiritual growth rather than strife with human opponents. An Atlanta minister who addressed Davidson College's Philanthropic and Eumean societies in 1892 offered a typical example of this older worldview. Casting his character-building exhortations in a mix of military and athletic images, the Reverend Dr. Strickler promised each of his listeners that "every difficulty overcome will be a captured gun for his ornament in the battle of life" and advised them that "conflict with difficulty is the only means of developing our power. Difficulty is the gymnasium in which real men are developed."[32]

The rise of intercollegiate sports marked a sharp shift in these visions of athletic contests, moving the ground from individual development to competi-

Two Trinity College football players pose manfully for the camera, 1890s. Courtesy of
Duke University Archives.

tive rivalry and placing a new emphasis on physical accomplishment. Throughout the South, religious leaders frequently condemned both developments.
Emory College president Warren Candler, joining in laments that regional
development gave southerners no "time to be anything more than money-
making or business machines," questioned the "materialistic psychology" reflected in concerns over winning or losing athletic contests. Other critiques
plumbed even deeper, casting the dispute in terms of fundamental questions
about human nature. Where John Franklin Crowell saw in football a "virile and
victorious sense of young manhood," religiously minded critics frequently denounced the sport in terms of an age-old spiritual war with the animalistic
temptations of the flesh, linking it with "mere animal currents" and "the lower
impulses of the physical man."[33]

   At Trinity the struggle over these competing visions of manhood came to a
head in the early 1890s. Although trustees were uneasy about the secular turn
apparent in many of Crowell's reforms, football became the dominant symbol
of the dispute. In 1892 North Carolina Methodists' Western Conference informed Trinity's trustees that football was "a source of evil, and of no little evil,
and ought to be stopped." Crowell ignored the warning and pressed on with his
program, mounting a staunch defense of the virtues of athletic competition. In
the fall of 1893, however, the trustees presented Crowell with a stark rebuke and
demanded that football at Trinity stop immediately. Crowell resigned shortly
afterward, becoming perhaps the first college president in U.S. history to lose his
job over a football dispute. Trinity would not resume the sport until the 1920s.[34]


Like the Livingstone College turnip planter, however, Trinity trustees sought to
stem a rising tide. The forceful physicality that staunch Methodists denounced
in terms of "animal currents" and "lower impulses" met with far greater favor
elsewhere in state and national society, particularly among a rising generation
of young white men. For members of the nation's Anglo-Saxon elite, who saw
themselves as the rightful leaders of U.S. society, the democratic tumult of the
late nineteenth century had sparked an alarming spate of self-recrimination.
As European immigrants and freed African Americans began to acquire political and economic power, Anglo-Saxon leaders worried about losing their influence over American society. Such concerns frequently surfaced in condemna-
tions of young men's physical condition. The circumstances of modern life,
particularly the many hours men had begun to spend at study or at an expanding range of professional desk jobs, often became the culprit of this scenario,
inspiring alarmist terms such as "nervous," "hysterical," "soft-muscled," "paste-
complexioned," "over-refinement," and even "womanized."[35]

The solution these worried young Anglo-Saxons seized involved indulging precisely those impulses that Victorian propriety had condemned, the "primitive" energies of physical force. "In a perfectly peaceful and commercial civilization such as ours there is always a danger of laying too little stress upon the more virile virtues—upon the virtues which go to make up a race of statesmen and soldiers, of pioneers and explorers," Theodore Roosevelt, the nation's most prominent exponent of this new vision of manhood, wrote in 1893. "These," he continued, "are the very qualities which are fostered by vigorous, manly out-of-door sports, such as mountaineering, big-game hunting, riding, shooting, rowing, football and kindred games." Like most of his contemporaries, Roosevelt drew on the newly popular philosophy of Social Darwinism, which cast human history in terms of competition not between individuals but between entire races, and he targeted his exhortations to develop virile virtues, including his advocacy of college football, specifically at Anglo-Saxon men.[36]

The intense emotion that football brought out in its defenders suggests the high stakes they held in the version of manhood that the game was seen to foster. As well as dismissing the sport's "tendency to excesses," some football supporters proved willing to accept even the violent deaths that had become a not-uncommon aspect of the game. In 1897, for example, a young man named Von Gammon died from injuries received in a contest between the University of Georgia and the University of Virginia, becoming one of more than a dozen young men killed playing the sport during its early years. Still, a resulting movement to ban college football met with stiff resistance, including from Von Gammon's mother. Invoking the symbolic significance that football was coming to hold for masculine development, Rosalind Burns Gammon urged the Georgia governor not to sign a bill banning the sport, arguing that her son would want the game to continue, because of his support for "all manly sports, without which he deemed the highest type of manhood impossible." Oliver Wendell Holmes Jr. put the matter more directly, claiming that football deaths were "a price well paid for the breeding of a race fit for headship and command."[37]

The risks that football's supporters were willing to run hinted at the depth of concerns about their place in a changing society. Such concerns were indeed palpable throughout North Carolina, as young white men pursued their own vision of racial redemption. They had lived much of their lives in the shadow of a lost war and in the economic wreckage it had produced throughout the region. Painful memories of the devastation suffered by their parents' generation intensified their determination both to raise their region from poverty and to reestablish control over their state. As industrial development became the watchword of a recoalescing white elite, spurred on by the rapid growth of a textile industry that would soon become the largest in the world, this new generation shaped a political vision that offered a formidable blend of industrialism and paternalism, with little room for doubt that a small corps of white men should lead the state's affairs.[38]

Daniel Augustus Tompkins, one of the state's dominant postwar industrialists, offered in his many speeches and writings a particularly striking vision of the masterful white man, articulating the policy that would become the creed not only of an industrial elite but of the state's Democratic Party. He advocated strict controls on voting, arguing that "platitudes about equality and natural rights do not alter race prejudices and laws of nature." He strenuously opposed legislative attempts to raise manufacturing wages or reduce the textile industry's twelve-hour working day, arguing that mill owners were far more qualified than outsiders or workers themselves to judge the need for spare time and the appropriate level of pay. He had particularly harsh words for the reformers who questioned the conditions of textile mill employment, singling out in particular "well-meaning, tender-hearted women, most of whom are living on incomes and have little knowledge of practical life."[39]

In contrast to such supposedly feminine sentiments Tompkins offered a stirring assessment of male competitive strife, presenting not simply an unruly melee of Darwinian clashes but a system dominated by assertive, successful, and unquestionably white men. "In a business man's every-day life he sees this law of the survival of the fittest at work, thinning out the ranks of his competitors, introducing new material," he announced in an 1890s speech that used such business metaphors to argue for the extension of "practical good sense and Anglo-Saxon superiority" to the Philippine Islands.

> And it would be the silliest kind of sentimentalism for the successful man of affairs to sit down and lament his past success and cease his efforts to widen his avenues of trade, because he may have been the indirect means of pushing to the wall some other business man, forcing him to assign or to go into bankruptcy, leaving his wife and children dependent on charity. Yet the like happens every day. Competition, the very essence of business life, puts down some and elevates others. The fittest survive. It must be so, else there is no life, no progress. Whatever the socialist and other sentimentalists may think, the survival of the fittest is, has been, and will always be the law of progress in national affairs, in business, and in all other walks of life.[40]

The confidence that rang in Tompkins's rhetoric, however, belied the struggle required to impose such a vision on his own state, in terms both of social status and of race. The melee that had erupted on the Davidson baseball field highlighted the tensions that ran through a society in great flux, where assertions of privilege were frequently met with sharp resistance. When a black man stepped in front of a white student at the game, the student did not ask him to move, he "ordered" him. The man, no longer willing to defer, did not immediately obey. When the student pressed the conflict by employing his riding whip, a highly charged symbol of domination, another African American stepped into the fray, uncowed by the young man's efforts to assert his own superiority. That incident was quickly settled, but there were more to come.[41]

An especially serious challenge to elite white privilege arose in the fall of 1894, sparked by a broad range of concerns about the industrializing path that D. A. Tompkins and his fellow Democrats had charted since "redeeming" the state from Reconstruction almost twenty years before. The aftermath of war, along with the growing vicissitudes of market agriculture, had wreaked havoc on the state's small, independent farmers—growth in the Tar Heel textile industry was fueled in part by the labor of a rising tide of refugees from agricultural disaster. By the 1890s, farmers' discontents had coalesced in a new political organization, the People's Party, which sought to shift public policy away from industry in favor of agriculture. In 1894 the surging Populists struck a Fusion alliance with the state's Republicans, who drew much of their support from African Americans. The resulting campaign wrested control of the state legislature from the ruling Democrats. Victorious legislators subsequently reversed a range of Democratic policies that had favored commercial interests over small-scale agriculture and curbed voter influence over many state affairs. Two years later the alliance won an even more dramatic victory, seizing more than three-quarters of the seats in the state legislature and placing a Republican, Daniel Russell, in the governor's mansion.[42]

In response to the 1896 defeat, a rising generation of young Democrats seized control of their stumbling party's affairs and began to shape a new strategy that responded to the vision of white manhood coalescing around vigorous sport and other "manly" activities. Along with adopting a newly aggressive tone in action and rhetoric, the Democrats promoted striking images of manliness and race, seeking to draw white Populists back to the Democratic fold. Even as the United States went to war in Cuba, a conflict that would be widely publicized as proof of revived Anglo-Saxon prowess, North Carolina Democrats urged the state's white men to stand up to African Americans, calling for "a white man's government." In speeches, leaflets, editorials, and political cartoons, party leaders combined old prejudices with the new philosophy of Social Darwinism to portray African Americans as apes, as "human devils," and—most significantly—as beasts who harbored uncontrolled desires to rape white women. A vote for the Democrats, they assured prospective voters, was an assertion of white manhood, a way to protect vulnerable wives and daughters from African Americans' evil designs. Such rhetoric, combined with a statewide campaign of physical intimidation, returned the Democrats to power in 1898 and helped solidify that victory in 1900.[43]

Those late-century elections would prove a watershed in state history, bringing the conflicts that had raged over the direction of state development to a decisive end. The victorious Democrats passed a disfranchisement amendment that effectively eliminated African Americans and many poorer whites from politics, leaving control of North Carolina affairs firmly in the hands of the state's industrial leaders. A series of Jim Crow laws further stigmatized black residents, pressing them to the margins of public life. Images of rapacious African Americans, vulnerable white women, and protective white men would dominate public life for decades, in North Carolina and around the South, stifling a wide range of efforts to alter the political and social status quo. The Democrats' grip on state power would go virtually unchallenged for more than half a century.[44]

For many of the party's young supporters, the 1898 success marked the kind of redemption offered by Theodore Roosevelt's much-celebrated charge up San Juan Hill, which had been widely cast as the defining moment of the Spanish American War. "The management of our political affairs has recently been rescued from the hands of a set of political demagogues who have disgraced the commonwealth and lowered it in the estimation of our sister states," one Davidson student rejoiced following the 1898 election. In journals such as the *Davidson College Magazine*, articles lamenting the state of political and social affairs soon began to give way to confident discussions of the policies that the victorious Democrats should enact.[45]

Any lessons that young North Carolinians might have learned from football probably had little effect on either the triumph over Spanish forces or the conduct of Democratic politics. Despite the numerous discussions surrounding the sport, the number of intercollegiate football games played by North Carolina schools before 1898 was relatively small. At the same time, as subsequent generations of athletic coaches would learn, ambitious rhetoric about the power of sports to shape participants' actions and ambitions did not necessarily translate to the players on the field. But even if football had limited influence on the political and military victories obtained through forceful action in the late nineteenth century, assessments of such triumphs helped to legitimize competitive athletics as a meaningful part of a young man's life preparation. In his widely read autobiographical writings, Theodore Roosevelt used his own successes as proof of the power of physical activity and urged a new generation of young men to prepare to "hit the line hard." Davidson professor W. J. Martin drew similar links when he exhorted Davidson students to join the school football team in the fall of 1899. "Yes it takes a *man*, but it *makes* men," he wrote. "Many a soldier that charged up that memorable hill at Santiago had been developed in courage, manhood and *nerve* on the football fields of our American Colleges."[46]

The political arrangements that crystallized at the end of the nineteenth century would profoundly shape athletic competition within the state. As North Carolina's modernizers pursued their industrializing course and the state became more thoroughly enmeshed in market economics, the connections football supporters had drawn between the demands of sports and those of life would only strengthen. At the same time, the state's exclusionary politics meant that different groups of North Carolinians would experience such connections in very different ways.

For young white college men, who looked forward to careers directing the state's political and economic affairs, athletics increasingly seemed to mirror the world in which they lived—the heated rush of political campaigns, the strategies of business endeavors, the mastery linked with power. With young women watching admiringly from the sidelines and with African Americans banished from the field of play, such athletic rituals would come to seem a confirmation of the existing social order, and discussions about plays, about players, and about the fortunes of one team or another would shade into larger debates over how and by what kind of men the state's affairs should be run. These sporting endeavors also assumed the mantle of regional revival, riding a rising tide of Confederate nostalgia that brushed aside memories of Civil War defeat and celebrated Confederate gallantry, courage, and determination. The pageantry of athletic contests lent itself well to such sentiments. Football games were frequently awash with Confederate symbolism, as officials and spectators alike asserted both racial and regional manhood by flying Confederate flags, singing Confederate songs, and punctuating the action on the field with well-practiced rebel yells.[47]

Outside these charmed arenas, in women's institutions, in working-class communities, and among African Americans, sports would take on other meanings. Competitive athletics, with its close symbolic ties to political and economic institutions, would offer a field in which many North Carolinians could develop skills and express emotions that they could only rarely indulge in the world beyond such games. A wide range of state citizens would seize these opportunities, further expanding the hold athletics was gaining on the heart of state society. In women's colleges, at black high schools, and in textile mill villages, North Carolinians would develop sporting institutions that offered myriad insights into alternate dreams, expectations, and debates, linking participants and spectators to the worlds from which they were excluded. At times such athletic pleasures would become a simple distraction, a momentary escape from the burdens of a workday world. But they would also nurture efforts to transform that world.

The promise athletics held as a way to challenge North Carolina's reconfigured social order first surfaced in the state's African American institutions, where leaders cautiously began to formulate an athletic philosophy. Athletics developed slowly at black schools for reasons that illuminated a number of the financial and political challenges African American educators faced as the century neared its end. Many of the state's black residents had made remarkable progress since Emancipation, and by the 1890s they were well on their way to establishing a thriving middle class, carving out economic niches as doctors, lawyers, ministers, teachers, business operators, and home owners. But African Americans' foothold in state society remained tenuous. The majority of the state's black residents were still extremely poor; black institutions suffered from chronic financial difficulties; and the racial stereotypes that populated popular culture and political rhetoric meant that black leaders still devoted considerable effort to establishing racial respectability. All these factors helped shape the experiences of black college students, down to the games they played.[48]

The meager finances and enormous needs of struggling black colleges meant that black students were required to devote much of their physical exertion to their schools' upkeep, whether through growing crops, laying bricks for new buildings, or doing the school's laundry. Free time was often limited, and even accounts of boisterous student behavior revolved around work. "The most unpopular industries at Livingstone have always been woodcutting and whitewashing," William Fonvielle wrote in his memoir of college life. "I have never known a student of the thousands I have met, who did not profess to having a horror for the whitewash brush. . . . Many a young minister and would-be physician—leaders of people—can testify that he has been knocked into a barrel of whitewash more than once."[49]

Lack of funds frequently hampered the development of extracurricular activities. In 1902, for example, early efforts to establish football at Raleigh's Shaw University were brought to a sudden halt when two members of the school's fledgling squad ignored warnings to be careful and kicked a football through a dormitory window. Contemplating the destruction, school vice-president N. F. Roberts became so enraged that he seized the offending pigskin and cut it into shreds. Only several weeks later, when Roberts relented and bought the financially strapped students another ball, did the sport resume at Shaw. The challenges and hardships African Americans faced could indeed seem to leave little room for play, as was suggested both by the agricultural assault on the Livingstone baseball field and by Booker T. Washington in his autobiographical *Up from Slavery*. "I have never seen a game of football," Washington declared. "I was asked not long ago to tell something about the sports and pastimes that I engaged in during my youth. Until that question was asked it had never occurred to me that there was no period of my life that was devoted to play. From the time that I can remember anything, almost every day of my life has been occupied in some kind of labor."[50]

Still, Washington himself felt the allure of athletics, concluding his description with the wistful declaration, "I think I would now be a more useful man if I had had time for sports." Many of the values that athletics claimed to teach—discipline, reasoned strategy, self-control—had in fact become cherished goals at African American institutions. Despite meager funding, black colleges were also more than able to pursue activities that mattered to them; lack of funds was not the same as lack of resources. In Livingstone's first decades, for example, some faculty believed so strongly in their task that they took jobs for little or no pay and made ends meet as best they could. Students made similar efforts, from washing out a single shirt each night to going hungry when they ran short of funds. The same energy would go into athletics.[51]

At North Carolina's black colleges, most early athletic efforts involved baseball. Baseball's rules had first been set down in New York in 1845, and the sport spread rapidly across the South after the Civil War, becoming especially popular among African Americans. Early in the 1890s Livingstone and Biddle began a series of Easter Monday baseball games, which students remembered with great fondness. "Everyone was smiling, happy and wearing their best clothes," Livingstone graduate W. F. Fonvielle noted of the contests, cheerfully recalling that "some how Livingstone always beat Biddle at the game in those days." Biddle's school colors—blue and gold for truthfulness and loyalty—were unveiled on Easter Monday in 1895. "Baseball seems to be the craze at present," the *Living Stone* reported in 1892. "Every-body that can lift a pound now hurls a ball viciously through the air. The excited pitchers 'holler' 'How is that,' even in their dreams." In 1901 Livingstone student George W. Bowles offered an ode to school athletics, using standard sporting language to argue that "athletics are essential in our colleges and higher institutions of learning," and that "we are able to use our mental attainments in proportion to our physical abilities." He also noted proudly that "we hope to have a very strong Base Ball nine this year."[52]

Football, however, was another matter. Throughout the 1890s, even as football became a powerful symbol of manhood at white colleges, African American schools showed considerably more reluctance to engage in the sport. The Livingstone-Biddle match had seemed a promising start. Players at Livingstone had chipped in to buy a football, affixed temporary cleats to their regular shoes, and padded old clothes for practice clashes. Livingstone's female students had sewed the uniforms. Similar preparations no doubt took place at Biddle. Despite a raging snowstorm that kept the audience down, obscured the field's lines, and created some controversy regarding scoring, the game was called a great success. Although Biddle triumphed 4-0, Livingstone's students graciously accepted the defeat. "The game between Biddle University and Livingstone College was played and very much enjoyed Tuesday, December 27th," the *Living Stone* magazine reported. "Our boys played well, as did the Biddle boys. It was a great game."[53] Students were also eager to schedule a rematch. "What's the matter with a football game on Thanksgiving Day?" a Livingstone student columnist asked in the fall of 1893. But none was played. No black college in North Carolina competed in another intercollegiate football contest for almost a decade, and Biddle would not play again until 1908. Throughout the country only a handful of black schools played even one football game before the turn of the century.[54]

This reluctance to engage in the increasingly popular sport highlights the uncertain position African Americans held in North Carolina society, where football offered large risks and only minimal rewards. Educators at African American schools, most of which were church sponsored, no doubt shared widespread concerns about the spiritual implications of intense physical endeavor as well as the violence football involved. Livingstone's earliest football efforts had been brought to a temporary halt after one player received a "paralytic stroke" in an intramural game, and the decision of Biddle faculty to ban football after the Biddle-Livingstone contest was in part influenced by parents' complaints about the sport's brutality. But these educators also faced dilemmas particular to African Americans.[55]

The young white men who embraced a newly assertive vision of manhood were reaching for a lost mastery, girding themselves for what many saw as a Darwinian struggle to reassert control over a state that seemed to be slipping from their grasp. African American leaders, for whom Social Darwinist thinking portended little but catastrophe, were less concerned with dominance than with respectability. "Nations are no longer governed by races, but by ideas," Joseph Price optimistically declared. In particular, North Carolina's African Americans focused on asserting their claims to the rights of citizenship they had so recently attained and on defending themselves against a range of ongoing efforts to confine African Americans to the lower rungs of southern society. Administrators at many colleges were especially troubled by the growing popularity of a movement termed "industrial education," which held that African American schools should adopt modest goals, abandoning most academic work and focusing on training black youth in the trades that would prepare them for what many whites saw as their "proper" positions at the bottom of the southern economy.[56]

Challenging presumptions of black inferiority was a daunting task, one that involved not only combating long-established stereotypes about black character and ability but refuting new theories of civilization that relegated African Americans to the lowest levels of cultural development. The effective racial rhetoric employed by North Carolina Democrats had drawn strength not only from white uncertainty about the future but also from a growing racial cast in U.S. culture. Throughout the country, blackface minstrel shows portrayed the antics of comical, contented slaves even as pseudo-scientific scholars such as Harvard's Nathan Shaler argued that release from the "civilizing" influence of plantation life had sent black Americans spiraling toward a previously savage state.[57]

Most of this rhetoric was grounded in assumptions about African Americans' physical nature. From minstrel show portrayals of foolish, dancing slaves to stump speech images of rapacious black rapists, popular images of blacks centered on physicality. Whether drawing on centuries-old theological distinctions between body and spirit, on recently popularized theories of human evolution, or on accounts of racial progress from "savagery" to "civilization," such depictions cast African Americans as closer to the instinctive physicality of animals than to the higher mental and moral capabilities ascribed to whites. At times the link was subtle, as when a *News and Observer* reporter described a Republican Party member as an "old negro with a long goatee and eyes like a lemur." But it was often more direct, as when the editor of Sampson County's *Caucasian* invoked Nathan Shaler's theories to argue of "the negro" that "his animal nature so preponderates over his intellectual and moral nature, that in the age of puberty, when the animal nature develops, that the moral and intellectual qualities are clouded by the animal instinct and not only cease to develop but really retrograde."[58]

African American educators were well aware of efforts to deny African Americans their full humanity by describing "savage" behavior or "animal" instincts. "For two hundred and fifty years," Joseph Price told an audience in 1890, "the white man of the South saw only the animal, or mechanical side of the Negro. . . . The man was overshadowed and concealed by the debasing appetites and destructive and avaricious passions of the animal." Many working-class African Americans sought to mark their freedom through exuberant physical display, through parades and fancy dress, and even through physical assertion, as when the black baseball fan challenged the Davidson student. In contrast, most middle-class black leaders adopted a strategy of respectability, determined to buttress their claims to citizenship through strict adherence to the sober, restrained ideals that constituted Victorian visions of civilized behavior. The fit of rage that led Shaw's N. F. Roberts to shred his students' football may well have stemmed less from concern about the damage it had done than from anger at their conspicuous lapse of self-control. Black leaders labored mightily to spread their gospel among African Americans at large. "Colored men, you have no money to throw away on circuses, minstrels, balls, frolics, whisky, and other nonsense," the *Star of Zion* told its readers in a typical appeal. "You have children that should be well educated, and wives whom you should make comfortable by purchasing homes. . . . You have a poll-tax that every manly Negro ought to pay. Prosperity and happiness awaits every colored family that is industrious, frugal and preserving."[59]

Such endeavors lent themselves far more neatly to the older metaphors of moral contest with an abstract foe—the biblical images of spiritually centered foot races and wrestling matches—than to the heated clash of football competition. A contributor to the *Star of Zion* caught this spirit in an 1897 contribution. "Thus far the Negro has done well, he has answered all questions," the contributor wrote with a confidence that contrasted sharply with the anxious tone of the Democrats' racist rhetoric.

> His destiny is to make his race the equal of the best race in history and to be distinct only as to color. To-day is the Negro's; there is nothing prior to emancipation but stripes, curses and despair. "It is high time to awake" and, putting on the whole armor of civilization, do battle with thrift and intelligence for the second emancipation; emancipation from hatred and scorn and prejudice. The first emancipation was a jubilee of liberty and blood; but the second, grander and better and differently achieved, shall be an everlasting jubilee of liberty, of peace and of the united American people.[60]

The mix of discipline and supposedly primal force that had proved so captivating to white men around the country thus held far less appeal for African American leaders or for the white administrators who guided many of the state's black schools during their early years. University of North Carolina president George Winston might proudly announce that "animal exuberance" abounded at his school. Administrators at African American schools, aware of the images such language would invoke in many readers' minds, would probably not have described their students in that way, preferring, as had Joseph Price, to demonstrate "the manhood of the Race" through intellectual development. The era's "scientists" of race remained divided on the question of whether blacks held physical advantages over whites, and African American athletes had not yet gained the renown that would prompt widespread twentieth-century speculation about the "natural" sources of black athletic skill. But as long as football was closely associated with animal exuberance or, in the words of Southern Methodists, "the lower impulses of the physical man," it remained a risky endeavor for black institutions.[61]

A brief article published in the *New York Times* in 1897 summed up in its five sentences all that black educators had to fear from college football. The article, which appeared on the front page, described a game between Tennessee's Knoxville College and an independent black team called John Singleton's Tigers. "NEGROES RIOT AT FOOTBALL," the headline ran, and the article continued: "The first football game ever played by Negroes in Tennessee took place here this afternoon between local teams. The game was not finished on account of the fatal wounding of Fred Staples and the serious injury of half a dozen other players. A riot concluded the game, when several drunken white men attacked the players because they could not make a touchdown. Hasty summons of the police prevented murder. A dozen chickens were offered as the prize, but the birds were stolen during the game."[62]

Although this contest took place in neighboring Tennessee, the account would have been unpleasantly familiar to many of North Carolina's African Americans. The facts of the game were alarming enough. In a period of rising racial tension, a sporting event had provoked a riot that seriously injured several young black men. (Fred Staples apparently managed to live for several years after his "fatal wounding.") The newspaper account added insult to those injuries. It portrayed not black accomplishment, but mayhem. Although whites had apparently begun the altercation, the headline read, "NEGROES RIOT." The black players' apparent inability to reach the end zone made them seem less than competent, and the report of chicken stealing invoked the thousands of condescending minstrel show skits that focused on the supposed black propensity for that particular activity. The article also made clear what a risky public effort football could be. An individual game could be a model of scientific efficiency. It could also degenerate into a test of brute force. Most games contained elements of both, leaving interpretation open to frequently unsympathetic beholders.[63]


Still, as football gained in prestige and respectability, it also offered some tantalizing possibilities for racial advance. The football-related image that would become an icon of American culture—the level playing field—held particular metaphorical power. When white North Carolinians invoked that image, it generally carried the same restrictions as other aspects of southern public life:

Shaw University football team, 1905. Most of North Carolina's black colleges, including Shaw, began to field football teams in the early 1900s. Courtesy of the University Archives, Shaw University.

the field might be level, but only whites could play. Viewed more broadly, however, it invoked the philosophy that would guide the efforts of generations of black North Carolina leaders, the idea that given a fair chance, African Americans would demonstrate convincingly that they had the same abilities and deserved the same rights as their white counterparts. African Americans would seek to make this point anywhere they could, from military service to medical research to the world of literature. But athletics, which drew a growing measure of public attention, would become a particularly charged arena for such endeavors.[64]

The interest black North Carolinians had begun to take in the broader meanings of athletic achievement was suggested in a lengthy description of a game between Harvard and the University of Pennsylvania published in the Charlotte-based *AME Zion Quarterly Review* in 1900. The article focused on W. H. Lewis, the nation's first black All-American football player, who had become a part-time director of the Harvard football squad. Lewis was a man of numerous accomplishments—in addition to his athletic honors and coaching skills he had become a successful lawyer and writer. But it was football that put him in the news. The *Quarterly Review*'s assessment, which touched on discipline and publicity, on calculated strategy, and on racial recognition, marked the long road North Carolinians had traveled since Livingstone's anonymous agrarian had made a last stand for the concrete virtues of cabbages and turnips. It also pointed toward some of the meanings sports would carry into the future.

"The betting was ten to seven in favor of Pennsylvania," the *Quarterly Review* explained. "And yet with a weak and crippled team Harvard was overwhelmingly victorious. And why? because W. H. Lewis, the colored coach had studied the methods of the Pennsylvania system and mastered them. He devised a system of defense which completely blocked Pennsylvania's team and made it almost impossible for them to score." The article went on to probe the meanings of Lewis's feat, noting, "The civilized world holds in high respect the trained and successful athlete. The best of the colleges of the world encourage athletics as a means of strengthening and adding to the health of students and of stimulating their mental powers at the same time." It then concluded with a prediction about the wider effects of his accomplishments. "The proud Anglo-Saxon admits that his superior has not appeared on the athletic field. . . . Our race is proud of him because in all his success he stands for us, and the higher he goes in the physical field of athletics or the mental field of law or literature, he must necessarily open the way for others, and lift us all up at the same time."[65]

## CHAPTER TWO

# Our Own Ability

## Sport and Image among
## College Women, 1900–1920

The first intercollegiate basketball game in the history of Charlotte, North Carolina, took place in the rain on the afternoon of April 8, 1907. At precisely 4:30 P.M. two teams spilled onto the outdoor field, accompanied by "a tumult of cheers and an avalanche of streamers." A large and eager audience ringed the court, standing along the sidelines or watching from the advantageous seats of horse-drawn carriages. Spectators unable to secure admission scaled nearby buildings to catch glimpses of the grounds. Although the game ended with the low score of 10-4, it became the talk of the city, prompting even the jaded reporter assigned by the *Charlotte Observer* to describe it as "a scene such as is not witnessed everyday in staid old Charlotte."[1]

The game that caused the fuss differed considerably from the contests that spark similar excitement today. The baskets were made of wood supports with wire mesh backboards, and a ladder was still required to retrieve the ball from the closed nets after a score. A jump ball was held not only to start each half but after every basket. The heavy laces on the leather ball made dribbling a risky operation. And the *Observer* reporter's information had come secondhand, "on good authority" he promised, because at this unprecedented public meeting between the young women from Charlotte's Elizabeth and Presbyterian colleges, male spectators were forbidden.[2]

Even as North Carolina's young college men sought some measure of salvation on the football field, the state's female collegians laid claim to the basketball court. Basketball had been invented in 1891 when a young YMCA instructor named James Naismith wrote down thirteen rules for a game that could be played indoors. The first women's contest took place less than a month later, and by the turn of the century basketball had become the most popular pastime at women's schools from Maine to California. A decade before North Carolina's men's colleges fielded their first varsity teams, basketball formed a central part of student life at many women's institutions, joining the panoply of activities that North Carolina's female citizens undertook as they worked to shape new roles and new identities within their changing world.[3]

The growing numbers of North Carolina women, black and white, who ventured off to college after the Civil War formed part of a broad expansion of women's activities. North Carolina's reconfiguring society, with its myriad new schools, shops, railroad lines, "manufactories," urban districts, and governmental institutions, presented its citizens with a wide range of challenges and opportunities. Women rose to the occasion, taking "public" jobs as well as mobilizing thousands of church and community clubs to work for causes that included temperance, child labor laws, and public school improvement. North Carolina's colleges encouraged this activity, designing their curricula to give their students the skills, confidence, and determination to confront the world around them. Physical vitality, so important to such efforts, quickly became a key component in the image of a "new woman" that began to emerge in North Carolina and around the nation. During the first part of the nineteenth century, argued Smith College instructor and women's basketball advocate Senda Berenson, "the so-called ideal woman was a small brained damsel who prided herself on her delicate health, who thought fainting interesting, and hysterics fascinating." But by 1901 an article appearing in the *Salisbury Daily Sun* (and reprinted in Livingstone College's *Living Stone*) could announce, "The 'old maid' has entirely disappeared completely, and in her place we have the breezy independent, up-to-date, athletic and well gowned bachelor girl, who is succeeding in business life or a profession and asks neither pity nor favors from her fellow men."[4]

The images that came together in the *Daily Sun*'s evaluation touched on many of the factors involved in women's changing social roles, alterations that had close connections to the broader transformations that were remaking North Carolina society. As college women approached new opportunities as schoolteachers and community organizers, they joined a broad trend in which citizens were shifting growing portions of their lives from extended family circles to a spreading realm of public life formed by factory employment, expanding state institutions, and the bustling activities on the streets of the state's booming towns and cities. As this new society took shape, North Carolinians of all kinds came to depend less on the support of family and neighbors and more on their own ability to negotiate this new arena, to create favorable impressions among strangers, and to tackle a wide range of challenges without the "pity" or the "favors" that were usually hard to find in this hotly competitive arena. Farmers who moved to town in search of factory employment, salesmen bent on convincing customers to buy new products, and schoolteachers who sought to fulfill demanding new state requirements all faced these dilemmas as they scrambled to find places for themselves in the new North Carolina.[5]

Just as football engaged questions about the kind of men required for such a world, so basketball touched on the issues that swirled around changing concepts of womanhood, including sexuality, self-confidence, racial difference, political rhetoric, and public image. Basketball was part play and part in earnest; like football, it allowed players to momentarily elude the pressures of their society, even as it helped prepare them to pursue new roles within the public realm. But women's sports also took on dynamics of their own. Women's actions remained circumscribed by concepts of women's proper social place and by the racial rhetoric that underpinned state politics, concepts that reached to some of the deepest levels of North Carolina society. As young women stepped into new jobs and new activities, they cautiously negotiated their changing roles, seeking to expand their realm of action while avoiding overt threats to the status quo. Competitive athletics, a realm so closely linked to men and manhood, proved a revealing test of the strategies that they developed, illuminating some of the diverging paths state women pursued, as well as the complexities of the images they crafted for themselves.

The health of female college students had become a national educational concern as soon as the first women were admitted to Oberlin College in 1837. Nineteenth-century physicians focused theories of women's health almost exclusively around childbearing, playing on widespread assumptions about female physical fragility and often suggesting that vigorous physical or mental activity posed great risks both for women and for their future children. As growing numbers of women's colleges opened their doors, administrators carefully stressed measures taken to safeguard students' physical well-being, often through moderate exertion. "Diligent care is exercised over the health of the pupils," the catalog of Charlotte's Institute for Young Ladies explained in 1876, adding that "rest and recreation, with a due proportion of physical exercise, are made as obligatory as study." Two years later, school administrators assured parents that their daughters would not be allowed to collapse under the strain of undue mental exertion. "So soon as any pupil's health appears to require it, there shall be on her part a complete cessation from study," the catalog stated, also assuring parents that in such cases their tuition would be refunded.[6]

Early exercise programs often consisted of an afternoon "walking period," which encouraged students to spend time outside. Soon, though, supporters of such activities created more systematic programs of "physical culture," or "physical education." Institutions such as the Boston Normal School of Gymnastics, founded in the late 1880s, developed calisthenics-based exercise programs and produced specialized educators such as Nora Jones, a Boston Normal graduate whose "careful and intellectual training" was prominently featured in Presbyterian College literature in 1899. Descriptions of these programs generally meshed with other attempts to portray women's institutions as centers of genteel respectability, evoking the images of dignified self-control associated with conventional ideals of well-bred ladies. "The aim of the work in Physical Education is to correct careless physical habits, develop the body symmetrically, and give to the student that erect, strong, reliant, dignified, and graceful carriage and deportment, that always characterize the cultured woman," ran a typical promise.[7]

Beneath such genteel language, however, lurked other concerns, as a growing interest in physical health combined with other goals. Advocates of women's rights worked to abolish cultural as well as legal restrictions and linked activities that encouraged greater physical movement to a growth in both self-confidence and independence. In the mid-nineteenth century, women's rights activist Amelia Bloomer sought to advance women's cause by designing what became known as the Bloomer Costume—a pair of Turkish-style trousers covered by a shortened skirt—that allowed women to move about more freely. In North Carolina, students at Greensboro's State Normal and Industrial College were known for their rejection of constraining corsets, and one of the school's early catalogs sang the praises of the ideal Normal student by announcing,

You can tell her by her manner
When you meet her on the street
For she walks as if she meant it
Treading squarely on both feet.[8]

When thousands of American women took up bicycling during the 1890s, Susan B. Anthony remarked that the sport did "more to emancipate women than anything else in the world," because it produced a "feeling of freedom and self-reliance."[9]

Driven by their movement's larger goals, the women who spearheaded physical education efforts promoted exercise with zeal, whether or not parents and students shared their enthusiasm for gymnastics and Swedish calisthenics. "Parents are particularly requested not to give permission, either written or otherwise, to their daughters to omit calisthenic exercise," the Charlotte Female Institute pleaded in 1886. "We cannot be responsible for the health of pupils unless we have entire control and direction of their hours of exercise. These exercises can by no means be injurious, but, on the other hand, highly beneficial, and no young lady can be excused except for good reasons." Physical educators met such challenges head-on, delighting in the changes that exercise worked in their students. Southern physical education pioneer Clara Baer exemplified this determination. She was particularly fond of recounting how the vigorous exercise routines she devised at New Orleans' Newcomb College compelled her students to "sweat off" their corsets.[10]

Across North Carolina, young women rose to the new challenge—and often stepped beyond it. While some students were at first reluctant to join even moderate exercise classes, others quickly became eager to move past walking and calisthenics to more stimulating diversions. College women embarked on their pioneering efforts with enormous energy, eager to experiment with everything their changing society had to offer. As men's college athletics sparked growing excitement around the state, "careful and intellectual training" came to seem a dull alternative. In 1899 students at the State Normal and Industrial College in Greensboro described a thoroughgoing revolt, with "some girls complaining of how 'pokey' we are not to have games, many grumbling about that stupid walking period, still others giving vent to their feelings and energy by writing spirited editorials on 'Our Need for Athletics.'"[11]

As the nineteenth century drew to a close, these restless young women found a remedy in basketball. "In athletics we are the progenitors of a new regime," members of the State Normal College class of 1900 proudly announced in their summary of class accomplishments. Previously, they continued, "the walls of the now elegant library enclosed all our efforts toward physical culture. There we wrestled in the dust with greased poles and dumb-bells, while 'all outdoors' remained unnoticed." But the class had taken action. "The enthusiasm ran so high over basket ball in the spring that a determined few lent themselves to the task of cleaning and preparing the grounds," they noted. "The athletic spirit spread until now every class in the school plays basket ball." Interclass matchups and yearly class tournaments quickly became a key component of student life at the Normal and at many other schools.[12]

The arguments with which students and administrators justified athletic games in many ways resembled those their male counterparts had employed. The themes of balance that resonated through male student writings also appeared in statements about women. "In this progressive age, the world is calling for men and women, symmetrical men and symmetrical women," a Livingstone College student wrote in 1901, later adding, "We admire the spirit of the young ladies in organizing an Athletic Association." One State Normal student invoked the familiar argument that exercise improved academic performance, couching her argument in scientific terms: "It has been proven by many experiments that the people, male, or female, who keep themselves in the best physical

Shaw University students take a break from study to pose for this basketball photograph that appeared in the school's annual catalog in 1909. Courtesy of the University
Archives, Shaw University.

condition . . . are capable of doing the greatest amount and best mental work."
Another student added, "A half-hour of basketball, tennis or golf every afternoon, when we forget that we even possess a head, could but be beneficial to the
physical and mental well-being of all of us."[13]

Like young male students, who cast athletics as a welcome balance to the
stresses of academic life, female college students were contending with heightened challenges. While many of the South's first women's colleges had focused
on turning out accomplished ladies, emphasizing skills such as art and music,
late-nineteenth-century institutions shaped their programs to meet greater demands. Many women aspired to become public schoolteachers, a profession
that required them to pass a demanding state exam in order to obtain a teaching license. At the State Normal College, for example, students often scrambled
to find ways to study during the mandatory 10:00 P.M. to 6:00 A.M. lights-out
curfew. Some women tiptoed into school bathrooms for after-hours cram-
ming, and for years students told the story of the young woman who got up

before sunrise, lost her way in the second-floor darkness, and fell through a skylight into the room below.[14]

For young women, however, the advantages of being able to "forget that we even possess a head" went well beyond relieving the stress of study. It also spoke to the stringent self-awareness so often demanded of women in New South society. While writers at the *Salisbury Daily Sun* might have been confident that old ideas of female propriety had "entirely disappeared completely," students at nearby Livingstone College could have offered contrary evidence. Livingstone women were apparently lectured on the importance of good behavior so often that finally a writer for the student magazine protested the discrepancy in expectations for the school's male and female students. "Much stress has been put upon the girls' character and carriage—the necessity of their demonstrating soul beauty through their charm and grace; what, oh what! about the boys?" the editorial demanded. "Are they faultless? Is it a high bred spectacle to see them while sitting in the class room or chapel hanging rag-on-a-bush fashion upon one another's shoulders? A loud and ranting tone of conversation, seasoned occasionally by a full and 'fat laugh' in the presence of the sisters is not a sign of much gentility."[15]

At the State Normal College, students had to answer to Lady Principal Sue May Kirkland, who used both lectures and individual reprimands to keep the students constantly aware of their appearance. Any young woman who wished to venture into town first had to pass the formidable Miss Kirkland's inspection, and on Saturday mornings a long line of students formed in front of her rooms, each anxiously awaiting judgment. As women at the Normal College prepared for their new social roles, they were also cautioned to monitor the effects of their activities on the rest of their behavior. When Mrs. John Van Landingham, the wife of one of North Carolina's rising textile tycoons, visited the school in 1902, she lauded students for their "education, independence and adaptability." But she also urged them to accept "the responsibility of sustaining the old Southern type of womanhood with its purity, dignity, gentleness and refinement, and to it adding the practical qualities demanded by the age, as well as the business knowledge and high culture now offered to the sex; without also a masculinity, an assurance, a loudness, and a 'new woman' arrogance."[16]

The strains of such continual self-inspection ran through an eloquently poignant piece written by Normal student Laura Weill in 1908. The article, titled "The Tomboy," described a young girl with what can only be characterized as longing:

> She stood on a forked limb of the knotted old tree, one hand resting on the
> trunk beside her, while in the other she held a bright red apple which she

munched eagerly. One could tell at a glance that she was a tomboy, and one could imagine, too, the looks of perplexity and even of despair, that would steal over the faces of the good ladies of the town when her name was mentioned; for could a girl, who preferred climbing trees and playing ball to sewing and cooking, ever grow into dignified womanhood?

The tomboy, however, was totally oblivious of them, as she stood high among the branches on that fresh October day. Her brown hair had once been braided, but now the tangled curls were streaming behind her. Her soiled blue dress showed many tears, and her stockings numerous snags. The shoes could boast of more spaces where there should have been buttons, than the actual buttons that were on them; but of these the tomboy was not conscious either.

There for a moment she stood, with all the freedom, light and sunshine of the out-of-door world reflected in her own happy face. Then at the sound of a distant whistle, and with an answering one, she swung easily from the tree with a sound of rending cloth, and quickly disappeared over the little hillside.[17]

The girl in the description was happy in part because she was not aware of her appearance and did not let concern about dress or hair or the "good ladies of the town" keep her from running and climbing and having a good time. As female students struggled to attain "dignified womanhood," this luxury of self-abandonment often seemed reserved for small children and for men. A short story published in the same magazine in 1903 had sounded a similar theme; in it a spectator at a college baseball game listened to the loud calls of the teams and then asked her companion, "Don't you wish you were a boy? it is grand to yell like that?"[18]

Basketball gave young women the chance to escape some of these inhibiting demands, through running, jumping, and cheering for their teams. The sport assumed particular prominence at colleges for white women, where it became part of a thriving, woman-centered culture. School annuals quickly filled with dozens of photographs and cheers, and campus visitors were struck by the expressions of enthusiasm. "The sound was like the breaking of a heavy surf on a rocky coast miles away, so loud was it and so tumultuous," the *Charlotte Observer* reported of a Presbyterian-Elizabeth rematch. When Elizabeth supporters celebrated their victory, the reporter continued, the excitement overflowed. "Had a tribe of Comanche Indians been turned loose [on the] campus, they could hardly have caused more confusion."[19] A group of Normal students struck a similar theme a few years later in a rhyming evocation of the school's annual interclass tournament:

Sing a song of tournament!
A week full of care,
Colors waving, rooters raving,
Balls in the air!
When the game is over,
The winning class goes wild!
They yell and squall like savages.
But the losers all are riled.[20]

The festive atmosphere of basketball tournaments may well have lent some measure of support to the stringent requirements of college women's daily lives by giving participants a chance to indulge in emotions normally kept under strict control. But students also linked the sport to self-assertion and to a growing confidence they felt about their abilities in many areas of life. At the turn of the century, for example, Elizabeth College students named their intra-mural teams the Amazons and the Olympians, invoking the powerful women who peopled classical mythology and hinting at the aspirations they had developed for themselves.[21]

At first college women downplayed this growing confidence through conventions of photography and public rhetoric. A 1901 photograph of the State Normal College's team showed the players grouped loosely around the school's elaborately constructed basket. Only two of the six team members looked at the camera; the others gazed off into some dreamy distance. The team's yell was spirited, yet somewhat vague; it cheered the team but did not directly mention competition.

Hoop-la! Hoop-la! Gold and White!
The Normal team is out of sight!
We are the stuff—tough, tough tough!
We play basketball and never get enough![22]

The subdued assessment that accompanied the photograph underscored this reticence, stating simply, "We feel sure that the strength we have gained by these physical exercises will contribute largely to our future career." Still, such careful presentation masked the intensity already stirring among the school's players. Many years later Berta Allbright Moore recalled that in 1901 her class adopted a distinctly less subdued attitude toward interclass competition. The sophomore team had been particularly good that year and had gloried in its own strength, anticipating easy victory in the annual school tournament. "The Duke-Carolina games can hardly stir up as much feeling," Moore wrote in a reminiscing letter. "We were so sure of the cup, and acted so arrogantly that the whole school lined

Basketball players at the State Normal College, 1901. At the turn of the century, basketball uniforms differed little from everyday garb. From *North Carolina State Normal and Industrial College Decennial*; photograph courtesy of the University Archives, Jackson Library, University of North Carolina, Greensboro.

up against us. And of course that was our delight—The more they detested us, the better we felt we were."[23]

Such a display of confidence was generally frowned on. The class of 1904 noted the next year that "we, profiting by the example(?) of last year's Sophomores, have endeavored to be a very quiet, unpretentious class."[24] In subsequent years, however, more assertiveness began to show in school publications. The Normal champions of 1910 (including team member Laura Weill) took a far more energetic stance toward the camera. They rolled their sleeves up to their elbows, crossed their arms, and projected a very different sense of athletic femininity. Their cheer ran to a driving rhythm, dealt directly with competition (they had beaten the sophomore team in the championship game), and acknowledged the players by name:

> Rip! Rah! Re! Rip! Rah! Rix!
> Here's to Stancill, Lambe, and Hicks.
> Boom-er-rac ree! Boom-er-racher rowers!
> Ho for Hassell, Cotchett, Powers.
> 'Tis for the Sophomores quite a trial
> To beat McWhorter, Wooten, Weill.[25]

As basketball became a college institution, the physical confidence the game helped to develop became much admired on women's campuses. In 1915 the yearbook description of Presbyterian College student Ashby Herron described her as a "tall, handsome girl, who walks with an athletic swing and an independent air." In 1907 Presbyterian's basketball team captain, Katharine Cramer, was chosen both college athlete and college beauty. The team portrait in the 1908 annual showed the players gazing at the camera with calm assurance, and the accompanying text noted that the team looked forward to the future "with perfect confidence in our own ability."[26]

Such confidence also had wide-ranging implications, as Senda Berenson suggested in one of her many writings on her favorite sport. Berenson lauded basketball for helping women develop "physical courage, self-reliance, quickness, alertness." She also touched on the game's potential role in the broader ambitions she passed on to her students. "One of the strong arguments in the economic world against giving women as high salaries as men for similar work is that women are more prone to illness than men," she wrote. "They need, therefore, all the more to develop health and endurance if they desire to become candidates for equal wages."[27]

In southern college publications such ambitions were rarely voiced so directly. But connections between sports and independence were often made through implication, as in the name Amazons or in the coupling of Ashby

The Presbyterian College team of 1908 confronted the camera with assurance. From *Edelweiss*; photograph courtesy of the Robinson-Spangler Carolina Room, Public Library of Charlotte and Mecklenburg County.

Herron's "athletic stride" and "independent air." As enthusiasm for woman suffrage built on college campuses, the campaign for women's right to vote developed associations with basketball as well. In Virginia in 1916 two groups of African American college graduates named their teams the Suffragists and the Feminists. An Elizabeth College class prophet, taking up the popular task of envisioning her classmates' futures, linked sports with suffrage through the expansive self-assertiveness of a loud yell. "It was a crowded street of a large city," she said of her vision. "At first I could not understand what the crowd meant, but looking down the street I saw a company of women marching to and fro. As the parade drew nearer, I saw the rowdy leader wildly wave her flag, and heard her shriek at the top of her lungs, 'Votes for Women.' I recognized that awful shriek as the same one that Jessica used to utter on the basket-ball field of Elizabeth."[28]

As young women gained confidence in their athletic abilities, their rituals began to press beyond assertions of independence into a more highly charged realm, hinting at a blurring of differences between the sexes. The 1910 Normal team set one of their cheers to the tune of the football song "Touchdown," and the assertive lyrics, which began "Smash, bang, rip them Senior Team," suggest they did not feel the need to soften the lyrics to fit a female endeavor.[29] That year's freshmen made even more explicit connections as they sang the prowess of their squad:

Rah, rah, rah, for the men so rare,
   They've got the rest of you beat;
Others may at times compare,
   But none with ours will ever compete.[30]

In 1910 these sentiments were not limited to athletic pursuits. That year the *State Normal Magazine* published a short story about a woman who worked up the courage to participate in a spelling bee that pitted her community's women against its men. She emerged victorious, besting her own husband on the final word. As they walked home together, she triumphantly informed him that "it would have been better for you if you had stayed at home with the baby."[31]

Still, the shifts in men's and women's roles implied by such student proclamations—assertions about which students themselves had mixed feelings—only rarely reached beyond college walls. Rather, they remained private affairs, limited to the pages of student magazines and, in the case of basketball, to the protective confines of intramural competition. Young women might run and jump and scramble toward victory with the same zeal as their male counterparts, but in the early decades of the twentieth century, their efforts would receive far less public notice. After its rocky nineteenth-century beginnings, men's varsity athletics at both black and white colleges expanded steadily through the first two decades of the twentieth century, drawing a growing share of public attention. Women's college athletics would travel a far different road, focusing on intramural play and remaining largely out of public view.[32]

The diverging paths taken by men's and women's college sports showed most strikingly at African American colleges, where men and women frequently studied side by side. Black female students, rising to the occasion, used the opportunity to move into new arenas and often extended calls for racial equality into arguments for women's equality as well. At Livingstone College, for example, women took part in debates; gave commencement addresses; enrolled in Greek, Latin, and theology classes; and played as prominent a role in college life as that of their male counterparts. Descriptions of college activities in the student-written *Living Stone* magazine generally reflected such equal expectations, referring to the student body as "sons and daughters of Livingstone." Competitive solidarity between male and female students on academic matters seemed to be expected, as when A. C. Platt, who would later star on Livingstone's first varsity basketball team, noted of his class, "Rivalry is existing between the girls and boys of the class in which they stand shoulder to shoulder, arm to arm, strong in faith as they march."[33]

Still, when detailed accounts of varsity and intramural sports became a regular part of the *Living Stone*'s monthly reports, such descriptions focused entirely on men. In 1901, for example, Livingstone student George W. Bowles lauded Livingstone's female students for organizing a women's athletic association, noting somewhat vaguely that "to become healthy and useful one must needs take plenty of exercise." He then segued into an animated discussion of the prospects for the school's male baseball team, describing it as "competent" and "splendid."[34] As African American institutions began expanding their support for men's varsity sports, this gap widened further. In 1912 Raleigh's Shaw University became one of the founding members of the Colored (later Central) Interscholastic Athletic Association (CIAA), the nation's first black college sports league. The CIAA reflected the lofty goals black colleges were developing in the athletic realm; one founder explained that the league was organized "to train students in self-reliance and stimulate race-pride through athletic achievement." But such goals, at least in sports, were limited to men, as CIAA competition included no women's events.[35]

At Livingstone the growing interest in men's sports was reflected in the *Living Stone*, which devoted increasing portions of its monthly issues to reports on varsity and intramural play and to frequent assessments of character-building potential. In contrast, those issues that survive in the college archives contain only the briefest mention of women's sports. Women's athletics was clearly beginning to develop at black schools. In a brief account of a 1913 field day competition at Fisk University, which featured track and gymnastics events, the *Living Stone* correspondent noted, "Those events are thoroughly representative for the young women did as much as the young men in making the occasion a success." By 1909 women's basketball had become significant enough at Shaw University to warrant a photograph in the school's catalog, suggesting that Shaw officials saw the sport not only as a popular campus institution but as a useful advertisement for the school. Still, the details of black women's competition remained muted. If, for example, the Livingstone junior women played the sophomores, or if the seniors challenged other schools, the *Living Stone* did not regularly report the results.[36]

Limited support for women's varsity sports at both black and white schools points toward some of the challenges that North Carolina women faced as they cautiously expanded the roles they played in state society. As elsewhere in the country, North Carolina's political and social institutions were built around assumptions of fundamental differences between men and women. The nineteenth-century concept of womanhood that reigned within the upper circles of North Carolina society had little to do with the sense of freedom or self-expression that athletics encouraged. Rather, it encompassed a vision of restraint and self-sacrifice—Mrs. Van Landingham's purity, dignity, gentleness, and refinement—that rested on a cornerstone of moral virtue. Such virtues were concentrated within the private realm of home and family, where women were expected to work their greatest influence on society indirectly, shaping husbands and children through moral guidance. A visiting minister at Livingstone College invoked this ideal in 1901. As the *Living Stone* reported it, the minister applauded women's moral strength, arguing that "man is as clay in her hands, she shapes and develops him as she will." Subsequently, "a strong appeal to women was made to make us just what we ought to be."[37]

By the turn of the century North Carolina's college women had stepped to the margins of this vision of womanhood, where they stood on shaky ground. Turn-of-the-century reconfigurations of politics and manhood had brought questions of female virtue to the forefront in both black and white communities, even as social and economic change pressed growing numbers of women to venture beyond the protective embrace of family and community. Although many North Carolinians supported women's expanding activities, with African Americans frequently in the vanguard, other state residents were more troubled by the change, envisioning a fundamental shift in the bedrock of social order. When State Normal student Fodie Buie ventured to the post office in her small-town home one morning, a neighbor confronted her with an apocalyptic assessment of her educational endeavors, exclaiming, "All you gals will come back from there a pack of infidels and the whole world will go to the dogs."[38]

As so often in women's history, concerns about female independence laid particular stress on sexual matters, engaging the central symbol of female virtue and self-control and reflecting the complex strains of thought entangled in the thorny definition of women's social roles. North Carolina's racial politics invested public discussions of women with unmistakable sexual overtones, turning deeply personal intimacies into highly charged symbols of moral rectitude and male authority. In public such discussions had focused on men's actions, emphasizing the dangers unprotected women faced from male aggressors. The rhetoric that undergirded the state's white supremacy campaigns held that white women who ventured beyond the embrace of white male protection risked assault from ravenous black men. Concurrently, black communities worked to shield African American women from the unwelcome attentions of white men, whose vision of white supremacy frequently involved disdain for black women's virtue. Fears of predatory white men in fact helped boost support for black women's education, as families sought to give their daughters alternatives to working as domestics in white homes.[39]

Still, reactions to women's athletics reveal concerns about the role that women themselves might play in such sexual dislocations. Images of pure, virtuous white women would fill state political rhetoric for decades, and assumptions about white female virtue would dominate state courtrooms any time a black man was on trial for assault. Black leaders vocally defended the virtue of black women at every opportunity. But in everyday life, more complex notions of women held sway. Even as North Carolinians cast women as guardians of virtue, descriptions of women's activities also invoked biblical conceptions of female moral weakness, raising the threatening possibility that unsupervised young women—like Eve—could lose hold of themselves and go astray. The heated emotions and intense physicality of sport could heighten such concerns. In the nineteenth century, when men were carried away by the passions of sport, their loss of self-control had usually been associated with potential violence. Similar lapses on the part of women almost invariably carried sexual implications.[40]

Contrasting concerns about athletic women as usurpers of male roles and as dangerously vulnerable to their own impulses showed clearly in a small pamphlet titled *The Taint of the Bicycle*, published by Livingstone College graduate W. F. Fonvielle in 1902. The work, which grew out of a popular series of articles that Fonvielle had written for the *Star of Zion*, focused less on political matters than on cultural upheavals, depicting a world turned upside down by the arrival of the newly invented "wheel." In a series of wickedly satiric observations, Fonvielle critiqued growing worldliness in church life (exemplified in the popularity of church-sponsored bicycle raffles) and the supposedly spendthrift habits of working-class African Americans (seen in his portrait of a barefoot cook cheerfully pedaling a bicycle worth many times her weekly salary). He also offered a striking image of female riders, based not on the vision of sexual equality so frequently invoked by black women, but on a reversal of conventional sexual roles.

"Then, sad regret—woman went 'a coasting,' and 'a scorching,'" he wrote. "For a time she rode her brother's bicycle—when he would let her; she rode her son's 'bike,' if she were larger and stronger than he; on her lover's 'safety,' if he loved her better than she loved him; and finally on her husband's 'wheel,' if he were a hen-pecked husband.... With stiff hat, laundried shirt, high collar, four-in-hand tie, low cut vest, cutaway coat, plus a substitution for pantaloons, she rode and pretended to be happy in her new role." The last sentence of the paragraph touched on the uncertainty engendered by such sweeping social change. "Perhaps she was happy," Fonvielle mused.[41]

As the story continued, however, Fonvielle offered a far different account of the effects that bicycle riding could have on women, turning from the usurpation of male possessions and attire to a highly feminized form of weakness in which physical freedom led not to fulfillment but to disaster. The final chapter of the work recounted the fate of Sadie Southwell, the star pupil of her home-town school who had gone on to graduate with top honors from a distin-guished seminary. After marrying a minister and settling into a new town, she acquired a bicycle and "joined bicycle parties of different sizes, shapes and sexes, having a thoroughly good time." The minister, meanwhile, let his protec-tive impulses lapse. He "never inquired as to when and how the young wife went and came," satisfied "that she was with her friends and enjoying herself." But one day she returned home highly distraught, and when her husband asked what was the matter, "bursting into tears, between sobs and much incoherent speech, she made a confession—told him all." Fonvielle never specified the nature of what he called her "sin," but the implication was obvious. The story ended with the deaths of both husband and wife, overcome by her unnamed transgression.[42]

Outside the realm of fiction, the tight connections that had developed be-tween public appearance, independent action, physical exertion, and sexual suspicions showed particularly clearly in the experience of State Normal stu-dent Fodie Buie. When Buie got a courthouse job in her small North Carolina hometown, she purchased a bicycle to ride to work. She later recalled the stir she caused when she rode her new possession through the town wearing the slightly shortened skirt that bicycling required. "Ladies did not go places alone," she explained, and "if one's skirts did not touch the ground, one was looked upon with suspicion, if not downright disapproval, and somewhat ostracized by the 'best ladies' in the community."[43]

By the end of the nineteenth century, however, disapproval was not the only reaction to changing female dress, a development that would introduce addi-tional dilemmas to women's sports. Young women found that while less con-straining attire gave them more freedom of movement, the combination could also turn them into objects of erotic fascination, particularly as they spent more time in public. Bessie Delany, who taught school in the black community of Boardman, North Carolina, in the early 1910s, encountered such reactions when she took advantage of her newfound independence to cast aside her father's rules on modest dress and make herself a blue silk outfit in the latest style. "Skirts were going up, and you could see the ankle when you walked," she recalled. "And when the men would see a glimpse of ankle, they would say, 'Oooooh-weeee!'"[44]

Female basketball players thus faced dual reactions, exemplifying the shifting cultural currents they sought to negotiate. By the early 1900s most state basket-ball players wore bloomers, the blousy trousers that had become the legacy of Amelia Bloomer's Bloomer Costume (while bloomers had proved too controversial for everyday wear, they quickly became an athletic institution). Bloomers could be criticized as a symbolic effort to appropriate male clothing, as when W. F. Fonvielle called them "a substitute for pantaloons." They could also spark great interest. The *Charlotte Observer* report of the 1907 Elizabeth-Presbyterian match dwelt particularly on the players' uniforms, offering a description in which details of the match itself mingled with a teasing hint of a fine spectacle missed: "The players, it is understood on good authority, were attired in abbreviated skirts, that nothing might impede the celerity or the alertness with which they leaped, dived heroically and sped determinedly toward their rivals' goal."[45]

In coverage of the Elizabeth-Presbyterian contest, in fact, any hint that competitive basketball might be somehow unwomanly was submerged beneath the event's sexually charged excitement. As well as being a fiercely fought competition, the game took on the flavor of a carnival, temporarily upsetting social conventions. The disruptions began as soon as supporters of the two schools descended onto the Charlotte streets, at which point the city's journalists "buried their tablets and pencils in their pockets and forgot to take notes," seeing "nothing but pretty, attractive faces, milk-white arms, dainty little shoes and becoming dresses." Although college officials had attempted to keep order by barring male spectators, the game created so much interest among the city's male population that the day before the contest officials felt compelled to announce that not only would men be barred from the grounds, but "a close watch will be kept to see that none enter in disguise." The *Charlotte News* suggested that if men were allowed to buy tickets to the game, "it would take an expert mathematician to figure out the amount of the gate receipts." The *Observer* predicted that "the coffers of the athletic clubs of the colleges would be filled with gold, for business would have been suspended and the populace would have turned out en masse."[46]

A number of the city's young men found the game's attractions stronger than even the threat of arrest, and they scaled the buildings around the field to catch forbidden glimpses of the players (despite the *Observer* reporter's claim of information had "on good authority," the enthusiastic detail in his description suggests that he was probably among the culprits). The *News* summed up the event with a cartoon that depicted observers with opera-glasses, a Keystone Kops policeman, and a bloomer-clad player whose clinging outfit suggested a considerable degree of wishful imagination. The *Observer* reported with similar amusement on those who spied on the game "in spite of the inhibition of those in charge," noting that the young men had been summoned to court, where they would be forced to "show cause why the penalty of death should not be imposed."[47]

A 1907 cartoon that originally appeared in the *Charlotte News* captured the carnival-like atmosphere that surrounded North Carolina's first women's basketball game played in public. From Queen's College *Caps and Belles*; photograph courtesy of the Robinson-Spangler Carolina Room, Public Library of Charlotte and Mecklenburg County.

A handful of adventuresome young sports were not the only Charlotte residents thrown off balance by the spectacle of female competition. In one of the New South's most seriously commerce-oriented towns, even the suggestion that business would have been suspended was significant indeed. Although the women's competition apparently failed to inspire the alcoholic excesses so common at football games, when the teams' supporters descended on the Charlotte streets after the contest, they sparked their own brand of inebriation. "Every girl talked at once and to every one in sight," the *News* reported. "No one took time to interpret what her neighbor said. Men stared, caught the contagion and began to act silly. . . . Little wonder that the latent spark of sport in their souls became suddenly rekindled and that they offered bets on the next game; on the supper hour; on the outcome of the aldermanic campaign; the Thaw trial—on anything bettable. The intoxication, once revived, was maddening."[48]

Descriptions of the young women carried a particularly strong air of abandon. The scene at the grounds was pictured as "gloriously incoherent and ecstatic." An Elizabeth College victory celebration appeared in print as an anarchic spree, with behavior more akin to popular stereotypes of Native Americans than to that of respectable young ladies. The erotically tinged account of one of Presbyterian's disappointed supporters suggested further lapses in ladylike self-control: "One flaxen-haired beauty came pounding up the streets, flirting a white and blue flag, stamping her little feet and giving vent to her disappointment by screaming at the top of her voice. She was red in the face and big eyed. Later she sat at a soda water table, and pounded the glass with her cute little fist."[49]

The young women who played for Elizabeth and Presbyterian betrayed little consternation at the stir they had created; in fact, they seem to have enjoyed the attention. Like Bessie Delany, who did not let either the comments of vocal bystanders or her father's disapproval dissuade her from showing off her ankles, they pressed ahead. The victorious Elizabeth students described the game with enthusiasm in their school annual, including a reprint of the *Observer*'s somewhat racy caricature. Presbyterian students took the loss in stride. "With material, the rawest ever, we got to work and turned out a creditable 'Varsity Basketball team,'" the school annual reported in 1908. "With what seemed monumental nerve we next challenged our sister college. What happened? Get trimmed? Well, we rather think we did, but on as close scores as you can see. But, notwithstanding, we're up and at it again this year."[50]

School administrators, on the other hand, were clearly less enthusiastic. A planned rematch between the schools the following year was canceled, and despite the "deep and all-pervading gloom" the cancellation created on the campuses, the teams did not compete again. The Elizabeth College physician who made the ruling referred to several "accidents" that had plagued the school's intramural games, a judgment that itself suggested concerns that the excitement of basketball could draw young women beyond the bounds of their own self-control. Still, the spectacle of the earlier competition, along with the sensationalized reporting it inspired, had done little to enhance the colleges' reputations as producers of well-bred southern ladies, and issues of public image likely played a role as well. In subsequent years, students at Presbyterian College made diligent efforts to schedule other matches but found few other colleges willing to accept their challenge.[51]

Concerns about public image would help shape women's basketball in many ways, influencing not only public competition, but the rules that women used and the uniforms they wore. Such careful attention to appearance reflected both the controversy that surrounded efforts to expand women's activities, and the growing significance that image and appearance wielded in North Carolina society. As North Carolinians moved to unfamiliar places and built new institutions, their fortunes increasingly depended on the impressions they created, the gestures, words, and images with which they presented themselves to acquaintances and strangers. This growing reliance on appearance, along with the constant self-examination it required, could be a source of great anxiety. But residents—especially those engaged in controversial endeavors—could also turn it to their advantage.

In North Carolina, most of the interactions that came to govern public life reflected the state's social structure, within which rich and poor, men and women, black and white, each occupied a designated place. The elaborate system of manners and encounters that developed in the state meant that such inequalities were embodied not only in the laws that dictated who could vote, sit on juries, or occupy the front section of a streetcar, but also in the customs of daily life. From the mocking stereotypes and demands for deference that circumscribed the day-to-day activities of African Americans, to the faded clothes and pale complexions that set mill workers off from more prosperous residents, to the modest dress and restrained behavior required of women who wished to be treated with respect, reminders of these relationships ran through citizens' daily lives in intricate patterns of behavior and expectation. The firm hold that white male Democrats had established over political and economic power meant that defiance of prevailing norms could be both futile and dangerous— perils most strikingly embodied in the ruthless violence visited on black men who even inadvertently stepped out of place. So dissatisfied state residents adopted other strategies; they learned instead to dissemble. Hidden behind smiles and pleasant tones and the civility for which the state would become renowned, they built identities that departed sharply from the existing code and took on projects that would eventually change it.

At times North Carolinians pursued such ends through elaborately crafted deceptions. In the first decades of the twentieth century, for example, the rise of white supremacy and the collapse of black political influence meant that the state's African American schools depended more than ever on the support of northern white philanthropists, who themselves increasingly subscribed to the idea of "industrial education" and encouraged black colleges to discontinue "impractical" academic endeavors in favor of programs focused on "the saw and plane and the anvil."[52] In response, many schools began to teach their students not only Greek and Latin but how to conceal intellectual aspirations from white benefactors. Rather than wholeheartedly embracing industrial education, colleges simply added courses in carpentry and brickmaking for male students and in dressmaking and laundry for women, and emphasized those activities in public appeals. In 1902 Shaw University issued a fund-raising pamphlet that typified such efforts. Although Shaw boasted law, medical, and theo-

Livingstone College students disguised as maids, 1910. From *An Appeal for the Girls'*
*New Building*; photograph courtesy of the North Carolina Collection, University of
North Carolina Library, Chapel Hill.

logical schools, the pamphlet revealed none of those endeavors. Instead, it
showed students in their proper "place," the men pursuing carpentry and
blacksmithing, and the women perched behind sewing machines. When Livingstone College put out a similar pamphlet in 1910, one of the most striking
photographs showed the college's female students dressed as maids, conspicuously displaying washtubs, brooms, and boxes of Gold Dust scouring power.[53]

In many women's endeavors, however, appearances were shaped in more
subtle fashion, woven into the dress and manners of daily life. Mrs. Van Landingham, who had advised State Normal students to maintain the air of southern ladies, touched on this strategy when she urged her listeners to preserve at
least the facade of dependence, underlining her words with a hint of warning.
"Let then no girl of today permit the earning of a living, nor the financial
gratification of 'the glorious privilege of being independent' relieve her brother
of his natural care, nor her lover of his gallantry," she cautioned. "Let not her
courage in threading her way through crowded streets on foot, bicycle or in
buggy, make her indifferent to protection and chaperonage, lest her disposition
suffer by too much confidence, her face wear the hardened expression of assurance, and the time come when she shall look for chivalry and find it not: for
things when unused, in time cease to exist."[54]

Female college students from both races, whose very pursuit of higher educa-

tion represented a step beyond dependence, quickly learned that their education encompassed not only academic subjects but lessons in the behavior that
would mark them as respectable ladies, rather than threatening rebels. The
dreaded inspections of Lady Principal Kirkland or the strict rules imposed on
Livingstone women served multiple ends, training young women in discipline
and self-awareness while also ensuring that their behavior would do nothing to
draw attention to the schools' potentially controversial missions. Such strategies were also evident in school curricula. As well as teaching students to
reason, to debate, and to aspire to public work, professors who themselves had
defied convention by choosing permanent careers offered instruction in the
mysteries of proper dress and refined manners. The self-consciousness this philosophy instilled (and from which basketball was such a welcome release) pro-
tected not only individual reputations but also the broader goals that women
were beginning to develop.[55]

For many women this concealment focused on demonstrating that their new
activities neither disrupted prevailing expectations of female discretion nor
usurped roles reserved for men. Even as women filled new jobs, took prominent
roles in efforts to reform prisons and child labor laws, and worked to transform
public education, they portrayed these interests in terms of traditional female
activities such as raising children, caring for the less fortunate, or pursuing
church missionary work. In many instances the veil of caution and restraint
produced the desired impression. When strong support for suffrage developed
at the State Normal College in the 1910s, the students kept their enthusiasm so
publicly discreet that when the state's governor appeared at a school function,
he lavishly and confidently praised the students for their good sense in resisting
the voting rights fervor. The suffrage-minded students hid their amusement
politely in their handkerchiefs.[56]

In the first two decades of women's college basketball, players adopted similar strategies, striving to clothe their new activity in restraint and respectability.
College officials frequently emphasized their students' modesty and sought to
avert any threats to reputation by adopting a variety of measures to conceal
female players. Elizabeth and Presbyterian authorities banned male spectators;
State Normal College administrators planted a hedge around the institution's
outdoor court; and all female athletes monitored the details of athletic dress.
"After players put on their 'gym' suits . . . they must put on long black stockings,
a top skirt which had a way of hanging down behind, and throw a coat around
the shoulders," one State Normal student recalled of the dash that turn-of-the-
century students made from dormitory room to gym class. "The rear effect of
the whole outfit reminded one of a rooster's tail feathers in wet weather, but we
were nothing if not sticklers to the strictest sense of modesty."[57]

Propriety was of even greater concern for African American women, who continued to contend not simply with the expectations of their own communities but also with the opinions of whites. At the end of the nineteenth century, as the rhetoric of white supremacy enveloped white women in a protective, if also stifling, mantle of purity, black women found themselves cast in opposing roles, characterized as highly sensual and with little control over their impulses. Such portraits became so prevalent that in a 1903 report to Shaw trustees, university president C. F. Meserve felt compelled to defend the honor of his students in general and his female students in particular. "At the present time, when race prejudice is so strong and attention so constantly called to some members of the race, I wish to put on record my belief which is derived from my own personal experience and observation," Meserve wrote. The statement is frequently seen in the press that nearly all colored women are lewd and that practically all colored people will steal and lie and that they generally condone these vices. . . . I have found the students at Shaw almost without exception clean, pure minded men and women, obedient and of earnest purpose." He went on to emphasize that "violation of the rules of the institution has received the condemnation of the major portion of the student body and this has been more marked even on the part of the young women than the young men." The sexually charged excitement of the Elizabeth-Presbyterian basketball game, in which young women were portrayed as "gloriously incoherent and ecstatic" and their behavior linked to stereotypical images of "savage" Native Americans, no doubt produced some consternation at the two schools. For African American institutions, such a public spectacle would have been disastrous.[58]

The stress placed on young women's reputations, as well as on their physical safety, showed in the rules by which black colleges governed female students' conduct and dress. General concerns about maintaining racial respectability meant that most black colleges imposed tight controls on both male and female students through rigid regulation of schedules and behavior. But women were watched with special care. Bessie Delany recalled that while she and her sister Sarah lived at Raleigh's St. Augustine's College, "We were not allowed to go off the campus without an escort. Matter of fact, we were not allowed to go to certain places *on* the campus without someone to go with us." Almost from Shaw University's inception, officials devoted part of the annual catalog to discussions of female students' wardrobes (the garb of men received no such attention). "Students are expected to dress neatly and modestly," ran one directive. Others forbade the wearing of velvet, satin, expensive jewelry, silk hose, "French heels," thin dresses without slips, and other fashionable garments. The policies were so detailed that many shifts in women's fashion could be discerned in the changing lists of banned attire.[59]

As late as 1916 Shaw University students remained well-concealed behind combinations of skirts and bloomers. Courtesy of the University Archives, Shaw University.

Similar caution was evident in athletic wear. Black college women faced few suggestions that they were too frail to engage in sport. The stringent work required of slave women and the heavy labor so many black women pursued following Emancipation had laid to rest most notions of black female frailty. But concern with public image showed clearly in black athletes' dress. The carefully composed basketball image that appeared in Shaw's catalog in 1909 offered no fuel for any criticism from either parents or skeptical observers. It showed a group of young women decorously arranged on a tree-lined grassy court, with no spectators in sight. It also showed that while students at white schools had adopted bloomers almost a decade earlier, Shaw women still played in skirts that brushed the grass around their feet. A photograph from 1916 pointed to continuing conservatism; the young women had switched to bloomers but still wore them only beneath concealing skirts. Although the skirts were abandoned the next year, modesty remained a definite concern, as the catalog instructed students to be certain that the bloomers they packed were "*very full*."[60]

Even as hedges and heavy material helped mute the sexual implications of women's sports, the games that black and white women pursued also downplayed potential concerns that athletics would tempt women to become too much like men. The choice of basketball itself invoked this issue. James Naismith had designed his new game with an eye toward teaching the strategic virtues of team sport while avoiding the violence associated with football. By directing player efforts toward shooting upward rather than running forward, by emphasizing passing (before dribbling was invented in 1896, basketball players were not permitted to run with the ball), and by banning all "shouldering, holding, pushing, tripping or striking," Naismith sought to shape a game focused around the artful movement of the ball rather than the forceful movement of the players. College men, caught up in the physical clashes of football, frequently disdained the new sport as a "sissy" game, and its early popularity at women's colleges gave it a distinctly feminine stamp.[61]

Once women's colleges took up basketball, they modified the game still further, minimizing exertion and reducing potential roughness through carefully designed "girls' rules" that clearly marked the women's game as different from the men's. The 1909 catalog photograph of Shaw University players offered a dramatic illustration of those modified rules. Not only did the players wear shoe-brushing skirts; they were dispersed in pairs across the court. The only action was taking place beneath the basket, where one young woman raised her arms to shoot and another, standing at a respectful distance, sought to screen her view. The large number of players on the court suggested the Shaw women were playing an especially conservative version of the game, devised by Newcomb College's Clara Baer and called, tellingly, by the feminine name "basquette." The rules of basquette divided the court into seven sections. A pair of players—one from each team—occupied each space and could not venture beyond its bounds. A more widely used set of regulations, drawn up by Senda Berenson and published as the official rules of women's basketball in 1901, split the court into three sections and employed five players on a team, with two players stationed under each basket and one in the center section. No player was allowed to dribble more than once, and in both sets of rules all physical contact between players was forbidden.[62]

North Carolina women's basketball was thus profoundly shaped by a range of expectations that governed female conduct, assuming a form that allowed young women to stretch their athletic wings while avoiding potential criticism. Still, concern about outside opinion was not the only force guiding women's sport. Women's basketball programs were frequently influenced by one final factor—a vision of society that diverged sharply from the Darwinian philosophy that had helped drive the growth of men's college sport. The activism that women's colleges had encouraged in their students belonged to the reforms of the Progressive movement, to a broad range of efforts that included temperance, child labor legislation, prison reform, and school improvement. Instead of championing the competitive tumult of marketplace economics or party politics, Progressive thinkers envisioned a more harmonious social order and focused their efforts on promoting efficient government, protecting "weaker" members of society, and softening the harshest edges of all-out capitalist strife.[63]

Progressive activists met with strong opposition, and the qualities that basketball had been designed to teach—discipline, teamwork, and determination—offered effective preparation for the challenges young women would face once they ventured beyond college grounds. For all the domestically centered rhetoric about nurturing schoolteachers and municipal housekeepers, young women who undertook teaching or community reform confronted situations that required a far broader range of skills: public speaking, placating suspicious parents, organizing community fund drives, directing reform organizations, living on their own in strange communities, negotiating with recalcitrant school committees or reluctant public officials. Still, Progressive women usually saw their goal not as defeating their opponents but as converting them, as helping "backward" individuals to see the modernizing light and embrace ideals of ambition, discipline, and self-control. "Let us get trained hands and cultured minds and hearts, and then go forth in God's name to carry sunshine and cheer into the thousands of homes where ignorance and vice reign supremely," Annie Kimball had exhorted her fellow Livingstone students in 1891.[64]

North Carolina's Progressive female activists also held tightly to ideas of female moral authority and carefully avoided any action that might endanger that position. The harshest critiques of women who showed their ankles or who screamed too loudly at a game had, in fact, come from other women, from the "good ladies" of North Carolina's many towns who saw breaches of conventional behavior as threatening a privileged female status. Even as many young women began to throw off ladylike constraints, anticipating the cultural and sexual transformations of the 1920s, other women continued to put the rhetoric of feminine morality to a variety of ends, justifying moves into public life, guarding the autonomy of women's organizations, and buttressing women's claims to authority in matters that ranged from public morality to political reform.[65]

This persisting vision of social order and female respectability established one of its strongest footholds in the increasingly elaborate physical education programs that were developing at many of North Carolina's white women's colleges—programs that would stand in sharp contrast to athletic developments elsewhere in state society. By the late 1910s, high-school-age girls had begun discovering basketball's many pleasures, and by the mid-1920s a combination of student efforts and a changing cultural climate would make varsity girls' basketball a fixture at many North Carolina high schools. As the state's black college women began to cast off some of the restrictions governing their conduct, many of them would also venture into varsity play. But physical educators would chart a different path, underscoring the varying conceptions of society and of womanhood developing within the state. While they promoted women's exercise, encouraging both gymnastics and games, in true Progressive fashion they placed strict controls on competitive endeavors, launched harsh critiques of intercollegiate sports, and emphasized the cooperative rather than the competitive aspects of athletics. Students might play games against one another, but the watchword was "moderation"; they would not be permitted the "excesses" that tainted varsity athletics.[66]

Within North Carolina the growing influence of physical education philosophy was particularly evident at the State Normal College, where deliberate attempts to downplay competition in favor of cooperation became clear during the 1910s. The confident class of 1910 stood at the peak of the school's basketball enthusiasm. After those years a combination of faculty actions and student decisions slowly displaced basketball from the pinnacle of the school's athletic activities. The descriptions of basketball games in student publications also took on a different tone, focusing on the sport's ability to inspire self-control and cooperative effort. "The spirit of co-operation, the team work brought about by athletics does inestimable good," explained the 1913 annual. " 'Athletic spirit' has steadily grown in our college because the students have come to realize that physical training gives them needed relaxation, poise, self-control and ability to work with others."[67] The description of the young woman voted college athlete underlined this emphasis on control:

> Here's to the girl that's strictly in it,
> Who doesn't lose her head even for a minute,
> Plays well the game and knows the limit
> And still gets all the fun that's in it.[68]

The 1914 annual specifically denied that a taste for competition ran through the school programs. At the annual class tournament, the writer emphasized, "the different classes contest for the cups and show fine class spirit, not of bitter competition, but of intense enthusiasm." By 1920, just after the State Normal College became the North Carolina College for Women, this new approach to physical activity would be consolidated in the state's first degree-granting physical education program, under the direction of an energetic young Virginian named Mary Channing Coleman. Like her colleagues around the country, Coleman came prepared not simply to uphold the honor of physical education but to actively promote the social vision that it embodied, setting the stage for a statewide conflict over sports, society, and womanhood that would go on for

decades. The influence wielded by physical education, she presciently promised, would be both "wholesome" and "lasting."[69]


Like their male counterparts, North Carolina's college women seized eagerly on
competitive athletics, rejoicing in the joy of movement and the discipline of
mastering athletic skills. But while men's athletics quickly became a major facet
of North Carolina culture and a cornerstone of twentieth-century male identity, women's sports were shaped by a far more constraining set of social expectations. As a result, most games took place in seclusion, and the exuberant
verse and confident photographs that depicted athletic activity were printed in
school annuals and student journals rather than in the state's major publications. The careful maneuvering that surrounded women's basketball offered
little direct challenge to the state's prevailing political arrangements or to the
assumptions about men and women on which they were based. Still, such reticence allowed basketball courts to become spaces where young women could
experiment with change, could test themselves, could try out competition and
determine where they stood. As a key component of a new kind of female
education, basketball helped prepare women for a remarkable spate of social
activism and a permanent transformation of their conceptions of themselves.

Even from his distant rooftop, the *Observer* reporter could read this mix of
ambition and restraint in the basketball game that unfolded on the Presbyterian College field, and his description serves as an admirable metaphor for the
work that so many southern women pursued in the early decades of the twentieth century. "The game throughout was clean and ladylike," he wrote. "There
was no slugging and there was no work for the stretchers or the ambulance. But
let it not be thought that there was nothing doing. If there was a dull minute
from the call of the whistle to the last biff of the ball, it would be hard to say
where it was. The girls were there to win."[70]

## CHAPTER THREE

# Preparation for Citizenship

## The Spread of High School
## Basketball, 1913–1934

I n the opening months of 1927, members of the girls' basketball team at Lincolnton High School arranged themselves on the school steps for a yearbook photograph. Lincoln County, North Carolina, was still a largely rural area, tucked into the foothills of a conservative southern state. But no one would have known it from the picture. Newspapers, magazines, and movies had spread the daring styles of the 1920s to even the most remote corners of North Carolina, and the Lincolnton team members sported bobbed hair, surprisingly low necklines, and brightly patterned socks rolled down below their knees. An accompanying description cast the team's efforts in terms that made clear that the factory rather than the farm had become the dominant metaphor in these young people's lives. "The basketball season this year has been a great success," the summary read. "Miss Hoke proved her ability as coach by taking an inexperienced team and, by hard and persistent work, managed to bring together a smooth-working machine which we were proud to have represent our school."[1]

Across North Carolina, at hundreds of newly built public high schools, basketball teams sat for similar pictures and made similar claims. Basketball swept through the state in the years after World War I, part of the wave of modern institutions that accelerated North Carolina's transition from a state centered around small farming communities to one focused on commerce and industrial production. Between 1905 and 1930 North Carolina's school officials opened more than 400 high schools as part of a broad-based effort to prepare the state's citizens for this new world. Within these institutions, students tackled the heightened academic challenges designed to fit them for the demands of jobs as clerks, secretaries, managers, sales representatives, and dozens of other new professions created by the state's expanding commercial economy. They also played basketball. The sporting craze that seized the nation in the first part

Lincolnton High School team, as pictured in the school yearbook, 1927. Courtesy of Lincolnton High School.

of the twentieth century had made its way into school systems throughout the country, spurred by both community interest and changing educational philosophy. Baseball was still the national sport, and football remained the pinnacle of big-time college athletics. But basketball called for less equipment, required fewer players, and was open to both boys and girls. By the mid-1920s James Naismith's invention had become North Carolina's most widely played sport, sparking widespread excitement and creating countless vivid memories.[2]

"Basket ball is one of the most popular games that is played to day on the school grounds," the school paper at Mecklenburg County's Dixie High School reported in 1916. "It is practiced in almost every country school of any standing. Basketball is the subject from morning until night; every one talks of it. If you ever see a small crowd of boys or girls standing talking together, you can guess they are talking about basket ball." Decades later many former players recalled their experiences with undimmed enthusiasm. More than fifty years after Lavinia Ardrey Kell donned the black bloomers and short-sleeved jersey that made up a Pineville High School uniform, she warmed quickly to the topic. "I would love to be young one more time, just to get to play basketball," she explained. "At that time that's about all I expect that we went to school for was to play basketball, we loved it so much."[3]

Throughout North Carolina, basketball inspired thousands of similar experiences, creating unforgettable moments for individual players as well as for family and friends. Basketball legends began to haunt every corner of the state, with winning seasons, big games, and impossible shots recounted over kitchen tables, in street-corner conversations, or on the steps of churches before services began. On one level these tales related deeply personal events, the almost timeless stories of courage, challenge, and self-realization that give sports so much of its tantalizing appeal. But through the accounts also wove more time-bound themes, reflecting the opportunities and dilemmas raised within a state increasingly dominated by cities and factories and bound together by newly paved roads, the spreading influence of large-circulation newspapers, and the newfangled invention of wireless broadcast. As in the nineteenth century, ideas associated with athletic rhetoric—discipline, precision, and teamwork—fit neatly with the pressing demands of commercial and industrial growth. Perhaps most significant, however, the fledgling system of high school sports competition also spoke to a broader set of issues regarding moral authority and social order, as state residents struggled with the tensions of a society that combined the rhetoric of democracy and equal opportunity with a reality that fell well short of those ideals.

Part of basketball's burgeoning popularity lay in its connections to the glamorous modernity that so clearly marked the 1920s, the whirl of automobile excursions, late-night dance parties, and other new excitements to which the bobbed-haired, bare-kneed Lincolnton players clearly aspired. As radio, magazines, newspapers, and motion pictures spread a newly daring national culture throughout the state, touching young and old, urban and rural, black and white, athletics attained new cultural heights. In a society fascinated by the speed and power of airplanes, automobiles, and other dazzling machines, talented athletes who exhibited similar qualities drew reverence and acclaim. Stars such as Babe Ruth, Jack Dempsey, and Helen Wills, who moved faster or hit harder than their predecessors, became figures of national adulation, and their achievements were recorded and promoted through the breathless tones that so marked the era.[4]

Basketball fit the tenor of those speedy times particularly well. When a renowned white Georgia YMCA team visited Charlotte, they were billed as "the

The speedy men's team from Charlotte's Second Ward High School, as pictured in the school newspaper, May 1927. Courtesy of the Second Ward High School National Alumni Foundation.

fastest in the South," and the *Charlotte Observer* writer who went to see them play wondered at the way "perfect precision, marvelous ease, lightning speed, eagle accuracy and various and sundry other elements of the game were flashed before the audience in kaleidoscopic fashion." Members of the 1928 boys' team from the city's black Second Ward High School impressed observers so thoroughly that the school newspaper reported, "It is said that they were so fast that the human eye was unable to follow them as they traversed the boarded floor." Elizabeth Stratford Newitt, who played for white Charlotte Central High in the mid-1920s, summed up the excitement young people felt when they balanced speed and skill in the heat of competition. "The thing of it, you have to be quick," she explained with enthusiasm. "And you have to be able to handle that ball just right. And get it where it belongs."[5]

But athletics did not become an integral part of North Carolina's public school system simply because state residents enjoyed playing or watching. Rather, its new prominence sprang from its links to the state's ongoing social transformations, and particularly from the way school sports supported state leaders' ambitious social goals, while helping to ease some of the tensions created by such broad-based social change. Sports thus became part of a new stage in North Carolina's public schooling, in which political and industrial leaders sought to use the state school system to shape the character of citizens in accordance with visions of economic prosperity and social order.[6]

The men who seized control of North Carolina government at the turn of the century saw the state's future in terms of industry and commerce, and they undertook a series of ambitious and wide-ranging attempts to modernize the state and its citizens. Rather than viewing North Carolina as a collection of autonomous communities, they began to talk of the state in the same terms that the Lincolnton basketball team had employed, as an integrated machine whose successful operation required hard work and coordinated effort from all residents. Following in the footsteps of northern-based Progressive activists, who used government and private actions to help order and direct the process of industrial development, North Carolina leaders launched their own series of wide-ranging social programs, including a nationally acclaimed Good Roads campaign, an innovative effort to eradicate the widespread and debilitating hookworm parasite, and a vast expansion of the public school system.[7]

As well as making physical improvements in the surfaces of roads or the health of citizens, these modernizers also embarked on a more ambitious effort, seeking to change the way that most North Carolinians regarded the world and their place in it. For more than a generation, members of the state's emerging industrial elite had schooled themselves in what they called "habits of industry," the Victorian-inspired mix of sobriety, restraint, rational calculation, and steady, disciplined effort with which they had responded to the rigors of industrial production and marketplace competition. In the early decades of the twentieth century, these new leaders sought to spread the gospel of individual transformation throughout North Carolina society. As well as touting the individual benefits to be gained by such behavior, they argued that any apparent drawbacks to rapid economic change—including skyrocketing farm tenancy rates and the problem of child labor—would be solved by the greater efficiency created when a wider range of North Carolinians adopted these ideals.[8]

The first large-scale attempts to encourage this kind of widespread social change were undertaken by the proprietors of North Carolina's burgeoning textile industry, the major force behind the state's rapid economic growth. As textile operations grew, and as more North Carolinians moved from family farms into the textile villages that sprang up beside most mills, managers began to seek out ways of introducing formerly independent individuals, accustomed to the seasonal rhythms of agricultural production, to the far different requirements of industrial labor.[9]

Such efforts often took the form of what industry executives called "welfare work" programs, which were designed to offer workers some relief from the monotony of factory labor as well as to instruct them in the rationalized ways of modern, industrial life. Participating mills offered an array of classes and activities that included "better baby" competitions, instruction in home decorating, demonstrations of "domestic science," and a range of sports and recreation programs. As well as helping to counter critiques of the sometimes deplorable conditions that low wages produced in many textile communities, welfare work was intended to teach discipline and ambition, encouraging workers to adopt the "necessary discipline and the close attention to details of manufacturing" and to aspire toward a level of material comfort that could be attained only by steady labor and a regular paycheck.[10]

North Carolina leaders saw the expanding system of public education as an ideal way to spread a similar gospel of training, discipline, and steady effort throughout the state, particularly to rural areas. In contrast to nineteenth-century educators, who spent a few months a year teaching children the handful of basic skills that would supplement lessons in farming and household management learned at home, twentieth-century instructors saw themselves as playing a far greater role in young people's development. State school officials instituted longer school days and stricter attendance regulations, as well as requiring students to cover a greater amount of academic material. They also transformed the school environment. Students at nineteenth-century schools focused on collective learning, embodied in the tradition of reciting lessons en masse and out loud. They monitored their own progress and left school whenever they or their parents felt that they had learned enough. The new system of graded education, in contrast, evaluated students according to a set of detailed state standards, with progress from one grade to another determined by how well they met those goals.[11]

As well as seeking to meet the demands of an industrial society, graded schools embodied a new approach to democratic opportunity. In the nineteenth century, faced with the challenges of rapidly growing and diversifying cities, northeastern educators had sought to create a uniform system of public schooling that would shape a wide range of students to fit smoothly into the emerging society. Along with stressing discipline, punctuality, and attention to detail, teachers and administrators encouraged the development of a worldview centered around competition, ambition, and determined effort, marked by carefully measured individual performance. As an increasingly professionalized society placed greater stress on education, these graded schools became powerful symbols of long-held visions of the United States as a land of opportunity in which individuals advanced according to their own merits as well as the efforts they put forth.[12]

In North Carolina, as elsewhere in the country, the democratic vision that graded schools promoted proved far more ideal than reality. High schools, for example, reached out to only a portion of the state's population. As late as 1933, state high schools enrolled less than two-thirds of eligible white residents and barely a quarter of eligible African Americans. Students from rural, African American, and textile mill families frequently found the need to contribute to family income more pressing than educational ambitions. Many students also met with structural obstacles. During the 1920s, African Americans often had to travel considerable distances to reach the scattered handful of black public high schools the state had begun, somewhat grudgingly, to support. The schools in many textile mill villages only went through seventh grade, forcing students who wished to pursue further education to pay tuition to high schools in nearby towns. Still, the gospel of effort and education prevailed in many corners of the state. Educators and converted students turned schools— particularly the new network of high schools—into centers for promoting high ambitions and unflagging efforts.[13]

Blanch Harris, a student at Claremont High School in Catawba County, touched on this transition when she cautioned her peers about the importance of the new institutions. "Men and women who are not trained usually have a hard time getting along in this world," she wrote in the *Hickory Daily Record*. "They are the ones who dig ditches, construct houses, wash dishes, scrub floors and numerous other things. Now why should we live such a life when we have such institutions for education?" An editorial writer for the school newspaper at Charlotte's Second Ward High School chimed in with the exhortation, "We must plant the seed of desire, water it with sincere faith. If you think you are beaten you are. If you dare not, you don't. If you want to win, but think you can't, it is almost sure you won't."[14]

Competitive athletics seemed to fit neatly with these new educational goals, and across the nation, secondary school educators began to show a growing interest in school athletic programs. Health concerns raised by the troubling physical state of many World War I draftees played a role in this new interest. In the words of two North Carolina professors, "America was astounded and shocked out of much of her complacency and apathy, when the draft revealed the positive fact that one out of every four of the young men who should have been in the prime of their physical manhood, were unfit to bear arms in the emergency call of their country." Physical educators also argued that a period of recreation offered an important balance to the increasing intellectual demands of classroom work. But the most compelling arguments drew on developing theories about the importance of play and games in young people's moral development, which gave scholarly weight to long-standing claims that athletic competition could encourage precisely the habits of thought and action that North Carolina educators idealized.[15]

Advocates of school sports promoted this philosophy throughout the state. In a 1926 pamphlet titled *Physical Education in the High School*, two of North Carolina's most distinguished professors of physical education lauded sports for teaching "precepts of good citizenship" as well as "sound character and right habits of living." "Educators realize that the playfields afford a laboratory for putting into practice these precepts, such as cannot be found any other place," they argued. While state officials focused most of their citizenship-building efforts on white schoolchildren and offered only limited support for recreational facilities at African American schools, the state's black educators promoted similar programs within their institutions, clearly marking their resolve to educate their students in accordance with the latest modern standards. "It should not require a very long argument to convince any one that athletics has its legitimate place in the scheme of the education of the young," Biddle University professor R. L. Douglass wrote in 1917. "Not only does it promote the development of bodily vigor, but moral strength as well; for those who succeed must first submit to a rigorous discipline, including avoidance of excesses, the cultivation of courage, self-control and resourcefulness. We submit, therefore, that a right use of the instinct to play, generally strong in adolescence, may prove a most powerful means of wholesome elevation."[16]

Seen in this light, basketball could seem a worthwhile social "laboratory." It also offered another powerful benefit, as school officials quickly concluded that sports contests were extremely popular with parents and communities. Some parents were cool to school athletics, particularly those who headed farming families that depended on young people's labor and who saw sports contests as a distraction from more immediate family concerns. Helen Shipman, who coached women's basketball at one of North Carolina's rural African American schools, would never forget the time one young woman's parents decided that picking crops was more important than a championship game, letting their daughter play only after Shipman mustered the entire team for a day of work in the family fields. But the rapid spread of sports teams and the statements of school officials suggest most families displayed greater enthusiasm. In 1923 a

Second Ward High School women's team, as pictured in the school newspaper, May 1927. Courtesy of the Second Ward High School National Alumni Foundation.

writer in *North Carolina Education* offered advice about promoting school endeavors, suggesting that a school newspaper might be used to spark interest "in any undertaking of the school." "This is particularly true in athletics," the author noted. "Announcements of contests, accounts of games, stories about the individual players, will do a great deal towards arousing enthusiasm and creating school spirit which can be done through athletics as in no other way."[17]

The interest athletics drew mattered to school officials because convincing communities of the value of a high school education often proved an uphill battle. For North Carolinians impatient to usher the state into what they viewed as a superior modern world, wide-ranging educational changes seemed essential. But for those citizens whose interests remained centered on family and community ties, such changes were far less attractive. A broad swath of North Carolinians believed in education. Public school funding had been an issue in the political struggles that shook the state in the 1880s and 1890s, and governor Charles Aycock had ridden to power in 1900 on a campaign that promoted both white supremacy and public education. Still, as privately funded community schools were replaced with an expanding system of state-supported public institutions, parents lost much of their ability to select teachers and set goals for their children, developments that dampened their enthusiasm for the new arrangements.[18]

The growing state role in public education was further complicated as the heightened expectations promoted in many high schools began to draw students out of their parents' world and into a very different one. Blanch Harris, the Catawba County student who lauded the advancements a high school education made possible, had clearly absorbed the ambitious rhetoric of the state's educational leaders. But her implicit condemnation of manual labor failed to acknowledge that the parents of most high school students had enjoyed no opportunity for that level of education and spent their days engaged in just the kind of activity that she disdainfully dismissed. Even when parents wished for their children to rise in the world, the reality that such advancement represented could contain troubling, sometimes painful, implications.

Community sports enthusiasm also pointed to another dilemma raised by the state's new schools. Sports became so popular in part because they embodied ideals of community and mutuality that often seemed missing from modern classrooms. A worldview that idealized ambition and individual achievement might have been a valuable asset for young people trying to make their way in the bustling economies of Charlotte or Raleigh. But such ideals also chafed against deep-rooted community values, which centered on cooperation and mutual assistance rather than competition. L. E. Lashman, who served as playground supervisor of the city of Raleigh during the 1910s, justified his work by highlighting the contrast between traditional ethics of reciprocity and the increasing emphasis that school curriculums placed on individual achievement. "The writer was once asked if he was 'folksy,'" he wrote of himself in *North Carolina Education*. "He was told people in a certain town were folksy and that he would be expected to be the same. Are the children taught to be folksy? What happens to Johnny if he whispers to his neighbor? How quickly in the classroom is every attempt to be sociable frustrated by the teacher's 'no whispering'? How is co-operation encouraged in the average class-room? . . . If Tom and Jack work together at the solution of an arithmetic problem it is called cheating and both are punished."[19]

While academic ambitions could push friends and family apart, school athletics brought communities together and gave parents the chance to take a more active role in school endeavors. Athletics could not take place without community support. Despite their grand ambitions, North Carolina's high schools usually had no funds for equipment, transportation, or facilities. Parents who themselves had not attended high school usually could do little to help their children with schoolwork, and many could not afford to contribute financially to school activities. But they could sew uniforms, help build gymnasiums, drive players to games, and cheer loudly for school teams. Behind the photographs of uniformed players and accounts of seasons that appeared in school yearbooks lay the efforts not only of players and coaches but of entire communities.

Shelby High School men's team, 1925. From *The Legend*; photograph courtesy of the North Carolina Collection, University of North Carolina Library, Chapel Hill.

Seen this way, memories of individual achievements blend into a dense net of community connections in which the details of how a player got to a game carry as much weight as what happened on the court. "We always had a way to go to ball games," Lavinia Kell proudly explained. "Because we lived four miles below Pineville, back of Pineville. We had a lot of boys and girls around here that played ball. We could have made up a team mostly from down here. So we always had our transportation. And in that day, transportation was an item, too. . . . The boys would take the cars, or sometimes one of the girls would take the car. Our coach always made sure we had transportation." Vada Setzer Hewins, who lived in rural Catawba County, echoed those words. "I lived like three miles out of Catawba. [The coach] always got you a way home. You didn't have to get out here and bum. He never left you stranded. He'd take you to the games, then he saw that you got home."[20]

One of the grandest gestures a community could provide was a gymnasium, and many went to great lengths to do so. In the Mecklenburg County community of Newell, white farming parents cut down trees, hauled them to the school, and constructed a sturdy, watertight log structure. The materials for the two large fireplaces that heated the building were painstakingly gathered by

The 1927–28 women's team from Pineville High School practices on the school's out-door court. Courtesy of Douglas Nisbet Davis.

the students themselves—for weeks every child who rode the morning school bus carried a rock to add to the collection. The Mary Potter School, a private African American academy in Granville County, undertook a similar endeavor when basketball fever swept through the institution. "At first basket ball was played on the second floor of the administration building, but that was about to prove deteriorating to the structure," a school history recounted. "Hence en-thusiastic, unanimous efforts to build a gymnasium began." The school under-took two major building projects in the 1920s. Money for a boys' dormitory was donated by a Pittsburgh church organization. But the community built the gym itself, using funds and time donated by students, faculty, and alumni. "The Mary E. Shaw gymnasium is a symbol of youth, built by youth, as a place of rec-reation and play for the generations to follow," the school's historian proudly recounted.[21]

The symbolic value of a brick, board, or log structure was reinforced by the supportive crowds that gathered at games, drawn together in spite of the many new diversions—radios, automobiles, and improved roads—that so often sent members of families and communities in different directions. When North Carolinians clambered into automobiles to embark on joyrides or long-distance excursions, their new mobility threatened to pull apart traditional social fabrics. When cars carried players and spectators to school basketball games, they could help to reaffirm or expand community connections. A stu-

dent engaged in a math test, as L. E. Lashman noted, sat alone, waging an individual battle with a set of state-determined expectations. A basketball player, as
Elizabeth Newitt recalled, performed a public drama in which spectators could
play prominent roles. "I never will forget my mother," Newitt said. "She attended. And one time I was standing ready to shoot a foul. And she said,
'Elizabeth! Put that in!' You could hear her all over the place. Everybody was as
silent as they could be. And here was this command from my mother. And I
did—I shot it and it went in. And somebody said, 'Well, what would have
happened if it didn't?' I said 'The Lord only knows. I don't.' "[22]

As the interests of students, parents, and educators converged around varsity
basketball, they sparked an explosion in the number of school teams and the attention sports received. In 1913 a group of professors at the University of North
Carolina inaugurated high school state championships for boys' teams from
white schools in several sports, including basketball. By 1924, when control of
league and championship play was turned over to the newly organized High
School Athletic Association of North Carolina (NCHSAA), more than a hundred schools participated in the competitions, with basketball the most popular
sport. African American schools organized their own association, which eventually became known as the North Carolina Athletic Conference. Many counties, along with some private organizations, inaugurated highly popular end-
of-season tournaments. Newspaper coverage of high school games expanded
from simple reports of scores to often lengthy accounts prominently displayed
on the sports pages that many of the state's newspapers had begun to publish on
a daily basis.[23]

As basketball programs developed, the combination of character-building
rhetoric and heightened community attention began to shape the game in new
directions. Many promoters of organized recreation, including basketball in-
ventor James Naismith, had seen sports largely as an arena of free play where
players exercised a creative spontaneity that was often difficult to achieve in
everyday life. Tournaments, newspaper articles, and growing spectator support
pressed teams not simply to play but to win. These new priorities cast sports in
terms of work rather than play, encouraging a focused pursuit of success that
laid far greater emphasis on strategy and calculation and in which coaches
gained far greater authority.[24]

James Naismith steadily resisted such developments. From his position as
physical education director and basketball coach at the University of Kansas, he
argued against strategies that he thought "mechanized the game" and tried to
minimize the influence of coaching, contending that his players gained more

when they made decisions (as well as mistakes) on their own. He often crit-icized coaches who took too large a role in games, as in an incident he included in his published retrospective on the sport. "The star player on a team left the defense to rush out and get the ball," Naismith recounted. "He was successful in his attempt, and taking the other team by surprise, dribbled down the floor and made a beautiful goal. The crowd wildly acclaimed this feat, but the boy was removed from the game for failure to follow exactly the instructions of the coach." Naismith then condemned the action, asking, "Why should the play of a group of young men be entirely spoiled to further the ambitions of some coach?"[25]

The memories of North Carolina's early high school players suggest that Naismith's philosophy had many adherents in the state during the 1920s. At first many students were happy simply to have a team. Jane Kuykendall, who at-tended high school in the small, mountain community of Mocksville, was delighted just to play. "The boys team was organized and we thought we had a pretty good season even though we lost every game," she wrote many years later. "Then the girls began to be interested in playing basketball and the interest grew until we felt we would die unless we could play! . . . I loved every practice even though I was not very good at the game. Somehow I managed to play in enough games to earn my letter—that big, all-important, bright yellow 'M.' I thought it was the most beautiful emblem in the world. I had just bought a navy slip over sweater and the 'M' looked wonderful on it. Never in my life have I been as proud as the first day I wore the blue sweater."[26]

Just as Jane Kuykendall's fondest basketball memory involved her pride in being on the team, other players focused not on practice periods or win-loss records but on other recollections: a surprise, half-court basket; the dinners host teams sometimes served their visitors; the home-court advantage a coun-try team that played on dirt had over city squads used to smooth board floors. Some schools had coaches who had played in college and could offer some strategy or technique, but many did not. Sam Ardrey, who played at Pineville High School in Mecklenburg County, recalled that any male teacher at a county high school, "regardless of any experience that he had or had not had," was considered a qualified coach. The Pineville coach was largely a chaperone: "He just went along, you know, kept score and that kind of thing." Many other players had similar experiences. In the early 1930s Elizabeth McCall Callaway played at the rural school of Sherrill's Ford with enough success to make the white all–Catawba County team. But she did not remember getting much ad-vice until she moved to Charlotte and began playing for a small business col-lege. "[That was] the first time I'd ever heard anybody say 'Use your hips to get them off of you,' " she recalled, laughing at the thought. "You know, under the basket. I can remember him saying that, and I never had heard that before."[27]

Even when coaches took their work seriously, their players did not always respond. "Seemed like I just played like I always did," Elizabeth Callaway recalled of her reaction to her new coach's efforts. "I don't think I ever did use my hips." John Thompson played for one of Mecklenburg County's legendary white high school teams, the Berryhill High squad of 1934. But when the school was invited to Raleigh for a state playoff, the coach they chose to accompany them suggested that a championship was not the only thing on players' minds. "We had two coaches at Berryhill that year," Thompson recalled. "Both of them were nice coaches, but one of them was strict, and the other didn't care much what we did. So we voted—and we voted for the one that would let us have a good time." The night before the big game, the coach told the team to go to bed early and then went off to visit a girlfriend. The players followed his example rather than his words. "We partied all night," Thompson explained. "We went from one dorm to the other and saw State players—just had a good time like crazy high school students would do. We didn't get any rest. The next day we should have beaten this team. We had a better team. But we just give out—they wore us down."[28]

As the Berryhill players learned, they, along with James Naismith, were swimming against a competitive tide. While limited coaching and supervision may have allowed for more self-expression, it rarely triumphed in a heated contest against a more thoroughly prepared team. Those coaches and players that adopted more focused strategies began to dominate the sport at both high school and college levels. Naismith's own place in basketball history reflects this change. While he is revered as the founder of the sport, assessments of his coaching career at the University of Kansas convey considerably less respect. His later career enters present-day basketball discussions largely as the answer to a trivia question about the only Kansas coach to have a lifetime losing record.

In North Carolina a growing focus on strategy, calculation, and rational efficiency could be seen in newspaper coverage of basketball games, which routinely included not only accounts of play but assessments of why the winning team had come out on top. Machine-related metaphors ran throughout such descriptions, with references to the "Trinity Machine" and the "Chapel Hill Machine" as well as descriptions of a successful squad as a "speedy, accurate, well-coached machine" or as "clicking on all cylinders."[29] Reporters regularly attributed victory to consistent, dependable play, which stressed high-percentage shots and eschewed more dramatic but less certain long-range tosses. In the first two months of 1921, for example, the *Raleigh News and Observer* praised the Shaw University team for its ability "to perfect preconceived plays" and lauded the Trinity team for "steady headwork" and "machine-like working." In contrast, it chided the North Carolina State team for its lack of systematic passing and scolded another squad for its reliance on long-range shots. "Trinity placed her dependence in consistent passing and took no unnecessary risks," ran a typical assessment.[30]

Such visions of efficiency and discipline, encouraged by multiplying rewards in the form of league, tournament, or state championships, strengthened views of basketball as a way to teach participants about the modern, industrial world. Such ideas also dovetailed with trends in the state's manufacturing industries. The 1920s ushered in a period of growing rationalization in U.S. industry, as the gospel of scientific management spread throughout the country. North Carolina textile executives, who were contending with fluctuating demand, uncertain cotton supplies, and fierce competition within their industry, made particular efforts to boost productivity. Throughout the 1920s they streamlined operations, introducing the latest machinery and demanding from their workers far greater levels of speed, precision, and endurance. Just as the metaphors of production had entered the realm of sport, some employers sought to use sporting language to cast their factories as competitive arenas where workers could urge each other on in friendly rivalry, "competing to do more or better work."[31]

Even as coaches and communities placed increasing stress on the efficiency that led to victory, however, they also imbued sports with a significance that went well beyond their ability to inculcate specifically industrial virtues. By the 1920s, sports participation had come to be seen as an important way to teach not only discipline and direction but also moral behavior. The latter aim was eloquently evoked by baseball commissioner Kennesaw Mountain Landis as he justified the harshness of the lifetime ban he placed on the Chicago White Sox team accused of throwing the 1919 World Series. "Baseball is something more than a game to an American boy," Landis declared. "It is his training field for life-work. Destroy his faith in its squareness and honesty, and you have destroyed something more; you have planted suspicion of all things in his heart."[32]

Nationwide concerns about the moral lessons taught by sports sprang in part from an awareness of the prominent place that athletic competition had assumed in national life. But they drew also on widespread fears that many of the forces that had previously helped shape young people's behavior were losing their influence. The exuberant youth culture of the 1920s, with its drinking, dancing, automobile rides, suggestive movies, short skirts, and hot jazz rhythms, deeply disturbed many observers. Concerns about young people's activities were voiced around the nation during this period, often in tones that suggested near-hysteria and portended complete social breakdown. Such worries about the direction of national morals were fueled by a series of highly publicized scandals that included the widespread flouting of Prohibition, along with its sensational gang violence; the Teapot Dome financial scandals that revealed corruption at the highest levels of government; and the "Black Sox" case itself, which made it starkly clear that even world champion athletes were willing to break the rules of the game they played so well.

In North Carolina, a state caught in the middle of a difficult transition from one way of life to another, concerns about social stability ran particularly deep. The state's newspapers kept up a steady stream of sensational articles with headlines such as "Erotic Music Befuddles Girls" and "Wall Street's Boy Wizard Indighted" that only intensified such worries. "Immorality Declared Frightfully Prevalent," warned the *Raleigh News and Observer* in a 1921 report on a Rotary Club–financed examination of one of the state's largest cities. Among other shocking conclusions, the study claimed that "night riding in automobiles had degenerated into the vilest debauchery, that dancing had in many quarters degenerated into disgraceful obscenity, that the moving picture houses were constantly presenting immoral and suggestive pictures." Such activities, combined with an apparent upswing in drinking and gambling, were producing results that ranged from "sin and shame" to "much dishonesty on the part of employees who handle money." The investigating committee's report recommended that parents "exercise a firmer discipline in the control of their children and young people" and urged "that all of our moral people take a firm stand at this time upon the side of morality and decency, of law and order." "It is no time to let politics, business or personal feeling lead us to take a low stand," it concluded. Not only is the world on fire today, but our house here is on fire."[33]

These concerns coincided with a broad shift in controls on individual behavior sparked by North Carolina's continuing urbanization, a process taking place in many other parts of the nation as well. Most North Carolinians had grown up in small communities where individual actions were shaped and guided by a strong set of community norms and where practical jokes, public ridicule, and other informal but effective measures kept deviations from a generally accepted order to a minimum. Religious faith provided the most widely invoked source of moral standards, but every church discipline committee could attest that divine sanctions were often most effective when backed up by the watchful eyes of friends and neighbors.

The rapid growth of North Carolina's urban centers and the influx of new people and ideas made maintaining social order seem a far more problematic endeavor. Urban growth proceeded at astonishing rates after the Civil War, as the spread of the textile industry as well as an expansion of commercial cotton and tobacco culture pumped money and people into what had once been small trading towns. Between 1870 and 1930 the city of Charlotte alone grew from less than 5,000 to more than 80,000 residents. As urban migrants throughout the world had learned, the relative anonymity of city life could offer city dwellers a welcome freedom from social and sometimes from fiscal responsibilities. One Charlotte resident portrayed such changes with detached amusement, suggesting that by the turn of the century, "a whole week, instead of a day, may be required to carry a choice bit of scandal into every part of the town. . . . The preachers no longer attend courts; plenty of people stay away from funerals; you may dodge a creditor for days without remaining in hiding." But other observers were more inclined to adopt the worried tone of the city's YMCA officials, who as early as 1887 had anxiously proclaimed, "Charlotte has nine churches and twenty-four saloons; about thirty five per cent of her young men attend church," and asked, "How can the others be reached?"[34]

As YMCA officials so often stressed, athletics offered a promising arena for such moral endeavors, and coverage of sports events suggests some of the ways that new institutions were attempting to replace older methods of shaping young people's behavior. The watchful eyes of observers, particularly sports reporters, were clearly being employed as a subtle form of moral suasion, serving as both a reflection of and a spur to public opinion. In 1926, for example, the boys' squad from white Maiden High School in Catawba County came in for a public upbraiding when the players apparently developed an inflated opinion of their abilities and indulged in the kind of self-promotion usually frowned upon in rural communities. An account of the team's loss to Claremont High in the county semifinals was titled "Maiden Stock Hits Decline," offering a perhaps unconscious juxtaposition between modern volatility and more substantial values. In the text, the reporter used a time-honored sarcastic edge to take the offending team to task.[35] "Thus the highly touted Maiden quintet saw all their hopes to annex a county title go a glimmering; for their self-styled county championship outfit offered only a passive resistance to the opposing team," the assessment ran. "Time after time Maiden's so-called famous crisscross offense went to pieces against the stiff guarding of the Claremont team, often losing the ball only to have it run back for a marker at the opponent's goal." A few years later an Asheville High School coach lost his temper during a much-anticipated game with Charlotte's Central High and refused to shake hands with the officials following the contest. After the coach apologized for letting the game "get the best of" him, the *Charlotte News* ridiculed his behavior by noting that he would prove a "drawing card" in future contests, attracting spectators interested in seeing not how good his team was but how well he would control his temper.[36]

The incident at Central High touched on one of the central lessons sports was designed to teach. The descriptions that accompanied the expanding array of basketball competitions suggested that while organizers may have been pleased by precise play and competitive spirit, they were more concerned with a different set of issues. Time and again, officials stressed the importance not of victory but of following the rules, lauding the combination of discipline, restraint, and respect for authority that had come to be known as sportsmanship. Officials of the NCHSAA, for example, promised "to foster good feeling and good sportsmanship in the North Carolina high schools; to stimulate, to control, and to direct along sound lines and on a high plane high school athletics in North Carolina."[37]

Similar sentiments were expressed at the first annual Southern Textile Association basketball tournament, held in 1922. By the 1920s many textile mills fielded their own basketball teams, and for decades the Southern Textile Association tournament would showcase some of the South's best male and female basketball talent. As in other competitions, officials sought to emphasize sportsmanship over victory. In 1922, tournament president W. V. Martin "reminded the players that while the capturing of a trophy was important the event was even more important in developing real sportsmanship and fellowship among the textile plants." The report of Martin's remarks, which appeared in the manufacturer-sponsored *Southern Textile Bulletin*, went on to praise the teams in language that would become part of a formulaic ritual at countless similar events. "Such spirit of co-operation and sportsmanship as was exhibited by every team interested in the tournament has never been witnessed in this city before," the writer noted, later adding that "referees were particularly impressed with the spirit and were often heard to wish that collegiate teams could be as well disciplined regarding the decision of officials."[38]

As the last sentence suggested, praise for sportsmanship was so lavish in part because good behavior could not be assumed. The developing system of athletic competition was creating enormous internal tension. Most communities were coming to view both sportsmanship and competitive ambition as desirable goals. But while the two were both associated with athletics, they had little connection to each other—and could in fact conflict. The increasing rewards for basketball success did indeed result in greater ambitions and a corresponding willingness to submit to discipline and embrace rational methods of preparation in pursuit of expanded goals. As such ambitions grew, however, it became increasingly difficult to contain them within the game's structural framework, which required that each contest have a winner and a loser and where the difference between the two often turned not on an obvious difference in skill or effort but, rather, on luck or on the judgment of a referee.

The complications faced by basketball referees were succinctly examined some years later by John B. McLendon Jr., legendary basketball coach at the

North Carolina College for Negroes (later North Carolina Central University), in an article titled "Pity the Poor Official." "Officials are put in an unreasonable position to begin with," McLendon argued.

> The implications surrounding Basketball Rules are that the game is one in which no contact is allowed. To play Basketball as such a game is impossible. . . . The problem comes in determining, not that contact shall not occur without penalty, but how much contact can occur without too many penalties interrupting the contest. Unless there is agreement between officials and coaches and players as to the amount and type of contact allowed without penalty there is bound to be some harsh talk about the officials and maybe some harsh talk to them as well, for such an agreement is seldom achieved.

The dilemma, McLendon continued, was heightened by competitive zeal: "A 'satisfying game' is a nebulous ideal seldom attained in basketball . . . because one side always wins."[39]

While most participants tried to control themselves, the emotions of heated contests led to on-court outbursts throughout the nation, often involving disputes with referees. James Naismith dramatically illustrated this dilemma in his account of a conversation with an official who "told me that whenever he refereed a basketball game, he was very careful to see that the window in the room where he dressed was left unlatched, in order that immediately after the game he could, if necessary, grab his clothes and leave unnoticed." During the 1920s, North Carolina newspapers reported a variety of such outbursts, including a hard-fought contest between Trinity and North Carolina State, which ended in a dispute that required the precipitous exit of one of the players. "Just before the final whistle, the fourth and disqualifying personal foul was called on Ripple, State College captain, who proceeded to strike the referee in the face," the *Raleigh News and Observer* reported. "Trinity students rushed upon the floor with dire threats, but Ripple was taken from the gym by a side door and serious trouble was averted."[40]

Although written accounts rarely suggested that referees were ever other than scrupulously fair, some of the complaints were apparently justified, pointing toward the uneven authority wielded by the game's rules. James Naismith made it clear that in basketball's early years not only did referees sometimes fear for their safety, but avid partisans frequently devised methods to assist their teams directly. The first backboards, for example, were designed not to aid in shooting but to keep spectators, who frequently sat above the basket, from participating in the game, often employing the same qualities of discipline and well-calculated strategy that basketball was supposed to teach. "I distinctly remember one boy about fifteen years old who used to come into the balcony and take a place directly behind the basket," Naismith wrote. "He came early in order that he might always get this seat. He patiently waited an opportunity to help his team by darting his hand through the rail at the proper time to help the ball into the basket."[41]

In North Carolina's early contests, particularly when teams made their own arrangements regarding referees, some squads seized on similar opportunities to circumvent the rules. As a high school senior, Elizabeth Newitt learned the hard way the extent to which an official could determine the outcome of a contest. In 1923, when her Central High School team played an unofficial state title game against a squad from outside Charlotte, she faced a decision that had little to do with any of the "wholesome" lessons that school sports were supposed to teach. Newitt managed the team, and when she discussed the upcoming game with the opposing squad, they made her a tantalizing offer.

"They wrote me a letter asking if it would suit us to be host for the game," she related. "And they would agree that we could be host, if we would agree to allow them to have the referee." The proposal was tempting. Newitt had prided herself on her ability to draw sizable crowds to her team's games, resulting in considerable revenue from gate admissions. A championship game offered even more lucrative opportunities. "I had great visions for making a lot of money," she explained. "And I did, that night." Such success, however, came at a price. "When the time came, that referee began to call fouls on our main team," she remembered. "He called fouls on every single one of them, and put them out. Put everybody out except me. See, I was the one handling the money. And I had to give them a percentage of it. So he didn't dare put me out. And here we were with substitutes. And we had one substitute—it was the last game, and she had never been put in. So she was up in the balcony with a boyfriend, without her uniform and everything. And I couldn't use her. And it was just another nightmare."[42]

The additional assistance carried the visiting team to a narrow victory. Newitt recalled that the school principal had "sent word to me for me to walk off the court," but she had decided not to. As she contemplated the game's dismal results, the team's coach took action. "Our wonderful coach, Dick Kirkpatrick, stepped up," she said. "He took that referee by the scruff of the neck. We were playing at the YWCA uptown. And they had tremendous steps down in front. He took that man and he kicked him all the way out, and kicked him down those steps, he was so furious."[43]

That day's contest, with its themes of finance, deception, anger, and violence, contained numerous lessons for an observant young person, lessons with a depth and complexity that went well beyond formulaic invocations of good sportsmanship. But they were not the lessons that supervisors of youth sports wanted young people to learn as part of an activity that was increasingly described as a "preparation for citizenship." Rather, they pointed toward the risks involved in designating the emotional and unpredictable realm of varsity sports as an arena for such lessons. Many educators pursuing character-shaping goals were, in fact, inclined to favor the more regulated atmosphere of gym class over varsity athletics. In part this preference came from the concern that athletic programs could rapidly grow beyond administrative control. "High School principals and superintendents are of the opinion that they should run High School Athletics, rather than have athletics run them," read a complaining note in *North Carolina Education* in 1922. But it also spoke to the nature of competition. A sports event, it quickly became clear, provided spectators with experiences that could spin out of control. Elizabeth Newitt was not the only North Carolinian to learn about the harsher realities of life in a competitive society through basketball.[44]

Similarly, while competitive athletics might encourage individual teams to develop disciplined strategies, varsity competition did not always promote state leaders' visions of North Carolina society as a harmonious, smoothly working machine. Rather, it could lay bare the divisions that had come to mark state life. By the 1920s, despite state leaders' frequent attempts to invoke a statewide unity of ideas and interests, it became increasingly clear that North Carolina was a highly diverse place in which such commonalities could not be assumed. Freed but disfranchised African Americans contended both with whites and with class-based divisions that developed in their own communities. Formerly independent farmers who succumbed to the difficult economies of cotton culture found themselves working as tenants or clustered in cotton mill villages, even as other North Carolinians visibly thrived in the new economy. The rush for industrial development pitted towns and cities against one another in their attempts to draw businesses and population. New norms of urban sophistication, which emphasized fine dress and familiarity with European high art forms, drew sharp cultural divisions between city-dwelling professionals and their less prosperous neighbors.[45]

School sports would draw part of their force from the way they played on such divisions, either confirming or undercutting the existing social order. Herman Cunningham, who competed for Monroe's black Winchester Avenue High School, touched on this issue when he recalled the particular pleasure Winchester fans and players derived from defeating larger, wealthier schools, victories that he interpreted by emphasizing character over resources. "We were just interested in playing the game, and we was determined to win," he explained. "And that's what made the difference. We played against a lot of teams that had the fancy, shiny uniforms and things. And ours would just be the medium uniform, but we had a good squad. Nine times out of ten we would bring the bacon back to Monroe." Most such contests stayed within the rules, with participants drawing satisfaction from their ability to triumph within conventional competitive frameworks. But incidents such as that related by Elizabeth Newitt suggested that some at least some loyalties lay not with the abstract moral structure such rules represented but, rather, with a community's own interest. A referee who became a villain in one community and a hero to another, or a conflict on the court that spilled over into fights among the fans, underscored sport's potential to exacerbate divisions as well as draw communities together.[46]

The larger questions raised by North Carolina's social divisions and by issues of allegiance to athletic and other rules struck a particular nerve in the early 1920s. The years that followed World War I had been marked by nationwide social turmoil, as the democratic expectations raised by wartime rhetoric clashed with existing social and economic inequities. American educators, who saw one of their tasks as molding the next generation of loyal citizens, faced this dilemma head-on. Like their counterparts around the country, the leaders of North Carolina's educational institutions, both black and white, had emerged from the victories of World War I with an excited sense of mission and a renewed faith in the values of American democracy. "The world has just been engaged in a life-and-death struggle between autocracy and democracy," North Carolina superintendent of schools J. Y. Joyner wrote at the end of the conflict. "It is now predicted that America will become the seminary in which the nations will find that instruction which will breathe this modern spirit of democracy into the old monarchical nations of the world, and that American colleges and universities will become the educational centers of the world during the period of reconstruction that is to follow." Teaching democracy would, however, prove a more complicated task than such patriotic rhetoric suggested.[47]

For North Carolinians consigned to the lower levels of the existing social order, who were particularly keen to expand democratic rights and opportunities, definitions of democratic education came easily to the pen. Edwin Johnson, who headed the black schools of Henderson, waxed eloquent when describing a system of school governance in which students helped to set and enforce school rules. "The world march toward democratic institutions, and the outlawing of unnecessary wars, will be greatly stimulated by cultivating in school children a spirit of toleration, sympathetic cooperation and intelligent respect for constituted authority," Johnson wrote in the *North Carolina Teachers Record*, the official publication of the black state teachers' association.

"Present-day life requires initiative rather than passivity, independent thinking rather than blind following of direction, and active participation in the world's affairs rather than a limited accumulation of facts apart from their use. The success of our teaching and administration should be measured by the degree to which we help children live in this democracy of ours and assume the responsibility necessary to a full, purposeful life."[48]

Educators with a greater stake in existing social structures, on the other hand, often had far more difficulty articulating such ideals. When a national committee convened in 1921 to chart the essentials of democratic instruction, the report it issued offered not the ringing endorsement found in Edwin Johnson's words but, rather, ten hesitating, highly qualified concepts, many of which seemed as concerned with containing democratic impulses as with promoting them. The second of these ideas typified the committee's approach. Titled "Equal rights and opportunities as distinguished from equal abilities and achievements," it stated, "If there is to be a saving popular faith in democracy each individual must be taught to distinguish sharply between equality in the sense of rights and opportunities, and equality in the sense of natural abilities and individual achievements. Many Americans scoff at democracy, because they assume that the Declaration contemplated an equality made possible by heredity; or believe in it because they confuse it with a communism which gives each individual an equal share in all things whether he earns it or not."[49]

Such concerns ran so strong precisely because despite the continual praise of U.S. democracy, its rewards were far from equitable. Just as basketball, despite myriad statements about the best team winning, often turned on aspects of chance, accident, or design that could transform games into narratives of great complexity, the rewards provided by industrial capitalism were distributed in a manner not always easy to explain or to accept. While the nation's political and economic leaders spoke often of democracy, many of them pursued a far more hierarchical vision, in which a handful of citizens directed political and economic affairs while the rest of the population was content to follow and obey. This philosophy was especially noticeable in North Carolina. From the pervasive Jim Crow legislation that sharply limited African American opportunities, to the autocratic direction of textile mill operations, to the growing disdain with which urban residents regarded the "backwards" ways of farmers and textile workers, social divisions had become patently and painfully obvious throughout the state.

Such disparities sparked turbulence across the nation in the years after World War I. For many of the country's less privileged citizens, the increased interest in democracy inspired by the war fueled challenges to the rules by which U.S. society had customarily operated, often setting off major social upheavals.

African Americans returning from military service became far more assertive about demanding equal treatment in civilian life, prompting responses that ranged from lynchings to full-scale race riots. In the hills of West Virginia, coal miners who had worked long hours and risked death to defeat German autocracy began to press their claims against mine operators who forced them to live in mine-owned housing, to shop at high-priced mine-run stores, and to work under conditions that made their profession more dangerous than serving in the army. The armed conflict between mine workers and company defenders that broke out in Logan County, West Virginia, in the fall of 1920 was only the most dramatic of dozens of large-scale labor disputes that disrupted life in communities around the country.[50]

In North Carolina such disputes became most visible in the state's prized textile industry. Southern textile mills saw their first major wave of union organizing during the postwar era, as workers began to challenge the wage cutbacks and productivity demands with which mill owners sought to adapt to the end of wartime prosperity. "We prate about democracy! We boast we have crushed autocracy," one textile union supporter wrote in 1919. "But we have an industrial autocracy right here at home." That February, operatives at Charlotte's Highland Park Mill joined the national United Textile Workers union and began a three-month walkout—an action that spread to the nearby communities of Belmont, Concord, and Kannapolis. After mill owners settled the dispute by agreeing to reduce working hours while keeping wages steady, Charlotte-based David Clark, editor of the influential *Southern Textile Bulletin*, sharply criticized the union. In his statement, he directly contrasted the divisions laid bare by the strike with a vision of a more smoothly working order, invoking "those days wherein the mill operative and the mill owners worked together in harmony and good feeling." But the 1919 conflict was only the beginning. Throughout the 1920s, mill owners' prized regimes of scientific management and productivity growth put increasing pressures on textile employees, and tensions between workers and employers continued to build. The late 1920s saw a second, more widespread wave of textile strikes, and by the 1930s, when the hardships of the Great Depression raised new questions about the workings of U.S. society, concerns about social order only intensified.[51]

In the volatile atmosphere of the 1920s and 1930s, with so many social arrangements thrown into troubling question, athletic competition could take on multiple meanings. Athletic contests could indeed highlight or even exacerbate social divisions. But the structure of organized sports could also offer a particularly comforting social model, especially when rules were obeyed and when coaches and referees served as respected figures of authority. The metaphor of American society as an athletic contest, in which individuals played designated roles in support of their various teams and in which an impartial set of rules sorted out winners and losers according to a single, common standard, bore close resemblance to the view of society as a well-oiled machine and offered a similar justification for the hierarchical rankings such a system produced.

The links many of North Carolina's white educators drew between the structure of sports and concepts of both moral order and social hierarchy can be seen in *Physical Education in the High School*. When listing the qualities sports participation could develop in young people, authors J. F. Miller and W. C. Parker specified motor skills (quickness of perception and quickness of action) and classic game-related talents (self-control, cooperation, self-confidence, and determination). They also included several highly charged moral concepts (fairness, truthfulness, courage, and loyalty) as well as the clearly hierarchical pairing of "leadership" and "obedience." In contrast, James Naismith's retrospective account was far less ambitious, focusing mainly on skills (agility, accuracy, alertness, skill, reflex judgment, and speed) as well as mentioning cooperation, self-confidence, self-sacrifice, and sportsmanship. Significantly, neither leadership nor obedience appeared in Naismith's account, and the quality that he placed first on his list—initiative—was missing from the North Carolina assessment.[52]

A more direct suggestion about the broader ways that sports and sportsmanship could be linked to social order was broached in a speech given by E. J. Coltrane, president of the white North Carolina Education Association, to the North Carolina Negro Teachers Association in April 1931. North Carolina's black educators were already developing their own responses to the economic predicament in which the country found itself, and their suggestions generally recommended a broader and more just distribution of social and economic resources. As it became clear that one result of the depression was the replacement of longtime black employees by unemployed whites, one educator fumed, "The great fight of American patriots today is not against the forces of red radicalism; it is against the forces of black obscuratism and militant ignorance." *North Carolina Teachers Record* editor Leland Cozart adopted a quieter tone but stressed a similar point. "If we would build wisely and well for the future," he editorialized, "we must build a philosophy which places the common good above individual achievement of success and the power which attends it."[53]

Coltrane's speech, however, acknowledged no such possibilities, focusing instead on an elaborately argued, urgently delivered defense of the status quo. "I am interested in the maintenance of our democratic institutions," he told the audience. "I am more interested, however, in the maintenance of a safe type of civilization. If there are certain evils in our democratic society which are conducive to the destruction of our civilization, then something must be done about it. *We must maintain our civilization.*" With a set of arguments in which formulaic invocations of student initiative were submerged in a palpable fear of approaching chaos, Coltrane cast proper education—including the encouragement of sportsmanship—as the key to maintaining social order, particularly in terms of teaching young people to peacefully accept whatever inequities the social and economic system happened to produce. "Taxes levied on corporations and public utilities for the support of schools are simply insurance for the stability of the future," he stated. "If you are disposed to doubt the validity of this argument I suggest that you take a map of the world and select the countries that have little or nothing in the way of schools. Then go back into their history and note what happens every time they decide they need a change of any kind in government. In almost every case they stage a revolution with all its loss of life and property, and then property rights go overboard and are not worth anything." The United States, he then explained, was different. "We have learned better. Our people are becoming educated. Their education is resulting in toleration. They are becoming good sports."[54]

As the widespread popularity of high school basketball made clear, E. J. Coltrane's effort to use the concept of sportsmanship to rally a group of African Americans behind his defense of "civilization" represented only one of the many interpretations that school sports could support. The complexity of athletics was, in fact, one of the most significant sources of its widespread appeal. The many components of the national popular culture that emerged from the social ferment of the 1920s and 1930s—institutions that ranged from Walt Disney cartoons to country music to the Amos 'n' Andy radio broadcast—gained strength because they were able to accommodate the complex and sometimes conflicting array of interests developed by the many members of an increasingly diverse society, coming to mean different things to different people. Basketball did the same thing. It reached back to elements of North Carolina's past even as it embodied many aspects of a changing present. It held out a sense of order in a troubling time but could support multiple interpretations and be put to widely varying uses. Even as one group of state residents used the language of athletic sportsmanship to justify a social status quo, the implicit declarations of equality embodied in the teams young women so avidly organized, or in the efforts African American parents poured into school uniforms and gymnasiums, suggested that the ambitions extolled by state leaders' rhetoric did not always stay in the channels that their advocates envisioned.[55]

Even as a diverse range of North Carolinians shaped sports to their own ends, however, athletics in turn shaped them. The Lincolnton High School women, proudly sporting their rebelliously bobbed hair, drew inspiration from the machine metaphors used to describe state society, even as they challenged the place they held within it. The spread of high school sports reinforced a powerful paradigm in North Carolina, weaving the ideas of head-to-head confrontation, of sportsmanship, and of victory and loss into people's daily lives. The continuing complexity of athletic games meant that the significance of this paradigm remained open to interpretation, resting on the ideas and actions of individual participants. But its influence would grow in subsequent decades, even as countless state residents worked to pattern sports—and North Carolina—after their own ideals.

## CHAPTER FOUR

# The Relationships of Life

## White Men, Competition, and the Structure of Society, 1919–1936

O
n August 9, 1919, Charlotte streetcar driver Roland Mc-Cachren walked off the job. That evening, 150 newly unionized drivers locked the city's streetcars in their night storage barn and announced that they would not resume work until they reached a settlement with their employer, the Southern Public Utilities Company. Running the bustling city's public transportation system was a steady job, and it carried far more prestige than work in the cotton mills that ringed the city and provided much of its wage employment. But the hours were long, and as driver Jesse Ashe later recalled, they "didn't have no money much." When requests for shorter hours, better pay, and union recognition fell on deaf ears, drivers turned to the kind of confrontation that directly contradicted the visions of competitive harmony put forth by the state's industrial leaders.[1]

Like many such disputes, the drivers' strike highlighted the divisions in North Carolina society, defining the interests of workers in direct conflict with those of their employers. Southern Public Utilities, a division of James B. Duke's powerful Southern Power Company, sought to downplay any such clash, casting itself as an institution that, when left to its own devices, promoted order, efficiency, and fairness for all. "The company has done everything possible to make working conditions as pleasant as possible, just as it has maintained the scale of pay at the highest notch possible," company president Z. V. Taylor informed the Charlotte public. "In our attitude toward the car men we have had in mind not only to give them a square deal always but to promote and maintain that sort of [personnel] and that degree of morale that makes for the most efficient and satisfactory service to the public." Still, this apparent interest in social harmony did not stop the company from acting forcefully in its own interest. On August 25, company officials used strikebreakers to put the cars back into service. That evening an angry crowd gathered outside the car barn. Just past midnight, Charlotte police chief Walter Orr was confronted by a resident of North Charlotte, where Highland Park Mill textile employees had recently staged their own walkout. Sixty years later, car barn night foreman Loy Cloniger still vividly recalled the melee that erupted. "It was a crowd around that lightpost in front of the barn there," Cloniger explained. "Chief Orr says 'Get back every damn one of you.' And the police come just shooting." When the gunfire ceased, five men had been killed, their bodies scattered on streets and lawns around the barn.[2]

Although the strikers carried on for two more weeks, they had clearly seen enough. Roland McCachren joined Jesse Ashe and Loy Cloniger on a five-man committee appointed to settle the strike. On September 8, a month after they had left their posts, the drivers returned to work under a compromise wage agreement and without union recognition. The day after the settlement, a *Charlotte News* article touched on the difficulties involved in challenging an institution as powerful as Southern Public Utilities. The brief piece noted that McCachren was the father of thirteen children and that the thirteenth, a boy named George, had been born the night of the car barn shootings, at a house barely two blocks from the events. "It's just naturally time for me to go to work," McCachren told the *News*. "Thirteen children isn't anything to make a man want to be idle."[3]

Roland McCachren had little time to weigh the long-term meanings of his action. Six months after the strike, following ten days of illness, the forty-seven-year-old driver succumbed to an abscess in his left lung, and his large family was left to manage on its own. But North Carolina had not heard the last of the McCachrens. In 1943 the University of North Carolina basketball team announced that George McCachren, the child born on the night of the car barn altercation, had been chosen captain of the squad. His election drew particular notice because he had been preceded in the position by three of his brothers. Dave McCachren had been Tar Heel captain in 1934; Jim McCachren, in 1936; and Bill McCachren, in 1939. Roland McCachren's efforts to improve his life had been thwarted by stubborn and sometimes violent resistance. His sons, pursuing an alternate path, found nothing but acclaim.

McCachren's oldest son, who graduated from Charlotte's Central High School soon after his father died, had seen college as a distant dream. Jonathan Mc-Cachren had gone to work at a local printing company, indulging his love of sports by playing, coaching, and refereeing at Charlotte's YMCA. But by the 1930s, athletic skill opened more doors. The state's universities had expanded both their academic programs and their student bodies, and organized sports had assumed a new prominence in college life. Coaches seeking to build winning

The basketball-playing McCachren brothers: Jonathan (back); Jim, Bill, and Dave (center, left to right); George (front). Courtesy of George McCachren.

teams could call on a variety of sources to help promising players pay their college bills. With such assistance and with the contributions of their family, the four younger McCachren brothers worked their way to coveted degrees, securing a foothold in the nation's expanding middle class. Their story, given added poignancy by their father's early death, became a Carolina legend, a frequently invoked icon of the realized American dream.[4]

At first glance Roland McCachren's labor action may seem to bear little relationship to his sons' athletic achievements. But both sets of experience were shaped by the same forces: the industrial and commercial expansion that was transforming North Carolina's society, economy, and culture. Such changes set off intense debates at many levels of state society as the men who had climbed to the top of the state's industrial pyramid sought to solidify their hold over the state. Even as industrialists championed the mix of unfettered economic action and paternal social concern invoked in Z. V. Taylor's antiunion editorials, residents with less faith in the benevolence of industry sought to curb its influence. By the 1930s, organized athletics had become a part of this dispute, most notably among members of the state's white male middle class, whose monopoly on political and economic power tied them particularly closely to the broader social narratives to which athletic contests were so often linked. Within the safely segregated spaces of school and industrial teams, white men's athletics became the focus for a series of struggles over competing values and identities as well as the social structures over which these men wielded such authority.[5]


For much of North Carolina's white male population, the lure of sports began in boyhood, often with the baseball teams that sprang up in communities around the state after the Civil War. At the turn of the century, for example, legendary Yadkin County pitcher Fred "Fed" Reinhardt became a hero to young men for miles around. "To be perfectly frank, there is one section of western North Carolina in which that name meant more and was known by more people, particularly young ones, than was the name of William McKinley or William Jennings Bryan at the time of their greatest popularity or ascendancy," *Charlotte Observer* columnist M. R. Dunnagan recalled in 1922. "Not one boy, but hundreds, in that section, if asked which of the three men mentioned they would prefer to be or to be like, would swell an inch larger and stretch a little taller, then, without hesitation or halting, would proudly reply, '"Fed" Reinhardt.'" Athletics also helped cement bonds between men of different generations; many athletes linked their early experience of sports with memories of their fathers. Textile mill player Frank Webster, for example, vividly recalled attending games with his father in the 1910s. "I was a little fellow around five or six when he carried me down there and held my hand," Webster explained six decades later. "I'd see these ball players playing and that kind of caught my eye."[6]

Community baseball players were particularly revered for the qualities of strength and toughness that meshed well with the realities of a farming economy. In his autobiography, Guilford County native and Hall of Fame major leaguer Enos "Country" Slaughter connected his baseball skills with the harsh demands of a subsistence farming economy, describing the rigors of farmwork, the strength he acquired preparing for community wood-chopping contests, and the accurate arm he developed while throwing rocks at rabbits during hunting expeditions, because his family could not afford to provide its youngest member with a gun. In a description of his father, a catcher who played both barehanded and barefooted, he tellingly conveyed the toughness such play revealed with a hint at one potential benefit of publicly displaying that brand of fortitude: "I guess Ma figured that a guy who wasn't afraid to handle speeding baseballs without the protection of a catcher's mitt or even shoes, had what it took to handle droughts, floods, and anything else that could get in the way of a farmer."[7]

As sports enthusiasm developed throughout the 1910s and 1920s, aspiring young athletes found an expanding range of outlets for their ambitions. Baseball, football, and basketball squads represented not only communities but also high schools, YMCAs, textile mills, professional leagues, and a variety of other organizations. While the fame of a player's exploits had once spread largely by word of mouth, in the conversations that passed time during evenings, weekends, or slow spots in the working day, such local discussions were supplemented by increasingly detailed accounts in state newspapers as well as in a variety of other publications.[8]

In this new context, sports often took on grander dimensions. Accounts of athletic contests attracted fans and readers by raising athletes to heroic heights, infusing games and individuals with a sense of moral purpose. The weekly adventures of fictional hero Frank Merriwell, who combined unspotted virtue with dramatic sports achievements and whose exploits sold nearly half a million copies between 1896 and 1910, exemplified the genre. The effect of such boyhood encounters with daunting obstacles, moral dilemmas, and last-second triumphs could be profound, as suggested when T. H. Higdon, a correspondent for the University of North Carolina's *Alumni Review*, penned a breathless description of the Tar Heels' upset of Kentucky in the semifinals of the 1932 Southern Conference basketball tournament. Praising the Carolina team as "the scrappiest, hardest fighting and doggedest aggregation that has ever represented Carolina on the Auditorium Court," Higdon rushed headlong into the action: "One minute Kentucky was ahead one point, the next minute a field goal would put Carolina ahead. For the last ten minutes of the game the lead alternated with each goal, and the pistol shot was just behind the last one run by the Tar Heels." It was a game, he concluded, "like the tales in the Frank Merriwell stories."[9]

Associations between sports and virtue assumed particular significance in the state's colleges and universities, where in the 1920s and 1930s intercollegiate athletics became one of the major centers of both campus life and state society. College athletes had once scraped together meager funds and performed before relatively small crowds. In the 1920s, however, college sports became a nationwide obsession. North Carolina saw a dramatic demonstration of such change in 1925, when 16,000 spectators somehow managed to crowd into Chapel Hill's 2,400-seat Emerson Field for a game with the University of Virginia. In 1927 the university remedied this situation by opening the much larger Kenan Field. For a quarter of a century Trinity College trustees had stubbornly refused to lift the football ban they had imposed in 1895. But in 1920, just four years before a massive contribution by tobacco magnate James B. Duke prompted a change in the school's name and an expansion of its purpose, football was permitted to resume. In 1929 Duke University completed its own massive arena, Duke Stadium, and in 1931 the school hired renowned coach Wallace Wade away from the University of Alabama, embarking on a decade-long quest for national athletic fame.[10]

The heady excitement of this new interest and the heroic tone of athletic descriptions came clear in an alumnus-penned account of the key moment in a game that pitted Carolina against rival Maryland. "Shorty Branch is not exactly an elf, but he exhibited sprite-like qualities, not to mention the attributes of a Houdini, as he recovered a Maryland punt on his own 6 yard line in the final few minutes of play Saturday, whisked through a horde of tacklers without being touched, eluded the safety man with a decidedly impish twist of the hips, sped the length of the field and across the goal line to give the Tar Heels a 28-21 victory in the most spectacular football duel that has graced the Kenan stadium since its dedication," wrote the correspondent for a special edition of North Carolina's *Alumni Review*.

Shorty the Great was the composite of the red-headed Galloping Ghost of Illinois, Army's Cagle, Thomason, Osterbann, Kipke—all the football immortals, as he swung into that magnificent run. It was the grand finale of an afternoon of scintillating plays, long passes, wide-end sweeps, deceptive formations, fumbles galore—all the elements of soul-stirring football drama. And over 7,000 spectators, including [North Carolina governor] O. Max

Gardner and a score of high state officials in the Governor's box, brazen football scouts and blasé sportswriters in the press box, tensely gripped the edges of their seats and alternately groaned and shouted as the forces of war vacillated in rapid succession.[11]

The turbulent scene; the crowd of thousands in the capacious stadium; the presence of politicians, scouts, and sportswriters; and the invocation of a panoply of gridiron gods marked not only the growing popularity of college sports but also a wholesale transformation of college life. In the years after World War I, North Carolina's white colleges and universities had joined counterparts around the nation in expanding their curricula and their student populations, seeking to meet the needs of an increasingly complex industrial economy. Rather than relying on managers and supervisors who had worked their way up from the factory floor, U.S. businesses were beginning to fill their management-level positions with employees who had specialized training in fields such as accounting or market management. In North Carolina's textile mills, workers saw the change in the growing numbers of college-trained managers directing their operations. In universities it became apparent in the enthusiastic response to programs that reached beyond a standard liberal arts curriculum to offer "practical" training.

The University of North Carolina became a prime example of this shift. The university founded a business school in 1919 and subsequently added programs in education, engineering, public welfare, psychology, and sociology, prompting President Harry Woodburn Chase to note in 1923 that "the conception of what a University is for has altered and broadened to an immense degree." As programs expanded and as a college degree became increasingly essential to securing a foothold in the nation's middle class, student populations changed as well. University enrollment, once limited largely to a privileged few, grew rapidly during the 1920s. The Chapel Hill student population increased from 1,200 in 1920 to more than 2,500 in 1924, and most of the new students pursued programs that lay outside the traditional liberal arts. Other institutions saw similar shifts.[12]

Such changes gave North Carolina's universities more influence within the state, as they reached a broader population and turned out growing numbers of alumni. But this wider net and expanded mix of goals also created conflicts that raised questions about both the purpose of higher education and the direction of state society. In many ways this debate recapitulated earlier discussions of the value of "book-learning" as opposed to the lessons drawn from extracurricular activities. But it also reflected a new context. Earlier discussions about college athletics, conducted during a period of political and economic tumult, had

In the 1920s and 1930s thousands of eager spectators flocked to the action at North Carolina's college football games. Courtesy of the North Carolina Collection, University of North Carolina Library, Chapel Hill.

focused on the concept of the well-rounded and determined individual and had involved only a general sense of the challenges that awaited graduates outside a school's confines. The version of the debate that unfolded in the 1920s and 1930s was set within a more clearly defined economic context, and it was often far more specific in its goals for students as well as its assessment of appropriate preparation. Such words rang particularly clear in the voices of alumni whose own economic prominence prompted them to speak with authoritative confidence about the business world.

Some of the ongoing tension between the view of college as a place for intellectual and cultural cultivation and that which cast the experience as a training ground for work was summed up in a pair of opposing vignettes printed in a 1928 *Alumni Review*. The first scene presented an alumnus who lamented that the jobs he had been forced to hold while a student had prevented him from taking advantage of the school's cultural activities. In an apparent attempt to dispel prevailing sentiments in favor of such real-world experience, he declared, "The fellow that works his way through is not a hero; the fellow that has plenty of money to spend is not absolutely different. They are both just ordinary fellows; neither to be worshipped or despised." The second piece featured an alumnus, "successful in his field," who unquestioningly supported the idea of work experience, bluntly stating, "It does a man good to work his way through college. It makes him appreciate the values of an education. It makes him realize just how things in life are."[13]

Many prominent alumni supported the latter position, casting a sense of "how things are" not only in terms of the difficulties of making a living but also as necessary for acquiring an understanding of what they called "human nature." Business success, they argued, thus sprang not only from individual virtues but also from the ability to assess and manage others. In the fall of 1927, for example, Alumni Association spokesman A. H. Graham admonished that year's freshman class, "Should you have to make the decision of choosing between making Phi Beta Kappa and engaging in college activities, take the latter. . . . For no matter how much book knowledge you have you will be handicapped in life if you fail to understand human nature." In May 1931 association president K. P. Lewis, then president of Durham's Erwin Cotton Mills, echoed such concerns. "It will not take long for you Seniors to forget much of what you have learned in books at Chapel Hill, except that part of your knowledge that you use in your life's occupation, but the benefits of your college life and training will never leave you," he wrote in the *Alumni Review*, later adding, "I can think of nothing more valuable in contributing toward a man's success in life than a knowledge of human nature and the ability to deal with his fellow man."[14]

Athletics fit well with both expanded enrollment and this new view of education. Athletic contests allowed students and alumni to come together in a common cause around a set of powerfully expressed masculine values. Sports became a significant forum for discussing moral conduct, since the many challenges that athletes and coaches faced during a contest provided material for countless assessments of character and competence. The way athletics mirrored the competitive strife that infused so many other aspects of U.S. society also fostered discussion of issues pertaining to those realms, including the limits of competition, the meanings of written and unwritten rules, and the best way to prevail over opponents. The graduates of North Carolina's major universities were coalescing into a new state elite. Collective assessment of the competitive dramas enacted on the state's college football fields not only threw the glow of heroism onto the more mundane tasks of business life; it became one way this group of powerful white men worked to define themselves, their actions, and their values. The significance of these conversations came clear in the obsessive fervor they sparked among many alumni. Football discussions took on such intensity that one North Carolina State alumnus with few athletic interests

As college football grew in popularity, football discussions, debates, and wagers became a familiar part of daily life. Courtesy of the North Carolina Collection, University of North Carolina Library, Chapel Hill.

noted that he rarely went to alumni meetings because "I do not remember having attended one where football, if not the only subject, was, at least, the principal subject of discussion."[15]

Such discussions covered a wide range of issues, dealing with such cherished modern concepts as "efficiency," "system," and "strategy," as well as individual character. Was a coach who cursed on the sidelines blessed with "spunk and spirit," or was he a bad influence to be eliminated? Did the decision to adopt an ill-fated passing attack represent noteworthy daring or contemptible foolhardiness? Was a football player who approached basketball with a "knock-down and drag-out" style making the best use of his talents or violating the spirit of the game? What failings (or ill-fortune) could best explain a loss to a supposedly weaker opponent? Such issues were discussed with a passion that often magnified the importance of athletics, as when Charlotte lawyer Marvin Ritch wrote University of North Carolina president Frank Porter Graham to complain that the university coaches were "absolutely inefficient" and to charge that their record belied claims that North Carolina was "the most progressive and forward looking State of the South."[16]

The rhetoric that surrounded midcentury athletics in many ways resembled the discussions of thirty years before. A Davidson College declaration spoke of developing "quick thinking and decisions, and the prompt co-ordinating of mind and muscle," as well as of "unrivaled opportunities for moral training in honesty, fair play, truthfulness, respect for others, cooperation, true sportsmanship, and fair dealings in all the relationships of life." When University of North Carolina athletic director Robert Fetzer spoke in favor of further expanding athletic facilities, he invoked long-standing ideals of strength and vitality, giving particular attention to the business world: "The University is being called upon to produce real, finished, he-men; men who are ready and willing to take their places in the world. Men who will not be forced aside in the duties of citizenship and business by a weak, ailing body, or a lack of character and stamina."[17]

Still, college athletics had also become significantly intertwined with the specific circumstances of the state's developing industrial culture, most notably its dominant textile industry. The spectacular growth of the southern textile industry—by 1933 more than two-thirds of the nation's textile workers tended looms and spindles in the Piedmont South—meant that the upper circles of North Carolina politics and society were dominated by textile-linked businessmen and professionals. Textile mill owners faced intense and at times cutthroat competition within their volatile industry. Efforts to cut costs and raise productivity met with challenges from workers, who contested such measures with bitter and disruptive strikes in 1921, 1929, and particularly 1934, when a South-wide general textile strike drew almost half a million workers off their jobs. At the same time, however, a persisting labor surplus gave managers the upper hand in most dealings with workers, and men who managed to prosper in such an intensely competitive environment developed enormous confidence in their methods and themselves.[18]

The importance that college football had assumed among the state's industrialists became clear in the fall of 1935, when University of North Carolina president Frank Porter Graham launched an effort to downplay football's significance and almost lost his job as a result. Graham, who had been university president since 1930, had already sparked his share of controversy in North Carolina. While his warmth, energetic spirit, and moral fervor had won him friends throughout the state, his ideals had also made him enemies. In his years as university dean and then as president, he had become one of the South's most outspoken liberal thinkers, gaining a national reputation by promoting principles that ranged from interracial cooperation to the right to unionize. Early in 1935, during a bitter labor strike in the nearby town of Burlington, he had drawn the ire of conservative industrialists for using his own money to bail

Frank Porter Graham called his attempt to reform college football "the hottest wire that I ever got my hands on." Courtesy of the North Carolina Collection, University of North Carolina Library, Chapel Hill.

a union leader out of jail. But until he challenged college football, he had never felt such fury. "I have picked up a good many hot wires in the brief years that I have been president of this institution," he wrote a friend, "but this is the hottest wire that I ever got my hands on."[19]

Graham's proposed reforms, which became known as the Graham Plan, dealt with one of the most thorny issues confronting college sports: athletic scholarships. The question of whether colleges should aid gifted athletes brought out one of the most significant components of sports as cultural ritual: the importance placed on winning. Unlike more traditional rituals, which were carefully crafted to guide participants toward a desired end, athletic gatherings remained contingent, much of their meaning resting on an outcome that could not be determined in advance. While such uncertainties gave athletic events a heightened level of excitement, they also demanded far greater preparation, as much of the power of such events depended on the satisfaction that came with victory. The best way to ensure such results was to attract fine athletes, an endeavor that many team supporters undertook with enthusiasm but which further heightened disagreements over the purposes that universities sought to serve.[20]

The staffing of college athletic teams had always taken on a certain ambiguity. In earlier, less regulated years, colleges sometimes added players to their team rosters without bothering to cloak such actions in educational concerns. Like many talented athletes, pitcher Fred Reinhardt found teams eager to secure his services for important games. "Reinhardt was never a college man," M. R. Dunnagan noted, "but he was at times employed by Old Trinity college, in several games against Guilford college, Bingham and other college teams." By the turn of the century, however, more stringent regulations were in place, and rather than hiring paid professionals or trying to turn students into athletes, team boosters sought to turn athletes into students. In many cases recruiters learned that their most persuasive appeals involved financial aid. Such incentives usually amounted to only partial assistance, even for the finest athletes. One of the University of North Carolina's best baseball players, good enough to win a contract with the New York Yankees, asked that his signing bonus equal the amount he still owed on his college bill. But in those days even a small amount of money could go a long way.[21]

Officially, universities in the Southern Conference, North Carolina's major white interscholastic league, did not give scholarships based solely on athletic skill. But if a promising young man wished to attend a certain school and lacked the financial wherewithal, coaches could draw on a variety of sources, including loans, contributions from interested alumni, or a variety of full- and part-time jobs, to help him pay his bills. In keeping with the official adherence to strictly amateur competition, however, this kind of assistance was not publicly discussed, existing, rather, in a vaguely defined space of hints and understandings. "I realize," Frank Porter Graham once noted, "that there is a twighlight zone in which men operate in all fields of life whether it be modern finance, industrialism, the making of war, or intercollegiate athletics."[22]

As Graham's comment suggested, this unofficial network troubled university officials, particularly as their changing curriculum began to challenge traditional ideas of universities as centers for intellectual idealism and dispassionate inquiry. Nationwide concerns about the growth of college sports and their place within broader educational missions broke into public view in 1929 with a report commissioned by the Carnegie Foundation for the Advancement of Teaching. In his preface to the 400-page document, Carnegie Foundation president Henry S. Pritchett summed up many of those concerns. "In the United States the composite institution called a university is doubtless still an intellectual agency," he wrote. "But it is also a social, a commercial, and an athletic agency, and these activities have in recent years appreciably overshadowed the intellectual life for which the university is assumed to exist." The report offered a wide-ranging critique of university athletics, raising questions about the academic performance of athletes, the effects of competition on relationships between schools, the ethics of athletic perquisites such as training tables, the profits derived from game receipts, and in particular, the practice of financial aid for athletes, which it termed "the deepest shadow that darkens American college and school athletics." A second report, issued in 1931, repeated many of the charges.[23]

In the fall of 1935, citing the Carnegie Foundation findings, Graham announced his plan to reform athletic practices within the Southern Conference, with specific focus on assistance to athletes. No student at a Southern Conference school, the Graham Plan read, could receive financial aid based on athletic ability. Students who wished to play on varsity teams could only benefit from scholarships awarded according to intellectual promise and that were open to competition from all eligible students. Each varsity athlete, the plan continued, would be required to sign a statement affirming that he had received no unauthorized financial assistance from any quarter.[24]

Frank Porter Graham was no enemy of sports. He had played football as a student, and he relished attending games. His first presidential address, the *Alumni Review* reported, was laced with athletic metaphors: "Using football parlance, he admonished the students always to 'keep your eye on the ball, and not let distractions side-track you from your main course of getting an education.'" But Graham still held to the amateur ideal, the idea that sports should be played for the sake of play alone, untainted by any hint of monetary gain. And he, like administrators around the country, had been troubled both by the exploding popularity of college sports and by the corresponding rise in "twilight zone" activities of recruiting and sponsorship. By forbidding outside athletic aid and by insisting that academic promise be the basis for scholarship assistance, the Graham Plan sought to place the school's burgeoning athletic programs firmly under university control and to reassert the primacy of intellectual activity.[25]

Graham had known his plan would anger some alumni. But he was not prepared for the scale of the response. The school was flooded with protests, many of which illustrated the broader social issues that the plan engaged. Not only did alumni enjoy both the pageantry and the symbolism of athletic contests, but the recruiting practices that the plan sought to eliminate closely mirrored the philosophy that governed business dealings in the state. Like business, recruiting had involved a championing of results-oriented practicality over abstract idealism, the significance of personal connections, and a vision of the existing economic system as a logical and appropriate response to prevailing circumstances, particularly the realities of "human nature" that alumni speakers had so often invoked. North Carolinians who took up their pens and mustered their influence to oppose the Graham Plan defended not just top-level college football but an entire vision of the world.[26]

The practicality to which so many alumni appealed could mean the ability to solve a given task. A regular *Southern Textile Bulletin* feature, for example, was titled "Practical Discussions by Practical Men" and offered monthly advice on technicalities such as card setting or keeping drop wires clean. But practicality was also invoked to justify a less-than-perfect status quo—an argument that pure ideals simply could not be achieved. Reactions to the Graham Plan consistently drew on this idea. A resolution passed by the alumni of New Hanover County called the plan "essentially idealistic and extremely impractical." Alumni in Davidson County concluded that current programs were "as near amateur as is possible of attaining." A Durham County resolution affirmed that participants' commitment to amateurism was as strong "as the circumstances and conditions will permit" and called the plan "a highly theoretical document, intricately woven with a very delicate thread of the most idealistic thought." Even one of Graham's supporters urged changes, noting, "I may be more liberal in my ideas than you are, but by the same token more practical."[27]

Supporters of "practicality" often focused on the competition that North Carolina universities faced from other schools, asserting that alumni and administrators elsewhere would do their best to circumvent the regulations and deprive North Carolina of prized recruits, relegating the state's squads to "the position of doormat before teams of other institutions." In a particularly pointed expression of this reasoning, K. P. Lewis invoked his own business experience. "I admire very much the motives of your action and your conscientiousness but I think your present program is entirely too idealistic. The other institutions simply will not play fair, or rather some of them will not," he wrote, going on to cite the price wars in which textile manufacturers engaged after World War I.

We have had a lot of experience, in business life, in co-operative agreements. Time and again we have endeavored to maintain a price on our products. We had no right under the law to make an agreement but we did have the right, which we exercised, of each person's announcing what he was going to hold his goods at. These efforts all came to naught, caused by various types of subterfuge and evasions, and the whole scheme completely flopped. These managers of sales were men of high character, certainly equal to the average coach or professor. The same thing exactly is going to happen in connection with your regulations.[28]

While this inability to come to collective terms clearly frustrated many industrialists, others cast such actions in a different light, invoking the theme of individual independence in the face of restrictive regulations. Such writers often cited the dramatic failures of Prohibition in support of their case, as when one alumnus concluded, "Prohibition taught that we cannot regulate by rule of thumb but must govern conduct by education and moral sentiment." W. A. Blount, of the Liggett & Myers Tobacco Company, invoked both the liberty of individuals and the attractions of his product, informing Graham that "the U.S. military academy once prohibited the smoking of cigarettes—but when they found they were making liars out of most of the cadets, they abolished the rule." Even as K. P. Lewis lamented the failure of price agreements, he also lauded the idea of strong, unfettered individuals, personified by the state's successful coaches. "I should think that Wallace Wade and Carl Snavely would both be open for consideration of other jobs if this matter is handled as you desire it," he wrote. "I would have a poor opinion of their independence and individuality if I did not think so."[29]

Although critics of the plan focused their arguments on matters of practicality, their comments also suggest that they were troubled by what they saw as Graham's apparent rejection of the paternalistic ideals that remained dear to the hearts of state industrialists. Paternalism had been a reigning metaphor for state industry ever since the late nineteenth century, when builders of cotton mills had justified their actions as the best way to care for a rural population struggling with the economic turmoil of modern life. One facet of that scenario involved identifying and encouraging young men seen as worthy of social and professional elevation—a role in which state leaders reveled. In November 1929, for example, *Southern Textile Bulletin* editor (and major Graham opponent) David Clark printed an admonition to encourage young boys, lauding the personal inspiration that influential men could wield. "The doffer boys in the mills or the boys in the mill village who have not yet reached the age for work will later grow into men and the kind of men they become depends to a considerable extent upon the treatment and encouragement given them by the mill men of today," Clark wrote, continuing, "An overseer may engage the most humble doffer boy in kindly conversation and perhaps his interest and word of encouragement may be an inspiration and may make that boy realize that he has an opportunity in life and that he can amount to something." Among the admiring responses that Clark received was a letter from K. P. Lewis, who reported that he had ordered it read throughout the mill he headed. "It is certainly a very strong expression of the duty of those higher up to the young man just starting out in his life's work," Lewis wrote, "and I am glad that you wrote such a strong and helpful editorial."[30]

Helping young men find the means to attend college was one way that successful North Carolinians played that paternal role. In troubled financial times even small contributions could make the difference in a young man's ability to pay for school and could help forge a powerful bond between individuals. More than half a century after future University of North Carolina president William Friday left Gaston County for Wake Forest College, he still recalled with fond emotion the moment when college dean Daniel Bryan granted him the fifty-dollar scholarship that made the journey possible. Letters written by alumni made clear that such pleasures were mutual. Restricting such assistance to scholarships that were open to widespread, academically based competition threatened this bond.[31]

The combination of practical and personal discomfort that the Graham Plan created was voiced with particular clarity in a letter from *Raleigh News and Observer* publisher Frank Daniels regarding young men from Raleigh's Methodist Orphanage. "Some of these boys, I presume, will go to college and it would be absolutely necessary for them to have help," Daniels wrote. "But if some good Methodist is interested in helping some of these boys—and this year there were three boys from the Methodist Orphanage on the Raleigh High School's championship football team—it would be impossible for such a Methodist to do what he feels like is his duty if your recommendations are adopted." As Graham pointed out in his reply, an athlete would be within the rules if he had secured an academic scholarship open to all residents of the orphanage. But that reasoning seemed to have little resonance with the personal connections Daniels described, with the good Methodists "interested in helping some of these boys," or with his mention of the personal side of athletic recruiting: "Incidentally, some of the alumni here in Raleigh had hoped to be able to interest some of the Methodist Orphanage boys in Chapel Hill but now, of course, they will probably go over to Duke."[32]

The importance of personal connections and the particular pleasure gained by an alumnus in supporting a successful athlete were also noted in a letter from Judge J. Will Pless Jr., who invoked "human nature" in suggesting that athletes inspired contributions that otherwise would not be made at all. "While a successful student deserves as much or more consideration and help than a good athlete, he just doesn't get it; and we can't change that unless we can also change human nature," Pless wrote. "But the good student is not being deprived of anything by the alumni; and the fact that one more boy of athletic ability is given an education does not harm the good student. Isn't it better to let one of two boys receive an education, for whatever reason, than to prevent him from getting it just because the other isn't?"[33]

The passionate outpouring of letters underscored the depth of the attachment university alumni had formed both to college athletics and to the multifaceted vision of manhood that it had come to symbolize. But the controversy also became a lightning rod for a far deeper conflict within North Carolina, one that involved the conservative economic road the state's industrialists had chosen to pursue. For North Carolinians who had chafed at Frank Porter Graham's liberal thinking, the football controversy provided a welcome opening. Even as some state residents made phone calls and wrote pleading letters, others began to organize more direct action. On February 29, three months after Graham had put forth his measures, the *Charlotte Observer* announced that it had learned of a movement to capitalize on opposition to the Graham Plan, as well as to other university actions, and oust Graham from the presidency of the University of North Carolina. The reasons listed for the move included "that Dr. Graham's administration of affairs at the University has been offensive to powerful influential and financial interests in and out of the State."[34]

The fierce opposition to the plan had already spurred some of Graham's supporters to advise restraint, fearing such consequences. T. E. Wagg Jr. of the *Greensboro Daily News* advised Graham to drop the fight almost a month before the *Observer*'s revelation, reasoning

> that in essence this is a minor issue. Certainly it is if the forces making cannon fodder of the restraining suggestions triumph and reduce Carolina more to their ideas of the purpose and functions of a university. I can easily imagine a North Carolina, with such eminent spokesmen as Mr. David Clark in a position to speak for it, descending to new low levels. I can imagine much of the precious freedom disappearing if the issue comes to a head. . . . I say that the academic freedom of the University, the atmosphere of the place, the contribution the University is making to North Carolina and the nation is of far greater importance than football, even if it is purely commercial football, and that to endanger these traditions is perilous.

Alumnus Nat Henry also urged Graham to put aside athletic principle in favor of more important issues, writing, "The arrogant, self-appointed gods of North Carolina industry in the interest of their pocketbooks want your university to stop telling young men that real value exists in human lives, unafraid thought, and in knowledge. If necessary you should put aside your ideals for the moment, for your presidency is more important than sportsmanship."[35]

As such worried comments revealed, the conflicts laid bare by the Graham Plan controversy involved not only economic and political issues but also the role the university should play in state society. Union-minded workers did not pose the only challenge to industrialists' hold over North Carolina's economic and political institutions. While academic ventures into fields such as sociology and economics could support business interests, they also made universities into potential competitors for authority over the direction of state development. When, for example, North Carolina reformers launched a series of campaigns centered on wages, working conditions, and especially child labor, many of the reformers had university connections, and universities had frequently produced the studies from which they drew their ammunition. Associations between universities and liberal social programs would become even stronger in the era of the New Deal, when Franklin Roosevelt and many of his associates drew heavily on academic expertise.

Resentment of university "meddling" in industrial affairs was often bitter, as suggested in a 1928 *Alumni Review* that carried a warning from a "substantial citizen" about the stances taken by university faculty. "The trouble with you people at Chapel Hill is that you've lost sight of the fact that the University is simply a part of the state's educational system and belongs and is responsible to the tax payers," the alumnus fumed. "You strut about and offer advice and criticism like the Lord Almighty." A barrage of similar denunciations appeared in the *Southern Textile Bulletin*, a development that proved especially telling. If Frank Porter Graham had become North Carolina's most prominent liberal, *Textile Bulletin* editor David Clark was perhaps its most outspoken conservative. The contrasts between the two men highlighted with particular effectiveness the diverging intellectual paths North Carolina's warring leaders had chosen.[36]

Graham had been nurtured by a strong liberal strain in North Carolina thought, by ideas that championed both education and social reform. He had grown up surrounded by committed educators, among them his father, Alexander Graham, who was superintendent of the Charlotte public schools, and his cousin, Edward Kidder Graham, who served on the English faculty at the University of North Carolina and eventually became the institution's president. As a child on his front porch and then as a university student, Graham had listened to countless ringing exhortations about the higher calling of academic labor. He also belonged to the cohort of state residents who subscribed to the Social Gospel, which held that faithful Christians should work to improve conditions in the world at hand rather than focusing on future heavenly rewards.[37]

David Clark embodied another, equally strong thread of Tar Heel philosophy. While Clark's father, North Carolina Supreme Court Chief Justice Walter Clark, had been known as a liberal thinker, David Clark cast his lot firmly with North Carolina's most conservative industrialists. After abandoning an early foray into textile mill operation, he founded the *Southern Textile Bulletin*, a Charlotte-based journal designed to appeal to mill owners and managers. Clark began the endeavor with a sharp declaration of his own independence, proclaiming that the publication was "Heir to Nothing." Along with outlining the latest developments in management and production techniques, Clark loudly and persistently opposed attempts to curb the textile industry's independence in any way, winning his most prominent victory when he spearheaded a series of lawsuits that succeeded in overturning federal standards governing the hours and conditions of child labor. In the early 1920s, as university researchers began to delve into industrial issues, Clark began a series of assaults on what he called the "communistic" tendencies of university faculty, voicing dire predictions such as, "Every year, thousands of young men who would, otherwise, develop into successful businessmen and manufacturers come under the influence of radical professors in our colleges and universities and have their minds so twisted that their careers are ruined."[38]

Like many of the Graham Plan opponents, Clark stressed experience over idealism. In the fall of 1930, in the wake of several bitter textile strikes, Graham had circulated a letter through the state that advocated changes in the industry. Among other points, he argued for "a national, non-partisan economic and social survey of the textile industry" and directly attacked industry practices, asserting, "Social adjustment must be made to industrial change and since, in our commonwealth, some social adjustments lag far behind the industrial advance, it is, therefore, the part of industrial and social wisdom to make such clearly needed adjustments as the reduction of the legal sixty hour week, the abolition of night work for women and children, the elimination of the fourth grade clause in the child labor law, and the adequate provision and enforcement of this social code by the commonwealth." David Clark mounted an angry defense, telling Graham, "You are paid a salary to teach the young men in the University of North Carolina for nine months of the year. You have no experience in industry or business. Why do you feel that you are especially qualified or chosen to tell the textile industry of North Carolina how to conduct its business?" He then went on to ask, "Would you like to become manager of a cotton mill and show the industry exactly how it should be run? I think I can arrange for you to become manager of a small mill if you wish to give a demonstration."[39]

The intense emotions involved in this intellectual split were also evident in rhetoric from the other side, as when a Rockingham attorney mused to Graham that "winning is secondary, because when one man wins another must lose, and sometimes it seems to me that the loser profits more, but I guess I had better detour from this line of expression, otherwise Dave Clark and his kind may allege that I too am socialistic or communistic." He went on to allude to both the state's social divisions and the staunch opposition Duke administrators had mounted to Graham's plan with a biting outburst: "Let Dave Clark with his hunkies and the money he has to spend for the Camels and the spenders of old man Duke's bounty spread themselves with their brand of football, and then we will thank God we have a few people in North Carolina, especially a fine boy at the head of our University, who had rather see them pay the tobacco farmers for their toil and sweat, and will fight to make them do it."[40]

But such views did not hold sway. Despite alarmist rhetoric about communism and radical professors, the university was generally extremely cautious when dealing with industrial matters. The scholars who were winning the university a growing reputation in the field of regional sociology expended most of their effort on critiques of the state's rural conditions rather than examinations of its industrial situation. The state-funded institution depended on the legislature to approve its budget, a particularly precarious position in the midst of the depression. And as Graham came to realize, the ideals that the Graham Plan espoused held limited appeal for a public already used to athletic fanfare and the pursuit of monetary gain.[41]

Charles Tillett, one of Graham's staunchest supporters and oldest friends, cautioned him about these broader attitudes in a lengthy letter that urged him to moderate his efforts. Tillett himself opposed intercollegiate football, proposing instead that colleges "rent their stadiums out each week-end to league football teams and use the money to buy books for their libraries." But he realized that few North Carolinians agreed with him. "The opposition, to state it bluntly, does not think monetary aid by alumni, to the extent of board, room and tuition, in and of itself, and by itself, contaminates," he wrote, adding, "Of course, the public generally does not think that the boys, by being parts of a tremendous commercial enterprise, will be hurt, because the public does not think that money, taken by itself, hurts anybody." Competition among colleges to attract top players, "in and of itself is not necessarily offensive because it is exactly what goes on all day long in America with respect to everything else."[42]

Faced with threats to his presidency and with a weakening of resolve among other Southern Conference schools, Graham backed down. Southern Conference presidents, following an intense lobbying campaign, had voted by a slim majority to accept some of Graham's proposals. But some presidents disagreed with Graham, and others faced opposition from their own alumni. Duke, which had worked to build a nationally prominent football program under Wallace Wade, was particularly adamant and threatened to leave the Southern Conference if the proposals were enacted. In December 1936, conference presidents modified the rules they had adopted ten months earlier, and in 1937 they reversed themselves entirely, voting to allow official assistance to athletes as long as the funds came from nonuniversity sources. Graham himself eventually gave in and followed suit.[43]

By abandoning the Graham Plan, Frank Porter Graham conceded that he led a divided university, one that served a variety of ends. T. E. Wagg, who had urged that Graham abandon the football fight in order to preserve other areas of the institution's independence, provided an apt metaphor. "What the University and Duke may contribute to North Carolina and the nation is immeasurable, provided of course, matters of the flesh do not intrude," he wrote. "And football, including the sale of tickets and the building of stadia, is a matter of the flesh." For the next quarter-century, university athletic programs would steer their own course, supported by alumni through tax-exempt organizations that included the Educational Foundation, founded by Chapel Hill alumni specifically to raise money for university athletics, and North Carolina State's Wolfpack Club, which counted David Clark among its founders and most active members. Under Wallace Wade, Duke's football team continued to prosper, winning coveted Rose Bowl bids in 1938 and 1942. College athletics was in place to stay.[44]

The new legitimacy the Graham Plan defeat conferred on athletic scholarships strengthened associations between athletics, industrial virtue, and social mobility, further complicating an already tangled web of relationships among the white men who occupied varying positions in North Carolina society. Wade had discerned these connections early in the dispute and challenged Graham's efforts with the assertion that the plan would have devastating consequences for what Wade called "the poor boy." Eliminating athletic scholarships, Wade argued, meant deserving young men of modest means would lose their only means for financing a college education. The cultural power wielded by the image of the poor-boy athlete came clear in the frequency with which it was invoked during the Graham Plan debate. It would be further strengthened by well-publicized real-life success stories such as those of the McCachren brothers.[45]

Interest in competitive athletics in fact formed one of the major points of continuity among white North Carolina men at different levels of society, a connection that became particularly evident in the athletic endeavors of the state's textile firms. Employers frequently saw company baseball and basketball teams as integral parts of broader efforts to promote employee loyalty and inculcate industrial discipline. For their part, employees eagerly joined industrial teams and often provided organizing impetus themselves. Textile mill baseball gained particular renown, developing devoted followings and nurturing remarkable talent. Southern textile communities provided professional major league teams with a steady supply of players throughout the first half of the century. When Chapel Hill–based researcher Harriet Herring embarked on a survey of North Carolina mills in the 1920s, she noted that most "take for granted assistance to baseball teams."[46]

By the 1920s Saturday afternoon baseball games had become fixtures in textile mill communities throughout the South, anticipated social events as well as displays of physical skill. "Everything in the whole country would be there," Eula Durham recalled of home games in the small community of Bynum. The Bynum team also had a strong road following, through a measure that further tightened connections between community and mill. "Ernest Wicker, a man that used to work around down at the mill, Mr. London would let him have that truck on Saturday to carry anyone to the ball game that wanted to go," Durham explained. "He'd pull it up down there at the store. Lord, every gal and boy in Bynum would be in that truck. Go off to the ball games. Have the best time. You didn't have to worry about how you was going to the ball games."[47]

Such baseball fever brought its own opportunities. Mills were often eager to improve their teams, and talented players found their services in great demand. When Frank Webster first took up textile work, the industry's best jobs—making women's full-fashioned hosiery—were extremely difficult to obtain. "At that time, a hosiery job, you almost had to live a lifetime to get one because people made good money on those machines," Webster explained. "They tried to stick with it. For a newcomer to work his way in, somebody almost had to croak out or die before you'd get a machine. In other words you'd have to wait for your time to come, and sometimes that was lengthy." But his baseball abilities gave Webster a considerable advantage. One day, he recounted, a friend suggested that he call on Ernest Chapman, who ran Burlington's Tower Hosiery Mill. "So I came down and talked with Mr. Chapman, and he wanted me to work for them because he knew I could play baseball pretty well. And they had a team here. This boy got hurt and this machine was open. That's what led me to getting a job at Tower Hosiery Mill." In 1936 Webster started on an Einesidel-Rheiner hosiery machine and at shortstop.[48]

Despite the growing celebration of "poor boys" who used athletic skill to gain college scholarships, many players were reluctant to leave such supportive communities for the unfamiliar surroundings of a college campus or for the middle-class life a college degree made possible. When Enos Slaughter was offered a minor league baseball contract, he took it and stuck with it despite the intense homesickness that he felt in his first assignment. But he had been far less willing to leave home for college. When Slaughter finished high school, his athletic talents had garnered him a scholarship offer from Guilford College. "This pleased my dad, who wanted me to continue my education," he later wrote. "But I didn't share those feelings. My mind was set on going to work for the mill and continuing to play second base for the company team. After he and I went back and forth a few times over the matter, he finally relented, saying: 'All right. If you can do what you want often enough, you ought to be happy.' "[49]

Despite the apparent similarities between college and textile sports, however, the two institutions took on very different meanings. For the present and future industrialists who watched college games with such satisfaction, athletic events provided a multifaceted mirror on an existing world, suggesting courses of action and models of behavior that they associated with their everyday activities of management and planning. For most wage laborers the autonomy and status they gained on industrial teams stood in welcome contrast to the realities of factory production and helped blunt the disdain with which textile workers in particular were often regarded. In this role industrial athletics became part of the complex politics of respect that suffused North Carolina, joining a range of political and psychological efforts to downplay the economic and social hierarchies that industrialization had produced in favor of standards that softened or sidestepped such distinctions.

Textile workers were hit especially hard by North Carolina's new industrial order. Not only did they endure long hours and low wages, but they were frequently dogged by the stigma attached to textile labor, by the gap between the standards of living in mill villages and those enjoyed in nearby towns, and by the deeply ingrained American assumption that such inequities resulted from a system in which deserving individuals clambered to the top and those left at the bottom could only blame themselves. The stares that textile workers encountered when they ventured into town, condescending references to "poor white trash" and "lintheads," and the taunts that textile mill children endured in school all made workers keenly aware of their low social standing. The anger that such disdain could produce erupted in Ralph Austin's account of a confrontation at a Charlotte baseball game. Austin was sitting with some companions, watching the game, when a fellow worker reacted to an insulting remark with a violent outburst. "We were in front of three or four fellows," Austin explained. "Somebody said, 'Sit down up there you linthead.' I've never heard any one man get such a cussin'. He would have really hurt that fellow if he'd a stood up. It made him so ashamed of himself he felt like crawling."[50]

Athletics offered a way to counteract such condescending assumptions, as a short article in a 1922 *Southern Textile Bulletin* suggested. "Those who assert that work in the cotton mills seriously injures the health will be hard pressed to explain the fact that the basketball team of the Highland Park Mills has so far

Highland Park Mill basketball team members as they appeared in the *Southern Textile Bulletin* in 1922. Photograph courtesy of the North Carolina Collection, University of North Carolina Library, Chapel Hill.

beaten every other team in the Charlotte City League," the *Bulletin* proclaimed. The article went on to emphasize the achievement these victories represented, noting, "The other teams in the City League are composed very largely of men who have been trained at colleges or in Y.M.C.A. gymnasiums and yet boys from the Highland Park Mills have walked away with each of their competitors in turn." It then added a visual component to the argument, explaining, "Elsewhere in this issue we are publishing a cut of the Highland Park Mills basketball team and we assert that they compare in appearance favorably with college and Y.M.C.A. teams."[51]

On the surface the article represented yet one more salvo in David Clark's campaign to counter charges that the long hours, low pay, and dangerous conditions of textile mill work posed grave health risks. But the circumstances of the story were far more complex. The Highland Park mill had been one of the most important battlegrounds in the labor conflicts that rocked North Carolina in the years after World War I. The plant's workers had gone on strike in 1919, and they had driven strikebreaking drivers out of their North Charlotte neighborhood during the streetcar strike. Barely six months before the article appeared, they had struck again, spending the entire summer facing Highland Park's owners over locked gates, picket lines, and sometimes loaded rifles. The 1921 conflict had ended in a standoff; the workers had not been able to restore the wage reductions they were contesting, but many felt their action had averted future cuts.[52]

In this context the Highland Park team's successes and the *Southern Textile Bulletin*'s enthusiastic endorsement offered a number of potential meanings. The cheerful account of the basketball team's successes provided a reassuring contrast to the mix of anger and confusion that had filled earlier articles about the strike. The previous year, southern mill owners had looked to their new, regionwide textile basketball tournament as a way to promote "real sportsmanship and fellowship among the textile plants." City league competition likely held out the promise that some such fellowship could be created among more diverse groups of people, helping them set aside troubling questions of social or economic status. Workers may have felt some of the same impulses; after months of work stoppage and impassioned argument—which eventually culminated in the arrival of the state militia—many workers probably appreciated the exciting but contained action of a basketball game.[53]

Seen through the eyes of the players who stared so confidently from the *Textile Bulletin* pages, however, the city competitions may well have taken on other meanings. Defeating a team of the college men who so often claimed a privileged position in directing government or economic affairs must have held particular satisfaction for the textile team and its followers. Such successes could also have future implications. The 1921 settlement produced only a temporary truce within the textile industry. Less than a decade later the textile South would experience a series of even more wrenching conflicts, culminating in the general textile strike of 1934, the largest labor action the country had ever seen. Maintaining a commitment to collective struggle required southern textile workers to sustain their sense of self-confidence, their conviction that despite the dismal stereotypes so often used to disparage their character and conduct, they possessed the skills and vision to shape their future. Within the textile villages religious faith, mutual support, and a vibrant, shared culture helped keep workers from succumbing to despair. Athletic success may well have played a role in this process as well.[54]

Victories over teams from higher social stations could indeed mean a great deal. Hoyle McCorkle, who worked at the Highland Park Mill in the 1930s and had painful childhood memories of being taunted by town children, recalled how he and fellow employees felt when new manager Arthur Jarrett put forth the effort to develop a star baseball team. "It was really a source of great pride to us," explained McCorkle, who played on the team. "We'd always looked up to the hosiery mill, but now we began to beat them at the baseball, and it did us a whole lot of good. . . . They made more money, and it was a nicer job, an easier job, a cleaner job, and they made a whole lots more money. And they belonged to this baseball league, but when Jarrett came here we began to win. We finally began to beat them pretty regular."[55]

Such alternative measures of respect were enormously important, allowing many North Carolinians to retain dignity and self-esteem even in circumstances that often seemed degrading. But they could also play problematic roles within state society, at least from the perspective of those who envisioned an alternate social order. This was particularly true in the late 1920s and in the 1930s, a time when workers faced intense competition for their loyalties. Throughout the era, textile workers were confronted by union supporters who urged them to band together in defiance of the existing system, while industrialists proclaimed they should be satisfied with their lot. As the Charlotte streetcar workers reasoned, unionization dealt directly with the inequalities of the economic world and sought to redistribute economic power in a way that gave workers more say in how the industries they staffed were run. Alternative sources of identity, such as sports or religion, could help build the confidence and communal ties required to support such efforts. But they could also ease the tensions that helped spark collective action, offering a welcome distraction from the hardships of textile work and building additional connections between workers and their mills.[56]

Of the many institutions that textile workers built for themselves, athletics stood in especially ambiguous relationship to the world of owners and managers. Management often had a heavy hand in athletic efforts, particularly where successful teams were concerned. Some employers left their employees largely to their own devices, as Ethel Faucette, who worked at Burlington's Holt Plaid Mill, recalled. "They had baseball games," she noted. "It was played back up yonder, at the other side of the old home place. Until Bob Holt gave them a ball ground and told them now they had to play up there. And so they did, they played up there." But others were often as interested in the teams as workers. Harriet Herring described one mill that "stopped aiding ball teams because it took too much of the superintendent's time, since he was always going with them on trips." Another company ceased its support because, in the owner's words, "everybody got more interested in ball than they were in the business. They would close down the mill for the afternoon and everybody go to the games."[57]

Ball teams gave managers and owners numerous opportunities to exercise paternalistic clout in forms that ranged from new uniforms to player recruitment to rewards for individual and team success. The assumption that such efforts maintained good feeling among workers and blunted interest in union-led activities was suggested by columnist Ethel Thomas Dabbs in a 1935 *Southern Textile Bulletin* as she described the exploits of a mill team in Greenville, South Carolina.

J. M. Bolt [the weaving overseer] is manager of the ball team, which won two cups and are the King Cotton Champions. Mr. Bolt and several members of the team went to see the World's Series played in Chicago, and spent three days there that they will never forget. The very best of feeling prevails around Brandon. The people are proud of the mill, the community and the chance to work and are ready to give a warm reception to any one who dares try to spread poisonous influences. The 'flying Squadron' [a group of union organizers that galvanized support for the 1934 strike] gave this place a wide berth.[58]

Like many other "welfare work" measures, team sponsorship rarely had such dramatic results, and the solidarity that teamwork forged could, in fact, be turned against mill owners. During a 1929 strike at Gastonia's Loray Mill, for example, members of the mill baseball team covered the "Loray" on their uniforms with their union's initials. But gestures of support for this important aspect of textile mill culture had considerable effects; worker memories of company teams were often interwoven with appreciation of management support. One of Jesse Ashe's most vivid recollections of the Southern Power Company team where he played alongside W. S. Lee Jr. was Lee's practice of providing players with a production bonus, an incentive that colored even Ashe's memories of a league championship. "Mr. Lee he'd give us five dollars a hit. And he'd mail me the check every time I'd get a hit, you know. . . . No, [it was] two dollars for a hit and five dollars for a home run. And that fellow from Clemson, during the playoff day, he got two home runs and one three-bagger. He got twelve dollars. . . . I didn't get a hit that day. But I wound up; I batted .301 that year."[59]

Hoyle McCorkle recalled how a successful baseball team brought new morale to Highland Park. But his appreciation of the team was closely intertwined with his feelings about Arthur Jarrett, whose efforts had built the field and recruited many of the talented players who helped produce the winning records. McCorkle drew a sharp contrast between life under Jarrett's watch and the years when Highland Park workers had constructed barricades in the North Charlotte streets and sent stones flying toward strikebreaking streetcar drivers. "There was a lot of things that was going on that weren't right and didn't make no money and the job was pretty tough and things like that. But after Jarrett came here, things began to change. People began to want to go see the ballgame instead of going to union meetings. Jarrett had a good idea there. That helped a lot." It is perhaps not surprising that although mill owners dropped most of their worker welfare programs during the 1930s, they usually retained their company teams.[60]

Throughout North Carolina similar stories unfolded. As union activities flagged in the face of stringent opposition and hard economic times, baseball games carried on, offering workers a measure of respect and a way to pass their time but prompting little change in other aspects of their lives. One year the Tower Hosiery team tied for its league championship, Frank Webster recalled, and mill owner Reid Maynard took the team to see the Yankees play the Giants in the World Series. The players spent one day in Washington and several in New York, staying at good hotels, eating well, and enjoying the chance to see their game played at its highest level. "He treated us like kings and all," Webster noted. But the transformation was only temporary, ending as soon as the team returned to Burlington. "Everybody was tired and hungry, sleepy. We got back off the baseball trip and work went on normal from there. I worked at Tower Hosiery Mill."[61]

As sports became a key component of white men's lives at many levels of North Carolina society, they offered them an engaging activity, community acclaim, and a powerful sense of self. The growing prominence of the state's athletic institutions sprang from a social situation whose complexities were rarely reflected in the celebratory tones of athletic rhetoric—large-scale athletics prospered at state universities largely because of a compromise struck by officials and alumni, while the cherished games played in textile leagues were far removed from the realities of mill work or the social structures of the nonsporting world. But men's sporting institutions continued to expand, providing multifaceted support for the state's social and economic order. College football games gave state leaders a chance to forge social ties and debate manly character, even as the action on the field helped endow competitive endeavors with a sense of masculine heroism. The athletic scholarships awarded to deserving young men such as the McCachren brothers became a widely celebrated model for social mobility that rested on individual ability and ambition, rather than on collective efforts to transform the status quo. While textile league sports fostered a sense of pride that could buttress industrial rebellion, they also forged ties between workers and management that could bind workers closer to their mills, blunting efforts at strikes or unionization.

Sports also maintained an almost mystical hold over North Carolina's white male population, influencing many men in ways they did not necessarily recognize or control. Yale president James Angell had invoked this power when he warned Graham that he faced "a long and hard fight in which even normally intelligent people will be against you on account of the wholly emotional attitudes that athletic contests seem to elicit." The many writings that supported

Graham were shot through with sporting metaphors, evidence that even as the writers railed against the emphasis given to athletic competition, they too were drawn to images of strong, capable, and heroic individuals, men such as Fed Reinhardt, Frank Merriwell, or a father who caught baseballs with no gloves and no shoes. An admiring article in the *Norfolk Virginian-Pilot* stated, "Graham is a little chap, but he hits like [boxing champion Jack] Dempsey when the time comes, and evidently the hour has struck." Davidson president Walter Lingle echoed that phrase, writing, "I hope you are feeling as strong as Jack Dempsey these days." Wiley Hurie, president of the College of the Ozarks, wrote Graham a letter that sharply denounced the existing state of college athletics but ended with the exhortation, "May you knock a home-run."[62]

Charles Tillett, one of Graham's staunchest friends and most thoughtful critics, turned to such language to assess the profound effects North Carolina's athletic institutions were working on the men to whom they meant so much. Tillett was particularly skeptical about the value of physical and mental strife. He would later become a nationally known critic of the use of force, opposing World War II and working tirelessly for world peace. In a lengthy letter written at the height of the Graham Plan crisis, he broadened his analysis of the situation into a critique of the role sports had come to play in education, highlighting some of its limits as a model for real life and warning Graham that even college presidents were far from immune. "Intercollegiate football tends to emphasize far beyond its merits the virtue of personal bravery," Tillett wrote.

As a result of intercollegiate football, ideals of personal bravery pervade the entire college community to the extent that the college product tends to consider the virtue of personal bravery the greatest of all virtues. While it is a virtue, it is a thoroughly primitive one. In the hierarchy of virtues, I think wisdom comes first and courage last. In fact, so many fool things are done as a result of courage that I at times seriously doubt that it is a virtue. It certainly partakes of many of the characteristics of vice. I am inclined to think that if the normal college student were presented with alternative courses of action, one having some wisdom and requiring the exhibition of physical or moral courage and the other being much the wiser but requiring no utilization of the virtue of physical or moral courage, he would choose the first named course every time; he would probably think he was a time-server if he chose to be wise rather than brave.[63]

Tillett, who had become a lawyer, went on to talk about his own experience, explaining, "When I got out of college, I found that I was definitely contaminated, and one of the most difficult tasks I had was, in the court house, to develop a restraint of my courage in order to act wisely for the benefit of my client."

He then pointed to Graham himself, noting Graham's own enthusiastic support for college football and suggesting, "I doubt if you yourself have been completely preserved from this same contamination. I am not at all sure but that your willingness to assume personal responsibility for the Plan when it was publicized and began to be condemned (an unwise thing to have done from the standpoint of gaining the objective sought) was the result of this contamination."[64]

With those words Charles Tillett offered a glimpse into the power that organized athletics had gained over North Carolina society, and particularly over much of its white male population, suggesting the extent to which athletics had indeed become a guide for life, shaping men's actions in ways they did not even realize. Athletics, of course, was not alone; the rhetoric of bravery and conflict infused the arenas of politics, of market economics, of war, and of union activity. But it was athletics that played out these ideals with such sharp, dramatic clarity, and athletics that wove them into daily life, game after game and season after season.

## CHAPTER FIVE

# It Was Our Whole Lives

## The Growth of Women's Basketball, 1920–1953

I n the spring of 1949, the twelve members of the Highland High School Ramlette basketball team packed themselves into an assortment of supporters' vehicles and embarked on the long and bumpy journey from Gastonia east to Durham. The Ramlettes had played a stellar season, had won the district tournament held in neighboring Bessemer City, and thus had gained the right to compete for the state championship, 150 miles away at North Carolina College. Before they left, the students from the close-knit school had packed the gym to cheer them on. "Go Thompson!" they had yelled. "Go Davis!" "Go Adams!" "We were pumped up," recalled Gladys Thompson, the Ramlettes' tallest player and top scorer. "We were going to win this."[1]

The Ramlettes met those expectations, bringing home the North Carolina Athletic Conference crown. Gladys Thompson found the victory particularly sweet. She had been a tall, clumsy girl, often called "Stringbean" or "Pole," who lacked the grace of a natural athlete. "When I started playing, I was afraid and awkward," she recounted. "They would tell me, 'You're awkward,' and I wanted to give it up." But she loved basketball, and she worked hard on her skills, challenging the equally determined players who starred for schools across the region. When the Ramlettes took the court in Durham, she was ready, scoring twenty-three points in the championship game and winning most-valuable-player honors. "I always think about that," she explained. "Because I scored the twenty-three points, more points than any girl on the team had ever scored. . . . And they wrote an article about me in the paper. I think that would highlight everything. There were good times and bad times, but this one sticks in my mind more than any of them. When we won that championship. And then the article written about me—and that came back to the school; it was on the bulletin boards and everything. I felt pretty proud of myself."[2]

With her performance Gladys Thompson reached a goal dreamed of by thousands of her peers around the state. Varsity athletic competition had become an integral part of life in the Tar Heel State, drawing larger crowds than any school event but graduation and offering students perhaps their major opportunity to earn respect and acclaim among their peers and within their communities. Throughout North Carolina, high school and college students envisioned starring for beloved institutions, playing before cheering fans, cradling championship trophies, and seeing their accomplishments acknowledged in the authority of newspaper type. Basketball had become by far the most popular U.S. women's sport, and for the many young women who played the game, it held particular appeal, carrying them past many of the restrictions that still circumscribed women's activities. "Just little things about it, you know," Gladys Thompson explained. "Getting to go places. Girls didn't get to go many places. I had a strict mom. She was strict. And to get to go to *Durham*, North Carolina. Or even *Bessemer City*. That was a long way for us. Girls now they have boyfriends that just drive. But see, they didn't have cars to take us places then. As a matter of fact, when I played basketball, I wasn't courting. My mama didn't allow me to court until I graduated from high school. She did not. You had a friend to take you to the prom, but that's it."[3]

Today the Ramlettes' accomplishments draw periodic notice largely because Gladys Thompson was eventually allowed to court, married classmate Ervin Worthy, and then had a son named James, who grew into one of the greatest basketball players North Carolinians had ever seen. Since Ervin Worthy never played the game, attempts to trace James Worthy's athletic background point straight back to 1949, to Gladys Thompson's record-setting efforts, and to the vibrant popularity that women's basketball attained during the middle of the twentieth century. From the 1920s into the 1950s, women's basketball was one of the most popular spectator sports in small towns and rural communities across the nation. The cheers that urged on Gladys Thompson and her teammates echoed around North Carolina, as communities gathered to watch young women dribble, shoot, and strive to win. "The gym was always full," recalled Mildred Little Bauguess, who starred for Catawba County's Claremont High School from 1947 to 1951. "Here in this town, sports was a big thing. That was about the only entertainment they had in Claremont. They had a ball game on Tuesday night, and one on Friday night. And everybody'd bring the whole family. I think it cost kids about a dime to get in. The girls played just right before the boys. They'd come in to one, and they'd stay all the way through."[4]

North Carolina women's basketball blossomed amid a series of cultural transformations that forever altered the world within which young southern women shaped their lives. During the 1920s, young women took advantage of a growing range of opportunities. They moved into clerical and secretarial work and aspired to new positions within the textile industry, most notably to skilled, high-paying jobs knitting the newly popular sheer rayon hose that would themselves become a symbol of changing womanhood. The Nineteenth Amendment, ratified in 1920, cracked open the political realm. By the 1930s young women could look to a new and powerful set of female role models, from First Lady Eleanor Roosevelt to educator and "Black Cabinet" member Mary McLeod Bethune to Texas native and eventual North Carolina resident Jesse Daniel Ames, whose Association of Southern Women for the Prevention of Lynching encouraged southern white women to openly challenge the assumptions of white female vulnerability so often used to justify both racial violence and political oppression. Such new opportunities meshed neatly with the images and ideas that populated the expanding realm of mass commercial culture, in which movies, magazines, and advertising copy offered a view of womanhood that stressed vigorous activity, adventurous spirit, and sexual appeal.[5]

Basketball courts formed one arena within which North Carolina women grappled with these varying influences, as they drew on community ethics and their own experiences as well as the tantalizing images of mass commercial culture to fashion identities that would fit their changing world. As basketball gained in popularity, a wide variety of young women eagerly seized the opportunity to step into the public spotlight and to stake a female claim to a series of actions and emotions—freedom of movement, physical confidence, competitive spirit, delight in individual accomplishment—previously reserved for men. Basketball's influence would have its limits, working more change on individuals than on North Carolina society as a whole. But the sport would help thousands of young women negotiate a dizzying array of transformations, linking them to worlds outside their own experience and introducing them to the pleasures and perils of public performance, while also anchoring them in family, community, and a strong sense of themselves.

In the fall of 1920, a few short weeks after the Nineteenth Amendment wrote woman suffrage into the U.S. Constitution, a group of young women at Charlotte's Central High School banded together and headed toward the principal's office to proclaim their basketball ambitions. Central High offered several sports for boys, but none for girls, a situation the students were determined to transform. "We elected ourselves to be the team," player Mary Dalton explained years later. "We didn't have a team. We had played together; we were friends. So we just decided we wanted to have a basketball team and we said: 'We'll be it.'" The caption beneath their yearbook picture linked the newly formed squad's efforts to women's expanding role in other areas of public life, announcing, "Man's age has been heretofore, but now woman's age is coming in, not only in politics but in athletics."[6]

Similar stories unfolded throughout the state. "The girls of old Lincolnton High have always done their part in boosting the school and are justly proud of the work of the boys' teams," the school's first female basketball squad declared in 1925. But the players expected to do more than cheer in future, adding, "We hope sometime soon to do our part in giving our school a high standing in athletics." The team's relative modesty reflected a difficult first season. Among a number of defeats, the school calendar recorded the night when "girls meet their 'Waterloo' in a basketball game with Charlotte, the score being 41-1." The next year, however, the players announced considerable progress. "This year Lincolnton High will have to bow to the girl's basketball team," they wrote. "Miss Hoke, being the best coach that Lincolnton could have secured, molded the girls into the best winning team that L.H.S. has ever produced. Of the sixteen games, the girls won thirteen, losing only one away from home. The total score was four hundred and twenty-five to our opponents' two hundred and eighty-four points."[7]

For these new basketball players, the game took on multiple meanings, intersecting at many points with the social and economic transformations sweeping the state. Elizabeth Newitt, who managed the Central High School team in 1923, worked hard to bring her team into the colorful tumult of promotion, profit, and energetic action taking shape around her. "I had a lot of ambition for us to grow and to be active and to be very much like the boys," she explained. "So I set out to have a lot of games, give it a lot of publicity, make a lot of money. Which we did. We had headlines in the paper, big headlines when we would have a game. We drew a big crowd. And we made a lot of money. I bought the uniforms for the girls. Had enough money to buy uniforms for the boys on the football team. And I just made money right and left."[8]

The short-sleeved shirts and abbreviated bloomers that Elizabeth Newitt so proudly purchased embodied not only her business skills but also the confident independence that players found in their new activities, mirroring broader shifts in female attire. In the powerfully symbolic realm of women's garb, less fabric meant not only fewer physical restrictions but also increased self-confidence, a willingness to confront the world without the shielding protection of heavy material. Along with her account of games won, skills developed, and money made, Newitt stressed that her team's players had the assurance to roll their stockings down below their knees. "We rolled out," she explained, pointing to a team photograph. "We wore hose, and if you see this picture, we've got our hose rolled down. You see how we did it."[9]

Women's team at Charlotte's Central High School, 1923. Elizabeth Newitt is third from right, with bow in hair. From *Snips and Cuts*; photograph courtesy of the Robinson-Spangler Carolina Room, Public Library of Charlotte and Mecklenburg County.

Like their turn-of-the-century predecessors, aspiring basketball players caused some consternation among citizens who still held to visions of womanhood characterized by dependence, sharp distinctions between men and women, and strict moral purity. For the young, white men who plied the state's major college gridirons, the widespread, almost unconscious association that had developed between sports and manly virtue meant that the era's sporting disputes were frequently fought on a broad social canvas, focused on questions not only of manhood but also of political and economic life. For women, however, such battles were more often turned inward, trained on bedrock concepts of women's physical, emotional, and sexual nature.[10]

Suspicions about female frailty lingered in some corners of the state. In February 1929, when Derita High School star Nell Fincher hit her head in practice and slipped into a ten-day coma, a number of Charlotte-area parents determined to pull their daughters off school teams. Some communities harbored concerns about the sexual implications of short sleeves, rolled-down socks, and especially the shorts that were beginning to make athletic fashion. Helen Shipman, a coach in one of the state's rural black communities, lost two players to a father's concern that her team's uniforms showed too much thigh. Vada Setzer Hewins, who played for white Catawba High, recalled the whispered disapproval that made the rounds of her community when the girls' basketball team abandoned their "great big blowsy bloomers" for uniforms with shorts. "I would just hear rumors, you know," she explained. "They didn't just come right up to me and say it. Of course I know the principal heard it, the coach and all." Still others were troubled by basketball uniforms less because of the flesh that they revealed than for the way they seemed to blur distinctions between men and women, a perspective from which even bloomers could seem unacceptable. "Mama and Daddy wouldn't allow me to play on the team," Charlotte resident Frances Bullard longingly recalled, "for the girls wore blue serge bloomers, navy blue and beautifully pleated. Wearing britches was a sin."[11]

Similar concerns about strenuous activity and physical exposure had led an earlier generation of educators to constrain women's sports, carefully minimizing exertion and shielding female athletes from public view. But such reservations would have less effect on this new generation of players, who often came from different backgrounds and who ventured onto the court in a very different social context. Women's basketball had made its first inroads in the state's women's colleges, during a time when educated women's conduct was governed by Victorian-infused concepts of female frailty and respectability. The sport's 1920s expansion brought women's basketball to communities where both economic necessity and the demands of daily life had helped to fashion broader views of female capabilities.

Despite political rhetoric that cast white women as frail and vulnerable, few white communities were prosperous enough to spare women from hard labor. "We were always working on the farm, and outside, and we were strong," Vada Hewins recalled of her Catawba County childhood. "We really worked the year round, unless it would just be pouring down rain. You know, cotton picking or working in the fields, hoeing and all that." North Carolina's dominant textile industry had drawn on these rural patterns to develop a family labor system in which every member of a household was expected to hold down a mill job. Within textile mills, single and married women put in the same long, grueling hours as men, developing a broad sense of their economic responsibilities and their role in industry affairs. In the 1920s and 1930s, when conflicts over wages and escalating productivity demands set off a wave of strikes across the industry, women frequently stood in the forefront of the action.[12]

Among African Americans the economic constraints of post-Emancipation life meant that most women had no choice but to work, laboring in cotton and tobacco fields, stemming and sorting in the state's tobacco factories, taking in laundry, or pursuing domestic service. Even those young black women fortunate enough to go to college were not spared physical exertion, as financially strapped institutions continued to depend on female students for tasks such as college laundry. The ongoing difficulty of such work was suggested by a 1937 appeal published in the school newspaper at Barber-Scotia College, which asked alumni for aid in purchasing laundry equipment. "All sheets, table linen, towels, and other heavy flat work are now done by the students, by hand," the article explained. "With a washing machine, one girl could do in a few hours the work which it takes at the present time, several girls two or three weeks to do."[13]

In many such communities, informal sports became an integral part of growing up, and young women regularly played alongside brothers and male neighbors. Vada Hewins was one of eighteen children, and on the family's Catawba County farm they "had a ball game all the time." Civil rights activist Ella Baker counted among her fondest childhood memories the mixed-sex baseball games she played while at grade school in Littleton, North Carolina, during the 1910s. "I was a talker, and also I would rather play baseball than eat," she told an interviewer. "While I was there we had a mixed team of boys and girls, some much bigger than I, and I played baseball at recess. I'd take my lunch with me and eat it on the way to school, rather than bother with having to eat during lunchtime."[14]

Basketball's acceptance was also smoothed by a nationwide shift in notions of appropriate female dress, changes that helped to mute concerns about the air of sexuality that frequently infused women's athletics. Amid the tight-laced sensibilities of the Victorian era—compounded in North Carolina by the broad reach of conservative Christianity—even the slightest departure from convention had carried an unmistakable erotic charge, causing considerable public stir. But the expanding popular culture of the early twentieth century—movies, magazines, popular novels, and other products of mass culture that had begun to circulate throughout the country—offered a far more open treatment of female sexuality, focusing on and generally celebrating sexual appeal. A growing number of well-publicized "bathing beauty" pageants, most notably the Miss America contest begun in 1921, paraded attractive young women clad in bathing suits before a national audience of newspaper and magazine readers. A constant stream of advertisements, the driving force behind a nationally expanding "beauty industry," promised to initiate young women into the secrets of cultivating physical allure. In North Carolina, this charged new sensibility soon made its way into daily life. Women hemmed their skirts steadily upward to reveal nylon-clad calves and ankles. Rouge and lipstick, once considered marks of actresses and prostitutes, became a common sight.[15]

Such shifts were particularly noticeable in the case of African American women. At the turn of the century, middle-class black women had shied away from any hint of sexuality, fearful of reinforcing stereotypes that cast African American women as highly sensual, lacking both self-control and moral virtue. By the 1920s, however, numerous publications were beginning to celebrate black women's physical appearance. Black newspapers and magazines published countless photographs of eminently respectable young beauties, accompanied by animated descriptions of "mysterious black eyes," "shapely limbs," and "wonderful colorings of flesh." African American institutions organized their own beauty contests, often at the behest of the expanding black beauty industry, which frequently sought to link female beauty with race pride. An advertisement for the 1925 Golden Brown National Beauty Contest, which claimed to have drawn 5 million votes in its hotly contested race, explicitly linked the skin-cream-sponsored competition to racial self-confidence. "We must develop, in every member of our group, that quality known as pride," the copy ran. "Let us prove once and for all that we have here in America some of the most beautiful women of the world."[16]

Basketball could still become the focus of erotically tinged male attention. In 1927, for example, when the Dimpled Darlings of the American Spinning Mill captured the B division of the Southern Textile Association basketball tournament, they were celebrated as much for their appearance as for their achievement. "If the tournament had been a beauty show as well as a basketball carnival, the Darlings would have won first prize for pulchritude," a local reporter wrote. "Prettier girls are not to be found in an Atlantic City bathing contest, and the beauty of the 'dimpled dolls' is the kind that won't rub off. They have found that exercise in athletics is better for the complexion than rouge or lipstick." As the reference to the Miss America pageant made clear, however, basketball had become simply one of many new activities that placed young women's bodies on display.[17]

Within this changing context, women's basketball gained numerous defenders. Despite Nell Fincher's injury, her father did not see her as a frail maiden requiring protection from athletic excesses. Soon after she began to recover, he stopped by the *Charlotte Observer* to make clear his views. The resulting article, headlined "Of Course She'll Play Again," explained that Nell would be returning to the court. "I heard today some folks say that they think they'll stop their daughters from playing basketball," Fincher's father declared. "Well, I don't see why. It was a pure accident and the game had nothing to do with Nell's getting hurt." The disapproving rumors sparked by Catawba High's new uniforms had limited effect, Vada Hewins recalled, as school officials "just went right on with it." A few particularly conservative parents, such as Frances Bullard's, held out against the new activity. But many more supported their daughters' efforts with enthusiasm, sewing uniforms, dispensing with household chores on big game nights, and traveling considerable distances to cheer on young women's teams. Jimmie Maxine Vaughn Williams, who would eventually become one of North Carolina's most talented players, recalled that when she was in school, "my parents would drive 137 miles and then go back just to see a ball game when I might foul out in the first five minutes."[18]

Even as young women formed their high school teams, enthusiasm for the sport reached into other institutions where women were asserting themselves with greater force. In 1925 the student magazine at Raleigh's Shaw University heralded the school's inauguration of black women's college basketball, announcing that Shaw's female students had formed two basketball teams and were prepared to assume "their rightful place among other college women in the athletic world." While North Carolina's black colleges had previously displayed limited support for women's varsity competition, the Shaw declaration marked a new era. Support for varsity basketball would take root in most of the state's African American institutions; in private academies like Greensboro's Bennett College; teacher training schools such as Fayetteville State Teachers' College; coeducational, four-year institutions such as Shaw; and single-sex junior colleges such as Concord's Barber-Scotia. White women's colleges would continue to demur, focusing on an increasingly elaborate array of physical education programs. But by the mid-1930s, North Carolina's African American colleges had formed the North Carolina Women's Intercollegiate Athletic Association to regulate their play, and by 1936 ten of the state's thirteen black colleges sponsored varsity women's ball.[19]

As well as drawing on changing ideas about women, black women's college basketball tapped into the new energy that swept through black communities after World War I, as the efforts of the black soldiers that fought to make the world "safe for democracy" inspired African Americans around the country to wage battles against discrimination with renewed force. Such new assertiveness frequently met with violent resistance, most notably in the race-driven riots that erupted in East St. Louis; Washington, D.C.; Chicago; and many other cities. Throughout the 1920s and 1930s, however, African Americans steadily gained visibility in national life through the musical expressions of jazz musicians, the literary successes of the Harlem Renaissance, and the growing political force of the many black southerners who were moving to northern cities in what became known as the Great Migration. Black women, who had already established themselves as community and institutional leaders, played prominent roles in these newly visible activities. During the 1930s the nation's most

Livingstone College women's team, 1934. Courtesy of the College Archives, Carnegie Library, Livingstone College.

noted black leader was Mary McLeod Bethune, a graduate of North Carolina's Scotia Seminary and the confidante of Franklin and Eleanor Roosevelt. In 1937 the freshman class at North Carolina Agricultural and Technical University (A&T) voted Bethune the nation's "most outstanding Negro," placing her above Booker T. Washington and Jesse Owens. Within North Carolina, no African American gained greater public influence than the Sedalia-based educator and reformer Charlotte Hawkins Brown.[20]

Within North Carolina, as racial assaults began to slacken and memories of earlier political violence began to fade, African Americans took some cautious strides back into public life, frequently with women at the forefront. While political intimidation remained high in the state's rural, heavily black eastern region, North Carolina's inland cities, where the small size of black populations posed little challenge to white authority, offered some relief. In 1920, when state registrars opened their voter rolls to women, hundreds of black women appeared at offices across the state, part of a well-organized campaign to put a foot in the voting booth door.[21]

During the 1930s, black college students in Greensboro gave public voice to this more assertive spirit by directly targeting racial stereotypes through a boycott of the city's movie theaters. Greensboro theater owners had joined counterparts throughout North and South Carolina in resolving not to show movies in which whites and African Americans appeared on an "equal social basis." Students organized to protest both the decision and the racial order it sought to perpetuate. The boycott, along with the theater picketing that accompanied it, drew as many as a thousand students from all-female Bennett College and from coeducational North Carolina A&T. Early in the twentieth century African American college students had sought to combat racial stereotypes largely by example, by striving to live up to the most exacting standards of middle-class manhood and womanhood. By the middle of the century they were ready to take more direct action.[22]

Students also turned their energies to black colleges themselves. During the 1920s students at black colleges across the country began to challenge some of their schools' more authoritarian practices, protesting conditions that ranged from substandard cafeteria food to the continuing promotion of industrial education to the widespread practice of entertaining white visitors with programs of spirituals. Young women played major roles in these rebellions, frequently targeting the nineteenth-century regulations that still governed female conduct. Along with pressing for greater freedom in academic and extracurricular activities, they targeted school dress codes, underscoring the role that dress and physicality had come to play in conceptions of women's independence.[23]

The symbolic significance that female dress acquired showed clearly in 1925 when rebellious Fisk University students laid out their position in a letter to the *Chicago Defender*. "The girl part of the student body might have been able to get along with the orders forbidding them to talk with the boys on campus or in college buildings," the letter ran. "They might even have been peaceful, but not satisfied, with the order which forbade them dancing with boys, but when they are to keep on wearing cotton stockings and gingham dresses, it was too much." Ella Baker, who became one of Shaw's most militant student activists, recalled that one of her first protests involved speaking on behalf of fellow students who were chafing at the school's ban on silk stockings. "I didn't have any silk stockings," she recalled, "but I felt it was their right to wear their stockings if they wanted to."[24]

Student efforts contributed to a significant burst of energy at many black schools, giving extracurricular offerings a new significance. A new array of African American administrators, who had taken over guidance of most schools, cast this shift in the sweeping tones of democracy and self-rule, arguing that activities such as student government, drama, and athletics gave students particularly useful opportunities to develop the discipline and self-reliance required of independent citizens. When Barber-Scotia College president Leland Cozart assessed the extracurricular programs that Barber-Scotia inaugurated in the early 1930s, for example, he stressed the ways that such activities helped students "exercise leadership qualities on their own" and inspired them to engage in "the pursuit of excellence as a contract with themselves." Cozart viewed athletics, which he thought fostered teamwork, "victory-centered" thought, and self-discipline as a key aspect of these endeavors, for women as well as men. Not only did students leap at the chance to compete, Cozart explained, but among his fellow educators an "obligation was also felt to provide an athletic program for women students, not only in colleges exclusively for women, but in co-educational institutions as well."[25]

Descriptions in the *Barber-Scotia Index* painted a vivid picture of the energy and emotion that black college women poured into their play, showing that within the confines of school grounds, students and teachers felt able to let down some of the ladylike guard that school officials had once monitored so closely. When Mary McLeod Bethune attended the school in the late 1880s, a headlong rush down the dormitory stairs brought her both a demerit and a lecture on the importance of creating a good image for her race. In 1933 the *Barber-Scotia Index* offered a far more tolerant account of student conduct in its report of a student-teacher basketball contest. "With the leap of wild animals, they dash for the ball," Ila J. Blue wrote. "Across the floor it flies, the players darting and dodging, perspiration dripping, frantically fighting for victory. . . . 'Holding and blocking!' yells the referee at Miss Cotton, who has made a fast get-away from the Freshmen and shot a long floating pass to Miss Sykes." The description went on for a breathless column and then ended on an equally dramatic moment. With the student team leading by two points, the teachers made one final effort: "Freshmen cover, and toss an awkward pass to the Seniors. Silence intercepts and tries for shot. Like a bullet the ball bursts through the air * * it's going * * it's going * * smooth as oil, right in the basket! The crowd cheers, horns toot, and the whistle blows!"[26]

Barber-Scotia women still saw themselves as community role models and racial representatives, taking great pride in their ladylike demeanor, and most accounts of women's basketball in the *Barber-Scotia Index* offered more restrained descriptions of "perfect passes," "good training," "fine sportsmanship," and "thrilling games." Still, the coverage betrayed few concerns about the effects that rough-and-tumble exuberance could have on either players' morals or their physical well-being. Two months after the basketball contest, for example, a narrowly avoided injury during a college baseball game became cause not for alarm but for a teasing jibe. "By the way, whoever it was that tried to disable Miss Cotton at the baseball game the other day picked the wrong arm," *Index* columnist "Skippy" observed. "She puts tests on the board with her right arm, not the left. Tish, tish. Skippy thought you girls could aim well."[27]

The new teams that sprang up at schools around the state received enthusiastic support from their fellow students as well as from surrounding communities. In 1930, after the Livingstone College women's team cut a 10-2 swath through its competition, the editors of the school annual rewarded the players' efforts by featuring them at the front of the sports section, ahead of the college's less conspicuously accomplished male teams. "The most successful athletic team on the campus for the past two years has been the girls' basketball team," the description unequivocally announced. During its late-1930s heyday as the best in the state, Shaw University's team could draw as many as 500 to 600 spectators to a game, at a school with an enrollment of only 400 students. In 1934 when Bennett College took the court against the Philadelphia Tribunes, a semiprofessional basketball team starring nationally renowned tennis player Ora Washington, more than 1,000 spectators made their way to Greensboro's sports arena to see the contest.[28]

At many schools the dramatic action of women's basketball carried an emotional weight that made clear the extent to which North Carolina's black educators had cast competitive sports as a suitable guide for the determination and mutual effort they sought to teach their female students. "A single instance will best describe the drive and unity of a team pursuing a laudable goal," Leland Cozart wrote of the larger symbolism he saw in Barber-Scotia basketball, investing his description of a victory over rival Bennett College with a force that marked the lasting impact of the event.

> The teams were matched in the Johnson C. Smith Gym on February 19, 1938. A workers conference held at Smith at that time had adjourned an evening session to witness this memorable game. The score was tied several times in rapid succession. . . . Three seconds of playing time were left when the captain of the team, Miss Ornetta Biggers from Belmont, North Carolina, got the ball. Standing at dead center of the court she spun the ball which, like a homing pigeon, found the waiting basket. The tie was broken. The game was over. Barber-Scotia had won. Arthritic oldsters threw their hats into the air. Pandemonium broke loose, and the very foundation beneath the floor shook with the threat of collapse.

Cozart then paused to commemorate the years of effort that led to the victory, the first that Barber-Scotia ever logged over powerhouse Bennett. "Miss LaVerne Boyer had built a great club," he continued. "And all her patience and experience in coaching came to focus in an historical event on this memorable night which Scotiaites of that period will not soon forget."[29]

Buoyed by building community and institutional support, a thriving network of women's competition took shape in North Carolina. Although the exuberant prosperity that accompanied the rise of high school basketball came to a crashing end with the onset of the Great Depression, women's basketball barely broke its stride. As entertainment such as cars and movies moved beyond many residents' economic reach, school sports became a major focus of community life. Teams initially run by students gave way to coached and focused squads that prepared with intensity for play in newly formed athletic leagues and in the many private tournaments that began to spring up around the state. The *Winston-Salem Journal-Sentinel* Northwest Basketball Tournament, which would eventually host almost 200 teams a year, inaugurated its female division in 1932, and many other competitions followed suit. Some big-city tournaments, such as the Charlotte competition sponsored by the *Charlotte News*, included only boys' contests, and the white NCHSAA, the state's dominant high school organization, refused to supervise girls' play. But the African American North Carolina Athletic Conference frequently sponsored a women's state championship along with the men's competition, and most small-town tournaments, both black and white, included brackets for both sexes.[30]

In many communities, organized women's sports began at an early age. "I started out in the fourth grade," recalled Betty Langley Carter, who grew up in a textile village in Lincoln County. "In grade school. And I was so small, they had to make me a uniform. They didn't have one that would fit me." In middle school, fellow Lincoln County resident Ramona Ballard Hinkle noted, players had to contend with the highly improvised transportation that was all their school could afford. "Our coach, in the eighth grade, he would take all of us in his car," she explained. "And we'd have to ride in the trunk of the car, so there'd be room for everybody. They'd hold the trunk up." But these and other inconveniences seemed a small price to pay for the game they loved so much. "It was our whole lives," Hinkle recalled. "I can remember when I was in grade school, we walked two miles to school, and we got there early enough to play ball. And when the older ones came, we had to quit. So you got there early enough so you could play a little while before the older ones came."[31]

As top women's teams became emblems of pride for entire communities, frequently eclipsing the efforts of less spectacularly successful male squads, young women reveled in the privileges such stardom brought them. When Betty Carter and Ramona Hinkle made the squad at top-flight Lincolnton High, they found that their basketball skills got them out of chores at home and gave them special status among both peers and teachers. One teacher collected chewing gum as fines from students who talked in class and then passed the gum on to the basketball team. When the Lincolnton team was invited to a statewide competition, local merchants eagerly raised money for their trip. The team's most prominent supporter was the Lincolnton mayor, who insisted on giving the squad a personal send-off for every road game.[32]

Coverage of women's basketball, which frequently attained the rhetorical excess that marked accounts of men's athletics, added to visions of a confident, vigorous, and flamboyant womanhood. "The swift and accurate Hickory Hi 'Tornadoes' blew with a biting cold that sent the Lincolnton 'Wolves' away from the door, the visiting girls walloping the local six after the Wolves had taken an early lead," declared the *Hickory Daily Record* in the spring of 1928. "Coming back after the intermission, the visitors uncorked a flashy brand of passwork and the whole machine swept into action, racing down the asphalt court to fill the basket with eight additional chalkers, and effective guardwork of the visitors prevented the 'Wolves' from obtaining but five points during the quarter." After a lengthy description of the action, reporter Charlie Pegram ended by recognizing several individual players, following sportswriting custom by using only their last names. "Hamrick, flying the 'Tornado' colors, held scoring honors with 10 points, followed closely by Ramsey, of the local delegation, who gathered eight units. Bright lights of this feature for Hickory were the passwork of D'Anna and Whitener, Hamrick's eye for the basket, and Shell's ability of effectively guarding."[33]

That same year the *Wilmington Morning Star* employed even more heightened rhetoric, likening the young women who competed for Wilmington High School to ancient warriors. "Leonidas' stand in grim Thermopolae pass called for no more courage than was exhibited by the Wilmington girls," one article ran, "and while their rally fell short of a tie by one lone field goal they had proved to a crowded gallery that fear is not theirs." The *Baltimore Afro-American*, which frequently covered North Carolina black women's sports, invoked a different war in describing a trip taken by "the brilliant and versatile girl basketeers of Fayetteville State Teachers' College" through South Carolina, Georgia, and Alabama. "Beginning with Allen University of Columbia, S.C. . . . and ending with Talladega College, Talladega, Ala.," the reporter wrote, "the fighting femmes from Fayetteville laid a path of hardwood destruction through the South reminiscent of Sherman's march through Atlanta."[34]

As the reporters' tone suggests, the young women who clambered into car trunks or spent hours shooting at backyard goals frequently took men's sports as their guide. They had little choice in this regard. The enthusiasm for spectator sports that marked the 1920s had elevated a few individual female athletes to national status. Tennis player Helen Wills had created a national sensation in the 1920s, and Ora Washington, who succeeded Wills as national women's champion, built a reputation solid enough to have the *Greensboro Daily News* describe her as an "indomitable, internationally famed and stellar performer" when she visited the city in 1934. From the 1920s through the 1950s the multi-talented Babe Didrikson Zaharias garnered her share of public notice with achievements in track, basketball, baseball, and almost every other sport imaginable. But women's team sports, including women's basketball, remained local affairs, giving young female athletes few national heroines to emulate.[35]

Connections to men's sports were also heightened by the way teams were coached. Although the varsity programs beginning to develop at African American colleges would eventually produce a number of skilled black female coaches, the focus on physical education at many women's schools meant that most female teachers had limited experience with competitive ball. As a result, most women's teams were coached by men, and the few women who ventured into the profession generally patterned themselves after male colleagues. "I learned all my coaching skills that I have from men, from being in the field," recalled Cramerton High coach Lib Rotan. "You know, you'd go and watch [the men's coach], what did he do in practice, like a pick, or a screen, or a give-and-go. You weren't taught that in college."[36]

In many cases male teachers took up coaching women with some reluctance, simply because their schools "had no one else to do the job." But most quickly came to love the sport, developing the same intensity they applied to men's teams. Lincolnton coach Jack Kiser had been a three-sport star in college, and he set high standards for his female players, with significant penalties for those who failed to meet the mark. "Our practice was the last period of the day, which was physical education if you played ball," recalled Betty Carter. "And he made you shoot so many foul shots. Ring so many of them before you could leave. And we had to run and get up on the line and get our shot to catch our bus home. Or we got left—we didn't have a way to go home. We had to catch our bus. We got to where we could hit them, just like this, so we could get out the door and catch our bus." In Catawba County, Bill Bost quickly overcame his concerns about young women's stamina and began a demanding regime. "I would take those girls and I would run them just like I did the boys," he recalled. "Same type practice, same length of time. . . . And we won most of our games because we just out-hustled them."[37]

When women described their play, they often referred to men, frequently making unmistakable claims to a level of equality. "While our sterner brothers are concentrating over the pigskin on these bright October afternoons, tackling the dummy and learning to run in a broken field," the *Barber-Scotia Index* proclaimed in 1934, "we find ourselves working just as hard, or perhaps harder, with a spherical member of the same pigskin family." Lavinia Kell, who played for Pineville High School in the 1930s, delighted in the way her basketball skills placed her on a par with an athletic brother, in terms of both school prestige and public notice. "I made the first team in the eighth grade," she explained. "And my brother Billy and I were in the same class at school, and he loved basketball. And we would get off the school bus in the afternoon and couldn't wait to get home to see the [Charlotte] *Observer*, to see which one had scored the most points [in] the night-before ball game. . . . It would come out in the *Observer* the next morning, the high scorer. Of the girls and the boys from Pineville High School. We'd run to see which one beat the other one. He was very good, and I thought I was good, too. . . . He was fast, and he was small. He was always the high scorer. And if I could just beat him I was in my glory."[38]

Young women at African American institutions, accustomed to striving for intellectual equality with their male peers, often took comparisons with men a step further, challenging the restrictions embodied in conventional "girls' rules." By the mid-1930s, women's rules allowed for greater movement than in Senda Berenson's original version, dividing the court into two instead of three sections and stationing three offensive and three defensive players in each half. But the implications about female abilities were clear. Charlotte's Alma Blake, whose talents had been nurtured by an athletic father, recalled the way she and her teammates at Baltimore's Morgan College rebelled against the idea that women should play a less taxing version of the game. "Three of us would just stand there waiting for the ball to cross the line," she explained. "We said we weren't going to play if we had to play like that. Then they changed the rules to boys' rules." During much of the 1930s most of North Carolina's black college teams used men's rules, and the pride that women took in their ability to play the more strenuous game showed clearly in a *Barber-Scotia Index* report on an intramural tournament. "In keeping with the custom in this section," the author carefully pointed out, "boys rules were used exclusively."[39]

Players who competed under women's rules found their own sources of satisfaction, frequently laying less stress on the limitations the rules imposed than on the added skill required to play within such boundaries. "When I was in high school, the women's games were just as exciting as the men's games," recalled Mary Alyce Clemmons, who played for West Charlotte High School in the late 1940s under the coaching of Alma Blake. "We had what you call a limited dribble. Which meant you tried to get as far as you could and cover as much territory as you could without that continuous dribble. So you really had to be agile out there, to put it that way, because of the contortion you had to go through to get the ball around the defender." Lincolnton player Nancy Boulware echoed Clemmons's assessment. "You could dribble, at first at least, only one time," she explained. "So you had to really cover a lot of court with that one dribble. And you had to know who you were going to pass it to, or where each other player was. Because there was no such thing as running towards the goal and shooting a goal—you couldn't do that."[40]

When young women described the lessons they drew from their play, they also focused on the same sporting virtues that had become so closely associated

All-Star team coached by West Charlotte High School coach Alma Blake (with ball). Mary Alyce Clemmons is number 7. Courtesy of the Robinson-Spangler Carolina Room, Public Library of Charlotte and Mecklenburg County.

with men's sports, emphasizing the solidarity of team play, the pleasure of movement, the excitement of competition, and the thrills of public achievement. "I liked the physical attributes of it," Mary Alyce Clemmons recalled. "I liked the mental part—you had to think. You couldn't just get out there and move without thinking. You had to know plays. You had to develop certain senses. Extra peripheral vision. And you had to know your teammates and what their moves were. You had to know that Roberta's going to be there. Even though I don't see her now, she will be there. And the anticipation. And I like to win. I liked the winning. The winning was the best part."[41]

North Carolina women's basketball reached a peak in the decade after World War II. The war itself had curtailed the sport, an effect that contrasted with the expanding opportunities the departure of male soldiers created for women in most other fields. Although High Point College followed the lead of wartime industry, gaining national publicity when coach Virgil Yow bolstered his depleted men's squad by recruiting top-notch Stanly County player Nancy Isenhour, shortages of gas and tires cut into play around the state. After the war, however, women's basketball returned with a vengeance. By 1950 high school women could aspire toward two new tournaments: the Twin States Tournament, which brought thirty-two of the best black women's teams from North and South Carolina to West Charlotte High School, and the Girls' Invitational State Basketball Tournament, based in Southern Pines, which billed itself as the first state championship for white women's high school teams. Changes in standard women's rules, including the introduction of a roving player, led to a huge jump in scoring, increasing the game's popularity and prompting Allen Stafford, principal of Pender County's Long-Creek-Grady High School to comment, "In double-headers, as most schools now play, the girls' game will draw the crowd."[42]

Even as postwar high school players set new standards for scoring and attendance, North Carolina women's basketball was taken to even greater heights by the women who competed for the state's textile mill teams. North Carolina textile mills had sponsored women's teams for decades—testament to the high levels of female textile employment—and they had been quite successful. Between the inauguration of the Southern Textile League basketball tournament in 1921 and its wartime suspension in 1943, North Carolina women carried off seventeen division titles (the state's men could only manage six). But women's textile ball took on new prominence in the postwar years, spurred in large part by Winston-Salem-based Hanes Hosiery, which in 1945 launched a high-level recruiting program that attracted female stars from across the South. Hanes became one of several high-powered white southern women's teams that dominated national amateur competition in the postwar years, belying any notions that most white southern women were especially delicate or retiring.[43]

As with most company teams, the Hanes Hosiery Girls were sponsored largely to foster employee enthusiasm, keeping workers tied to the company by more than just their jobs. Hanes president James Weeks built a 2,000-seat gymnasium for the plant's teams, and the facility regularly filled with cheering employees. "It gave everybody in the company something to talk about and look forward to," Hanes player Eckie Jordan explained. "Back then, that was the thing to do—to go watch the Hanes Hosiery boys and girls play." But while employees cheered for both men and women, it was the women's team that brought Hanes national renown. While industrial men's basketball had begun to lose ground to the rising popularity of men's college ball, women's industrial squads remained among the nation's best. Hanes officials took full advantage of the public relations opportunities the women's reputation offered, scheduling an extensive series of league matches, exhibition games, and community workshops that effectively showcased the active, energetic womanhood linked to the company's most famous product.[44]

The Hanes women were destined for stardom from the start. When Weeks decided to start a women's team in the mid-1940s, he hired Virgil Yow, the coach who had recruited Nancy Isenhour for the High Point College team, and backed a high-level training and recruiting effort that made Winston-Salem a magnet for regional talent. Eckie Jordan grew up "teething a basketball" in Pelzer, South Carolina, and after she finished high school, she headed for Winston-Salem, determined to win a place on the Hanes squad despite her 5'2" stature. "Coach thought I was too short to play," she explained decades later, "but I proved him wrong." High school tournaments also became recruiting grounds. In 1951 Mildred Bauguess was still basking in the glory of a stellar performance at the *Winston-Salem Journal-Sentinel* tournament when the Claremont High principal walked into one of her classes and handed her a telegram inviting her to the Hanes spring tryouts. Yow spent two years wooing 6'2" Eunies Futch after she caught his eye in an exhibition match Hanes played against her independent team in Jacksonville, Florida. Futch waited until she finished high school but then took Hanes up on its offer. "I graduated Wednesday night, January 15, 1947," she recalled. "I caught a Greyhound bus Friday night."[45]

Young women made the trek away from home and family in part because they loved their game so much. "Eckie and I would have gone to the moon to play in a basketball game," Futch explained. Although players were required to work regular mill jobs and got no extra pay for their athletic efforts, they poured enormous energy into the team. During their season, which ran from Thanksgiving through March, players got off work at 5:00 P.M., headed over to practice, and sometimes did not come off the court until 9:00 P.M., both worn out and exhilarated. Before the season started, Mildred Bauguess recalled, they would scrimmage the Hanes men's team once a week "and get just as rough as they did." The concentrated effort allowed players to develop a skill and cohesion that had not been possible in high school and that stood them in good stead against most of their opponents, producing a 102-game winning streak in the late 1940s and early 1950s. Intensive practice also brought out the players' competitive drive. "The hardest games we had were in practice," Jordan explained. "We would just about kill each other. Because nobody wanted to lose."[46]

As the 1940s drew to a close, Hanes Hosiery's efforts paid off handsomely. In the absence of widespread women's college competition, the winner of the national tournament held by the Amateur Athletic Union (AAU) was widely considered to be the best team in the nation (as with many such "national"

Hanes Hosiery takes on Chatham Mills at the national Amateur Athletic Union tournament. Eckie Jordan is shooting. Courtesy of Eckie Jordan.

contests, however, before the mid-1950s only white players were permitted to compete). The Hanes team received its first invitation to the AAU tournament in 1948 and reached the quarter-finals. Hanes beat out the Blanketeers from Chatham Mills, based in Elkin, North Carolina, to take third place in 1949. Two years later, the squad finally captured the national crown, defeating the Wayland Baptist College Flying Queens 50-34. Hanes players repeated their feat in both 1952 and 1953, firmly establishing themselves as the best team in the country. Winston-Salem officials and citizens eagerly embraced the distinction that Hanes's successes brought the city. The *Winston-Salem Journal-Sentinel* gave extensive coverage to the team's play, and when the Hanes women won their third straight national title in 1953, the *Journal-Sentinel* headline proudly claimed, "Hanes Team Turns Twin City into 'New Women's Cage Capital.' "[47]

The many North Carolina women who ventured onto courts throughout the state claimed new ground for their sex, offering dramatic demonstrations of the physical confidence, self-assertion, and competitive spirit that had been so

closely linked to men's sports. The sight of Barber-Scotia players fighting sweat-
ily for victory or of Hanes team members sweeping down the court embodied
this new version of womanhood in succinct, compelling style. The cheering
crowds that filled gymnasiums at Shaw, in Winston-Salem, and at hundreds of
high schools throughout the state made clear that such expanded horizons had
widespread support, particularly when such efforts brought communities regional and national renown.

Still, despite the great popularity women's basketball achieved, it did not
mark a wholesale transformation in popular conceptions about female nature
or about the place of women in society. As in the past, the new ideas and images
that allowed women to expand their range of action did not wholly obscure
older visions of appropriate female conduct. Rather, young women occupied a
space where a variety of possible identities competed for their loyalty. As players
left the playgrounds and backyard games of childhood and entered the more
public realm of high school, college, and industrial competition, they become
prominent representatives of womanhood, of race, and of individual communities. Most found they were expected not simply to win but also to live up to
numerous conventions of ladylike behavior. Like many of their peers, basketball
players responded by fashioning collages of womanhood, mingling the exuberant energy of their new activities and the daring sexuality found in commercial
culture with older concepts of deference and restraint. Their shifting combinations of assertive action, deference to authority, physical attractiveness, and
careful self-control only emphasized the cultural complexities of the world in
which they lived.

The AAU tournament, at which Hanes Hosiery achieved such great success,
offered a particularly striking example of such juxtapositions. The tournament, which had begun in 1926, showcased skill, strength, and determination as
players scrambled for balls, frequently fouled out, and periodically sustained
significant injuries. But the events around the competition also promoted a
very different vision of women. During the weeklong tournament, one evening
was devoted to a player beauty contest, in which participants were judged on
the same basis as contestants in Atlantic City. Photographs of the victorious
queens highlighted the incongruities apparent in judging women by two such
different standards, as young women in basketball uniforms, complete with the
knee pads designed to protect them during falls, sported the diamond tiaras,
long velvet cloaks, and victory bouquets that invoked the more sedate, ceremonial privileges of royalty.[48]

The competing expectations of the beauty contest and the tournament itself
were abundantly clear to players and coaches, and they generally considered the
contest, as 1944 winner Maxine Williams put it, "just a little something extra for

the sponsors." "We were always more interested in the free throw championship, you know, that's part of the game," Eckie Jordan explained. "Our coach, he
discouraged any of us from participating." Margaret Gleaves's coach felt the
same way. "We didn't have any beauties, but anyway, he always discouraged us,
saying, you know, 'You're basketball players,'" she explained. But players were
far from immune to the images of made-up glamour that imbued popular
culture. Photographs from the era show that high school players adopted many
of the new female styles, displaying the same carefully coiffed hair, deep red
lips, and feminine poses favored by movie actresses and advertising designers.
While some AAU players challenged such ideals, showing up at the tournament
in jeans and boots, many did not. "The girls I played with were really feminine," Margaret Gleaves recalled, "primping, curling their hair, the lipstick and
everything."[49]

Many teams, in fact, were careful to cultivate feminine images, even as they
encouraged intensive play. Chatham Manufacturing player Catherine Whitener
Salmons, who grew up outside Winston-Salem, recalled that when she was
young, her athletic interests were connected to a broader effort to become part
of her older brother's male world. "He got some knicker pants and that's what I
wanted. I wanted those pants," she recalled. "I shot marbles and I beat him and
his gang and I was just a regular tomboy. I wanted to be a boy so bad. . . . My
hair was curly and I finally found a man that was a mulatto that my daddy went
to to have his hair cut and he took me and he didn't cut my hair like a boy but he
would cut it off and the first time I did that I thought my mother was just going
to die." Salmons was able to overcome her mother's objections and pursue her
boyish ways. But when she joined the team at Chatham Mills, she faced a far
stricter set of guidelines. Although players competed fiercely on the court,
when they appeared in public after the games, they followed a dress code that
mandated dresses, heels, hats, and gloves, presenting an unimpeachable vision
of conventional femininity. Many high school teams had similar rules for their
female players' dress. "We were called the Ramlettes," Gladys Worthy recalled.
"We had the Rams and the Ramlettes. And we'd always have to wear bows in our
hair. You'd have to wear a white bow in your hair, and white shoes, and make
everything just nice."[50]

As well as responding to a growing popular emphasis on female physical charm, basketball players accommodated deep-seated cultural assumptions
about appropriate female behavior, ideas tied up with the concepts of modesty,
deference, and self-control that had been a cornerstone of southern womanhood. Such expectations showed particularly clearly in the experience of players
from two-time state champion Lincolnton High School. The Lincolnton squad
plied the court in short, satiny shorts, but they kept their shirts tucked in. "Your

The Highland High School Ramlettes. Gladys Worthy is number 36. Courtesy of Ervin Worthy.

shirt tail was always in your pants," Betty Carter explained. They dribbled, shot, and guarded with zeal, but they deferred to the men who coached and refereed their play. "You never questioned anything a referee said," Billie Martin recalled. "Never talked back to coach," Nancy Boulware echoed. And while they at times gossiped privately about opponents, in public they worked to maintain the gracious charm that had become a hallmark of southern womanhood. "You were not ugly to your opponents, never said a word to them," Billie Martin noted. When the team was invited to the state championship tournament in Southern Pines, chaperone Hazel Smith cautioned them that their appearance was as important as their play. "When we went to the state tournament, I can remember Mrs. Smith saying, 'Now girls, remember, you've got a reputation to keep up when you go down the street,'" Ramona Hinkle recalled. "And they'd tell us, 'Everybody says that Lincolnton team is the best-behaved team down here.'" Billie Martin summed up the expectations the team faced in language echoed by women who played around the state. "You had to be a lady," she recalled. "You really did have to be a lady."[51]

In discussing the requirements of ladyhood, players were careful to distance themselves from images of women too concerned with their appearance to undertake strenuous activity. "Being a lady does not mean being prissy," Bennett College player Almira Henry explained. Her words were echoed by Hanes

Hosiery player Mildred Bauguess, who noted, "You can't be prissy and play much ball." But throughout North Carolina, expectations and admonitions kept players firmly rooted in womanly conventions, even as their efforts on the court at times defied strictures of femininity. "We were ladies," Bennett player Ruth Glover Mullen explained. "We just played basketball like boys."[52]

The collagelike methods with which North Carolina women formed identities and institutions reflected the increasingly fragmented nature of the culture in which they lived, where local tradition and experience combined with broader social change and with the growing influence of commercial culture to bring disparate influences to bear on individual lives. Visions of women as paragons of modesty and self-control had deep roots in North Carolina culture, drawing on nineteenth-century domesticity, on religious traditions, and on political rhetoric that ranged from calls for white supremacy to justification for the female activism of the Progressive Era. Respect for female strength and assertiveness responded to the realities of daily life in many North Carolina communities, where economic and other demands drew women beyond Victorian bounds. New standards for female beauty were driven in large part by expanding fashion and cosmetics industries, which devoted large sums of money to advertising their products and which exercised considerable influence over the images that filled popular media.[53]

Women's basketball illuminated these disparities with particular clarity. As basketball players responded to varying influences, they fashioned lives in which their ideas of womanhood reflected less a single, coherent concept about female nature than a set of shifting responses to an array of frequently unconnected expectations. In the 1920s, for example, basketball developed links both to acceptance of female strength and to new standards of female dress—the short skirts and bobbed hair that became such potent symbols of female physical freedom. But the two concepts did not have to go hand in hand, as illustrated by Nell Fincher, the young Derita star who played with enough energy to land her in a coma. Although Fincher had taken to basketball with zeal, unlike many of her peers she had not bobbed her hair, a contrast that her father pointed out when he joked with a reporter: "Nell has long hair and that's probably what saved her life. It's a pity more young girls nowadays don't have long hair—that is, if there's any danger of them slamming their heads against the floor."[54]

For the young women who reveled in basketball competition, the concept of multiple identities was, in fact, familiar, part of a long-standing rift between domestic ideals and the reality of many women's lives. Working women, both black and white, had long negotiated the disparate roles of wage earner, wife, and mother as well as the diverging realms of weekday work and weekend leisure, in which a woman could hold down a dirty, demanding job during the day and present herself as more sensuously feminine at night. For the black college women who competed with such zeal, for example, basketball became part of broader maneuvers among diverging roles, in which students and faculty members combined demanding academic classes and preparation for community leadership with fashion shows, tea parties, and instruction in housekeeping, dressmaking, and cake decorating.[55]

These multiple identities also affected interpretations of women's sports. For many of North Carolina's young men, particularly those fortunate enough to attend college, competitive sports had developed powerful symbolic associations with mainstream male ambitions, embodying ideals of prowess, strength, and triumph that meshed smoothly with concepts of business or political success. For young women the fit between athletics and adult life proved far less neat. In the 1920s, 1930s, and 1940s, women moved into the workforce in greater numbers and expanded the range of jobs they occupied. But such shifts had limited effects on prevailing assumptions about women's responsibilities to home and family—responsibilities built around domestic ideals of care and nurturing rather than the public clash of competition. At the same time, women's employment remained generally confined to factory floor jobs or to supporting roles such as secretary or executive assistant, positions with which competitive sports had little symbolic resonance.

Women's work in textile mills, like that of most male workers, was more about routine than spontaneity or competitive drive. Many women would work the same production job day in and day out for decades. As the experience of Catherine Whitener Salmons showed, basketball skills did not necessarily translate into productive labor of that kind. When Chatham coach Russell Plaster recruited Salmons out of high school, she had no trouble performing on the court. Mill work was a different matter. "I was left-handed, and nobody wanted to do anything with me because I was backwards from everybody else," she recalled. "I know I started and they were going to let me fold blankets and of course I couldn't ever do what I was supposed to do." She worked briefly in the sample room, "and then I went into the cloth department [where] you had to pull it down and see all these specks and stuff in it. I didn't do that too well. And then when they decided to build the 'Y' they asked me to go down and work on the membership drive. I think they wanted to get me out of the mill so I wouldn't have all these women upset."[56]

North Carolina women, in fact, built their basketball institutions during a time when many women expanded their horizons, both in North Carolina and around the nation, but raised few direct challenges to prevailing ideas about female nature or women's social roles. After winning the battle for woman suffrage, the national women's movement developed significant divisions over how best to take advantage of the victory and lost much of its national influence. Many women, pleased with the gains that they had made, and facing stiff opposition to further efforts to press women's rights, turned to other issues. In 1937, for example, Bennett College professor Merze Tate argued to a meeting of the National Association of College Women that "in the light of rapid historical progress," colleges no longer needed "to turn out an army of feminists." In the South, activists such as Charlotte Hawkins Brown or Jesse Daniel Ames devoted much of their attention to racial issues. In textile mill communities, women focused their energies on labor organizing.[57]

In many ways women's basketball followed a similar pattern. Intense engagement in competitive sports expanded team members' own realms of action. But most players did not push beyond those gains to directly challenge fundamental concepts of female nature. The approach that the Lincolnton High School team took to the question of whether they should play during their menstrual periods—a long-term point of contention in women's sports—offers a telling example of this strategy. Rather than openly challenging chaperone Hazel Smith's effort to enforce the regulation, the team engaged in a series of covert negotiations, explained in rapid-fire dialogue by Ramona Hinkle, Billie Martin, and Betty Carter:

Ramona: [Hazel Smith] kept a diary of the girls' monthly periods. You'd get your monthly, and you'd try your best to hide it from her. If you was in cramps and everything else, you didn't want her to know it. And she'd look at you and she'd say, "You don't have anything wrong with you today?" And you'd say, "No, I'm fine."

Billie: Because you wanted to play. I never missed a game because of that.

Ramona: We would lie about our monthly, and I'd really get mine confused sometimes.

Betty: I always had mine on Friday night.

Billie: After the game.

Betty: She'd let you play after three days. So Tuesday was our next game.

Ramona: And I was so mad because Betty Snipes hadn't started yet, in the eleventh grade.

Billie: She hadn't even started having her monthly, so she didn't have to lie about it.[58]

The players' actions offered an implicit challenge to the regulation, as well as to its assumptions about female capabilities, and their success helped give them a new kind of confidence. Still, their covert strategy left the rule intact.

The limited connections between female athletes' actions and more systematic movements to transform women's social roles meant that women's basketball generally had its most lasting effect on individual levels, in the role it played within participants' lives. Perhaps most significantly, it helped build the self-assurance that would become enormously important in a rapidly changing society. When, for example, Ella Baker reflected on the creative determination that had made her such an effective community organizer, she included athletics among her list of influences. "I think maybe a couple of things were positive assets for me," she said. "One is, as I told you, I had grown up playing baseball, and my man-woman relationships were on the basis of just being a human being, not a sex object. As far as my sense of security, it had been established. And also, I guess, my ego; I had been able to compete on levels such as scholarship without attempting to. And I could stand my own in debate. And things of that nature. I wasn't delicate."[59]

Hanes player Maxine Williams focused her assessment of her play on the way that basketball had widened her horizons. Williams grew up on an isolated Tennessee farm, where she developed her love for basketball through hours of practice shooting at a rim nailed to a tree. Her skills took her to Nashville, to Atlanta, and then in 1948 to Winston-Salem, where she played on Hanes Hosiery's championship teams, married, and settled down. "It broadens your thinking, adjusting to different situations," she explained. "I think it was an education that I probably wouldn't have had otherwise. I would've probably gotten a job in a little town . . . and I'd have probably married there, stayed there, built a house on part of my folks' farm, and been there. But when you get a taste of what it's like out of that, then I think you want to achieve that for yourself, or part of it."[60]

The confidence that athletics could build took on particular meaning within the structure of midcentury North Carolina society. As elsewhere in the country, state institutions and popular media championed the lifestyles of the white urban middle class, with the privileges that accompanied skin color, disposable income, and connections to the leisured world of elite culture. Women's basketball had flourished in precisely those areas that lay at the margins of this world—in rural regions, working-class neighborhoods, and African American communities—and it could help give its participants a source of confidence and self-respect that did not depend on financial success or ladylike privilege.

For Lincolnton star Betty Carter, who grew up in a mill village during the difficult depression years, basketball colored memories of privation with the pride she took in determined improvisation. "When I was younger, I got a

Lincolnton High School's 1951 state championship team. Billie Dysart Martin is in the center, with ball. Ramona Ballard Hinkle is number 25, to Martin's right. Courtesy of Billie Dysart Martin.

basketball for Christmas, and that was my only gift," she recalled. "Which my kids and grandkids can't comprehend at this time, that you only got one. And my little grandson said, 'Well, where was your basketball goal?' And I said, 'We had two electric wires coming out from the back side of our house. They were separated about this far. And that was my goal.'" Vada Setzer Hewins's farm-work tanned her skin and roughened her hands, and her family's farming income gave her little opportunity to imitate the alluring beauties that populated magazine covers and movie screens. But on the basketball court, a different set of standards ruled. "I really liked sports, like basketball and baseball," she explained. "And the different games like you could play outside. The coach made the statement once, said, 'Them Setzer girls plays like boys.'" His pronouncement, she continued, made her feel "pretty good."[61]

In African American circles, basketball players frequently saw their athleticism as setting them above supposedly frailer white peers. While women's teams outside the South occasionally played integrated games, most southern black women had little contact with white athletes, and black players drew their own set of assumptions from those circumstances. Students at Bennett College described the lack of intercollegiate competition at nearby white colleges with some disdain, remarking of white collegians that "they were little Southern ladies, that was too rough for them." Missouri Arledge, who grew up in Durham, recalled that when her black college team arrived at the newly integrated AAU tournament, the players felt immediately confident of victory. "When we got there and we saw that all the teams were white, we just thought that for sure we're going to win," Arledge recalled. "I don't know why, but we thought we were going to win the tournament because I guess we lived a sheltered life in college. We didn't see too many—well I don't remember seeing any—white girls playing basketball. All you saw were black girls playing basketball."[62]

The privilege athletic stardom could confer, including exemption from some of the restrictive regulations that black colleges continued to impose on female students, could also carry players well beyond any notion of racial hierarchy. When Bennett College player Almaleta Moore explained how much she and her teammates enjoyed the team's travel, a luxury rarely granted to black college women, she included a telling story of the confident exhilaration the experience inspired. "We would be riding along the highway and you'd meet some white fellows thumbing," she explained, "and we'd hang our heads out the window and say: 'Jim Crow car!' "[63]

In the complex world that North Carolinians had entered, individuals forged their own identities by grappling with images, ideas, and experiences that came from many different sources—a milieu within which it was often difficult to hold one's own. Basketball offered young women the means to confront this new world largely on their own terms, experimenting with the pleasures of heated competition and public acclaim while remaining rooted in communities and in themselves. Gladys Worthy loved the thrills of tournament trips and the prestige of being featured in the press. But the center of her story remained the skills she had developed and the community that sustained her. When the Lincolnton High team journeyed to the state championship tournament, they reveled in the attention they received. But when the game was on the line, Ramona Ballard listened not to the spectators' roar but to teammate Billie Dysart, and she drew not on newspaper accounts of national idols but on her own experience of female strength.

"I remember one night I was going to take a foul shot," she recounted. "And Billie came up to me and said, 'Mona, if you miss, it's all right.' And I thought, 'What makes you think I'm going to miss?' And that was just all I needed. I had four older sisters that made me a fighter. We only won by one point. And the headlines were 'Ballard Goal Good for Win.' "[64]

## CHAPTER SIX

# A Special Type of Discipline

## Manhood and Community in African American Institutions, 1923–1957

Amid the mountains outside Charleston, West Virginia, in the mid-1940s, North Carolina College basketball coach John B. McLendon Jr. found himself facing an angry young white man and a potentially explosive situation. McLendon and his team had boarded the bus after a game with West Virginia State and discovered only one seat open. Under the protocols of segregation, white riders had filled the front of the bus, and black riders had gone to the back. The lone empty place sat right on the dividing line, next to a young white woman with a baby in her arms. After a quick conference the team concluded that center Henry Thomas needed the most rest and should sit down. Thomas asked the woman if he could sit next to her, and she said she did not mind. The bus driver, however, had a different view. "I can see him now," McLendon recounted. "He looked up in the mirror, and he saw Henry Thomas sitting beside this girl. So he came back. And on the way back, I said to the players—they were all lined up, hanging on—I said, 'Don't forget, now, I'll do the talking.'"[1]

The bus driver ordered Thomas to get up. McLendon refused. "He's inside the law," he argued. "The law says we seat from the back, they seat from the front. It's the last seat on the bus, and he can sit in it if he wants to." The woman next to Thomas repeated that it was fine with her, which in McLendon's words "burned the bus driver up." The driver went back to the front of the bus, sat for a minute, and then returned and repeated his demand that Thomas leave the seat. As McLendon and the driver stared at each other, the other passengers became restless. "Go sit down and drive the bus," McLendon recalled them saying. "Come on bus driver, we've got to get where we're going." "Get on, and let's get out of here." "Drive the bus." As the complaints mounted, the driver turned away, went back to his seat and started the engine. But when the bus got into the mountains outside of Charleston, he pulled off the road and returned to the back. "He can't sit there," he repeated. "I'm not moving this bus till he gets up." As the passengers renewed their complaints, and as the driver's face grew red with anger, McLendon made his move. "I'll tell you what," he announced. "Since this is such a big problem to you, [and] these people have to get where they're going. . . . Ladies and gentlemen, I'll tell you what we're going to do. We're going to get off this bus."[2]

For the bus driver the team's exit may have seemed a victory, a successful reassertion of the code of white supremacy. But McLendon and his players had a different view. McLendon's strategic retreat had made his point, preserved the team's dignity, and averted violence. Most important, it had been the bus driver, rather than his African American confronters, who had become lost in a public display of disruptive and irrational emotion. After disembarking, players joked with each other and tossed rocks into the woods, waiting for the next bus to come along. "They laughed about it," McLendon recalled. "They really thought we had won. Because you can see what kind of position you can put that kind of person in. That you're better than he is—if that's what the problem is. He's not making any points by doing that."[3]

Almost a half-century after the encounter, McLendon laid out the rationale that governed his actions, explaining the complicated contests he played with white authority and with his young players' sense of their own dignity. "One of the best ways to play the game is avoid confrontation," he explained. "The next is to make the adversary ridiculous. . . . It's a matter really of learning how to maintain a position of respect. And to do this you do try to avoid confrontation. Because if you're made to lose your dignity, stripped of your manhood in front of your players, you can't be in a position to tell them to be a man. About life, about anything. That's what you're trying to make of them, men who can handle life well. You might have to almost be ready to sacrifice your life to maintain that position in their respect."[4]

Along with coaches and educators around the country, John McLendon sought to use the discipline and strategy of competitive athletics to prepare young people for the challenges of adult life. For coaches such as McLendon, athletics performed that role in many ways, fostering individual expression, teaching players how to work with others, building self-confidence, and harnessing the exuberance of adolescence in the service of a focused set of goals. "The biggest kick you get out of it—most of these kids have turned out to be decent citizens," explained legendary Winston-Salem State coach Clarence "Bighouse" Gaines. But as the West Virginia incident made clear, black athletes and educators living in the Jim Crow South also faced contests that tested character in other ways and in which victory and loss were defined by a far

Like most African American coaches, John B. McLendon Jr. taught his players far more than plays and strategy. Courtesy of the North Carolina Central University Public Relations Department.

different set of rules. In black athletic programs, standard lessons about discipline, teamwork, and determination mingled with other interests, as educators sought to gird young people against the obstacles of Jim Crow, to promote racial respect, and to transform the pageantry of school athletic events into a force that helped unite diverse and potentially divided black communities behind common goals.[5]

In the decades between the dawn of segregation and the evening when the North Carolina Eagles stepped onto the West Virginia bus, North Carolina's African Americans had fashioned a broad and varied network of communities around their state. Countless black residents pursued their lives and livelihoods in rural areas where families still farmed with mules and where small, wooden churches rang with the centuries-old sounds of lined-out hymns. A smaller number inhabited comfortably middle-class neighborhoods ruled by the gospel of sober self-discipline and the call of elevated, European culture. Still others eked out their livings in the unpainted shotgun shacks that clustered in most cities' swampiest terrain, where residents labored on the lowest, most uncertain levels of the state's economy and frequently drew status and identity from an expressive culture that emphasized improvisation, self-assertion, and dramatic flair.[6]

As members of these varied communities moved between their largely segregated worlds and the more racially mixed arenas of commerce, employment, and public institutions, they met additional complexities. Jim Crow legislation might set forth absolute racial divisions, embodied in concrete designations of "Colored" and "White." But the realities of segregated southern life encompassed myriad more ambiguous encounters and exchanges, in which African Americans took the measure of an oppressive world and looked for opportunities to assert or to maneuver, to press for advantage, or to step right to the edge of the Jim Crow line. Black schools, which sat at the crossroads of these many cultural currents, became one arena where young people learned to grapple with these many challenges, fashioning the strategies and identities with which they would confront adult life.[7]

On the surface, schools offered a tangible example of Jim Crow inequalities. In many communities dilapidated, drafty buildings, secondhand textbooks, and lack of bathroom facilities served as daily, painful reminders of the racial divide. "It was never the hardship which hurt so much as the contrast between what we had and what the white children had," Durham resident Pauli Murray recalled, focusing particular attention on the difference between the bare clay yard where black schoolchildren played and the facilities at a nearby white school. "Their playground, a wonderland of iron swings, sand slides, see-saws, crossbars and a basketball court, was barred from us by a strong eight-foot-high fence topped by barbed wire," she wrote. "We could only press our noses against the wire and watch them playing on the other side." Throughout the state, white officials guarded such disparities as a cornerstone of white supremacy. In 1947, when the school sanitation officer in the small town of Tryon refused to run a sewage line to the Tryon Colored School, white antilynching activist Jesse Daniel Ames offered a pointed assessment of the symbolic import she saw behind the action. "The sanitarian holds the views of some of the 'best' citizens here," Ames wrote. "Negroes get more than they deserve. They will ask for more as they get what they ask for. Soon, they will be demanding social equality, to be invited to our homes to eat and then to marry our daughters. All this as a result of our request for sewage connection for the school."[8]

Student recollections, however, make it clear that black schools were far more than the sum of their so frequently inadequate facilities. After the Civil War, many African Americans had seized on education as the most promising means for racial advancement. In the decades that followed, public schools became a major focus of community life as parents donated cash and labor to make up for state shortcomings and flocked to school plays, recitals, graduations, and sports events. Black public high schools, which North Carolina first began to build in earnest in the early 1920s, assumed particular significance. "See, it was a community thing," explained Burrell Brown, longtime teacher and coach at Hickory's Ridgeview High School. "Ridgeview was the community's activity. Wherever you lived in Hickory, and most of the people lived close to that area, they were tied up in what went on in Ridgeview." Within school walls, well-educated teachers poured their energies into their pupils, seeking not simply to educate individuals but to uplift an entire race. "There was a real sense of achievement," recalled Arthur Griffin Jr., a graduate of Charlotte's Second Ward High School. "And a sense to get a quality education. And the teachers—they'd look at you, almost as if they were wanting to *will* a good education into your head." West Charlotte graduate Patsy Rice Camp recounted a similar experience. "By the time we got to high school, we *knew* that education was serious for a black child," she recalled. "We knew that you could not be average and be black. You had to be good at what you do."[9]

Like their counterparts around the country, African American educators found athletics an uncertain ally. Athletic programs at black schools suffered from many of the same problems that plagued those at white institutions. Teachers and principals regularly voiced complaints about recruiting, eligibility violations, athletic fund-raising, and the academic performance of star athletes. Among the supportive letters that arrived at Frank Porter Graham's office following the announcement of the Graham Plan was a missive from Shaw University president William Stuart Nelson. Nelson lauded Graham's efforts, described ongoing attempts to reform college athletics among members of the CIAA, and bluntly stated, "There is no question but that the health of our educational institutions is dependent in large measure upon fundamental changes in our athletic ideals and program." Disagreements over the place of sports in high schools became a regular subject at meetings of the North Carolina Negro Teachers Association, with strong opinions both in favor of and against high-level competition. At the 1939 annual meeting, for example, association members voted to eliminate both sectional and state high school tournaments. When the tournaments were restored in 1940, the decision came only after a discussion that "went on for hours with the most fiery arguments on both sides of the question."[10]

But in a world where young African Americans faced a particularly broad array of psychological challenges, the lessons that athletics had to offer could also take on heightened significance, as teachers sought to gird their students emotionally as well as intellectually for a Jim Crow world. As Bill Finger, who came out of segregated Nashville to star for the powerhouse Loyola of Chicago basketball team, made clear, athletics could play a powerful role in fostering self-confidence. "You need some talent: be able to shoot, play defense, be quick or something," he explained. "But more than that, it's a matter of developing pride. It's something you have to feel. It's got to be within you."[11]

Ridgeview graduate Walter Childs echoed this theme in a heartfelt tribute to Ridgeview High instructors. "Not only were the teachers and coaches expected

The West Charlotte Lions, 1946. Rudolph Torrence is at center. Courtesy of Mrs. Gloria P. Munoz-Martin and the late coach T. M. "Jack" Martin.

to educate or train, they also became surrogate parents, advisors, and builders of character and dreams which instilled in us the belief that we could not fail if we followed their guidance," Childs recalled. "They took second-hand books, sports equipment and instruments and a building that needed improvement and accomplished the impossible. They created an atmosphere where students thirsting for knowledge were united with teachers who were willing to go the second mile to insure that they not only quenched that thirst but they also made it possible for us to achieve and experience success." His description laid particular stress on the school's athletic coaches. The men and women who ran practices, plotted strategies, celebrated victories, and consoled players after losses "instilled a special type of discipline in us that was a vital part of the sports that we played."[12]

As with their counterparts in many fields, supporters of school sports programs had to scrimp and improvise. Most schools had trouble finding funds for basic needs, with little left over for luxuries such as athletics. Rudolph Torrence, who attended West Charlotte High School in the 1940s, recalled that funding for the school's basketball team ebbed and flowed, depending on the quality of the team. "We made the state championship my senior year. And we won the state basketball championship that year," he recalled. "That year we had a pretty good team, and we did a lot more traveling than we had done in previous years, because we were winning. And our principal loved to win. And when you won, he would make sacrifices so that you could go to the next level. But by the same token, if you lost, he'd say 'I ain't spending a *dime* on you.'" Even in good times, teams and coaches found themselves responsible for raising money to provide uniforms, equipment, and transportation. As Burrell Brown succinctly put it, "Everything was just about from your pocket. There was no money any kind of way, really."[13]

Black school athletics in fact became a major lesson in doing much with little, and the ability to succeed with limited means became a point of pride. At Charlotte's Second Ward High School, student editors filled their school newspaper with descriptions of economic disadvantage overcome. "Basketball prospects around Second Ward High School appear very encouraging thus far," students reported in 1934. "Although the team has many obstacles confronting them, they will do the best they can. The players proved this when they agreed to bring enough money to purchase a ball so that they might begin practice early." Two years later a call for female players emphasized the importance of determination over both wealth and appearance. "The Second Ward Girls' Basketball Team has just been organized," the article ran. "We are planning to do something no other Second Ward team has ever done—win every game that we play. We want students from all classes. We want fat ones, skinny ones, short ones, tall ones. . . . The only requirements are tennis shoes, shorts, and the will to win. If you don't have the first named two, come anyway, if you have the third, because you can wear soft leather or rubber soled shoes and any kind of a short skirt. Come on girls and help us make our wish come true."[14]

Although neither state funds nor private donations provided much support for coaches or athletic facilities, African American educators at all levels developed their own programs and their own governing organizations. By the late 1920s, teams of both boys and girls were traveling the considerable distances between the state's new high schools to defend the honor of their institutions and communities. By the 1930s a statewide organization that eventually became known as the North Carolina High School Athletic Council governed school competition and had begun sponsoring state championships. The CIAA, which regulated competition for most of the state's black colleges, saw steady expansions in funding and in public notice, particularly as its member schools emerged from the hardships of the depression and began to find more funding for athletic activities.[15]

This developing athletic system held particular significance for young black men. African American communities warmly encouraged young women's athletic endeavors—"The same crowd who came to see the guys was there to see us play," Mary Alyce Clemmons recalled—and young women reveled in the joys of physical exertion and athletic rivalry. But while female athletes often viewed their sporting endeavors as one element in a multifaceted sense of womanhood, athletics formed a cornerstone of black male identity, immersing its participants in a multigenerational male world that linked grade-school boys with college players, and high school athletes with fathers and grandfathers. In arenas set well apart from the repressions and restrictions of a Jim Crow world, young men throughout the state fashioned athletic games into powerful sites of self-discovery and individual expression.[16]

Rudolph Torrence, who grew up in the Charlotte neighborhood of Cherry in the 1930s, recalled that he was on the football field from the time that he could "walk, talk, whatever." On the playground, where pickup games were ruled by "instinct and gut," the hard-contact game of football was considered the man's sport. "On the side of town that I was reared on during that period, it was kind of sissified to play basketball, as opposed to being very masculine when you played football. It was a little more prestigious with the male community," Torrence explained. Aspiring athletes started out as "peewees," playing only minor roles: "What would happen, the larger boys would organize. They would take $x$ number of peewees to balance it off. So actually I was just a balancing act at the beginning. . . . The big guys they'd say, 'Well, I'll take this peewee, and that peewee, or whatever.' And that was the way that we did it." The peewees' contributions consisted largely of hiking the football or "piling on" the other players after tackles had been made, but they were proud to be included in the masculine endeavor. "You wanted to participate, and whatever you could contribute in whatever way, then you did," Torrence said. "Mostly, you would be the person who would center the ball—a noneventful kind of position. But it gave you an opportunity to participate in the sport."[17]

As young men grew, their developing size and strength became a source of considerable pride. Bill Finger explained that in his early teenage years, "I can remember really being misused, elbowed. I was very timid." But as he kept playing, his confidence began to build. "I got over being timid," he continued. "I was starting to get big, was able to bluff somebody. I learned how to fight back. Guys were getting a little scared. That gave me a little confidence. From then on, I think I was alright." Such physical confidence was frequently paired with the pleasures of self-expression, particularly as basketball began to gain new status. Growing up in Charlotte in the 1940s and 1950s, future West Charlotte star Paul Grier spent much of his spare time in the company of fellow basketball devotees, devising dramatic feats in the alley behind his house. "I just put up a goal," Grier explained. "Now it wasn't a goal, it was a tire rim. I started with a tennis ball. Then I found a volleyball in the creek, and pumped it up some kind of way, patched it up, and started to shoot. And then when I got a basketball—good God that was it then. We put the rim about high enough where we could dunk it, and we'd just try everything on it. And then we'd raise it a little bit from time to time." On city streets and playgrounds such play became a colorful and competitive assertion of self. "When you're playing street ball," Charlotte resident Titus Ivory noted, "it's you against the other guy, which makes it: 'Hey, I've got to do my thing, because if I don't, I'll get had. If I do, I'll have somebody else.'"[18]

In black communities around the state, athletic contests became both glue and challenge, weaving sports events, both formal and informal, into a rich verbal culture of rivalry and exchange. Walter Holtzclaw, who attended Second Ward High, explained that games with crosstown rival West Charlotte took on particular importance because of the local status they conferred. "The rest of the games didn't matter as much as West Charlotte, because of the difference in the side of town," he said. "It was like a bragging right. Or if you lose, you've got to listen to it all year long." Such bragging rights, Titus Ivory recalled, were one of the sweetest parts of victory. "It was so good to be on top," he explained, "especially when we started out in junior high school. Most of the junior high schools were in a pretty close perimeter. And in that perimeter it was like bragging rights. If you beat Irwin, you had the bragging rights for this side of town. If you beat J.T. then you had the bragging rights for the whole city, because you beat the two top teams that existed at that time. . . . We'd have parties and at the parties the guys who would be on the winning side would usually come in with their chests all hung out, you know. It was like you were on top of the world at that time, because you had beat your opponent."[19]

High school coaches tapped into these sporting networks, keeping their eyes on promising young men and encouraging them from an early age. Titus Ivory recalled the pride he felt in being noticed by legendary West Charlotte football coach Thomas "Honey" Martin when Ivory was still in grade school: "I think the first time I ever saw him was when my grandmother was in the hospital, and he came to visit my grandmother," Ivory recalled. "And he looked at me and said, 'Gee, you are getting *big*.' Said, 'I'm going to make you a football player.' And the next year I went out, and I played a lot, because he saw that I was going to be a large guy." Such ambitions were also encouraged by players themselves, who took pride in grooming their successors. "It just so happened that in Hickory we had quite a nice little gathering of athletes," Burrell Brown explained. "And, well, we worked with them. We worked with the boys who played with us, and the boys who played with us worked with the other little fellows. They taught our system to the other little fellows. The little fellows would come and tell us, 'When we're old enough, we're going to play for you.' We'd smile. But they were telling the truth."[20]

At times this athletic interest could stray from the broader goals that most black educators held. Just as some educators were more concerned with community power and prestige than with the quality of their schools, in some athletic programs the local status that came with athletic victories took precedence over long-term goals. Athletes themselves could also reject the discipline and self-restraint promoted by coaches such as Brown, Martin, or McLendon, drawing instead on the values of a developing urban street culture, within which masculinity was frequently defined through defiant physical courage and dramatic self-assertion.[21]

Mary Mebane, who grew up near Durham in the 1950s, recalled a concealed romantic attachment to a player on her school's team in a description that both hinted at this alternate form of manhood and summed up the level of community tolerance athletic skill could engender. "He was a basketball star, and to all intents and purposes that was the only thing he had to recommend him, for even in the eleventh grade he could hardly write his name, depending instead on his prowess on the courts to get him through school, for the principal, a basketball nut, was also the basketball coach," she wrote in her autobiography. "For some reason, I became infatuated with him. It could have been his grace on the court as his lean, very black body went up for a shot. And he was the best scorer on the team, even though he was not the tallest of them. Or it could have been his insouciant manner, never really seeming to care, and being supercool in his conversation. Or it could have been the sense of danger he exuded, for he came to our country school from town, having been expelled from the city schools, and talked of dangerous and sometimes illegal activities on the weekend."[22]

More often, however, coaches imposed a far more rigorous discipline, seeking to add new layers of significance to the lessons of the playground. As players moved into high school, games that had once been ruled by "instinct and gut" gave way to more systematic strategy, as coaches worked to blend the exuberant energy of playground ball into disciplined team effort. Such efforts stressed a different side of manhood; coaches tempered young athletes' outer confidence with an emphasis on inner discipline, focusing on restrained dignity, rigorous rationality, and rapid, calculating thought. Charles McCullough, who took over basketball coaching responsibilities at West Charlotte in the 1950s, became one of many coaches renowned for his discipline. "He had that kind of respect where ain't nobody going to do nothing wrong in front of him," recalled former player Willie "Scoopie" Joplin. "Because they know he ain't going to deal with that. He'll tell you, 'Son, you can't play for me.' And that's that. And when he said that—you might be the best player in the school. But he would do that, he wouldn't let you play."[23]

Coaches taught their lessons through even the smallest details of the game. Second Ward High player Kenneth Diamond Jr. recalled the way his coach's insistence on the rationality of substance over style manifested itself on the free-throw line. While Diamond and his teammates favored the overhand free throws that were coming into vogue, their coach held fast to the older method of underhand shooting, a technique that could look clumsily old-fashioned but gave most players a better angle at the basket. Players had to stick to these rules, Diamond recalled, unless they could prove the coach's calculations wrong. "They used to make us shoot the underhand free throw," he explained. "You don't see that any more—in fact, some people refer to it now as a granny shot. . . . My coach made all of us shoot that way, unless you could make nine out of ten the way you wanted to shoot. If you could make nine out of ten with your style, he would let you shoot it your way. If not, everybody had to shoot the granny shot."[24]

This kind of discipline, which laid out a set of principles but also gave players room to prove themselves, was a common coaching technique, aimed at teaching students self-reliance rather than strict obedience. "I didn't have a lot of rules," Bighouse Gaines explained. "But I respected them, they respected me." When faced with a talented but flamboyant playground athlete, John McLendon did not bar the player's signature moves but set clear limits on their use. "He was kind of a hot dog, let's put it like that," McLendon explained. "I told him, 'The first time you make a bad pass going behind your back I'm going to pull you out.' "[25]

Titus Ivory recalled the ways that Thomas Martin sought to conceal his authority and build up his players. "Coach Martin used to take us aside and he used to talk to us individually," Ivory explained. "I ended up being the captain on my senior team. Which meant that I had to share in the leadership role. But he would always take me aside and tell me to transfer information from him to the players. . . . I knew that he would do that to me sort of to build my confidence, and to make it seem as if the instructions were coming from a fellow player, instead of coming from him." Ridgeview coach Burrell Brown built player involvement into a system that he described in a contribution to a national coaches' magazine. "You can't induce the average American boy to do your bidding willingly without showing him your need for cooperation," he wrote. "That is why, during the playing season, we have many squad meetings and encourage participation in strategy planning and schedule discussions. Even though player suggestions might not be used, there is created a feeling of being an integral part of an interesting project, rather than that of being a pawn selected to follow a master's inflexible instructions."[26]

An interest in flexibility and self-reliance also extended beyond the playing field. In 1938 George W. Cox, an energetic and many-talented director at North Carolina's most conspicuously successful black-owned business enterprise, the North Carolina Mutual Insurance Company, addressed a banquet celebrating Hillside High School's state football championship. In his remarks Cox laid particular stress on flexibility, lauding, in the words of a *Carolina Times* reporter, "the mind of the Negro boy as being versatile, that is being able to change from one thing to another with the greatest of ease." Burrell Brown also hinted at this broader view when he talked about the discipline Ridgeview coaches sought to instill. "You've got to learn discipline," he said. "You've got to learn to think quickly. You learn to know when to get out of the way of trouble. There's just so many ways you can give it to them, and that's the way we taught it."[27]

As McLendon's encounter on the West Virginia bus made clear, thinking quickly and avoiding trouble were particularly important skills for young black men. Black athletes and spectators could appreciate strategic thought both for its sheer mental pleasure and for the larger role it played in their everyday existence, where tasks ranging from securing a bank loan to walking unmolested down the street were often accomplished only through planning, foresight, and diplomacy. *Carolina Times* editor Louis Austin caught the spirit of this outlook in a 1938 editorial, when he described every African American's "necessity of being alert and using his mentality to carry him through many difficult situations that would destroy the average human." At the same time, the discipline of self-restraint related to the realities of a world where even slight breaches of racial etiquette could spark a violent response. Athletic discipline thus became part of a broader cultural array of warnings and strategies that ranged from the tales of tricksters who devised inventive schemes to avert direct confrontations, to the fast-paced exchange of insults in the verbal dozens, which encouraged participants to develop both verbal eloquence and cool self-control.[28]

Athletics also touched on a final facet of the mental discipline that was crucial to black educators' efforts: the ability to maintain self-assurance in the face of mental as well as physical challenge. George Cox's address to the Hillside High School banquet praised not only mental versatility but also emotional resilience. "In the game of sport is found the best example of how one conducts himself, so much that he can be or may be the supporting character in his community," Cox asserted, going on to quote Rudyard Kipling's "If," whose series of conditional clauses had become an icon of U.S. sporting culture: "If you can lose and start again at your beginnings and never breathe a word about

Ridgeview High School state championship football team, 1962. Courtesy of Samuel W. Davis.

your loss. . . . If you can meet with triumphs and disasters and treat those two impostors just the same." The writer who reported on the evening summed up the racial spin that Cox gave to the verse as he overturned conventional inter-pretations of Kipling's popular poetry as the highest expression of a specifically white manhood and invoked visions of sport as a proving ground for African American ability. "His point was don't be afraid of resistance that the color of the skin makes no difference. In connection with this he spoke of Joe Louis and Jesse Owens, Negro athletes of today."[29]

Viewed from this perspective, Kipling's "If" in fact seemed especially suitable advice for young black men, who confronted a world in which they were frequently portrayed through demeaning stereotypes, where whites regularly projected their own fears and anxieties onto African Americans, and where every facet of public life, from the Bibles used in courtrooms to the bathrooms in railroad stations, embodied the assumption that some groups of human beings were more deserving than others:

If you can keep your head when all about you
    Are losing theirs and blaming it on you,
If you can trust yourself when all men doubt you,
    But make allowance for their doubting too;
If you can wait and not be tired by waiting,
    Or being lied about, don't deal in lies,
Or being hated don't give way to hating,
    And yet don't look too good, nor talk too wise. . . .[30]

Such lines spoke to a number of the conditions with which young African Americans contended as they moved from their own communities into a wider world. Specifically, the verse advocated distancing oneself from irrational emotions and ideas and cleaving to an inner, rigorously rational core. As such, it was as much a discipline of thought as action. John McLendon waxed eloquent on the importance of such self-awareness and its application both on the court and in the world. "What it meant: you have to maintain yourself, all you are capable of, at all times," he explained. "You can't lower yourself to be a marginal playing team, dirty tactics. If you are in the right, well, you're going to prevail. Even though the system appears to be against you, it's really not you being any less, it's because somebody's worried about you already being much more than they want you to be. You play the game of life the way you play this situation." Herman Cunningham, a graduate of Monroe's Winchester Avenue High School, offered a similar assessment when he recalled his coach's strategy for dealing with the small size of one year's football team. "The coach, you see, he taught us discipline," Cunningham explained. "He said, 'Weight don't mean anything. Use your head.' "[31]

Their prestigious community positions, their connections to the outside world, and their close work with their players made athletic coaches, like many of their teaching colleagues, into powerful role models for young men, particularly in communities where high rates of mortality and difficult economic circumstances often played havoc with family dynamics. "Most of the kids that I grew up with were single parent kids," Rudolph Torrence explained as he talked about his high school coach's influence in his life. In his case the combination of his mother's early death and his father's work as a plasterer, which kept him on the road, had profound effects on family relationships. Although the elder Torrence always provided for his children, he remained a distant figure in their lives. As coach Thomas Martin spurred Torrence on to greater efforts and offered a wide range of advice about both sports and life, "he was filling the slack for the father role, for me and for most of the other guys."[32]

The deep-seated poverty that beset most black communities further expanded coaches' responsibilities, which frequently extended to providing necessities as basic as clothes and food. "We had a training schedule that we wanted followed," Burrell Brown explained. "Which included—even though your parents can't get you steak—we used to go and get pills that were supposed to have all this in it. Now it may not have, I don't know, but some of those kids didn't have a meal. And we'd say: 'All right, take some of these pills.' . . . Some of these kids just didn't have a meal." Bighouse Gaines recalled one strategy he used to give some of his more impoverished players extra food without threatening their sense of dignity. "You make it convenient to have him come home, help you pick up two leaves out of the driveway or something, and meanwhile say, 'Clara's got a ham in here. . . .' "[33]

Even as high school coaches worked to keep their players fed and to prepare them for life after graduation, they also sought to expand their opportunities by helping them win college scholarships. In many ways black athletes with the talent to gain scholarships played for higher stakes than their white counter-parts. White athletes who indulged their athletic inclinations at the expense of study or career preparation could turn to manufacturing work, public utility employment, or sales jobs that offered relatively secure livings—often trading on local acclaim or on their potential contributions to company athletic teams to win coveted positions. African Americans faced far more restricted possibili-ties and far greater competition for those jobs that were available to them. As a result, as Burrell Brown put it, "In that day and time, if you went to college your chances for getting the better jobs, whatever were open, it was better for you."[34]

Coaches worked hard to interest their players in college. As well as coaching, Thomas Martin refereed high school and college games, and he frequently brought players along to his assignments. "He'd always take one or two guys with him, to give you that exposure," Torrence recalled. "If he was going to call a college game on Saturday, then we rode with him. And we got that experience and exposure of watching a college game, plus being in that college environ-ment. And it just gave us something to look forward to." High school athletes did not always see such an array of opportunities and perils, focusing more on the immediate pleasures of their sport and on the acclaim it won in their communities, as well as among young women. "The boys wanted to go to college just to play some more ball, and if possible maybe get a job, maybe get a wife, whatever. But the big thing they wanted to do was see themselves in the picture where they played ball," Brown explained. Still, their coaches stayed focused on the larger view. "Even though I talked around to them that way— 'yeah, you might get you a wife'—I wasn't thinking about a wife," Brown continued. "I want you to have a future."[35]

In pursuing their ends, coaches also worked closely with the communities around them. At Ridgeview, for example, coaches Burrell Brown, J. C. Johnson, and Samuel Davis tapped into the male networks that fostered athletic interest, as well as into the cherished tradition of bragging rights. Ridgeview teams were inspired "to perform to the maximum," Walter Childs recalled, through tech-niques that included "comparing one team to last year's team, bringing back former members to practice and assist the team, and always having the practice open for parents, usually fathers, to watch. All of these things as well as the 'bragging rights' system used by former players to motivate the team to match or beat their record created the need for the team to be the best."[36]

In close-knit communities such as Hickory, discipline was both highly per-sonal and woven into community consciousness. Like many black coaches around the state, Ridgeview coaches laid down curfews, which they personally enforced. "Back in those days, we worked on the floor, and when we were off the floor, we were all in the same area," Brown explained. "So we might happen in on them. So they had to be kind of looking out." The coaches were aided in their job by watchful community members, particularly when the stakes were high. If an athlete failed to come home on time, or if someone in the community spotted a star out on the town the night before a big game, the phone would often ring for Brown, Johnson, or Davis, who would then head out to locate the offenders and send them home. In the relatively compact black community of Hickory, they usually had little trouble. "You know, kids didn't have cars like they have now," Brown explained. "So they'd be somewhere in the area. Might be having a little party or something, hanging out. In the area. You'd find them. If we could beat the person to them that was going to tell them so they could run."[37]

Athletes had such trouble dodging curfews in large part because athletic prowess had become a major source of pride in communities around the state, focusing the energies and interests of a wide spectrum of individuals. The spectators that crammed into Second Ward High School's gymnasium, James Ross recalled, represented the full spectrum of Charlotte's African American society, from school principal A. G. Grigsby, with his meticulous conduct and attire, to the less-than-respectable young men who sat in a back corner and "had cheers that cheerleaders couldn't do." At Second Ward, as at schools around the state, this multifaceted participation could help turn games into pageants of both community cohesion and racial pride, as coaches, players, cheerleaders, and members of the audience all contributed to the event.[38]

Cheerleaders established the initial tone, sending the undulating rhythms of their cheers throughout the crowd and setting spectators swaying to sounds that echoed the latest rhythm and blues hits. Rhythm and improvisation were the hallmarks of top-level cheerleading, Ross recalled, and the audience expected a good show. "These were not just rah, rah, rah," he explained. "You would have to take whatever the latest song was, or the latest dance was, and then come up with some cheers that incorporated your school's name and some other things and put all that stuff together. . . . And you couldn't do the same things every year. I mean, nobody wanted to hear that stuff you did last year. And so you had to come up with new cheers."[39]

As game time drew closer, the crowd became more active. As soon as the visiting team stepped onto the floor, the young men who sat in what Ross termed the "hoodlum corner" began to indulge in the long-standing community tradition of elaborate verbal taunts. Their barbs became particularly sharp when visitors hailed from country or small-town schools and could be mocked

Second Ward High School team, 1949. Courtesy of the Robinson-Spangler Carolina Room, Public Library of Charlotte and Mecklenburg County.

for their hair, their shoes, or any other departure from the latest heights of urban style. "The minute the other team came in, then you started to get on them," Ross recalled. "It was brutal what they would do to people from the other teams." The ongoing din intensified as the crowd joined in the game, responding to successful plays, seeking to throw opposing teams off balance, and at times almost obliterating distinctions between players and spectators. "When they were shooting, you would stomp on the bleachers," Ross continued. "The gym was so small. . . . I'm guessing you could get four hundred people in there. And if the fire marshall came, he probably would put everyone in jail. But you had those wooden bleachers that folded back for P.E. And so when you started stomping, I mean the noise in there would just be deafening."[40]

As the crowd moved to the rhythms of the games, the teams on the floor—women as well as men—put on a multifaceted show of systems, plays, and strategies. West Charlotte's Alma Blake schooled her female players in the arts of deception. "We'd do everything to confuse our opponents," she explained. "Don't ever let them know. If you look this way, pass that way. Sometimes, you know. If you look one place, pass it over yonder. You just had to know how to confuse your opponent." For the Ridgeview Panthers, even the gymnasium floor became part of the game. "We had a young man—his name was Marshall Sudderth—who played for us," Burrell Brown explained. "He drew a panther in each corner of the gym. And that panther had a lot of meaning to us. Certain spots on that panther, I'd tell the boys when we were practicing 'Here's where you'd better shoot.' So they could get an eye for the basket. We had kids then who could shoot the three-pointers that you shoot today." The panthers drove opposing coaches wild. "There was one guy, he used to tell his boys: 'Don't let them get in that corner. Don't let them get there.' "[41]

By the late 1940s, men's basketball began to generate particular excitement, drawing on a new energy developing around the sport. Starting in the late 1930s a series of alterations in rules and approach had begun to work wonders on James Naismith's game, transforming it from a character-building exercise into a major spectator event. Officially the changes included reducing the basketball's circumference, eliminating its heavy laces, transforming the way fouls were assessed, and eliminating the center jump once held after every basket. On the court players transformed the new rules into fancier ballhandling and far faster play, shifts that in the words of one advocate, turned "a dull, slow and unexciting game" into "a game of speed, skill and rhythm; a sport that is also an art; a game that is now filled with emotion." Black players quickly embraced the new approach, transforming deep-seated community aesthetics of drama and improvisation into elaborate dribbling patterns, sudden dashes to the basket, and infinite variations on a maneuver becoming known as the slam dunk. On courts around the country the new mix of discipline, enthusiasm, and aesthetic flair showed to spectacular advantage.[42]

This new version of the game first took hold in the basketball stronghold of the Midwest and in big cities such as Chicago and New York. But it soon arrived in North Carolina, spreading through the state's black colleges and the net of connections created by the Great Migration. Every summer North Carolina was inundated by youthful visitors from other states, among them a young Wilt Chamberlain, whose mother hailed from Halifax County and who spent several summers playing pickup games on North Carolina dirt. Northern students enrolled at southern colleges had given the South's African Americans their first taste of basketball, and when North Carolina's institutions began to offer athletic scholarships, the state became a frequent destination for northern or midwestern athletes who found that colleges in their home states showed interest in only the most spectacularly talented African Americans. Newspaper accounts of North Carolina college games soon filled with the exploits of stars who hailed from "the Metropolitan area" or "the city of Brotherly love" or who sported nicknames such as "The Kansas Kangaroo."[43]

North Carolinians responded eagerly to the new style, and dozens of young men began to spend their afternoons devising colorful moves and dunking tennis balls through bicycle tire rims. Basketball also sparked eager enthusiasm from black sportswriters, who recounted contests and discussed various strategic "systems" with great gusto. "A thousand thrills—the thrills that come only once in a lifetime, were felt. . . . Saturday at A. and T. College gym as the sphorical shaped ball bounced against the waxed hardwood all day, there was an exchange of leather for leather, and magnificently trained young men battled each other on the courts and in the ring," wrote *Carolina Times* reporter J. Archie Hargraves of a high school tournament held in Greensboro, an event in which spectators "packed the gym from doors to windows and the lattice overhead." Later, in describing one of the games, Hargraves emphasized the systematic play that proved the key to victory. "The Aggies were unable to get started as guard after guard and forward after forward faltered in the adjustment required to meet the Panther system of play."[44]

Soon high school and college fans had the opportunity to see a wide range of approaches challenge one another on the court, offering a multifaceted vision of African American styles and abilities. In 1950, for example, one CIAA match became an offensive battle that contrasted the differing styles of the North Carolina College Eagles and the Mountaineers of West Virginia State. "Never perturbed, maddingly calm, the Mountaineers engineered basket after basket with the precision of men who knew what they were about," a *Carolina Times* columnist wrote, contrasting their "ring-around-the-free-throw-circle" style with that of the Eagles, who "had put a complete emphasis on speed," racing and shooting with the "drivingest, fightingest play ever seen in drafty Uline Arena." After the Eagles' narrow triumph, Ronald Foreman continued, "spectators took their limpness back to hotel rooms and neat apartments with a feeling that furious competition had reached its zenith and controlled, defensive play had fallen to the nadir of its fortunes."[45]

Basketball fans could also revel in a strategy that centered on not scoring—on skillfully "freezing" the ball to protect a lead in those pre-shot-clock days. When overused, the technique was deadly dull to all but the most committed strategists. Employed at the right moment, however, it could prove as dramatic as any scoring drive. When the *Carolina Times* asked renowned Morris Brown coach H. B. Thompson to name his most memorable game, he pointed to the low-scoring triumph of his Purple Wolverines at the 1949 Southern Intercollegiate Athletic Conference tournament. Morris Brown, the article recounted, led by a single point with a minute and forty seconds left and opted not to shoot. "The Atlantans 'froze' the ball the entire minute and forty seconds!! 4,500 howling fans created pandemonium in their excitement as the struggling and valiant Tigers of Tuskegee fought but failed in their last desperate efforts. Morris Brown won their first crown 55-54 in true championship style."[46]

The new style of play worked wonders on spectators, frequently building

The North Carolina College Eagles, playing an exciting, fast-break style, helped spark interest in basketball among the state's African Americans. Hickory native and Ridgeview graduate Ernie Warlick is in the air, with ball. Courtesy of Ernie Warlick.

support to a fever pitch. In 1950 competitive fervor at North Carolina College games ran so high that John McLendon issued a written admonition to his fans. "For the emotional Basketball fan whose feelings of loyalty and rivalry and elation and depression are so pronounced during the game I prescribe H. R. Peterson's Tenets," McLendon wrote in the *Carolina Times*. He went on to list a few examples: "Basketball is a game—not a battle or a fight. Basketball is played for the fun and enjoyment it produces—not to provoke bitterness and sorrow.

A Basketball game is not a matter of life and death. Basketball is a game from which there must emerge a victor and a loser. In general, only a few points separate the two. The victors deserve congratulations; the losers respect. Victory should develop a spirit of tempered elation mixed with tolerance."[47]

Despite McLendon's words, however, tempered elation was generally in short supply. When Ridgeview High played rival Newton, spectators filled the small gymnasium to overflowing, and those who could not find seats or standing room waited eagerly outside. "Some of them had to be outside the door," Burrell Brown recalled. "Couldn't get them all in. They'd stand around wanting to know—someone would tell them what's going on. It was something." When Second Ward and West Charlotte met in the Second Ward gymnasium in Charlotte's Brooklyn neighborhood, similar enthusiasm filled the space. "Brooklyn was just like a town in itself," explained Second Ward player James Truesdell. "Everybody would show. The barbers, or whoever. People would close their business to come see us play." Fellow Second Ward player Walter Holtzclaw echoed Truesdell's words. "It was standing room only," Holtzclaw noted. "We had to have policemen here to keep people back off the court. So you were really playing around this black line here. It was just like that. They packed as many as they could in. And it was just a high that you can't explain. You really have to be there."[48]

When a wide spectrum of community members demonstrated a collective interest in the fortunes of school teams, the ties such actions created could play particularly significant roles within black communities. As elsewhere in North Carolina, a growing emphasis on formal schooling, with its corresponding promotion of middle-class ambitions and ideals, created its own tensions, as educators' efforts to "uplift" their fellow African Americans at times grated against local values, identities, and forms of expression. Officials at black colleges had looked to sports to build race pride and solidarity in part over the frustrations they developed when they realized that many African Americans showed little inclination to follow their cultural lead, turning instead to activities that took different forms and served different ends. Even as black teachers sought to inspire their students with Shakespeare, symphonies, and related forms of "elevated" culture, other African Americans congregated in juke joints, at evangelical church services, or in other alternate spaces, voicing dreams, joys, and sorrows through sounds and gestures influenced more by folk tradition or by the latest styles of an expanding commercial culture than by educators' cultural aspirations.[49]

The capacity of school sports to bring together sometimes-conflicting interests thus had particular meanings within African American communities. Sports events brought the drama and collective spirit of vernacular black culture into educational institutions, incorporating local style into a structure that emphasized the disciplined organization that middle-class educators prized so highly. Such cultural amalgamations, along with similar balances struck in pursuits such as school bands or dramatic productions, could help acknowledge and strengthen racial ties even as the artistic power they so frequently displayed sparked pride in what many considered a distinctive and dynamic black cultural style. For black intellectuals who spent much of the first part of the twentieth century publicly wrestling with their cultural past, an institution that combined a creativity rooted in vernacular culture with education-linked activities offered a solution to a troubling dilemma, making it possible to claim allegiance both to middle class ideals that cut across racial boundaries and to a specifically black heritage. At the same time athletic contests gave community cultural endeavors a place within the symbolically potent sphere of educational pursuits. If ongoing attempts to build black institutions depended on creating spaces where black citizens could both agree and argue, where they could work to at once fashion and critique understandings of their racial heritage and their existing circumstances, school athletics became one such arena.[50]

Charlotte's Queen City Classic, the fall football game that matched West Charlotte and Second Ward, served as a clear example. A large portion of the city's black community turned out for the game, with wealthier citizens driving newly polished automobiles to the city's Memorial Stadium and others walking up the streets, dressed in their Sunday best, for an event that would dramatize both rivalry and connection. The heated rivalry between the schools made for a volatile atmosphere. "There would be fights—there were always fights," James Ross recalled. "All kinds of things were settled at the Classic." Yet when young Arthur Griffin looked around him, he also saw a kind of unity. "You could just walk up Seventh Street . . . all the way up to the Park Center," he explained. "And right behind Park Center was Memorial Stadium[, and it] was this huge event for little kids to even think about looking at something as great as the Queen City Classic. Your two black high schools, West Charlotte versus Second Ward. It would fill up Memorial Stadium. And so for us growing up, that was the event. All these black people just filling up a big, huge arena was just—it was just unheard of."[51]

In white communities the cross-class associations that sports could create at times proved problematic, connecting working-class athletes to a set of social structures and assumptions that did not always operate according to their best interests. In black communities, conversely, such connections had the potential to contribute to a push for changes in North Carolina's racial order. The role that school athletics could play in building community bonds, as well as the uses to which such connections could be put, was suggested in one of the ways that supporters of Greensboro's Dudley High School reacted to the Supreme Court's landmark *Brown* decision. Dudley was considered one of North Carolina's top academic high schools, with a strong student body and a highly trained corps of teachers. But when black Greensboro organizations began to use the threat of *Brown* as leverage for improvements at African American schools, a vocal and united front of Dudley parents and administrators focused their initial efforts on demands for a new school gymnasium.[52]

On an individual level the mix of discipline, community support, and intergenerational connections that athletics fostered could make the experience particularly powerful, encouraging precisely the kind of confidence and deep-seated self-awareness that young African Americans needed to make their way in a challenging and often hostile world. Herman Cunningham attempted to explain this often ineffable sensation while describing his experience playing football for Winchester High. "The guy who lived right behind me, he played . . . and one up the street there, he played," he said. "It was a number of them played, and were good athletes at that time, and motivated us. It was a carryover all the way, step by step. From down in the lower echelon grades up. The guys that were coming up the channels of the school when we were playing, they were inspired to come in after we got out. And it just passed it on, just cycled all the way down." He concluded with an assessment of the broader meaning of such connections, which suggested the significance that sports could hold in that kind of community context. "By doing this, it made a good motivation for them to enjoy themselves playing, because they had the whole person into the game. Not just there for publicity or something like that. It was for real."[53]

By the late 1940s, even as black high school athletics helped build up communities and individuals, sports were beginning to take on broader ramifications in North Carolina colleges. Nowhere did these efforts show more clearly than in CIAA basketball, where a new group of talented coaches and players was taking the game to new heights of skill and recognition, reaching toward regional and national renown. The CIAA climb began in 1939, when Durham's North Carolina College hired John McLendon as its basketball coach. McLendon, a Kansas native, had responded to the new style of basketball by abandoning slow-paced, complexly patterned half-court strategies in favor of a hard-driving, attacking style that dominated the entire court—an approach that would eventually become known as the fast break. McLendon could trace his athletic heritage back to James Naismith himself—Naismith had been his advisor at the University of Kansas—and he drew much of his inspiration from Naismith's own interest in athletic spontaneity. In explaining the origins of his approach, McLendon once described an afternoon when he and Naismith happened on a group of Kansas players. "He asked them for the ball. 'Whenever on the court you had it, that's there where your offense begins. And whenever the other team has the ball that's where your defense begins,' he said. I took that to mean that you played basketball on the entire court. Your offense started off the boards or whenever you got possession, that's when your offense begins. You don't come down the court, stop, and decide 'O.K., now I'm going to run and play this and that.' The same on defense, if you get the ball anywhere on the court, you don't retreat, you attack."[54]

McLendon absorbed the lesson and took it a step further. Naismith had not believed in coaching, preferring a free-flowing form of play. McLendon developed conditioning drills, complex plays, and a wide-ranging strategic philosophy. "Contrary to its reputation," he later wrote, "the fast break is not an 'aimless,' 'helter-skelter,' 'run and shoot,' 'fire horse' game except in the appearance of its rapid, often demoralizing, action. It is a planned attack with multiple applications; it is a designed offense which can be utilized in one or more of its several phases each time a team gains possession of the ball." In McLendon's estimation the style also influenced its practitioners in ways that raised versatility to an art. While fast-break basketball was "a winner at the turnstiles," he wrote, "more importantly, it is a game of increased challenge to the young contestant. . . . The challenge lies in the player's learning to make the most of the many choices confronting him. The high-speed game requires quick sound reactions, lightning-quick decisions, and corresponding physical and mechanical adjustments to meet the ever-changing situations."[55]

The fast break carried the North Carolina Eagles on unprecedented scoring sprees. In February 1943 Rudolph "Rocky" Robinson scored fifty-eight points against Shaw University to break a single-game scoring record held by Hank Luisetti, the Stanford legend whose passing skills and one-handed jump shots had helped spark the new basketball style back in the 1930s. A year later, in another game with Shaw, the Eagles racked up sixty-seven points during the second half, another national record. The team began to draw enormous crowds. In the fall of 1952 North Carolina College proudly unveiled a 4,300-seat gymnasium with a million-dollar price tag. Barely two months later college officials announced that the press of spectators wanting to see the school's games was so great that they would begin radio broadcasts for the fans unable to secure seats. The accomplishments of the Eagles also set other teams scrambling to keep up. "I know we got to the finals in a tournament with McLendon's team—'49 I guess it was," recalled Bighouse Gaines, who would go on to win 828 games with Winston-Salem State and join McLendon in the Basketball Hall of Fame. "Shaw had a new gym. We thought we'd done a heck of a job coaching and got beat 119 to 65. . . . We looked at each other and said 'Let's go get some basketball players.' "[56]

CIAA coaches were not, however, content with local fame. Rather, they avidly sought ways to showcase their talented squads before a wider public. At the close of World War II a group of coaches and administrators revived a prewar plan for an end-of-season basketball tournament, as "a grand way of celebrating the play of the season by bringing the best teams together." Such an event, supporters argued, would serve many purposes, making possible "a time for fellowship with those from other member institutions, a great social occasion, a time for some Presidents to show off their best athletes and coaches . . . a time for some students and alumni to brag over their team, a time to crown the best tournament team, a time for the big pro scouts to see most top athletes together, a time to make the necessary money to operate the association and finally the time for the news media to extol the merits of the occasion and let the fans in other parts of the country know what the Association has achieved."[57]

In 1946, with a $500 budget, the inaugural contest opened in the Turner Arena in Washington, D.C. It did not disappoint. A week of stellar play was capped by a championship game that went into triple overtime as the underdog North Carolina Eagles battled the powerful Virginia Union Panthers. The game saw fourteen lead changes and was tied ten times as the small but speedy Eagles contested the methodical Panther play. In the second overtime the Panthers led by four points with less than a minute left. But the Eagles rallied to a tie, and the third overtime was all theirs. "In the final five minutes of overtime play, the 'whiz kids' romped and cavorted just like it was the first half of the tournament game," reported Norfolk Journal and Guide sports editor Lem Graves Jr., who called the game his "all time sports 'thrill-of-a-lifetime,' " despite the loss by his home state team. "Passing with lightning precision, and cutting into the basket in magnificent form, they dropped in four baskets in succession and then put on an 'ice' show to run the time out." The Eagles triumphed 64-56. North Carolina assistant coach Leroy Walker, who would go on to worldwide renown as a coach of track and field and an ambassador of sports, later explained, "I remember thinking that a better script . . . couldn't have been written by Hollywood."[58]

As it grew into a major event, the CIAA tournament became a celebration not simply of the players on the field but also of the thousands of students and graduates in attendance. During the tournament's stint in Durham, from 1953 to 1959, the Carolina Times gave lavish coverage not only to the games but to the many social events scheduled around them, highlighting the achievements of the many distinguished African Americans in attendance. "Dozens of parties were given by Durhamites at all hours of the tournament," the paper noted in 1955, and it gave particular emphasis to the array of entertainment hosted by the Carolina Guardsmen, one of the state's most exclusive social clubs. "Socialites attended the first Guardsmen's social weekend . . . by the hundreds from key cities throughout the East," the *Times* explained, describing events that included a "fashionable supper," an invitation-only formal dance, a "Bal d'Etoile," and a "brunch and cocktail party" covered by "accredited society editors," at which "organ music will be played and orchid corsages would be presented ladies."[59]

The pride black college graduates felt in their successes showed even more strongly during the games, when thousands of cheering spectators, dressed to the hilt, packed the stands. Legendary player and coach Al Attles, a 1960 graduate of North Carolina A&T, recalled the impact of his first CIAA tournament by describing the exhilarating effects of "the unbelievable spirit," the "fashions exhibited," and the "outstanding parade of great players." He also laid special stress on the racial accomplishment the tournament represented: "The most important aspect, I feel, was the pride of this small segment of the educational world showing what Black people can do with their own energies and determination." The mix of pride and excitement, as well as the opportunity to meet up with old friends and acquaintances, made the CIAA one of the most beloved events in North Carolina, with thousands of devoted fans returning every year. In 1970, more than two decades after the inaugural event, one such fan expressed this loyalty in no uncertain terms, declaring, "I would rather chew nails without teeth, testify against the Mafia, and vote for Lester Maddox than miss a C.I.A.A. basketball tournament."[60]

The growing prominence of the CIAA tournament became part of a broad-based postwar shift in African Americans' visions of their place in U.S. society—a shift that had also influenced the growing interest in high school play. The years that followed World War II brought a new energy to black communities around the country as African Americans took advantage of expanding national prosperity and a shifting racial climate to launch new efforts for recognition and equality. CIAA president George Singleton made such determination clear at the association's annual meeting in 1945, the year the league approved the tournament plans. After listing the CIAA athletes who had been killed in military service, he urged his audience to carry such efforts forward. "These young men and thousands of others have died in this gigantic struggle to bring about conditions of lasting peace," he told the gathered members. "They have died that all men everywhere might have the right to walk the world with dignity, to worship and speak with freedom, to enjoy freedom from want and fear, to enjoy equality of opportunity for gainful employment and preparation therefor, and to a decent and respectable standard of living. They have died in order that the philosophy of the master race shall forever be eliminated from the thinking and actions of the people of the earth."[61]

Singleton continued his address with a forceful reassertion of the belief that athletic talent could be used to further African American efforts to implement at home the principles of democracy they had fought for abroad. "The important part which athletics can play in breaking down the barriers of discrimination has already been demonstrated conclusively," he argued. "Negro heroes of the nation's gridirons, courts and tracks have undoubtedly served as ambassadors of inter-racial good will in the past. You must prepare them for an even greater future role in this regard. In every phase of American life, economic, social, political, religious, and educational, we must see to it that the principles for which these young men have died shall be translated into practical application here at home. We must see to it that they shall not have died in vain. That is our responsibility to them."[62]

Singleton's forceful celebrations of athletic strife joined an array of postwar pronouncements that brought talk of competition to new heights within black educational rhetoric. Despite a long-standing interest in the potential of sports to shape individual character and promote racial understanding, throughout the first half of the twentieth century many black educators remained skeptical about the broader value of school athletics. Athletic disagreements broke into view in the 1920s and 1930s, as student rebellions ushered in a far more vibrant college social scene, and as administrators such as Shaw's William Stuart Nelson became part of the nationwide debate over the relationship between athletic programs and academic missions. While alumni and administrators at majority white schools frequently turned questions of "intellectual" versus "practical" training into debates of the merits and shortcomings of industrial capitalism, at African American institutions such discussions also involved the role athletics could play in furthering racial interests. As with the athletic debates among North Carolina high school teachers, there were "fiery arguments" on both sides.

Supporters of college athletic programs frequently argued that sports drew black institutions closer to mainstream society as well as developing impressive representatives of their race. Others, however, had turned a jaundiced eye toward such opinions, taking up Joseph Price's turn-of-the-century assertion that both individual and racial interests were best advanced through intellectual pursuits. W. E. B. Du Bois became a particularly strong critic of black college athletics. In one of his many statements on the subject, he gave his faith in intellectual attainment and his critique of capitalism a potent racial spin as he denounced the black college student who "has swallowed hook, line and sinker, the dead bait of the white undergraduate, who, born in an industrial machine, does not have to think, and does not think." Such a student, he continued, "deliberately surrenders to selfish and even silly ideals, swarming into semi-professional athletics and Greek letter societies, and affecting to despise scholarship and the hard grind of study and research."[63]

In places like North Carolina the competitive rhetoric that was so tightly tied to athletic endeavors also held an uncertain position in many circles of African American society. While African Americans throughout North Carolina enjoyed the clash and drama of competitive sports and had rejoiced in the triumphs of black athletes such as Jesse Owens and Joe Louis, within many communities faith in competition was far from a driving force. The meager resources available to African Americans could encourage a strife-oriented view of life, particularly in urban areas. Burrell Brown, who grew up in Baltimore, credited "the school of hard knocks" with sparking his competitive drive. "I was a very poor person, and I came up in a hard time," he recalled. "Back in the days of the Depression. It's just something that became a part of me early. If you want to succeed, you have to beat the other guy to it." In other corners of black society, however, economic hardship had fostered a deep commitment to mutual endeavor, which frequently combined with a Du Bois-style disdain for a social system that promoted the welfare of some citizens at the expense of others. North Carolina educators, faced with both limited resources and a treacherous political climate, spent the first decades of the century stressing cooperation. Many teachers used their classrooms to pursue group-centered endeavors that resonated with community traditions and avoided any direct challenge of the racial status quo, while also offering a subtle critique of a society that had clearly not been organized with the good of all in mind.[64]

After World War II, however, the rhetoric of competition began to assume new prominence at black institutions. When Morgan State University's Martin Jenkins addressed the 1950 meeting of the North Carolina Negro Teachers Association, for example, he began his talk with an optimistic description of growing opportunities in colleges, the armed forces, and athletics. "In light of this trend we must now, everywhere, educate Negro children for full participation in American life," he told his audience. "This means that the children in your school, your children, must come out prepared to compete on equal terms with all other citizens; to ask no quarter; and to exercise fully their rights and responsibilities as American citizens." A few years later *North Carolina Teachers Record* editor W. L. Greene continued to press competitive themes, invoking the "greater freedom of the individual to participate in the opportunities offered by a dynamic society" and criticizing older modes of education in which " 'cooperation' was often stressed as a way to success." Educators, he wrote, "must meet the challenge of adapting our operations to the growing needs of society and we must also train youth to enter into society without fear and with the will to meet the competition of their contemporaries in all areas of employment."[65]

The postwar period brought a corresponding growth of athletic programs, sparked both by increases in school funding and by the new attitudes of players and coaches. This new restlessness appeared in details as small as team uniforms, as many high school coaches began to challenge the tradition of playing in uniforms passed down from white schools. When Burrell Brown arrived at Ridgeview High in 1947, shortly after finishing a stint of military service, he immediately joined with fellow coach J. C. Johnson to improve the school's teams, starting with their uniforms. "We were in bad shape for uniforms," Brown recalled. "We were using castoffs from Hickory High School for football, and they had I don't know what for basketball. We came in here, the [Ridgeview] colors were orange and blue, and they were playing in blue and gold. . . . So Johnson and I got together immediately. And we started getting them uniforms. . . . We knew it was important. It'd make the young players feel better. Make them feel like somebody, if they went out there in brand new uniforms occasionally instead of somebody else's castoffs." When Brown explained his new interest in this outward mark of status, he pointed directly to the changing times. "They had had people who didn't mind," he concluded. "We were a little younger at that time, and we minded."[66]

As Ridgeview partisans sold ice cream and conducted raffles to raise money for orange uniforms, other coaches planned even bolder actions, working to schedule integrated matches and beginning to press for equal participation in national athletic organizations. While even the most daring coaches did not openly flout restrictions on integrated competition within North Carolina, they laid plans to advance the issue elsewhere. By the early 1940s, following a celebrated set of games between the Panthers of Virginia Union and the renowned Blackbirds of majority white Long Island University, black college coaches eagerly sought contests with white teams. At North Carolina College, for example, John McLendon arranged matches that included Brooklyn College, the marines of North Carolina's Camp LeJeune, and even a team representing the Duke Medical College, which made an undercover trip to the Eagles gym in 1944.[67]

At first, McLendon recalled, his main goal was to build his players' confidence both in themselves and in the methods that he was using. "Because of the exclusion of blacks in sports, if you were practicing the games that other people were playing, you really had no way to decide whether you were really playing it well," he explained. "Because [the white teams] were the ones you read about in the newspapers. You read about some of our teams once a week in the weeklies. . . . I was kind of a hard taskmaster, tried to do it tough-love style, that's what they call it these days. And get my fellows to achieve. But they weren't sure that they were coming up to the standard that I had set. . . . It's almost like, you're in another world and you don't know whether you're really doing what you're supposed to do or not. So the only way to prove that is to play them." When the Eagles emerged triumphant from their first integrated game, a 1942 match with Brooklyn College, McLendon saw immediate results. "When we played that game, and our guys won the game, they felt like, 'Well, we're really playing basketball. Coach is a real coach here. He's not just coaching a game that only we play, but he's coaching a game that they play, and all these pictures we see on Sunday—we're better than they are.' "[68]

By the 1950s black institutions around the country were actively pursuing bids for national recognition, sending applications to national athletic associations and pressing to be included in national tournaments. Such efforts met with initial resistance, particularly from the NCAA, whose rules gave black schools little chance to prove themselves worthy of inclusion in the organization's national tournament. While the NCAA rated schools according to their performance against major opponents within their own districts, CIAA teams fell into the all-southern District Three, where ongoing prohibitions against integrated sport made full intradistrict competition impossible. In 1950 John McLendon blasted this policy in an uncharacteristically emotional column that reflected both his frustration at the NCAA's recalcitrance and his confidence in his team's abilities.

"A few teams in the East will play CIAA opponents," McLendon wrote. "However, there is not a single team in District Three which has the nerve, spine, backbone, or guts to play a CIAA opponent. Not a single institution in District Three will play a CIAA opponent on any terms since every one of them is bound by the chains of negative inter-racial practice. Some which are not so steeped in this phenomenal stupidity are afraid of the loss of athletic prestige which would naturally result after CIAA prowess on the court enacted its inevitable toll." He concluded with a final statement: "The NCAA may mean NATIONAL COLLEGIATE ATHLETIC ASSOCIATION to some people, but to us it means NO COLORED ATHLETES ALLOWED."[69]

A year later, after the NCAA thwarted black coaches' opportunity to make their case by holding its 1951 annual meeting at a segregated hotel in Dallas,

Texas, McLendon and his colleagues turned their efforts to the more sympathetic National Association of Intercollegiate Athletics (NAIA). After two years of discussion, NAIA leaders voted to consider eligible black colleges for tournament berths and to allow the winner of a new black college tournament to participate in its national championship contest. In 1953 the Tigers from Tennessee A&I State University became the first black college team to take part in an integrated national tournament. In 1957, after John McLendon had taken over coaching duties at Tennessee State, the Tigers took the NAIA crown, the first integrated national title won by a historically black school. The same year North Carolina A&T became the first historically black institution to play in an NCAA tournament, taking part in the inaugural "college division" event, which would eventually become the Division II tournament. A decade later Winston-Salem State, coached by Bighouse Gaines and starring the peerless Earl "The Pearl" Monroe, would bring the first NCAA basketball title ever won by a historically black school back to North Carolina.[70]

With their direct challenges of national athletic organizations, North Carolina's black institutions began to realize decades of hopeful talk about using college athletic teams to foster racial respect. Throughout the 1950s, efforts at athletic integration within the state and in the South at large would proceed at a snail's pace. But confidence in the institutions and the athletes that black schools had developed would prove an ongoing spur to action. Such an approach showed clearly in the spring of 1952, when the NCAA informed A&T coach Cal Irvin and athletic director William "Bill" Bell that their membership application had been approved, making A&T one of the first African American schools accepted by the organization. Students and administrators rejoiced at the news, seeing the recognition as "another step in the emancipation of colored athletes." School sports columnist Richard Moore joyously summed up A&T's achievements, concluding with a prediction which suggested that the "best citizens" of Tryon, North Carolina, had indeed calculated accurately when they denied the Tryon Colored School its sewer hookup, reasoning that, in the words of Jesse Daniel Ames, "They will ask for more as they get what they ask for." "These are only a few of the advancements made over a number of years," Moore wrote. "So you see, we are grateful indeed for our own accomplishments. Realizing that the fight is not nearly over, we are more determined to continue."[71]

## CHAPTER SEVEN

# The Big Time

## College Hoops on the Rise, 1946–1965

I n the winter of 1947 a group of students from rural Claremont High School made a hundred-mile trip to see a basketball game. The ride from Catawba County to the state capital in Raleigh remained a formidable journey on North Carolina's still-developing highway system, but the excited students paid little attention to the road. Word had begun to filter through the state that the team from North Carolina State College was playing basketball almost too good to be believed, and the Claremont players wanted to see it for themselves. They were not disappointed. Almost half a century later, one squad member sat back in his living room and recalled that night in words shot through with still-fresh amazement. "I remember the first time I'd ever seen a jump shot," Bill Bost explained. "I believe it was Sammy Ranzino. He was an All-American at N.C. State. He shot a one-hand jump shot. And I was in high school, and everything at that time was a two-hand set. Everything. And I was awed—I'd never seen anything like it. And of course just as soon as we got back to the gym, everybody was attempting this one-handed shot."[1]

That group of Claremont players, trying in their cracker-box gymnasium to leap into the air and launch one-handed revelations, stood with thousands of their fellow citizens at the beginning of a new era in North Carolina sports. The speedy, athletic style that was transforming basketball around the country had taken hold in northern cities and midwestern towns and was fast becoming standard fare at several of North Carolina's African American colleges. But until a band of Indiana hotshots descended on North Carolina State, few of the state's white residents had ever seen it played. For Bill Bost and for tens of thousands of North Carolinians who followed the state's postwar teams, jammed college arenas, and crowded into airports to greet victorious squads, basketball became a window opening onto a larger world, offering possibilities of which most state residents had never dreamed.

In the 1940s and 1950s, one-handed jump shots and other stylistic innovations favored by players from the Midwest and Northeast transformed North Carolina basketball. Here UNC's Pete Brennan takes a shot. Reprinted with permission of the *News and Observer* of Raleigh, North Carolina.

As college basketball began to reach a broad national audience, a handful of locales took the lead, bringing playing technique to new heights, developing devoted followings, and claiming a place in an exalted realm known as "the big time"—an arena in which schools vied for national recognition rather than regional or local fame. North Carolina, where several schools developed top-level programs, began to reach toward such heights. As the exploits of state basketball teams garnered a national reputation, they became a cherished symbol of broader Tar Heel ambitions, of efforts to join in the economic and cultural transformations of postwar life. But even as a series of outstanding teams and individuals brought the state new status in the ever-expanding realm of national mass culture, college athletics once again became the focus of internal cultural and political disputes. In the early 1960s, when a point-shaving scandal shocked residents throughout the state, the ensuing debate revealed deep cleavages over issues that included manhood, Cold War politics, the meaning of economic prosperity, and the effects of competition on individuals and society.

North Carolina's rise to basketball fame began, ironically, with the dismal performance of teams representing North Carolina State, the state's major land-grant institution. In pre–Cold War days, State's basketball teams were known as the Red Terrors; but they had historically produced little fear of any hue, and they fared particularly badly in the 1940s. Between 1943 and 1946 State's squads dropped fifteen straight contests with Duke and Chapel Hill. Football team fortunes fell even farther—the team lost so much ground it did not even bother to play Chapel Hill for several years. Such performances produced widespread consternation among the school's alumni, who fought an uphill battle for recognition against the graduates of more prestigious institutions, and they proved particularly galling for alumnus David Clark, champion of free enterprise and open competition, who poured enormous energy into fund-raising and promotional efforts and who peppered coaches and administrators with suggestions and critiques.[2]

When college athletics resumed in earnest after World War II, State football ambitions were hampered by the difficulty involved in hiring a nationally known coach. North Carolina State remained under the jurisdiction of the state's consolidated university system, which centralized administration of State, Chapel Hill, and Women's College in Greensboro. Although Frank Porter Graham's earlier foray into intercollegiate athletic administration had not succeeded in curbing scholarship aid to athletes, university officials still sought to contain athletic programs where they could, paying particular attention to football. In 1953, when a rumor began to circulate that State was considering hiring renowned Maryland grid coach Jim Tatum, university president Gordon Gray squashed the idea in one angry phone call. But basketball, which had yet to make an impact as a major college sport, was not so closely watched. So when North Carolina State officials set their sights on a newly discharged navy commander who had a reputation as one of the best basketball coaches in the country, not a word was said. In the fall of 1946, on a one-year contract with a $5,000 salary, Everett Case began his North Carolina career.[3]

Everett Case and North Carolina State proved a fortuitous combination. Case had never coached college ball, but he had become known as the finest high school coach in basketball-crazy Indiana. North Carolina State, with little

Everett Case celebrates a victory with one of his beloved North Carolina State teams.
Courtesy of Burnie Batchelor Studio, Inc.

basketball history to speak of, offered Case the chance to build his own program beyond the shadows of the coaching legends that haunted schools such as Stanford or Purdue. Fifty years after Case's arrival, North Carolina college basketball had become so much an institution that enthusiasm for the sport seemed almost natural, prompting speculations on the nature of state water or on the color of the sky, which so suspiciously resembled Carolina Blue. But in the twentieth-century United States, natural forces rarely wielded such influence over cultural transformation. Rather, basketball became a North Carolina obsession through a combination of ambition, effort, and promotional skill, which took advantage of developments such as road construction and television broadcasting to reach out to a broad swath of the state's population. And while historians have learned to tread cautiously when attributing historical change to a single action or individual, North Carolina's current status as a college basketball powerhouse can clearly be traced to the initiative of a handful of people, starting with Everett Case.

Case became North Carolina's most prominent advocate of what was coming to be called fast-break basketball. By importing high school stars from his home state of Indiana and pitting them against the nation's top teams, Case quickly gained the statewide notice that had eluded John McLendon, North Carolina's fast-break pioneer. While McLendon's teams had been successfully employing the new game for several years, black college teams rarely received much mention outside African American communities. Everett Case had the advantage of working for a high-profile white school that drew far more attention from newspapers, radio, and eventually television—coverage that would spread word of the game to every corner of the state.[4]

Case's teams were a hit from the start. The 1946 squad began its season with more wins than State supporters had seen in years, launching an undefeated national tour in which the team vanquished powers such as Georgetown and Holy Cross, as well as chalking up the first of what would be fifteen straight victories over Chapel Hill. Sportswriters, most notably *Raleigh News and Observer* columnist Dick Herbert, stood firmly behind the cause, and by January newspaper columns rang with rhapsodies to the sport. "The free-scoring machine which has been molded at State under the cage-wise Case, a product of the basketball hotbed of the mid-West, has stamped itself as a power to be reckoned with in the Southern Conference," a typical *News and Observer* piece announced in January 1947. By then excitement was running so rampant in Raleigh that it far outstripped the capacity of the school's 3,200-seat Frank Thompson gymnasium.

The furor reached a dramatic peak on the night of February 25, when fan excitement literally swamped the game itself. The Red Terrors were scheduled for a rematch with Chapel Hill, and Raleigh's fire chief, already nervous about the potential for disaster, had declared that the crowd could not exceed the stadium's seating capacity. When the last seat was taken, an hour and a half before the game, arena employees locked the doors against the swelling crowd outside. Tardy reporters presented identification and were allowed to crawl through one of the stadium's windows. Other would-be spectators had to be more resourceful. Amid the press and clamor of hundreds of excited fans, enterprising individuals jimmied basement windows, set up a ladder to reach a second-floor opening, and eventually pulled one of the arena doors off its hinges in their zeal to get inside. State player Norm Sloan was standing at a urinal in the players' bathroom when "the window broke right above us, and here came a girl crawling through the window. She didn't slow down at all. She just came right on in, ran right by us and went upstairs to the court." By 7:30 P.M., the school newspaper reported, the gym presented a remarkable sight: "Every inch of space was occupied with students and 'visitors' standing in the aisles, hanging from rafters, railings and anything else that might lend a reasonable amount of support." When requests to clear the building came to no avail, the fire chief announced that the contest had been canceled. He had to be escorted from the building by police, but the order stood and the game was never played.[5]

The crowds who so taxed State's facilities kept growing because the school's teams delivered on their promises. In Everett Case's first year the Red Terrors won their first Southern Conference championship in almost two decades and secured their first postseason tournament berth, at the prestigious National Invitational Tournament (NIT) held at Madison Square Garden. A third-place finish in that contest whetted appetites for further glory. University officials, sensing the importance of this national exposure, instructed coaches to give up the nickname Red Terrors, and from then on, State's teams were known as the Wolfpack. After three more Southern Conference titles, State received its first NCAA bid and reached the national semifinals before losing a close game to City College of New York, which was on its way to becoming the only squad ever to win both the NIT and the NCAA championships in the same year.[6]

State's teams not only won, but they did so in style, with exciting shots and come-from-behind finishes. Everett Case had the same flair as his players; he became known for his fiery half-time exhortations, witty comments, and consuming love for his chosen sport. He became especially beloved in the city of Raleigh, a previously sleepy state capital to which Wolfpack basketball brought both national prestige and a new topic of conversation. Soon after Case arrived, the News and Observer named him Tar Heel of the Week, noting, "Since the little man came here from Indiana . . . basketball has almost supplanted politics as the favorite topic of discussion in the North Carolina capital." The accomplishments of Case-coached teams were particularly sweet for State graduates, who often felt their school slighted by the more prestigious campuses in Durham and Chapel Hill. Since the Civil War, the rural eastern counties from which North Carolina State drew many of its students had watched the balance of state power and prestige tip toward the industrializing Piedmont region. The postwar growth of State basketball hinted at a possible reversal of that process, and Wolfpack teams became an obsession in the east, reaching the point where some claimed the outcome of a Saturday night game could be read "by the expressions on the young men's faces on Sunday morning at Sunday School."[7]

For many State fans the new prominence that basketball brought to their school was symbolized not only by the dynamic teams that took the court but by the arena in which they played. The massive, 12,000-seat Reynolds Coliseum was begun in 1943 and completed three years after Everett Case arrived in Raleigh. Construction of the giant structure had halted during World War II, and when Case visited the campus in 1946, he saw only the steel girders designed to hold up the largest arena roof in the Southeast. Now-hallowed legend claims that it was this massive skeleton that convinced him to take the job, suggesting that while State's partisans had little history to draw on, they entertained far greater dreams. The coliseum had originally been designed with 9,000 seats, matching the capacity of Duke's arena. Case persuaded university

Massive Reynolds Coliseum, site of the Dixie Classic, was a major point of pride for North Carolina State supporters. Courtesy of the North Carolina Collection, University of North Carolina Library, Chapel Hill.

officials to expand it to 12,000 seats, making it by far the largest facility in the state.[8]

To North Carolinians unused to such large buildings, the structure's effect was dazzling. One State alumnus recalled coming to Reynolds as a high school student, clambering up a still-incomplete elevator shaft to sneak into the 1949 Dixie Classic Tournament, and thinking it must be the grandest arena in the world. State officials cherished that symbolism, regarding Reynolds with the kind of pride that spilled out of a 1960 press release. Titled "A Monument to Sportsmanship: A Symbol of the New South," the release explained,

> There is one spectacle that surpasses all the color and glamour that this hall of the people and palace of spectacles can produce. It is the expression on the faces of a school-bus-full of young boys and girls from a country high school

on the banks of the Yadkin or the shores of the Chowan as they walk into the north balcony of the gigantic building and gaze south cross its 12,500 silent seats to the southern balcony 400 feet away. No convention or ice review or basketball classic or college dance can match the color and the thrill of young Tar Heel eyes viewing for the first time their State College Coliseum—the largest building of its kind in Southeast America.[9]

Of the many events staged within Reynolds's grand confines, the most celebrated was the Dixie Classic basketball tournament, held the week after Christmas from 1949 to 1960. The Classic pitted North Carolina's Big Four schools—State, Chapel Hill, Duke, and Wake Forest—against four teams selected each year from around the country. The Dixie Classic soon gained a reputation as one of the nation's best holiday tournaments, and it became a gala event complete with ceremonial banquets, city tours, award ceremonies, and a great deal of other fanfare. The tournament, combined with the huge crowds that filled Reynolds for regular season games, meant North Carolina State could boast of the nation's highest on-campus basketball attendance for ten straight years, allowing Raleigh to proclaim itself "world capital of basketball."[10]

The Classic quickly became a cherished Raleigh institution. "Dig out from under the Christmas wrappers. It's time for Dixie Classics now," a society column urged its readers in 1959, and the newspaper soon filled with descriptions of the visitors who were making their way to town for the big event. As the tournament's reputation grew, schools began to clamor for invitations. The process reached a peak in 1958, when four of the eight participants boasted top-ten national rankings. As well as offering good basketball, the Classic also gave the city a chance to show off both its hospitality and its modern efficiency. The News and Observer proudly reprinted admiring comments from the dozens of national reporters who descended on the city for the event, and it used the 1958 tournament to showcase the skill of its photographers and the technology of its new typesetting machines, which could be operated over telephone lines. As that year's Classic began, the paper filled with dozens of dramatic action shots and with articles sent "Direct From Coliseum Via Teletypsetter."[11]

The Dixie Classic gained prominence so quickly in part because North Carolina participants grew stronger by the year. For the first few years of Everett Case's tenure, State dominated its local opposition, amassing a record that included five straight Southern Conference crowns and its vaunted winning streak over the rival Tar Heels. But this ascendance would not last. Alumni and administrators at other schools quickly determined that they, too, wished to excel in this newly prestigious realm and began their own nationwide searches for coaches and players. They focused particular attention on New York, where

UNC coach Frank McGuire, center, brought North Carolina a stream of New York players and a national championship. Dean Smith, McGuire's assistant coach and eventual successor, is to his right. Reprinted with permission of the *News and Observer* of Raleigh, North Carolina.

college programs had recently been rocked by a highly publicized point-shaving scandal, leading officials at schools across the city to drastically reduce their basketball support.[12]

In 1952 Chapel Hill officials announced that they had persuaded Frank McGuire, the talented coach of the St. John's team, that a bright future awaited him in the Tar Heel State. Like Everett Case, who had used his Indiana connections to bring his "Hotshot Hoosiers" to Raleigh, McGuire began channeling top-flight New Yorkers to Chapel Hill. North Carolina's white schools were still politely but firmly rebuffing any suggestions that they begin to recruit the outstanding African American athletes who were making an increasingly large mark on national college sports. But a stream of other players began to move South. Five years after McGuire arrived in Chapel Hill, a *Sports Illustrated* article playfully joked at this reversal of a more renowned migration, dubbing the route taken by three-quarters of the then-undefeated Tar Heel squad "Basketball's Underground Railroad." Accompanying the article was a cartoon that showed Chapel Hill's renowned Old Well transformed into a subway stop. "Whatta ya know," exclaimed one of the young men emerging into the North Carolina sunshine. "Th' Mason-Dixon Line is just an extension of the IRT!"[13]

Like Everett Case, Frank McGuire was a charming, likable man who devel-

This cartoon by Willard Mullin pokes fun at the Tar Heels' imported squad. Frank McGuire kept a copy hanging in his office. From *Sports Illustrated*, February 4, 1957; reprint permission granted by the Estate of Willard Mullin and Shirley Mullin Rhodes.

oped friends off the court as well as respect on it. And like Case, he did not disappoint. The first State-Carolina contest of his coaching tenure, a game played in Reynolds Coliseum, ended in a 70-69 Tar Heel victory, snapping State's five-year winning streak. Duke and Wake Forest also put new energy into their programs, expanding their recruiting efforts and searching for new coaches. Wake Forest hired playing legend Bones McKinney in 1958, and Duke took on former Case player and assistant Vic Bubas in 1959. These many talents were showcased in another of Case's innovations, the Atlantic Coast Conference (ACC), which he and other coaches organized in 1953 to bring together the region's strongest basketball contenders. Basketball fever escalated to the point that little could be accomplished in the state during big games. When sports reporters protested the poor Western Union service at the 1955 ACC tournament, State's athletic director apologized, explaining, "It seems that people working the machines got more interested in the ball games than in getting out their stories."[14]

In the fall of 1956 North Carolina's strongest team to date took the floor, a talented Chapel Hill squad led by All-American Brooklyn native Lenny Rosenbluth. By the Dixie Classic, the Tar Heels had yet to lose a game, and they maintained their perfect record through the ACC tournament, drawing national attention and prompting one longtime observer to predict that "there should be no immediate ends to the basketball worlds the talented Carolina team can conquer." The team won its opening NCAA tournament matches in Philadelphia, returned to the cheers of an enormous crowd, and then prepared for the final rounds in Kansas City with what an eager reporter termed "the enthusiasm and optimism of youth" as well as "the tireless energy of the early pioneers." A semifinal win that stretched into three overtimes stopped traffic in Chapel Hill as hundreds of students poured out of their dorms and formed a giant conga line. Two days later, when the Tar Heels captured the national title in a second triple-overtime win over a Kansas team paced by college sensation Wilt Chamberlain, almost the whole state rejoiced. Standing among a huge crowd waiting at the Raleigh-Durham airport to greet the returning champions, a *News and Observer* reporter groped to find events of comparable significance. He first characterized the gathering as resembling "a Fourth of July celebration and the Easter parade combined" but later upped the ante, noting that "when the announcement came that the plane was overhead, a loud roar went up. Youngsters, as excited as if it were Santa Claus and his reindeers overhead, shouted 'There it is. There it is.'" The paper's editorial page lauded the "magnificent display of grit and stamina" and noted, "This week we can go to bed on time."[15]

With their win the Tar Heels roused joyful enthusiasm not just among

North Carolinians mobbed the Raleigh airport to welcome the UNC Tar Heels home after they captured the 1957 national championship in Kansas City. The signs reflect both regional pride and state citizens' embrace of the team's out-of-state players. Reprinted with permission of the *News and Observer* of Raleigh, North Carolina.

alumni but in countless other North Carolinians, who for the first time in their lives watched basketball on television. Televised basketball games were relatively rare phenomena in the 1950s. Athletic administrators were still leery of the medium, fearing that televising games would discourage fans from buying tickets. "I am scared to death of television," North Carolina State athletic director Roy Clogston wrote in 1954, and such concerns would linger for almost a decade. The broadcast schedule for the 1957 championship was finalized less than a week before the contests. But the response was remarkable. "The record which the Tar Heels won by the widest margin is not in the books," *News and Observer* editors wrote the day after the championship game. "That record was in the number of persons to see the team play. It was the first time a North Carolina team participated in a televised national event and both the novelty of the event and the sheer drama of the concluding games drew people to the television screen who ordinarily would rather be caught dead than looking at a basketball game."[16]

The new medium drew even lukewarm fans, as seen in the experience of Mabel Johnson, an eighth grade teacher in Halifax County who "pulled for Carolina's Tar Heels in the Eastern Regionals, and admits she cheered at the television set during the victory over Syracuse, although her interest in the sport is of recent origin." (Mrs. Johnson, who happened to be Wilt Chamberlain's aunt, refused to say whom she would root for in the finals, smiling and demurely answering, "I'd better not commit myself.") The sense of statewide connection that televised experience made possible, both by attracting new fans and by allowing them to see the action for themselves, was suggested in the *News and Observer* the day after the championship, when the paper ran a photograph of a man pushing a baby stroller that bore the slogan "I Was Never Worried" and noted beneath it, "He's the only one."[17]


As they cheered on their teams, North Carolina basketball fans became part of a national trend in which big-time athletics was gaining a yet greater hold over American culture. Starting in the 1940s a broad range of national media—movies, magazines, newspaper columns—began to present the public with athletic narratives that reached far beyond standard accounts of physical fortitude and formulaic virtue. Films such as *Knute Rockne: All-American*, along with profiles in publications such as the newly founded *Sport* magazine, offered richly rendered athletic stories shot through with dramatic interest. These new athletic visions, often aimed at women as well as men, depicted athletes whose lives were shaped not simply by sporting ambition but also by a wide range of relationships and responsibilities—by their connections to parents, spouses, teammates, communities, and country. In most such stories, whether fictive or factual, the central figure traced the classic lines of heroic development, encountering setbacks, temptations, and defeats before mustering the moral fortitude to rise to personal and athletic challenges and emerge triumphant.[18]

By the 1950s such athletic tales had become closely intertwined with notions of patriotism and of specifically American virtue. Some of the era's most influential sporting narratives—most notably films such as *Knute Rockne* and the Lou Gehrig biography *Pride of the Yankees*—told tales of immigrants who became Americans through sports, giving added significance to long-held conceptions of athletics as an avenue into U.S. life. Links between sports and patriotism had been strengthened during World War II, as noted athletes joined the armed forces to great fanfare and as the language of sports—of teamwork, sacrifice, and heroism—became that of war. Such connections drew even tighter after the conflict ended, as heightening Cold War rhetoric linked athletic competition even more closely to the structure of U.S. society, offering contrasting visions of a vibrant, competitive U.S. meritocracy and a sluggishly complacent Soviet socialism.[19]

The significance athletic prowess had acquired as evidence of U.S. moral and political superiority showed clearly in a 1956 *News and Observer* article that compared U.S. and Soviet Olympic basketball squads through metaphors of warfare, as well as portraits of American resolve, ingenuity, and progress. "The two teams play a wholly different brand of the game," the article ran.

> The Americans are very aggressive. They delight in stealing the ball. They can hit from outside or drive in with low dribbles, and throw bullet-like passes. . . . The Russians, who give the Americans full credit for inventing and developing basketball, play a brand familiar in the United States 20 to 25 years ago. The Russians seldom go for the fast break. They do not like to be guarded closely. They seldom try set shots from outside, usually preferring to work the ball in or pass to the pivot man under the basket. In seven games in the Olympics they have been forced to give ground every time when faced with aggressive play. Their plays are stock stuff and they lack sufficient team speed to be able to play on the major college American circuit.[20]

Within North Carolina, commitment to such profoundly satisfying portraits of U.S. athletics was compounded by the welcome sense of possibility with which basketball success colored the state's rocky transition to the postwar world. The prosperity that swept the nation during the 1950s did not come easily to North Carolina, where leaders and citizens were forced to realize that while they enjoyed a good reputation within the South, they lagged well behind other regions. Slow economic growth in the years just after the war did little to improve this outlook. A series of school studies placed North Carolina near the bottom of the nation in school funding and attendance. One 1950 survey ranked the state forty-seventh among the forty-eight states in the percentage of population in college, with barely half the national average of college-attending youth. Wages and income were losing ground as well, and growing numbers of citizens were leaving the state for better opportunities elsewhere. In 1961 the state's slow population growth forced the humiliating loss of one of its congressional representatives. Politicians campaigned for office invoking potential crises, calling for unprecedented state actions that included expansions in educational support and attempts to use state funding to lure new, high-technology industries.[21]

As North Carolinians struggled to improve their national reputation, basketball achievement stood as a symbol of the state's promise. Although most of the star players hailed from Indiana, New York, and other parts of the country, the "underground railroad" that brought them made clear that North Carolina was a place to come to as well as to leave, and the many players who remained in the state after graduating further underlined the potential appeal. And it was North Carolinians who had built the imposing Reynolds Coliseum, North Carolinians who organized and managed the nationally renowned Dixie Classic, and North Carolinians who supported their squads in such grand style, filling the state's arenas to capacity, pouring through the streets in giant conga lines, and cheering on their squads with the kind of noise that provided a celebrated home court advantage for their talented teams.

Even as big-time basketball brought welcome national notice to the Tar Heel State, the broadened team loyalties made possible by radio and television coverage also helped to ease some of the effects of increased postwar mobility. The postwar years saw numerous shifts among the state's population, as more people moved out of their native counties, more children left home to attend college, and more residents departed the state altogether. Teams whose exploits were broadcast throughout the state, and sometimes across the nation, gave newly mobile residents something to share, a way to maintain links with distant friends and relatives. This feeling ran particularly strong among Dixie Classic followers. "As the people of our state have come together for this Classic from all areas of the state, and countless others have followed it in various media, there has been created a closer bond between the people of our state," wrote one tournament enthusiast. "There has been a unity of pride in this event that has carried over into other areas." Another fan spoke of the Classic as a "way of life" for basketball fans. "People who could not rationalize a long trip for one game found the week following Christmas to be just right for a weekend away from home with family and friends," he wrote. "The trip to the Dixie Classic was more than just an excursion to watch basketball, although this was the magnet which kept them coming back year after year; but it was also an opportunity to meet and mingle and talk with old friends who shared the same interest in sports, especially basketball, and in outstanding players and teams."[22]

This sense of connection, combined with the excitement of the on-court action, made attending college basketball games an almost transcendent experience, perhaps best symbolized by the moments when students, alumni, and other fans let loose their collective emotions in a resoundingly satisfying din. At Reynolds Coliseum, Everett Case devised a meter that reflected the sound of the crowd through a series of ascending lights, and spectators eagerly responded. "They put that applause meter in there," a former Wake Forest player later recalled, "and you could hear them in Yancey County." Basketball games thus came to encompass a complex, dramatic mix of emotion and collective fervor, as well as a multifaceted male virtue. Reporting on a dramatic overtime win in 1950, *News and Observer* writer Frank O'Brien noted the meaning of the "little things" that made up the experience:

> The unbridled joy of the victorious players who stream onto the court, jump and shout and embrace in that moment when the battle is won . . . the heartbreak dejection and tears of the losers. Each a quick and complete picture showing the impact of a game that not even Hollywood could capture . . . and . . . the moment of huddle when a coach offers kind words to his losing team . . . and . . . a lonely figure, Sam Ranzino, no less, walking unhurried across the court, outwardly unexcited and the trace of a satisfied smile sneaking across his face . . . whilst his teammates hold an impromptu celebration, delirious with victory . . . with 11,000 pairs of admiring eyes watching happily.[23]

The excitement of watching such contests was underscored by the sense that the young men on the court were indeed enacting dramas of American ideals, combining the determination of "the early pioneers" with the speed, daring, and dexterity of the modern world to mingle meaning and excitement in moments that sent spectators wild with glee. Each North Carolina team boasted a history filled with such examples. In 1961 State player Terry Litchfield, who had worked to overcome nearsightedness so severe that he had once been pronounced legally blind, "tossed in a dramatic 25-foot shot from the side with only two seconds remaining to give State a pulse-pounding 61-59 victory over third-ranked Duke." Delirious State fans hurdled over benches and press tables in their rush to lift Litchfield onto their shoulders and carry him off in triumph. One of Duke's most memorable triumphs came in 1956, when the Blue Devils vanquished vaunted Kentucky for the first time. "Bobbie Joe Harris stalked Kentucky's Vernon Halton with sheer larceny in mind. And 6,000 people watched," a *News and Observer* reporter wrote, describing the final moments of that contest. "Halton, the Wildcats' All America candidate was holding a basketball—and then suddenly he wasn't. Somehow, Harris darted in, stole the ball from the hands of one of the best guards in the country and shot a pass to Bucky Allen. With a Kentucky man all over him, Allen let fly a half-hook from the left of the basket, in close. It dropped. And Duke had an 85-84 win; its first ever over the Wildcats. The 6,000 all but tore down Indoor Stadium in joy. Duke had done it again."[24]

The enormous appeal of North Carolina's postwar teams helped build college basketball into one of the state's most beloved institutions, making James Naismith's game a cherished component of Tar Heel identity. Still, basketball's

The spectacular feats of North Carolina's talented new basketball players conveyed multiple meanings about manhood and American society. Reprinted with permission of the *News and Observer* of Raleigh, North Carolina.

ascendance did not go unchallenged. Even as North Carolina teams pursued their winning ways, and as dramatic plays and come-from-behind victories inspired rhapsodic praise, a series of other developments gave some residents pause, suggesting that the portrait of athletics that so many people found so appealing contained basic flaws. Starting in the late 1950s, a series of troubling incidents drew big-time basketball into an intensifying debate over the state's broader ambitions and priorities, a controversy that would eventually encompass questions about the purpose of sports, the nature of moral corruption, the role that universities should play in public life, and the shape of postwar society.

In December 1956, during the height of Dixie Classic fever, the guests at a Tip-off Club luncheon were treated to "a little skit featuring toastmaster Billy

Carmichael and a husky, muscular male with knobby knees who was dressed as a woman—or at least as a woman claims she has to dress when she's trying to justify a new frock." A *News and Observer* reporter recounted the action in the amateur drama, describing how the principal character "came forth dribbling a basketball and demanding a seven-year medical education for herself and a five-year scholarship for her boy friend." He left no doubt as to the point of the performance: "Any resemblance between this gal, played by insurance man Ted Dick, and the sweet-voiced Louisiana lass who got State in hot water with the NCAA was purely intentional."[25]

The somewhat strained effort at humor attempted to make light of what had, in fact, become a serious problem for North Carolina basketball. In the fall of 1956 the NCAA launched an investigation into North Carolina State's recruitment of Louisiana high school star Jackie Moreland that culminated in the school's suspension from postseason play. The star witness was Moreland's girlfriend, Betty Clara Rhea, who broke the code of silence that so often surrounded recruiting discussions by testifying at a closed NCAA hearing that State assistant athletic director Willis Casey had offered to pay her medical school bills if Moreland donned a State jersey. The Jackie Moreland affair became only one of several basketball-related incidents that revealed the extent to which the on-court magic that so entranced North Carolinians was often accompanied by off-court actions that held far less appeal, raising questions about the sport's new incarnation and, by extension, about the society that had nurtured it.[26]

Many of these concerns centered on player recruitment, which took on enormous importance in the big-time era. Despite effusive rhetoric about character and heart, it was impossible to win at top levels with character alone. A team had to have talent, and quite a lot of it. As more colleges sought the prestige of the basketball spotlight, competition for that talent intensified, drawing increased attention from the NCAA. The association, founded in 1906 as part of an attempt to reduce football violence by revamping the game's rules, had been a relatively ineffective guardian of athletic integrity for much of its existence. After World War II, however, a series of new regulations gave it more teeth. Starting with the 1948 passage of what was called the Sanity Code, NCAA members set out a series of rules on issues that included amateurism, financial aid, and eligibility, and they began to build a mechanism to enforce such regulations. These efforts culminated in the creation of the powerful Committee on Infractions. Almost immediately, NCAA regulators found themselves investigating a constant stream of alleged violations.[27]

Players' academic records became one source of concern. While many players worked hard at their classes, the academic records of a number of others suggested that they had not yet accepted the idea that a college education had become the key to future success. Soon after Roy B. Clogston became North Carolina State's athletic director in the late 1940s, he wrote to an old colleague, pleading for help in finding recruits. "Our basketball setup for next year is in a precarious predicament," he explained. "We should not lose any of the boys, but the way events are happening, we may be lucky to have any of them for next year. Some of them are playboys, and others are not good enough students to pass their college work." Many State athletes majored in the institution's equivalent of physical education, and Thomas Hines, head of the school's recreation department, fought regular battles with both alumni and the athletic department over the program's requirements and athletes' performances. Despite rhetoric about scholar-athletes, the temptations to recruit based on talent alone remained great, as suggested in a letter Clogston wrote to David Clark in 1950 noting the drawbacks associated with a potential star. "His associates are two little weasely runts that haven't even gone to high school," Clogston explained. "He lives in a questionable district in South Chicago and isn't particularly interested in bettering himself. However, he can play basketball, and I consider him a tremendous prospect."[28]

Recruiters were also tempted to win an athlete's favor by offering more than simply a four-year scholarship. Because of constraints on official university representatives, recruiting strategies often involved mustering a murky assortment of athletic department officials, alumni, and independent "scouts," who developed elaborate rituals designed to improve their university's chances at snaring a prime recruit without technically breaking NCAA rules. North Carolina State's longtime director of alumni affairs H. W. "Pop" Taylor offered some insight into this process when he recalled a phone call he made in the 1950s to a New York alumnus who had been enlisted to entertain a potential recruit. The young man had expressed an interest in studying engineering, and after urging the alumnus to treat the player well, Taylor hinted at the possibility of additional incentives—a request the alumnus immediately understood and eagerly granted.

" 'There is something else that I want to know; this young man may not be very affluent and he may be in great need of some summer employment and I wonder if you have anything like that available,' " Taylor recalled saying. "Fred said, 'Yes, I'll give him a summer job. I tell you I will do more than that. If he will graduate with a satisfactory record in mechanical engineering he has got a job with us. And, furthermore than that, if he doesn't want to work for us I'll guarantee to get him a job anywhere in the world he wants to work.' I said, 'That is just wonderful.' " Everett Case had listened to the conversation but, sticking to the letter of NCAA regulations, had not said a word, a fact he was careful to emphasize once the call was over. "After I hung up the phone," Taylor recalled, "Everett said, 'Pop now you be sure and remember that you said that and I did not say it.' "[29]

When the elaborate dance of college recruiting drew the eye of *Sports Illustrated* writers in 1957, North Carolina schools took center stage. The magazine's article focused on a group of New York "talent hunters" who spent much of their time trying to guide the city's promising players to one of the schools with which they had somewhat vague connections. Two of the most prominently featured "sportsmen" were "Uncle" Harry Gotkin, who scouted for Frank McGuire, and Howie Garfinkel, who recruited for North Carolina State. Gotkin was described as an old friend of McGuire's; Garfinkel's relationship to State was less well defined. The article made clear that the process of recruitment involved not only discussions of the competing coaches and schools but also a series of other gestures and favors, often involving varying amounts of cash. "I wouldn't trade it for anything," one unnamed recruit was quoted as saying. "Guys take me to lunch. They take me to dinner. They buy me a beer when I want it. And they don't give me a funny look. If I need a couple of bucks for a date, there's always some scout who'll give it to me." The article ended with a graphic example of one of these small gifts, describing a player besieged by scouts who dangled yet another set of promises before him.

> The prospect laughed. He was used to fabulous offers that were rarely backed up. "Why don't you guys lay off me? I've made up my mind to go to North Carolina. Now why don't you leave me alone for a while?"
>
> For a moment no one spoke. Then Garfinkel slowly pulled a fountain pen out of his inside pocket, possibly to cross the boy's name off his list of prospects. The boy watched him.
>
> "Hey, that's a nice-looking pen Howie," the boy said.
>
> "You want it?"
>
> "How does it close?"
>
> "Like this, see. You want it? Take it."
>
> "Thanks Howie."
>
> "That's O.K., kid. Anything for a basketball player."[30]

Along with the problematic publicity such attention provided—the *Sports Illustrated* piece did little to improve the image of anyone involved—North Carolina's universities were also having to deal with more direct consequences of recruiting. In 1950 the NCAA began a series of investigations into North Carolina State's recruiting practices. In 1956 State was placed on four years' probation after NCAA officials concluded the school had made illegal offers to Jackie Moreland. In 1960 Chapel Hill was the NCAA target in an examination of the relationship between Frank McGuire and Harry Gotkin that focused on McGuire's reimbursement of Gotkin for "expenses" that apparently included money spent entertaining potential recruits and their families. In 1961 the Tar Heels were also placed on probation and barred from a year of postseason competition.[31]

Team supporters often regarded such investigations less as a search for wrong-doing than as another weapon wielded in the ongoing fight for recruits and rankings. Many State boosters viewed the Jackie Moreland case as the revenge of Kentucky coach Adolph Rupp, who had apparently called for the investigation after losing the fight for the talented player. When North Carolina was being investigated in 1960, Frank McGuire apparently saw the presence of Columbia University's graduate school dean at the head of the NCAA committee as a bad sign, expecting that the man would take the opportunity to pay McGuire back for the defeats he had inflicted on Columbia while coaching at St. Johns a decade earlier. Coaches loudly insisted that they had committed no violations—or at least no serious ones. "If you're going to convict schools on charges like these, I can tell you that there wouldn't be many left—to play basketball, or anything," Everett Case complained during the Moreland case, adding, "They are getting mighty thin, splitting hairs, grasping at technicalities." But such reasoning nei-ther lifted the sanctions nor removed the stigma they conferred.[32]

Even as the newly intensified competition added to recruiting complications, a series of incidents at games raised questions about the effects that big-time basketball was having on its many followers. In March 1957, as the Tar Heels were marching to their national title, a group of State students went on a rampage amid cars parked outside Reynolds Coliseum, leaving in their wake slashed tires, smashed windshields, and one overturned vehicle. Some of the two dozen students arrested in the incident claimed to have been angered because ACC tournament-goers had illegally blocked the entrances to student parking lots. But many observers drew more troubling conclusions, expressing reservations about the emotions the event stirred up. The editors of the *Greens-boro Daily Record*, noting that the State team had suffered a first-round loss to Wake Forest earlier that evening, remarked, "Outside observers cannot help wondering whether the causes did not go deeper. Are such demonstrations to be tied in with big-time athletics and the spirit which they generate? State College was not used to losing as it lost this time." Such concerns echoed around North Carolina as other editors offered similar assessments and ques-tioned whether the many nonstudent fans at the game meant that basketball now catered more to the interests of businesses and alumni than to those of students.[33]

Similar incidents touched every Big Four campus. On February 12, 1959, a game between Chapel Hill and Wake Forest ended in a virtual riot, with students and players embroiled in conflict on the court. According to ACC commissioner James Weaver's later reconstruction, the incident began with less than a minute remaining in the game, when a ball rolled loose on the floor and players for both teams dove after it. The players tangled with each other as they were getting up, and tensions that had been building throughout the game broke out in a fight. Players from both benches spilled onto the floor, and as coaches and officials tried to restore order, spectators joined in and "made a difficult task an impossible one." Two years later, in February 1961, a similar incident broke out at the end of a Duke–Chapel Hill contest. The melee, which the television cameras that had been covering the game broadcast throughout the state, resulted in the suspension of players from both teams and further questions about basketball's effect on students.[34]

In his report on the 1961 incident, Weaver drew a specific contrast between the quality of basketball in North Carolina and the behavior of basketball fans, writing that "basketball in this area has developed tremendously during the past decade; player technique is at times phenomenal. It is regrettable that spectator conduct has not kept pace." That incident also moved *News and Observer* sports editor Dick Herbert, one of big-time basketball's staunchest supporters, to lament that "most of the present student bodies have no sanity in their traditional rivalries," adding, "The players have a far greater respect and regard for their rivals." Frank McGuire, in an unguarded moment, fanned the emotional flames by suggesting that more lay in store at the team's upcoming rematch. "It's going to get worse," he told a reporter. "It can't get any better: Our students saw what happened tonight. . . . Despite anything you can do, it's going to get worse."[35]

In an era already fraught with concern about the conduct of young people and rife with phrases such as "juvenile delinquency," such demonstrations were enormously troubling, particularly when some participants demonstrated little remorse. The day after the Chapel Hill–Wake Forest brawl, one newspaper offered a relatively lighthearted assessment: "Spectators were trying to decide after it was all over whether it was worse than the free-for-all at the end of the game in 1956 at Chapel Hill. There was no agreement on this except that it was felt more people were on the court at Chapel Hill and that here there was more real punching." The Duke–Chapel Hill outbreak produced some similar analysis. "Many people have commented that the slugfest which erupted in the waning seconds of the basketball game between the University of North Carolina and Duke at Durham Saturday night was the 'best' they had ever seen," the *News and Observer* fumed, adding, "This is about the worst commentary that could be made on the brawl. It is another way of saying that an unusual number of people were doing some real slugging and that it is a wonder somebody didn't really get hurt."[36]

After stern warnings from both coaches and school officials, the Duke-Carolina rematch ended peacefully. But in one sense Frank McGuire's prediction of future troubles was on the mark. A few weeks after the outbreak, officials of the Federal Bureau of Investigation announced that several North Carolina players had been implicated in a point-shaving conspiracy. Back in 1951, when college basketball was rocked by its first major point-shaving scandal, North Carolina basketball was barely visible on the national horizon, and game-fixing centered largely on New York teams. By the late 1950s, however, the growing prominence of North Carolina teams had made their games logical targets for a new group of gamblers who sought to manipulate huge sums of wagered money. Eventually twenty players throughout the country were charged with agreeing to manipulate game scores—frequently by conspiring to win games with lower-than-expected margins of victory, and thus allowing gamblers to win bets based on point spreads. Six more, including New York playground legend Connie Hawkins and Chapel Hill star Doug Moe (whose recruitment had been featured in the 1957 *Sports Illustrated* article), were charged with accepting what was called "softening up" money—gifts meant to establish a friendly connection between a gambler and a player but that involved no game-fixing promises. Chapel Hill player Lou Brown was fingered as one of the main connections between players and gamblers. The trouble had apparently gone so far that when one fix went bad at the 1960 Dixie Classic, armed gamblers had confronted players outside Reynolds Coliseum to demand their money back.[37]

The charges were a devastating blow to North Carolina basketball fans. Recruiting irregularities could be chalked up as "splitting hairs," and "grasping at technicalities." A postgame melee could be attributed to an excess of youthful emotion. But there was no way to explain away fixed games. The scandals prompted both soul-searching and debate, as residents struggled to understand why the scandal had happened and to decide what to do about a problem that had once seemed comfortably confined to far-off urban centers. During the point-shaving investigations of the 1950s, university president William Friday noted, "The scandals seemed to be centered in New York City and were regarded as having affected only a few institutions remote from North Carolina." By 1960, however, "it became apparent that we were not immune to the influences which were affecting the sport in other parts of the country."[38]

Some assessments of the scandal picked up the theme of big-city corruption, reflecting a persisting unease about the many out-of-state stars North Carolina schools had recruited. The ethnically diverse group of Catholic and Jewish players that brought the state so much acclaim had done a great deal to tame strains of anti-Semitic and anti-Catholic feeling in the state. Support for northern-dominated basketball teams also pointed toward an easing of sectional strife, a change suggested by the *Sports Illustrated* cartoon that transformed a line drawn to represent irreconcilable differences into a subway connection. But tensions over outsiders could still flare, as they did in statements that ranged from remarks about "the Pope's emissaries and the refugees from the Synagogue," to a state senator's comment that "he might be able to pronounce the names of the Duke players if some of them had been from North Carolina." When the Tar Heels won the national crown, *News and Observer* editors expressed the hope that such an achievement would "stimulate interest in basketball all the way down to the grammar school level," cautioning that "in the future, North Carolina colleges who want to retain popular favor would do well to devote more attention to home-grown talent." A deeply shaken Everett Case, when first confronted with the scandal, voiced this concern directly. "Maybe the sense of values of New York boys is all screwed up," he surmised in one interview. "I don't know, but North Carolina boys would certainly be loyal."[39]

Such sectional aspersions, however, formed only a minor note within a broader condemnation of the recruiting practices that brought the implicated individuals to the state's cherished institutions. Dozens of newspaper columns, letters, and public comments cast the parties involved in the scandals as "bad apples," blaming the incidents on "some sorry conduct on the part of some fast-moving gamblers and a few gullible kids who tossed honesty and integrity to the wind." The roots of the problem, this argument ran, lay in the moral turpitude of the players involved and in the laxity of coaches and administrators who had yielded to the temptation of accepting individuals who did not belong in college in the first place. "Coaches are going to have to concentrate more on recruiting athletes with something besides basketball ability," wrote *Durham Morning Herald* columnist Jack Horner in a typical assessment. "Instead of looking for the best shooter and the fanciest ball-handler and dribbler, they must put more emphasis on finding youngsters with character."[40]

Although shortsighted recruiting had indeed caused its own problems, however, a closer examination of the athletes who participated in the scheme suggested that choosing players who would resist temptation was not as easy as such arguments seemed to imply. While some of the implicated players came from troubled families, had struggled in school, or had been involved in questionable activities, many of them had seemed to distinguish themselves both in the classroom and in campus life. Stan Niewierowski, one of the North Carolina State participants, had been elected Wolfpack captain in 1960, and Everett

Case had offered high praise for his leadership ability. Terry Litchfield, whose fight to overcome nearsightedness had drawn so much fan admiration, was a good student whose father was YMCA director for the state of Kentucky. Don Gallagher, accused of accepting several thousand dollars in bribe money, had graduated from State with honors, had been awarded the coveted Alumni Athletic Trophy after being voted the school's best senior athlete, and was serving as a lieutenant in the army when the scandal broke.[41]

The involvement of such well-regarded individuals raised questions that proved almost impossible for many avid basketball supporters to entertain. The point-shaving scandal had forced sports fans to abandon, at least in part, cherished portrayals of athletes as exemplars of manly virtue. But while it had been possible to consider that athletic skill might have a limited connection to moral fortitude, some supporters found it far more difficult to criticize sporting institutions themselves, or to concede that the big-time system that produced such extraordinary play might also be offering extraordinary temptation. Such confusion was dramatically illustrated in a Dick Herbert column in which the normally eloquent writer struggled to come to terms with the scandal in a disjointed paragraph where a lack of logical coherence pointed up his inability to develop a satisfactory solution to the problem. "The first suggestion would be to take more care in recruiting," Herbert wrote. "The fringe case or the questionable young man should be avoided. This is no guarantee of immunity. But it offers some protection. Some young men who rated high on character and background were involved in the fixes."[42]

Observers with less emotion invested in the moral symbolism of big-time basketball had less trouble responding to the scandal. Even as many assessments of the events decried the lapses of the individuals involved, other comments targeted the institution of big-time basketball itself, clearly expressing a long-standing frustration with the sport's statewide prominence. "The scale of values may canonize some young lout who can drop an inflated skin through a net, and his exploits may inflate the pride of school and the pride of state," wrote editors at the *Charlotte Observer*. "But this is no reason, no excuse; it is only misplaced emphasis." Such skewed priorities, the Raleigh *News and Observer* suggested, seemed to reflect a broader set of problems that plagued the nation as a whole: "It may indeed be that the big news in this story is the disclosure of a sort of sneaking corruption of American society itself which has reached the areas in which America is supposed to be doing most to build the intellectual and moral quality of its future."[43]

Such observers found much to criticize about the position that athletes had attained in North Carolina society. Not only did athletic skill seem to carry more weight than academic performance; it at times appeared to overshadow moral standards as well, as in a notorious case where Chapel Hill's prized honor court acquitted a basketball player of cheating but convicted another student on identical evidence. Critics also expressed concern about the multifaceted role that money had come to play in college athletics. While athletic scholarships had gained widespread acceptance, some observers clearly felt that even this form of compensation tainted school sports. *Charlotte Observer* editors followed their attack on the state's problematic priorities with a sharp critique of monetary rewards. "The people who watch the bouncing ball have demanded, and received, a professional show," they wrote. "But they have paid the price by seeing college kids turned into professionals. Many of these youngsters were corrupted by the public long before the crooks came slipping around." One disgruntled alumnus was even more direct, writing Chapel Hill chancellor William Aycock that "if you pay boys to play you should not be too surprised if someone else pays them more to lose."[44]

Examination of the individuals involved in the scandal revealed that money did indeed play many roles in the events and that the ideals of school loyalty and individual honor were buffeted by a crisscrossing series of other needs and desires related to the world outside the court. Lou Brown, who grew up in a working-class New Jersey family, attributed his actions to his longing for the growing range of consumer pleasures that had become such a celebrated part of postwar culture. "At college, he wanted to live like the kids who drove the Thunderbirds," ran one of the headlines in a confessional-style article he wrote for *Look* magazine. The piece, ironically, was set amid a series of glossy advertisements for Buicks, encyclopedias, outboard motors, and other consumer playthings, and it was subtitled "The candid confession of a young man to whom money meant too much." Elsewhere the scandal highlighted stresses in the era's cherished ideals of family responsibility. One article argued that a number of the implicated players, among them Don Gallagher, succumbed because they needed the extra cash to support wives and children. " 'One of the best all-around boys' went wrong after he married and became a parent," a headline explained.[45]

Such revelations played into more general concerns about the glorification of material gain that many citizens felt had permeated U.S. society at the expense of more elevated goals. "America's idealism has dissipated. Her greatest boast now seems to be that she makes more dishwashers than any other country," *Daily Tar Heel* editors lamented in 1961, echoing comments heard around the country as Americans sought to tap the meaning of the explosion in consumer goods and services that marked the 1950s. A number of national scandals, from quiz show and payola investigations to revelations of bribe-taking by General Electric executives, raised broader questions about the moral tone of national culture, suggesting that a society that purported to champion discipline, honesty, and fairness had become obsessed with an unruly rush for material goods.

From this perspective, the point-shaving scandal seemed not an aberration but a logical development. Lumberton resident Elmer Simkins laid out this argument in a letter to the *News and Observer*. "In this era of the 'fast buck' many of their elders have not set them shining examples of morality," he said of the implicated players. "Before we too severely condemn the young men who are involved in the basketball scandals, should not each and every one of us seriously consider our own lives, and see if we too are guilty of chasing after the 'fast buck?'"[46]

Whatever the cause of the scandals, however, university officials viewed them as the last straw in a decade-long series of events that had regularly embarrassed the institutions and absorbed far too much time and effort. Where sports had once been seen as a way to build discipline, honesty, and self-control, they were now regularly associated with deception, scandal, and unruly behavior. Led by William Friday, university administrators opted for wholesale change and devised a plan that targeted several aspects of the programs at their constituent schools. The reforms, quickly approved by shaken trustees, cut basketball schedules almost in half, permitting no more than fourteen games a season. They sought to curb both recruiting and out-of-state influence by mandating that no more than two scholarships a year could be awarded to players from outside North Carolina. And to the dismay of many fans throughout the state, they canceled the Dixie Classic.[47]

University officials accompanied these measures with a series of public statements in which they bent over backward to emphasize the new approach, often minimizing the potential contributions of athletics to college life and questioning some of the state's most cherished sporting institutions. When North Carolina State chancellor John T. Caldwell gave a speech on intercollegiate sports in March 1962, he argued that any preference given to athletes was "offensive to any true educator," and he characterized athletic scholarships not as a reward for a valuable skill but as a necessary evil: "The so-called 'scholarship' or grant-in-aid based on athletic ability, is not defensible educationally but must be tolerated and for one principal reason; it reduces to a minimum institutional dishonesty." He also leveled a direct blow at Reynolds Coliseum's proudly vocal partisans, asking, "Is not the 'home-court advantage' cultivated in violation of the spirit of true sportsmanship?" A few months later, when alumni began to grumble about the relatively undistinguished career of Chapel Hill football coach Jim Hickey, Chancellor William Aycock bluntly stated that "no coach will be fired just for losing."[48]

As with Frank Porter Graham's reform plan, this effort to curb college sports sparked heated debates across the state, pitting university administrators against sports-loving alumni. But as the conflict unfolded, it took on a very different tone. Alumni of the 1930s, perhaps chastened by the economic hardships of the Great Depression, had made their case for college scholarships largely in terms of practicality—imperfect measures for an imperfect world. Arguments of the 1960s often struck a far more heroic note, drawing on Cold War associations that linked athletics, manhood, American patriotism, and capitalist endeavor. In letters, newspaper columns, and television editorials, they described U.S. society in terms that echoed turn-of-the-century Darwinism, portraying a fierce struggle in which achievement was forever challenged, uncertainty was given little quarter, and purely moral victory could be cast as a sign of weakness.[49]

Similar arguments had already surfaced in athletic rhetoric, as a number of coaches began to avow with a new openness that sportsmanship alone did not measure a team's worth. Renowned football coach Jim Tatum, who had been hired by the University of North Carolina shortly after he was barred from State, had become a prominent advocate of such ideas, claiming in 1957 that "you can't build character with losing football." Such sentiments echoed in many corners of North Carolina, as opponents of reform constructed their own portrait of worldly challenge and manly resolve. "Whether you accept this reasoning or not, life is one victory after another," wrote an anonymous member of the class of 1958. "Success in everything depends on winning; not losing." Another alumnus asserted that "losing a piece of business does not improve my character," and noted in passing, "When you are on top, you expect some rocks to be thrown. This is part of the price you pay for success." In a column titled "Winning Doesn't Hurt," *Charlotte News* columnist Max Muhleman took issue with the statement that the state's college coaches would not be fired simply because they lost. "The hard facts of intercollegiate athletics say that coaches most certainly are, have been and will be fired for losing," he wrote. "There is nothing unhealthy, shameful or un-American about it. The same principle applies to every job: If a man isn't doing the required work he is dismissed."[50]

University officials had sought to pull away from such a struggle, casting their efforts in terms of maturity and moral vision. Supporters of reform frequently invoked a vision of manliness that harked back to the mature reserve of Victorian ideals, and they contrasted their efforts with images of childish emotionalism, as when former North Carolina governor Luther Hodges told the *Charlotte Observer*, "It's about time the aging rah-rah boys . . . grew up and let up." They also drew clear lines between the university and the society around it. "We must not accept the mediocrity of society as a standard of our leadership," William Aycock proclaimed in the wake of the initial point-shaving accusations, describing the university as "a citadel of truth." The institution's status as a moral beacon, the *Greensboro Daily News* commented, made the basketball scandals seem especially heinous. "The bribers and the fixers we shall

# Max Muhleman

# Winning Doesn't Hurt

For some time now I have had the sneaking suspicion that the basketball fix scandal scared the daylights out of the powers that be at the University of North Carolina.

When University Chancellor William Aycock took it upon himself this week to proclaim that "No North Carolina coach is going to be fired just for losing" he nurtured the suspicion almost to the point of confirmation.

**The hard facts of intercollegiate athletics say that coaches most certainly are, have been and will be fired for losing.**

There is nothing unhealthy, shameful or un-American about it. The same principle applies to every job: If a man isn't doing the required work he is dismissed.

The hitch in the coaching profession, particularly the football coaching profession, is that while the university or college hires the man it is the alumni money that supports the program. As any senate investigator will tell you, you don't accept money from anyone without a degree of obligation.

\* \* \*

## —UNC Has Never Won ACC Title

IF THE GRADS who make a big-time football program possible want a winner to show for their investment and support, they have a certain right to expect one. This is not to say they have reason to expect an all-consuming winner, a machine which grinds out foe after foe, but rather a representative team—one that has a chance of beating any opponent; one that occasionally wins a conference championship.

Supporters of big-time basketball frequently expressed themselves with hard-nosed force, as evidenced by this 1962 Max Muhleman column in the *Charlotte News*. Reprinted with permission from the *Charlotte Observer*. Copyright owned by the *Charlotte Observer*. Copy courtesy of the University Archives, Wilson Library, University of North Carolina, Chapel Hill.

always have with us. They are part of our society," the editors wrote. "But why are North Carolina's great citadels of learning linked with this scandal? Why has the corruption spread to the very centers of the citadels of truth?"[51]

The letters and comments that disputed de-emphasis took a dim view of that reasoning, portraying the decision not as an assertion of higher principle but as a cowardly reluctance to confront the realities of postwar U.S. society. The arguments, which in part reflected the long-standing inclination to value experience over classroom training, once again held up the sphere of business as the appropriate example to follow, portraying a world in which temptation and scandal were met with heroic, problem-solving determination. "Why would it have been wrong for them to use the same approach which successful businesses use every day?" asked one alumnus, adding, "The only answer that I can find is that the officials evidently do not feel that they are big enough to cope with the problems of big athletic programs." Such comments were echoed in numerous other letters, such as the one that argued, "If business people always discarded the whole, because part became contaminated, this would be a small world to live in."[52]

Echoing the assertion that university officials did not feel "big enough" to handle their basketball programs, many comments turned the questions of manhood on university officials, offering an alternative assessment that stressed physical fortitude and assertive resolve. At times such advocates suggested that critics of school sports secretly envied the physical prowess athletes displayed. One staunch Dixie Classic fan suggested that one of the reform's supporters "probably prefers elimination of inter-college athletics in favor of intramurals, where he very likely unexcelled in his college days at Wake Forest." They also invoked a timidity associated with women and children. One alumnus began his letter with a familiar childhood verse: "From Ghoulies and Ghosties, / Long Leggitie Beasties, / And Things that go Bump in the Night, / Good Lord Deliver Us!" Another described the trustees who upheld the university plan as "an irresponsible resolute bunch of teen-agers." Max Muhleman revealed his "sneaking suspicion that the basketball fix scandal scared the daylights out of the powers that be at the University of North Carolina." A letter written to a state newspaper brought up the issue in no uncertain terms: "Let us all hope too many college presidents and chancellors will not begin meddling with athletics as most of them are sissy-pants and know as much about athletics as Coach Everett Case does about being Miss America."[53]

Issues of manhood segued easily into those of politics, as some dissenters described the reforms as a rejection of the cherished American principles that had become so closely associated with competitive sports. "Anyone who enjoys sports, which are innately competitive, almost always plays to win," asserted an editorial in the *Daily Tar Heel*. "And what's wrong with playing to win? Is it such a base, foul desire? If so, we might as well do away with our entire political system while we're at it." De-emphasis provoked similar trepidation even among supportive alumni. After the reforms were announced, N. P. Hayes, president of Carolina Steel Corporation, wrote William Friday to express both his support of the plan and his concerns about some of its possible implications. While he did not support the idea of "victory at any cost," he wrote, "I am not in favor of an athletic program for exercise and pleasure, only. While athletics are far from being the most important thing in the life of a student at the University, it does have its importance. Winning within the framework of the new program is very desirable. For one thing, as far as I am concerned, a desire and a dedicated effort to win is a part of the American way of life."[54]

Harsher critics went further, linking their concerns about de-emphasis with long-standing suspicions about the supposedly radical politics of university professors. Among the university's most prominent critics was a television commentator named Jesse Helms, a longtime political operative who was building a statewide reputation with his vigorous, cleverly reasoned defenses of the social and economic status quo. "There was deception afoot amidst the pious pretense that the nationwide basketball scandals justified the de-emphasis, if not the complete elimination, of competitive sports," Helms warned in one television commentary, going on to question the broader motives of university officials. Other observers warned that the university was making a serious mistake. "Sir, what we need in this America of ours is more strength and virility and more emphasis on winning," one alumnus wrote William Friday. "Let's teach our boys that winning is important, that strength is important, and that moral fibre is paramount," he added, warning of the danger that "we shall all be engulfed by the hordes of Communism."[55]

Concerns about business and Communism, about academic isolation, and about the links between sports and society all came together in a particularly revealing letter from an alumnus living in Jacksonville. The missive also touched on university connections to the building civil rights movement, a development that contributed to distrust of university endeavors in many circles. "My love and concern for the great University of North Carolina prompts me to write this letter," he began. "I am much concerned about the group of people others refer to as Liberals, Academic Freedom Riders, and other names that may or may not be more descriptive taking over the school and warping the minds of these young people and which will take them until they are 28 or 29 years old before they get straightened out. This is about the age when they usually get concerned about paying the bills and the flaming desire to change things are then recognized for what they really are."[56]

He then turned his critique to the school's athletic teams, showing both his frustration with the current situation and his sense that the athletic department would be more responsive to his interests than faculty members would. "I cannot do anything about [faculty] except to pray for a revolution among the trustees and to oppose them until they reach the dawn themselves," he continued. "I can do something about the sad athletic picture. I have been accustomed to buying season tickets which I shall discontinue until some very POSITIVE actions are taken that will clearly let the public know that the greatest university in the greatest nation realizes that the American system is to try to win and that this university will once more get on the trail of athletic excellence."[57]

But perhaps the most pointed assessment came from Jesse Helms. He agreed that the scandal reflected broader social problems, commenting, "The kids who got caught were merely looking glasses for all the rest of us, and the thugs who corrupted them were ghouls standing as the symbols of an era." But he saw the problem not in materialism or the drive to win, but in the upbringing of the participants, which left them unable to confront the pressures of money and fame. "It wasn't commercialism and professionalism that corrupted basketball," he argued. "It was weak citizenship and deficient educational policies and deteriorating family life—all of them combined." Then he held up the Dixie Classic as a major symbol of national political and economic institutions. "The Dixie Classic is not as important as the principle that demands that it be resumed," he continued. "What is involved here is more than an exciting interlude between Christmas and New Years. It is a question of whether we will face up to our obligation to make certain that competitive affairs can survive without being tainted with corruption."[58]

Arguments such as these drew the basketball scandals into the ongoing debate over the nature of a variety of social ills that seemed to plague southern and American society, questions of whether problems such as poverty or inequality should be traced to individual shortcomings or to more systemic questions of social and economic organization. This issue had run through the statewide disputes over unionization as well as debates about the expanding civil rights movement, drawing a new intensity from the polarized politics of the postwar era. By holding up an ideal of triumphantly resolute manhood against the supposed weaknesses of point-shavers or officials who sought to lower competitive stakes, one group of big-time basketball supporters made athletics into a central metaphor for a conservative vision of U.S. society, transforming the game into one of the contested institutions that helped to define the turbulent conflicts of the 1960s. Emotional appeals to revive the Dixie Classic would continue unsuccessfully for the next three years, increasing popular suspicions of university officials in numerous corners of state society and adding fuel to the broader political conflagration.[59]

As well as playing into intensifying political disagreements, big-time basketball also illuminated some of the dynamics and dilemmas of postwar culture, giving new meaning to long-standing concerns about the wider social import sports had gained. Increasing basketball ambitions at the state's major universities ran parallel to efforts to expand the scope and prestige of academic programs, with particular attention to the science and technology research that was coming to define Cold War academic endeavors. Still, the furor over the scandals and reforms emphasized the extent to which college basketball had ceased to be primarily a component of an educational experience and had instead become a potent symbol with meaning in many corners of society. It also highlighted the ways in which the image of an institution was now shaped less by its own actions and priorities and more by the aims and interests behind the national magazines, radio programs, and television broadcasts that were claiming a growing share of Americans' attention.

Supporters of big-time events such as the Dixie Classic saw this media attention as a welcome opportunity, and they employed the language of advertising to describe how a successful athletic program could enhance a university's reputation among a broad public. "Who built up the University of Maryland?" asked an anonymous letter, "The President or Jim Tatum?" Max Muhleman argued that the 1957 national championship "helped make the University of North Carolina one of the most distinguished institutions in the land"—apparently using "distinguished" to mean "well-known." Supporters of resuming the Dixie Classic almost always pointed to nationwide publicity as one of the tournament's most significant components, as when state representative W. C. Harris Jr. told William Friday that the tournament "did more to spread the fame of and to create interest in North Carolina State than all other efforts of all of our public relations experts."[60]

Widespread recognition was undoubtedly a boon to either a business or a growth-hungry state, which could use the ensuing "goodwill" as an opening for new economic ventures. Still, such publicity was less obviously related to the internal goals of educational institutions. National publicity rarely reflected university priorities. The decision to glorify accomplishments in basketball rather than in philosophy or science was made by the people who wrote the stories or scheduled the broadcasts, with little university input. And while public interest in university affairs opened the possibility of more widespread support for university activities (a welcome development for a state-financed system), it also raised the specter of greater political interference in university affairs.[61]

The theme of advertising brought up yet another issue that disturbed many thoughtful observers of postwar U.S. society. As their horizons expanded, citizens had less direct experience of the institutions in which they took an interest. Rather, they pieced together their understanding of a broader world with fragments of experience and information gathered from many different sources. In a culture increasingly saturated with advertising and with the images of a visually oriented popular culture, such judgments were often made on the basis of appearance, in which a partial understanding or experience was extended into judgment about a greater whole. The idea that any virtues displayed by a basketball player competing for a Tar Heel school brought credit to the state itself encouraged citizens to take the part for the whole, to extend symbol to reality.[62]

The powerful effect that sports competition had on participants and observers made athletics particularly susceptible to this form of reasoning. An intricate, dazzling play, whether experienced directly, seen in person, or followed on television, could spark profound reactions that gained added force from the complex associations linking sports with U.S. culture and with male ideals. Such emotions were a cherished part of big-time sports; athletics came to play such a significant role in postwar mass culture in part because of their ability to retain, or even enhance, their emotional impact under the mediating influence of television. One criticism leveled against the university reform plan charged officials with seeking to remove such feelings from human life, comments that cast athletic emotion as a mark of genuine experience. When Everett Case retired, Jesse Helms lauded him in part because "he added a dash of excitement and color and pride to our area life," making "a giant coliseum throb with enthusiastic cheers." Helms then went on to charge, "There are those, of course, who disdain the enthusiasm and the competition of college athletics. If they had their way, they would diminish the emphasis to the drab point of dullness and disinterest."[63]

The sense of compelling reality that such forceful experiences created could, however, crowd out other facets of an increasingly complex institution. W. C. Harris Jr. could thus sit in Reynolds Coliseum surrounded by North Carolina State supporters, be overcome with emotion, and later write to William Friday, "I closed my eyes and vividly relived some of my great moments at the Dixie Classic. There were the great Wolf Pack teams with Dick Dickey, the amazing Sam Ranzino, the Tarheel team which went on to the national championship, interesting teams from Yale, Princeton, Cornell, Oregon State, Iowa, Brigham Young, Cincinnati, Northwestern, Tulane, and for a moment I could see players like Bob Pettit, Oscar Robertson, Lenny Rosenbluth"—going so far in reverie that he mistakenly claimed that no point-shaving had ever occurred at the tournament. And sitting in his university office, Friday could read the letter, recall the moment when he had been informed of the armed confrontation outside Reynolds during the 1960 Classic, and dryly note in the margin, "not the only thing he closed his eyes to."[64]

The point-shaving scandal cut directly to the heart of the dilemma posed by the expanded significance given to appearance and emotion: the potential separation between even the most powerful experience and its underlying reality. By making it possible to manipulate game scores while preserving the thrills of victory, point-shaving deliberately severed links between the game itself and any broader moral meanings it might have offered, suggesting that the implicated athletes had already abandoned their belief in such connections. Lou Brown provided a case in point when he described the recruiting tactics used by gambler Aaron Wagman. "He had a favorite sales story," Brown explained in his magazine confession. "He used it on me, and I heard him use it later. It was a true story, but the player involved, who has not been arrested, must be nameless." The player, the story went, was playing in a game where the gamblers' point spread favored his team by two points. "With two seconds to play, his team was losing by one point. He drove in for a basket that won the game. The students poured out of the stands, lifted him to their shoulders and carried him off. He was a campus hero, yet he was shaving points." That story bore painful similarity to the case of Terry Litchfield, who had scored the heroic winning basket in the emotional victory over Duke barely two months before he was implicated in the point-shaving scheme. It also undercut associations between athletic success and broader notions of virtue, raising questions about the extent to which players and fans had, whether consciously or not, come to value the experience of victory as valuable in itself.[65]

The point-shaving scandal and its aftermath had immediate effects on North Carolina basketball. The state's two big-time pioneers left their programs shortly afterward. Frank McGuire, who had been sternly lectured by university officials and who realized that Chapel Hill was no longer committed to supporting a top-level team, announced in 1962 that he would leave the Tar Heels to coach a professional squad (although he subsequently returned to college coaching at the University of South Carolina). He held publicly to the bad apple theory, characterizing Lou Brown as a minor player and a sloppy dresser who, unlike the other members of the team, refused to attend church. Everett Case was more deeply affected. He remained loyal to his adopted state and school, but he never recovered from the blow. Health problems forced him to retire halfway through the 1964–65 season. Before his death in 1966, he willed his possessions to his former players and asked to be buried in a cemetery overlooking the road from Raleigh to Durham, so that "when the boys go over to play Duke, they can wave to me."[66]

De-emphasis did not, however, produce the drastic change its opponents had envisioned. Point-shaving and other scandals had raised significant questions about postwar society, as well as about competition itself. Still, few in the university administration or in the state at large were prepared to seriously question either the value of competition or the basic structure of U.S. society. And while the growing distance between players and spectators left room for deception, it also made it easier to confine athletes to an ideal realm, paying more attention to the action on the court than to the frequently less appealing maneuvers that took place off of it. The compelling vision of heroic young men who combined physical prowess with emotional commitment to coach and teammates, who brought prestige to school and state, and who enacted profoundly American dramas of aspiration and achievement proved remarkably resilient. Those North Carolina schools that had escaped the scandal, among them Duke, Wake Forest, and a newly insurgent Davidson College, continued to pursue top-level basketball with unflagging zeal. Although university officials steadfastly refused to resurrect the Dixie Classic, pressures from fans and alumni soon prodded them to relax many other measures. The inexperienced assistant who had replaced Frank McGuire—a young man named Dean Smith—proved a better coach than almost anyone had reckoned, an irony that would spawn a mythology all its own. As State and Carolina teams returned to top-level form, and as North Carolina basketball reached toward ever-greater heights, the dilemmas raised by the point-shaving scandal faded in the glow of growing national renown.

## CHAPTER EIGHT

# From Amazons to Glamazons

## The Decline of Women's Basketball, 1936–1956

O n the afternoon of March 12, 1951 the members of the women's basketball team from Lincolnton High School stood waiting in the wings of the Southern Pines High School gymnasium, poised to defend the championship they had captured in a surprise run through the inaugural Girls' Invitational State Basketball Tournament the year before. As the players shifted nervously from foot to foot, the lights dimmed, the packed gymnasium grew quiet, and a spotlight illuminated the center of the floor. An announcer began to call each player's name, and Lincolnton forward Ramona Hinkle savored the mingled sensations of tension and excitement. The Lincolnton High players, by far the most successful athletes at their school, were used to special treatment—favors from parents and teachers, attention from town officials, admiring coverage in the local press. But the thousands of spectators that flocked to the weeklong Girls' Invitational, and the pageantry that accompanied the events, lifted them to even loftier heights. More than four decades later Ramona Hinkle broke into a smile as she described the scene. "That was elegant," she explained. "That was just wonderful," chimed in teammate Billie Martin. "That was big time."[1]

The Girls' Invitational had been designed with just such effects in mind. The event's founders, Aberdeen coach Robert E. "Bob" Lee and Southern Pines principal A. C. Dawson, sought to usher high school women's basketball into the statewide spotlight, giving young women a prominent place amid the array of postseason tournaments—the CIAA championship, the NCAA competition, the newly organized white men's high school tournament—that were turning the final weeks of March into a season of basketball obsession. The Girls' Invitational, drawing on the state's rich tradition of women's basketball, got off to a strong start, with close, high-scoring games and plenty of spectator enthusiasm. "The thrills came fast and furious with all the excitement of a see-saw battle offered right away," *Greensboro Daily News* reporter Bill Gallagher observed after the first round of the 1952 competition, in which Rockwell defeated Biscoe in a 70-65 overtime contest and Reeds conquered Jasper, 68-65. "They kept right on coming through the second and third games last night and tonight there was more of the same." The 1951 Lincolnton team created plenty of its own thrills, squeezing through the tournament by defeating Herring 55-51, downing Lowgap 53-52, and then rallying from a 9-point deficit to take the championship game from Goldston, 52-51. For some Lincolnton fans the excitement rose so high that it became too much to bear. "Our superintendent of schools, he and his wife went with us," Ramona Hinkle recalled. "And we didn't know this till afterwards, but he got so excited one night he had to go outside and throw up."[2]

The sport's widespread popularity, along with the quality of play, drew spectators from around the state and inspired rhapsodic praise. The tournament quickly began to outdraw the boys-only NCHSAA tournament, an achievement that was not lost on the reporters covering the event. "Who says women have lost their charm?" *Greensboro Daily News* writer Irwin Smallroad noted three days into the 1952 competition. "While the state schoolboy basketball tournament was drawing only 800 fans at Durham Thursday night, the state girls' tourney was played before 1000 at Aberdeen. The Aberdeen crowd Wednesday night was 1,300." Another writer linked the tournament's success to broader female gains in public life. "Women won the right to vote back in 1919 and now A. C. Dawson and his comrades here are campaigning to liberate the gals in North Carolina's high school athletic program," columnist George Webb observed in 1951, blithely adding, "The proposition is paying off like A.T. and T. stock. Except for Wednesday night's preliminary round tussling, this beautiful new Southern Pines High gym has been crammed to capacity rivaling a sardine can."[3]

Despite this promising start, however, North Carolina's female basketball players would find the 1950s far more daunting than would AT&T. The thriving statewide network of women's basketball embodied a belief in the value of competitive sports and in a vision of womanhood rooted in the relatively egalitarian ethics that pervaded many state communities, an attitude that came clear when Bob Lee defended his efforts by pointing to the men's state tournament and "saying that if it was good or bad for the boys then the same thing applied to the girls."[4] But women's competitive basketball also had powerful opponents, who looked at sports and womanhood from a far different perspective. Proponents of "physical education," who had established themselves in the state's women's colleges in the 1920s and 1930s, had been fighting competitive women's basketball for almost half a century. In their first decades of effort, a

These players from Kannapolis show the energy and competitive effort that North Carolina's high school women poured into their games. Courtesy of the Cannon Memorial YMCA.

time when women's sports meshed neatly with the demands of daily life in communities around the state, physical educators saw limited success. By the 1950s, however, a series of shifts in both state government and national culture would combine to tip the balance in their favor, a move with far-reaching consequences for women and for sports.

In February 1936, the organizers of North Carolina's Gold Medal Amateur Independent Basketball Championships for Girls received a letter from Mary Channing Coleman, the longtime director of physical education at the North Carolina College for Women in Greensboro. "You will perhaps allow us as possible participants to ask for some details as to the objectives of the tournament," Coleman began, continuing in a manner that made clear that she was less interested in learning about the event than in influencing it. "You are, of course, familiar with the National Amateur Athletic Federation, the standard organization concerned with the promotion of women's sports in the United States," she wrote. "The platform of this organization states explicitly their position on the commercialization and exploitation of women's sports through competition concerned with gate receipts as a primary objective. We shall greatly appreciate your acquainting us with the objectives in the minds of the promoters of the tournament."[5]

The letter went on for two pages, recommending a restricted schedule ("our standard sports organizations prohibit more than one game per day"); stressing a preference for female officials ("May we ask you to assure the public that this standard will be observed"); and questioning the trophies and medals that sponsors planned to award (" 'Recognition and not reward' is the accepted procedure in modern sports"). "The topics we have brought up have no doubt been cared for by the members of your committee," Coleman concluded, "but they are so fundamental in matters of promotion and protection that you will understand our asking to be assured of our agreement regarding them." She ended the letter with a formidable array of personal credentials, signing herself "Mary Channing Coleman, Charter Member, National Amateur Athletic Federation; Member, National Committee for Women's Sports; State Committee, Amateur Athletic Union; Immediate Past President, American Physical Education Association."[6]

Mary Coleman's letter, with its mix of admonition and credentials, reflected the growth of the national women's physical education movement, which championed "moderate" exercise over high-level competition and which had grown from modest nineteenth-century beginnings into a firmly established component of the nation's educational system. During the 1920s, as the expansion of physical education into public schools created a demand for trained instructors, and as female college enrollment rose, women's physical education grew into an integral part of young women's education, with many larger schools creating full-fledged, degree-granting departments. Committed physical educators such as Mary Coleman, who came to Greensboro in 1920; Anna Hiss, who joined the University of Texas in 1919; and Maryrose Reeves Allen, who was hired to direct Howard University's physical education programs in 1925, settled into long and influential careers both within their immediate communities and in the national associations physical educators organized to spread their influence.[7]

While school varsity athletics developed growing links to the Darwinian tumult of market-oriented commerce, physical educators sought to promote alternative ideals, emphasizing the values of harmony and order that had marked the Progressive Era. As well as organizing athletic and gymnastic programs, they often promoted innovative studies of modern dance. They championed intramural rather than varsity competition, encouraged as many students as possible to participate, and limited spectators to members of a college's own community. In the 1920s, as they began to reach outside college walls, they created state-administered scoring systems through which high school students could earn the equivalent of varsity letters by amassing points for achievements that included good posture, class attendance, and schoolwork as well as athletic activity. Finally, they sought to replace varsity matches with "play days" or "sports days," in which young women combined games of various kinds with social activities.[8]

"We invited the entire basketball group from Chapel Hill to be our guests at a party and game," Mary Coleman explained in a 1940s radio talk touting the virtues of a play day that involved students from Greensboro's Curry High School and Chapel Hill High.

> You understand that I put the PARTY first and the game second as that is the way we wanted it. We played a game and instead of playing six girls from each school we played twenty. . . . Each girl who had come out for basketball in each school had an opportunity to play at some time in the game. After the game, the Curry High School boys and girls held a reception with refreshments and dancing in honor of the guests from Chapel Hill. The game lasted three quarters of an hour and the dance lasted two hours. We hardly remember what the score was—because it was by far not our first interest. Everyone had a good time.

Writing for the Women's Sports Day Association, which sponsored similar gatherings among African American colleges, Maryrose Reeves Allen described

Players from Winthrop College and Women's College in Greensboro show considerable restraint in this "play day" match. Note the distance between the players as well as the "pinnies" they wore in lieu of uniforms. Courtesy of Winthrop University.

specific goals for such events, aiming to "develop in women the qualities of poise, beauty, and femininity by affording each individual who participates an opportunity to play in an atmosphere of dignity, courtesy and refinement."[9]

As their words suggest, physical educators held a view of womanhood that diverged from the one that energetic young women had fashioned on North Carolina's basketball courts. By espousing sedate games played largely in private, educators harked back to long-standing middle-class concerns with order and decorum as well as to the Victorian philosophy of separate spheres, which held that women should separate themselves from the ills of an emerging industrial society and seek to exercise moral influence over a world too often tainted by a brutish struggle for superiority. At the same time, however, physical educators pursued a developing critique of twentieth-century U.S. culture. Specifically, they linked the excitement of public competitive strife to an expanding national culture that focused on monetary gain and that all too frequently encouraged excesses in behavior and emotion, overemphasizing the twin goals of triumphing over others and gaining the approval of a crowd. Mary Coleman frequently condemned the mass emotions associated with spectator sports, pointedly attacking the "rallies before and after games, yell leaders to tell us when to applaud, hysterics after victory, or melancholia after defeat, excursion trains, banners, broken school days because of games, expensive cups and sweaters, large stadia, over exertion and extensive publicity."[10]

Such critiques took on particular meaning for young women. Shifts in U.S. popular culture promised women greater freedom and self-expression, suggesting that they could refashion both themselves and their destinies through creative engagement with new fashions and activities. Growing public acceptance of these new visions of womanhood had given women's sports a welcome boost. But they came with costs as well. The movies, magazines, and popular fiction that brought mass culture to places such as North Carolina rarely portrayed a broad spectrum of American womanhood. Instead they focused almost exclusively on images of youthful exuberance, urban sophistication, and sexual appeal, and they encouraged young women to judge themselves largely through the reactions they produced in others, emphasizing "popularity" and attractiveness to men. The highly visual nature of this new cultural realm stressed physical appearance in particular, creating a new set of concerns for young women. Less confining clothing, for example, could reflect a new sense of self-assurance. It could also spark greater self-consciousness, heightened by a rush of advertising that presented sensationalized accounts of the social consequences of physical "defects" and offered solutions in the form of makeup, toothpaste, hair straighteners, skin creams, nylon hose, brassieres, and a wide range of diet plans.[11]

In contrast to this focus on appearance and approval, physical educators urged young women to turn inward, developing a more independent sense of their own worth. Maryrose Reeves Allen had her own interest in feminine attractiveness. But she rooted her philosophy of beauty in a wide-ranging program of physical, mental, and moral endeavors and urged her students to turn away from popular culture notions of femininity, which she associated not only with sexualized superficiality but with narrowly Anglo-Saxon standards of appearance. Her ideal woman, her writings made clear, inspired not popularity but hushed respect. "I would like to mould every one of my girls into a mould," she wrote, "so that wherever they go the world will whisper, 'I can always tell a Howard woman when I see one because she walks in such beauty.'" Mary Coleman was particularly critical of the vagaries of fashion, which she associated not with reasoned inner decisions but with attempts to conform to the judgment of others. In one of her many public lectures, she disdainfully described a letter she once received from "an anxious mother asking me not to require Mary to wear gym shoes, as it would make her feet big and lessen her chances at being supported in the style to which she was not accustomed." In contrast, Coleman noted, the discipline and energy drawn from physical education would teach Mary to support herself.[12]

As Mary Coleman's letter to the Gold Medal tournament organizers made clear, physical educators were not content with building programs at their own institutions. Rather, they sought to expand their influence, and they made women's varsity basketball one of their main targets. They would prove formidable opponents. True to their credo, most physical educators were energetic, independent, highly organized women, and they went about their work with missionary zeal. Mary Coleman, for example, began promotional work as soon as she arrived in Greensboro, meeting with representatives of local high schools and beginning to give the speeches for which she would become famous. In one two-year stint she delivered almost sixty addresses, speaking to fellow educators, Parent-Teacher Association meetings, local recreation councils, high school students, and radio audiences. She created a comprehensive and demanding physical education program at Greensboro that turned out dozens of future high school and college physical education instructors. She helped to form the first statewide organization for women's high school sports, the North Carolina High School Girls' Athletic Association, which espoused physical education philosophy and which by 1930 had almost 100 member schools. She worked tirelessly for physical education requirements in public schools, successfully lobbied for the creation of an official state coordinator of girls' high school athletics, and secured the appointment of one of her protégées, Margaret Greene, to the influential position.[13]

Coleman and her colleagues met with considerable success at high schools in the state's larger cities, where relatively wealthy school districts could afford to hire trained physical educators and where members of a growing middle class were increasingly inclined to draw sharp distinctions between male and female activities. By the late 1920s, for example, newspaper coverage of women's high school basketball in many big-city newspapers differed enormously from the support in small-town publications. In contrast to the *Hickory Daily Record*, which spoke of the Hickory High Tornadoes "walloping" the Lincolnton Wolves and referred to players as Hamrick, Ramsey, and Whitener, a 1929 *Charlotte Observer* article on basketball at Central High School not only included the courtesy title "Miss" but struck a condescending note: "Miss Marjorie Bonitz has a fine little team this year." That same year, as Central High captain Nell Presson discussed an upcoming game with rival Derita High, her determination (and her mastery of sporting lingo) showed clearly in her words. "We are mean, tough and ready," she told the *Charlotte News*. "It's not a case of one girl wanting to win, but twelve. We promise those who turn out for this classic, they'll see plenty of action and a game they'll never forget." Still, the comments of reporter Randy Edmundson suggested that he had not taken the comments as seriously as they were meant. "Miss Presson was in a talkative mood," Edmundson observed. "Never have we seen anyone so excited over a coming athletic attraction as little Nell. She has been talking up the game since Derita defeated Central several weeks ago, at Davidson."[14]

In the early 1930s Central High School became a textbook case of physical education success. Despite the confident predictions printed in the 1921 edition of the school annual, in which female players asserted that "woman's age is coming in," the 1930 volume clearly differentiated the athletic activities of male and female students. "Be it gridiron, hardwood, or diamond, Walter Dennis Skidmore is all there to instill into his charges the knowledge, skill and ability that makes champions," ran the description of the highly successful coach of the school's male teams. The account of girls' coach Marjorie Bonitz took a very different tone, suggesting that amusement rather than achievement was the main goal of the women's program: "One has to be a jack-of-all-trades to keep the girls busy, but whether it is baseball, basketball, hockey, archery or whatnot, Miss Bonitz knows." By 1933 a physical education program was in full swing. "Central's girls participated in a new type of athletics during the 1932–33 season," that annual reported. "Miss Effie Lively, director of physical education here, installed with the school's direction, intra-murals, involving the three large classes in every sport." By 1935 the girls' varsity basketball team had vanished entirely.[15]

By the late 1930s, physical educators' efforts were also bearing fruit at African American colleges, shifting the balance the state's black female students had struck between competing visions of womanly behavior and offering a particularly telling example of the issues at stake in debates about female athletics. During the 1920s and 1930s North Carolina's black college women had bridged many of the boundaries between the energetic public action embodied in competitive basketball and the controlled refinement championed by physical educators, mirroring the wide range of activities they pursued in other realms of life. But while basketball players saw their athletic activities as both reflecting and promoting their community involvement, some African American educators were less enthusiastic. Black female educators in particular walked a fine cultural line, seeking to prepare female students for community leadership while keeping a careful eye on the reactions of both their male colleagues and white society at large. At the same time the gospel of refined moderation preached by black physical educators—many of whom had earned degrees at the same northeastern schools that trained their white counterparts—also struck sympathetic chords among many black women's organizations, which often had their own roots in Progressive Era reforms and whose members were equally committed to both the idea of female moral influence and the ends to which it could be put. As a result, physical education had considerable appeal. Even as North Carolina's African American colleges had embraced women's competition, some of the country's most prestigious black institutions, including Howard, Spelman, and Fisk, had turned to physical education instead.[16]

The common combination of ambitious goals for women and a stress on female distinctiveness showed clearly in the philosophy of Howard University's influential dean of women, Lucy Diggs Slowe. Slowe held expansive ideas about women's capabilities and about the role women should play in African American communities. In a 1931 address, for example, she called for fewer regulations on female student conduct; held that young women should throw themselves into the study of economics, sociology, and political science; and assured her audience that "this present day life demands that women must be ready to make their contribution not only to the home but also to the economic, political and civic life of the communities." In other talks, however, she held up an additional set of standards, echoing the turn-of-the-century admonitions directed at Livingstone and State Normal college students. "Our women should be taught that in spite of their new found freedom that modesty, refinement, reserve and integrity are still worthwhile," she told one audience, and she urged another to focus on "the healing and inspiring ministry of beauty" through "music, drama, literature, and painting and sculpture."[17]

By the late 1930s, questions about women's activities had taken on particular urgency at African American schools, as educators negotiated tensions generated by expanding professional and educational achievements. Black women rose from one-fifth of black college enrollment in 1920 to more than half in 1940, and by 1950 almost 60 percent of black professionals were women. In 1937, when Bennett College social science instructor Merze Tate addressed a Bennett-based meeting of the National Association of College Women, an influential group of black college alumnae, the "whole vexed question of woman's 'sphere'" formed the center of her talk. "Now that woman has by general consent attained the right to the best that man has, she must seek a training that fits her own nature as well or better," Tate told her audience. She championed the education found at women's colleges such as Bennett, stressing the significance of instruction in "the cultural and esthetic." She also sought to negotiate a careful balance between calls for women's rights and assertions of feminine distinction, eschewing both "the ultra-feminism of women's rights forever, and the ultra-femininity in the idea of women always to serve the men, to produce the race, and to keep the home."[18]

As formal restrictions on college women's behavior fell away, administrators also expressed dismay at the course many female students seemed to be steering, prompting energetic efforts to promote more conventional models for some aspects of female student behavior. While Merze Tate urged her audience to "give to our girls as to our boys every intellectual opportunity that the twentieth century offers," she also asserted that "there are some things in the first century that can never be outgrown." The Association of Deans of Women and Advisors to Girls in Negro Schools directly addressed concerns about female student conduct in its 1940 meeting. "What can be done to encourage culture and dignity?" participants in one session asked, citing issues such as "failure to acquire feminine culture," "promoting better decorum," and "problems of loud noises made by so many energetic girls."[19]

The official actions association members took that year made clear that they were maneuvering among multiple concerns, including interests in well-mannered decorum, in female distinctiveness, and in the images of African Americans that appeared in mainstream culture. They commended a "Charm Movement" inspired by North Carolina educator Charlotte Hawkins Brown and recommended Brown's recently published etiquette guide, *The Correct Thing to Do, Say, and Wear*. They laid plans for an exhibit of student artwork "as means of bringing about a better appreciation of the contribution of Negro women to American culture." They wrote letters to commend the radio broadcast *Ford Hour* for hosting singer Marian Anderson and to protest *Time* magazine's "objectionable use of the word 'pickaninny' in an otherwise timely and commendable article." And they reasserted their opposition to varsity basketball, voting to "use our efforts as an organization to eliminate from our schools intercollegiate athletics for women, urging the substitution of a more constructive program of intra-mural contests and intercollegiate non-competitive play activities."[20]

By the late 1930s, championing physical education over varsity athletics in fact offered a variety of benefits that addressed many of the dilemmas that black female educators faced. Physical education allowed female educators to promote decorous behavior, to put a distinctive stamp on female education, and to identify with the practices of the nation's most prestigious educational institutions, both black and white. It also gave them a chance to seize the higher moral ground. As Frank Porter Graham learned to his chagrin, men's athletics proved stubbornly resistant to reform despite revelations about athletes who avoided study, disregarded rules of sportsmanship, and accepted money from alumni. The language in the Association of Deans of Women resolution, which referred to "more constructive" intramural activities, suggested that women were able to exercise more control over their programs and themselves. Maryrose Reeves Allen used even more direct language in her response to a 1939 attempt to reform varsity athletics at Howard, vigorously defending her department's autonomy and her focus on nonvarsity activities. Pointing to a long list of concerns about the well-documented drawbacks of male varsity competition, she adopted a somewhat condescending tone as she explained that members of her department "most heartily agree with leading women educators elsewhere that once intercollegiate athletics for women gain a foothold, college women might become involved in the same athletic predicament as their brothers."[21]

Despite the popularity that women's basketball had attained at North Carolina's African American colleges, the state's educators were far from immune to physical education's multifaceted appeal. Such influence became evident in the mid-1930s as North Carolina schools strengthened their ties with national organizations, as expanding female enrollment and changing state teacher requirements fostered more comprehensive physical education programs, and as physical educators succeeded in giving their activities an air of both progress and prestige. At Charlotte Hawkins Brown's Palmer Memorial Institute, for example, women's varsity basketball met its demise in the mid-1930s. Pictures of both male and female basketball teams were prominently featured in the school's 1931–32 bulletin. A note in the 1936–37 edition, however, explained that "in line with the latest ideas of physical education, the athletic organizations have been rebuilt to permit every student to participate, instead of limiting the activities to just a few members and teachers, as was formerly true." The reorganization appeared to have its greatest effect on women's activities. The next year the bulletin's "Yearbook" page juxtaposed pictures of male football, baseball, and basketball teams with images of young women clad in ethereal white gowns engaged in an elaborate dance production.[22]

North Carolina A&T's varsity basketball program came to a similar end in 1937, after the school hired University of Illinois graduate Ordie Roberts to direct the athletic activities of female students. Roberts, a robust woman with a fondness for dancing and tennis, went at her new job with the energy that typified physical educators' efforts. She expanded the school's meager physical education offerings, adding classes in physical education instruction, folk dancing, and modern dance as well as a "Correctives" class for women unable to keep up with regular instruction. She organized a Women's Athletic Association, designed "to encourage athletics of all types, to be appreciated and participated in by all women students." She took over the school's annual May Day celebration, expanding the festivities and turning the event into a forum for displaying physical education activities. And she moved forcefully against var-

Many physical educators encouraged modern dance instead of competitive sports. Here a dance group performs in Wellesley Auditorium at Palmer Memorial Institute in Sedalia, 1947. Courtesy of North Carolina Historic Sites, North Carolina Department of Archives and History.

sity basketball. In the spring of 1938 she laid out her position before the school's athletic committee. Her argument touched on long-standing issues of female health, contending that "intercollegiate athletics produce a harmful physical effect upon the woman participants." Roberts also appealed to the committee's sense of prestige, arguing that "all of the leading colleges and universities in the country have taken the same steps in regard to the matter." Persuaded by her presentation, committee members "voted unanimously to discontinue intercollegiate athletic competition for women students of the College."[23]

Although other state colleges maintained their varsity teams for several more years, black women's college basketball was clearly on the wane. The year after Ordie Roberts won her victory at A&T, basketball powerhouse Bennett College became the first North Carolina college to join Maryrose Allen's Women's Sports Day Association, which had been established in 1938 in response to what organizers touted as "a national trend towards de-emphasizing intercollegiate sports competition among women students." Bennett hosted its first Sports Day in 1940, inviting women from several schools and then dividing them into temporary teams that engaged in friendly competition over tennis, volleyball, and darts. Soon afterward Bennett dropped its support for varsity basketball. Other schools followed suit. By the mid-1940s the games that had created so much excitement during the 1920s and 1930s had been almost entirely replaced by sports days, gymnastics exhibitions, and intramural play.[24]


In many ways black colleges were a ready target for physical educators' efforts. The young women at North Carolina's black schools had a foot in each of two worlds and thus in two visions of womanhood. Although most of them came from modest backgrounds, communities where women were accustomed to the rough-and-tumble demands of daily life, their education was designed to usher them into the middle-class realm of refined uplift, creating a balance that proved relatively easy to tip in favor of physical education. Physical educators would find their task more difficult in North Carolina's high schools, which remained more tightly tied to the standards of their surrounding communities. Until the 1950s, physical educators' influence remained largely confined to white schools in urban areas, while rural districts, textile towns, and African American communities maintained strong support for women's varsity competition. Most African American high schools still fielded their varsity teams, and a 1951 poll of more than 400 white high schools showed an almost even split over support for regional and state championship tournaments for girls.[25]

In 1952, however, the tide began to turn, as physical educators received a major boost from a newly assertive state board of education. In the late 1940s, as a national economic boom began to gain momentum, North Carolina officials launched a broad series of efforts to help bring the state in line with more prosperous regions of the country. Along with commissioning new rounds of highway construction and laying plans to attract high-technology industries, state officials worked to raise the level of instruction in the state's public schools, which lagged badly behind national averages. State school officials restructured curricula, sought funding increases, and began a round of high school consolidation. They also decided to rein in high school athletics, which were seen as drawing money and attention from academic goals.[26]

School officials, both black and white, had fretted for decades about the power that school sports could wield, and efforts at athletic reform drew widespread support from many corners of the state. In 1952, when a committee of state-level administrators set out to centralize the state's "jumbled" athletic programs, the *Greensboro Daily News* linked the effort directly to the state's broader social and economic aspirations. "It was something needed for a decade, something which had been in force in other states for many years," the article ran, asking rhetorically, "Was North Carolina actually this backward in education, in athletics, in community co-ordination?" Apparently it was. In 1952, arguing that "the athletic activities in the public schools of the State are

causing dissatisfaction and in many instances disruption in the successful ex-
ecution of instructional services," the state board of education adopted its first
high school athletic code.[27]

The code covered a broad range of issues, ruling on eligibility, grades, and
financial support and placing specific limits on competition in all sports. But
the measure dealing with women's basketball was particularly harsh, clearly
reflecting the influence that physical educators had gained within the state's
educational bureaucracy. Although male teams were permitted two postseason
tournaments, which included state championship play, women's teams were
limited to only one such contest. And rather than acknowledging the successes
of statewide tournaments such as the Girls' Invitational, the code banned them
altogether, specifying, "There shall be no regional or State championship games
for girls."[28]

That provision touched off a statewide debate over the nature of women's
athletics, as supporters and opponents wrote letters, lobbied state officials, and
aired their positions in the press. A public hearing held in April 1952 set out the
battle lines. At the hearing, Bob Lee stressed the advantages that competitive
basketball offered young women and argued for equal treatment, making his
claim that "if it was good or bad for the boys then the same thing applied to the
girls." A group of college-based physical educators, among them Mary Coleman's protégée Margaret Greene, countered that women should be treated
differently, invoking long-standing arguments about the need to guard young
women's health and reputation. The disagreement produced a "lively discussion" in which "points of view backed by statistics and scientific studies over
many, many years, were discussed." In the end, however, the physical educators
prevailed. When the code was formally adopted, the rule remained intact.[29]

The Girls' Invitational would be held one last time, thanks to a group of
legislators concerned about state government's expanding reach. Representatives from North Carolina's rural counties were already chafing at the growing
centralization of state school authority, and they had been particularly disturbed by a wave of high school consolidation that gave students access to a
wider range of academic programs but provoked enormous resentment in
many communities. This simmering dissatisfaction erupted when Representative William Copeland introduced a measure to exempt coastal Camden
County, which sponsored a popular, five-county women's contest, from the ban
on regional tournaments. Legislators from the state's 100 counties listened to
his arguments and then launched a supportive stampede in which "the name of
one county after another was added by that county representative until the
House total was 81." The legislators cast the issue as a clear question of state
versus local authority. "Our people and the county board feel they are fully

qualified to regulate the sports activities of their daughters," Senator A. P. Godwin Jr. of Nash County declared.[30]

The legislation cleared the way for the 1953 state tournament, at which Bob Lee's Aberdeen team won its first and only crown. But physical educators did not give up the fight. That spring, after emotions had cooled, they persuaded a sympathetic legislator to introduce a modified tournament ban. North Carolina's legislators had never distinguished themselves by their support for women's rights; they had refused to ratify the Nineteenth Amendment and would not vote in support of woman suffrage until the 1970s. The ban became law in the waning hours of the 1953 spring session, and North Carolina women's basketball would never be the same.[31]

The advent of statewide standards governing school sports was one of several postwar developments in which the spreading influence of state and national institutions boded ill for women's basketball. The sport had flourished in tight-knit communities where close family connections and a dearth of other social activities had made local institutions the center of community life. But after World War II, as North Carolina's cities began to attract more of the state's citizens and as improved roads and increased car ownership added to residents' mobility, high school basketball found itself competing with a variety of new entertainments. The widespread high school consolidations of the 1950s struck another blow to school athletic programs, disrupting traditional team rivalries and loyalties. Simultaneously, the advent of television broadcasts brought a new, remarkably powerful influence to bear on North Carolinians' lives, with major implications for a range of spectator sports.

The most immediate effects of such transformations could be seen in textile basketball. In the late 1940s, North Carolina women's textile teams had reached unprecedented competitive heights, a rise that climaxed when the team that represented Winston-Salem's Hanes Hosiery plant won the national AAU championship in 1951, 1952, and 1953. But the very next year, Hanes management disbanded the team, citing a drop in game attendance. The decision, which echoed similar moves at companies around the country, marked the end of an era in industrial sports. "All of a sudden we had competition with television," Hanes player Eunies Futch later explained. "Everybody had a car. . . . You could see it coming."[32]

Men's sports suffered as well. Attendance declined for men's textile teams as well as women's, and minor and Negro league professional baseball teams fell on hard times. But women's sports sustained by far the greatest damage. Dwindling audiences at local athletic events reflected not a waning interest in spectator sports, but rather a growing concentration of attention on those sports able to gain broad-based appeal. Even as minor league baseball suffered, for example, the major leagues increased their audience, boosted both by television broadcasts and by the black fans drawn to newly integrated teams. Television helped transform professional football from a minor sport into a national obsession and contributed to the surge of popularity enjoyed by men's college basketball. Women's sports, conversely, played almost no role in this new cultural alignment. Aside from an occasional spectacular individual, such as the multitalented Babe Didrikson Zaharias, U.S. female athletes had almost no national reputations and received little publicity outside their immediate communities.[33]

The reflected allure of big-time sports, boosted by a growing number of college athletic scholarships, helped maintain interest in men's high school sports. As North Carolina's major colleges began their rise toward national renown, drawing on star players from the basketball hotbeds of Kansas, Indiana, New Jersey, and New York, they also nurtured homegrown talent. "We made talks at all the schools in the state trying to get them new gyms," recalled North Carolina State assistant coach Carl Anderson. "We would go around to the Ruritan Clubs and the other groups trying to encourage people about building a facility where they could have town meetings and such. Really we just wanted them to build a gymnasium so we could get some boys from North Carolina. . . . Our idea was to get the gyms built and to let the game grow so we could recruit in the state."[34]

The program for the 1951 NCHSAA championship tournament underlined the extent to which excitement about men's college ball could translate into interest in boys' high school play. In the introduction to the tournament program, writer Bill Strickland dwelt less on the games than on the players' futures, explaining that "the prep school boys seem to get that old college try in their systems early nowdays" and noting that "there'll probably be plenty of the state's college coaches down looking over future prospects." Previous player successes, he continued, underscored the tournament's merits. "Taking a look at the college rosters this year, we found Bull Newsome playing for Lenoir-Rhyne, Eddie Morris and Bobby Goss on the N.C. State varsity, Jippy Carter at North Carolina, Conrad West at High Point, Bobby Hodges and Sonny Russell at East Carolina, Dick Crowder right here at Duke, John McGraw at Clemson and Milly Mason at Wake Forest—all graduated from these high school tournaments during the past three years."[35]

The year before, North Carolina State coach Everett Case had offered his own rhapsodic paean to the basketball fever spreading throughout the state. "Everywhere you go now you find youngsters imitating these players, and they are learning the game that way," he said. "Now when you travel around the state, you

see hoops hung on pine trees and backboards and baskets on almost every va-
cant lot. The sporting goods stores have told me that during the past Christmas
season they sold more baskets and backboards than they ever had before. Indiana, New York and New Jersey became leaders in basketball because the youngsters played at every opportunity. Now they are doing it in North Carolina."[36]

But while the state's young women might have been inspired by the new
brand of ball, might have hung hoops on backyard pines, and might have
spurred themselves to master one-handed jump shots and rapid-fire passes,
they found fewer and fewer opportunities to exercise such skills. Although
support for women's basketball remained strong within many communities,
even successful teams could not ignore the growth of the men's game. In 1951, as
state school officials were beginning to weigh the merits of women's play, some
college basketball enthusiasts began to suggest that interest in women's basketball was keeping North Carolina's homegrown male players from reaching their
full potential. *Greensboro Daily News* columnist George Webb, discussing the
controversy over the girls' state high school tournament, made note of "the
feeling expressed by one prominent college coach in the state who blamed girls'
basketball for causing a lack of interest around North Carolina in boys' play."[37]

In a state with limited resources, the growing interest in men's basketball
began to squeeze the women's game. Bill Bost, the Claremont player who had
been so inspired by Sammy Ranzino's one-handed shooting, encountered this
unexpected consequence after he graduated from college and began a high
school coaching career. Soon after he started to coach a women's team, he
discovered that one of his tasks was simply keeping his players on the court.
When he was in high school, the Claremont women's basketball team had been
the most celebrated squad at the school, packing the gymnasium and garnering
statewide recognition with tournament victories and phenomenal win-loss
records. His senior year, when he and All-State guard Mildred Bauguess were
voted "Most Athletic," his reputation paled beside her statewide fame. But by
the late 1950s, girls' teams throughout the state were defending themselves from
ambitious boys' coaches, who coveted the gym time the women used for practice and who sought to turn the prestigious institution of Friday night basketball into an all-male affair, eliminating the women's game in favor of showcas-
ing the boy's junior varsity. "When I first started coaching girls, they tried to do
away with it," Bost explained. "Boys' coaches especially. They wanted to have a
J.V. boys, and a varsity boys. And they would say: 'Well, if you want to play a
girls' game, play it on Wednesday afternoon.' "[38]

Even as growing interest in men's basketball placed pressure on remaining
women's teams, the dearth of women's athletic scholarships excluded women
from the powerful equation that so profoundly linked male athletic skill to

Ridgeview High School forwards Barbara Derr, Fannie Gaston, and Minnie Sue Full-wood, 1951. Although Ridgeview coaches warmly supported women's basketball, the lack of college scholarships for women meant that coaches poured their greatest efforts into men. Courtesy of Barbara Derr Fish.

social, educational, and economic opportunities. Young women such as Cath-erine Whitener Salmons had confronted those constraints in earlier decades. When Salmons told her parents she had been asked to join the Blanketeers of Chatham Mills, her mother responded, "You are not going to any mill and work. You're going to get you some kind of education."[39] After the war, as athletic scholarship opportunities expanded and as a broader spectrum of Americans aspired to higher education, this difference encouraged parents and coaches to focus their efforts even more closely on young men, whose skills could bring them not simply community acclaim but also a coveted college degree.

Burrell Brown, who coached both boys and girls at Hickory's Ridgeview High School, lavished attention on his male players specifically so they could win college scholarships. But despite his strong support for women's sports, he adopted a different approach with women, including his own daughter. "I had some discipline," he explained. "It was the type of discipline that if I wasn't coaching no coach would want. My daughter made first team. She was first team. And her grades fell. From A to B. And she had to get off the team. That was my discipline. At that time there was nowhere they could go to school on scholarship. And we wanted scholarship aid, and we got it because she became an A student again. It hurt her I imagine in that respect. It hurt me inside—I wouldn't let her know it. But she did graduate from college. And she's working—she's a teacher now." The accumulation of pressures and decisions throughout the state led to a drop in the number of women's varsity basketball teams and in interest in women's sports. While women's teams maintained community support in some corners of the state, most had trouble generating as much excitement as their male counterparts.[40]

The decline of women's basketball dramatically transformed local sporting culture, a shift suggested in the diverging experiences of Gladys Worthy and Mildred Bauguess. Worthy's sons grew up amid the heady atmosphere of big-time men's college ball, and even though the Worthys never built a basketball goal at their Gastonia home, the boys found plenty of places to play. Mildred Bauguess, who starred for both Claremont High and Hanes Hosiery, saw her own athletic legacy persist within the small community of Claremont for decades. "Right now, I can walk downtown, and at least eight out of ten people will say: 'You're the one who played ball,'" she recalled in 1993. "This many years off, forty-some years ago. . . . 'You're the one that played ball.'" But like many of the women who had fashioned such athletic history, she found that her daughters had little interest in the game. Despite their parents' efforts, their priorities lay elsewhere. "We had put the basketball goal up, and had it fixed to official height and everything else," Bauguess explained. "And all the boys in the neighborhood played, but they never played. Neither one of them."[41]

On the surface this widespread decline of women's competition represented a significant victory for physical educators, who now had women's sports almost to themselves. In reality, however, this triumph proved largely hollow. The women who so adamantly opposed competitive basketball had wagered that the demise of varsity women's sports would increase interest in what they saw as the more substantive benefits of physical education classes. "As long as emphasis is placed upon the game of basketball for girls as a spectator sport . . . the development of a real girls' physical education program in North Carolina will be retarded," wrote one supporter of the state tournament ban. But that is not what happened.[42]

Rather than sparking greater participation in physical education, the decline of women's varsity play instead cleared the field for a third set of female sports-related activities, a shift highlighted in a decision made by the NCHSAA in 1952. Even as many state educators were arguing that girls should not be permitted to compete in a state basketball championship, the athletic association promised to add "a note of color" to the boys' state tournament by instituting both a cheerleading contest and a "Tournament Queen" beauty pageant. Cheerleaders deserved this honor, a *Greensboro Daily News* writer explained, because "take away the cheerleaders from the hundreds of high school basketball games in the state and what do you have? Just a dull display of physical prowess." School officials, the article continued, "recognize the cheerleaders as a vital part of their athletic program, the part which puts 'school spirit' into the student body." The prize would be awarded to the "best and most enthusiastic" squad, which then could "put its claim as 'state champion' in its own right."[43]

The new prominence accorded cheerleaders and beauty queens highlighted yet another facet of North Carolina's developing sporting culture. In the 1920s and 1930s, as eager young female players were establishing basketball teams and as physical educators were seeking to solidify their hold over state institutions, growing numbers of cheerleaders, majorettes, and homecoming queens were making their own claims on the athletic world, with considerable success. In 1931, for example, the student newspaper at North Carolina A&T pointed out the many roles that the school's newly admitted female students were beginning to play in college life. As well as noting that female students had come out in large numbers for the women's basketball team, the *Register* explained that "plans are under way for a Popularity Contest, under auspices of the Y.W.C.A. On this occasion the students' choice for 'Miss A. & T.' will be made. It will be well for every student to return after holidays with their favorite in mind, so that the contest may be carried out successfully and the most popular co-ed be elected." A decade later, A&T no longer had a women's basketball team. But the contest for Miss A&T, who also served as the school's homecoming queen, had become one of the most significant events on campus. "The selection of Miss A. and T. must be a wise one, for she is the official lady representative of the student body for the coming year," the *Register* cautioned in 1942, adding that the titleholder should "be a living example . . . of a lady with charm, mental ability and physical beauty."[44]

The *Register*'s insistence that Miss A&T be not only intelligent but also beautiful pointed to a key feature of the developing cultural assumptions that helped shape women's entrance into twentieth-century public life, as well as one of the major factors behind the popularity of female cheerleaders. Cheerleading had its roots in the same men's colleges that first instituted varsity sports, and for the first decades of its existence it was largely an all-male activity. Female cheerleading, which began to gather strength in coeducational high schools during the 1920s, sparked concerns similar to those prompted by women's basketball. As well as questioning the propriety of public physical display, critics asked whether women would be able to perform the acrobatic stunts that male cheerleaders had developed and worried that loud chants and yells would damage female voices. As with women's basketball, women's cheerleading developed strong supporters who defended young women's abilities. But advocates of female cheerleading could also draw on a different argument, one that resonated with the growing cultural emphasis on female appearance and defined cheerleaders' accomplishments less through measurable skills than through their effect on an audience. While young women might not be up to the acrobatic challenges met by male cheerleaders, argued one midwestern advocate, they had advantages of their own: "Girls are more magnetic in appearance and will become the center of attention for the crowd and the leading of cheers will, therefore, be easy."[45]

This conclusion, which privileged appearance over skill, would be frequently invoked in North Carolina. The Greensboro publishers of a short-lived college basketball magazine, for example, opened their inaugural issue with a photograph of their designated "Queen of North Carolina Basketball," a young woman named Norma Jean McMillan. "Miss McMillan is a freshman at Guilford College," the description ran. "She is also a cheerleader, but she was chosen by PREVIEW because we think she is a very pretty young woman. No other reason." Similarly, when editors at the *Register* designated the school's majorettes "Students of the Month" in October 1950, the description that accompanied the women's picture focused specifically on their looks. "Though the majorettes are vivacious and talented, they add beautification to our campus as well as the band," the writer rhapsodized. "When our majorette marches before an audience, an inspiring thought twirls in our minds that A. and T. has beauty as well as talent."[46]

The celebration of cheerleaders, majorettes, and a variety of homecoming and tournament queens meshed neatly with the emphasis on gender distinction that emerged with renewed force in U.S. popular culture after World War II. While wartime female images had blended glamour with accounts of strength and independence, after the war U.S. women were bombarded with a new wave of movies, magazines, and television programs that cast feminine virtue in terms of marriage and physical allure, featuring women with large bosoms, tiny waists, carefully styled hair, and increasingly elaborate applications of makeup. Such images also began to reach a broader swath of the U.S. population as a wide range of advertisers touting beauty products targeted beneficiaries of postwar economic expansion.[47]

A newly discovered teenage market inspired numerous teen-oriented publications, such as *Seventeen* magazine, which rhapsodized at length about romantic love and featured articles and advertisements that urged readers to become more popular by purchasing products that fit fashion trends or corrected physical defects. African Americans also drew new attention, as suggested by the national successes of *Ebony* and *Jet* magazines as well as by the pages of A&T's *Register*, which sported a new crop of advertisements that portrayed classic 1950s images of attractive people having a good time while consuming name-brand products. In 1950, for example, a typical ad featured Sheila Guyse, a light-skinned, elegantly coiffed "Glamorous singing star of motion pictures and Broadway." Beneath the picture, ad copy touted the popularity of Chesterfield cigarettes in a set of phrases that posed significantly different aspirations for men and women. "They're MILDER! They're TOPS! In America's Colleges. With the Top Men in Sports. With the Hollywood Stars."[48]

Relationships between such images and portraits of female students were evident in the *Register*'s pages as well. In the summer of 1934, for example, the paper featured Sammie Sellars, a South Carolina native who had been chosen Miss A&T for the coming school year. The picture showed a plainly dressed young woman with a serene look, a simple hairstyle, and no visible makeup, and the article focused on her membership in school organizations, which included the basketball team. In contrast, a 1950 photograph of student-of-the-month Helen McWilliams in many ways resembled that of Sheila Guyse. The accompanying description mentioned McWilliams's suitability as a future Miss A&T, noting specifically that she was "keen featured and well proportioned." Her accomplishments were listed in suggestive order, emphasizing popularity over substantive accomplishment. " 'Miss Co-ed' for the year 1949–1950, and 'Sigma's Sweetheart' have been two of her most noteworthy positions held. She has also been or is Secretary of the Fellowship Council, President of the Y.W.C.A., Secretary to the Dean of Women, Member of the Business Club, Sunday School Teacher and Chairman of the Condolence Committee." According to the writer, she also knew how to cook.[49]

As suggested by the growing prominence of basketball queens such as Norma Jean McMillan, the spotlight on men's sports—particularly college basketball—made significant contributions to this crystallizing vision of male and female roles. Like many other tournament organizers, Dixie Classic officials each year conducted an elaborate search for a tournament queen, who received airfare to the tournament, lodgings, a prominent position in newspaper articles, and a fresh corsage each day. Again, physical attraction served as the main criterion, although other factors occasionally played supplementary roles. "We have finally been able to select our Dixie Classic Queen, and we are enclosing several pictures which we believe are indicative of the young lady's true appearance," organizer Harry James wrote in a 1956 press release, noting that Marie Barlow was a Mormon who possessed a figure that measured 35-23-35. "We had twenty-nine contestants," James continued, "and the girl we picked was one whom we felt would be a fine representative, both from the standpoint of beauty, and also due to the fact, she comes from a famous University of Utah basketball family."[50]

Even more than cheerleaders, tournament queens underscored divisions between men and women. Queens sat well removed from the melee on the court, replete in fresh corsages and flawless, feminine outfits. They set a tone by the charm of their appearance, while also contributing to the erotic electricity that postwar culture was beginning to build around a set of ever-sharper male-female distinctions. The *Greensboro Daily News* account of the high school tournament queen competition, which dismissed the pure athletic contest as simply a "dull display of physical prowess," suggested the growing significance of sexual appeal in postwar culture. At times such erotic dynamics could even overshadow sports themselves. Perhaps the most memorable Dixie Classic queen was Tulane student Sarah French, who presented Sammy Ranzino with the 1950 championship trophy and then kissed him with such fervor that he dropped it.[51]

A growing emphasis on similar pageantry at high school sports events made clear the wide-ranging influence that college basketball was beginning to have on high school play. A few days before the 1952 NCHSAA competition, for example, officials proudly announced that "Duke's Dick Groat and State's Lee Terrill, who have opposed each other three times during the past basketball season, will be on the same team here Friday night during the fifth annual state high school basketball tournament. Teaming with Wake Forest's Tunney Brooks, the two all-time Big Four greats will serve as judges in the contest to select the schoolboy tournament queen." Five days later, newly crowned Mary Trepke, representing High Point High School, handed the championship trophy to the winning team from Raleigh High, which had edged Greensboro by the score of 51-49.[52]


Young women seized on cheerleading, as they had on basketball, because it offered a prominent, public role in a major community institution as well as a

Dixie Classic Queen Sarah French brought an unmistakable erotic charge to Reynolds Coliseum when she kissed Sammy Ranzino at the close of play in 1950. Reprinted by permission of the *News and Observer* of Raleigh, North Carolina.

challenging activity. Cheerleading encompassed its own range of skills, requiring young women to work together, develop poise and coordination, and learn to handle the pressures of performing before large crowds. The activity also appealed to some physical educators, who saw in it the values of cooperation that were so central to physical education programs. While Mary Coleman had spoken disdainfully of "yell leaders" who "tell us when to applaud," Maryrose Reeves Allen embraced the activity, and supportive descriptions of Howard cheerleaders became a fixture in her annual reports. "This group was made up of about twenty very talented faithful young women and they exhibited a sense of love and loyalty to the University at all times," Allen wrote in 1956. "Too much praise cannot be given them. The department is looking to them for the kind of cheer leading squad that will always be spontaneous, creative and representative."[53]

Finally, just as the physical challenges of basketball had resonated with the broader experiences of its rural, working-class, and African American participants, the emphasis on well-groomed female beauty that cheerleading embodied meshed neatly with the less boyishly robust notions of femininity that prevailed in urban, middle-class communities. At Lincolnton High School, one player recalled, the difference between young women who played basketball and those who cheered on the sidelines was particularly clear. Basketball players at the small-town school usually came from rural areas or textile mill communities, she explained. In contrast, "The city girls got to be the cheerleaders."[54]

As cheerleading was redefined to encompass female participation, it began to lose its appeal among young men. Although cheerleading squads often retained a handful of male members, by the 1940s young women clearly dominated the ranks in many North Carolina institutions. This shift dismayed some people who had been proud of male participation in this school-boosting activity, including A&T chaplain Cleo McCoy. In 1947 McCoy "made many heads hang in shame" when he lamented that "A. and T. College used to be an all-boys school. What do you think the alumni will think when they come back here Saturday, and find twice as many girls on the cheering squad as boys?" Three years later McCoy remained dissatisfied, complaining that "only one or two men" had gone out for cheerleading, even though men outnumbered women on the campus by almost four to one.[55]

The shifting relationships between athletics, cheerleading, and masculine and feminine ideals were highlighted in changes that took place at Charlotte's Central High School. Elizabeth Newitt, a star basketball player who sought "to be very much like the boys," was voted the school's most attractive student in 1923. The school's 1939 annual, however, told a very different story. The most striking section of the publication featured full-page photographs of fourteen

Cheerleading squad, Winston-Salem Teacher's College, 1945. By the mid-1940s young women dominated cheering squads at most North Carolina schools. Courtesy of the University Archives, Winston-Salem State University.

students described as the school's most appealing examples of female beauty. The sexual current running through the choices was unmistakable, as the women had been selected "not by a beauty expert from photographs, but by a host of beauty experts, the boys of Central." While the chosen fourteen included two of the school's three female cheerleaders, not one of the twenty-eight women basketball players made the cut.[56]

Women's sports had the potential to encompass physical appeal as well. By the mid-1950s, however, a growing polarization between "masculine" and "feminine" activities, which contributed to widespread associations between "mannish" female athletes and suspicions of lesbianism, made it increasingly difficult for female athletes to blend athletic skill into socially acceptable versions of femininity, particularly when they no longer defended a school's honor in high-level varsity competition. Nationally, top-level female athletes had frequently come under sexual suspicion. Such critiques reached their height in the case of Babe Didrikson Zaharias, whose remarkable exploits were met with considerable admiration but also sparked ongoing innuendoes concerning her physical womanhood. The advent of the Cold War, which invested men's athletics with such potent moral force, had the opposite effect on women's sport. In the 1950s, U.S. sportswriters scrambled to explain the dominance that Soviet female athletes enjoyed in Olympic competition, eventually seizing on the reassuring theory that "strong Red ladies" could be contrasted with "frail Red males." Soviet women were compared disparagingly to less successful but more "feminine" U.S. competitors and were described with charming sobriquets such as Hefty Heroine or Tank-Shaped Tamara.[57]

As well as affecting women's competition, the growing split between athletic activities and more overtly feminine endeavors began to hamper physical educators as well. Their deep commitment to their athletic pursuits, along with a tendency to remain single, meant that physical educators themselves diverged from sharpening feminine conventions. Many found themselves beset by growing innuendoes of lesbianism, even as they faced droves of young women who had limited interest in athletic activity of any kind. Concerns about their public image, along with a growing nationwide uncertainty about how best to handle frequently rebellious young people, complicated physical educators' efforts to vigorously promote their athletic vision. Advice to educators during the 1950s frequently suggested that teachers adapt to what were seen as young people's own priorities. In the case of women's sports, such recommendations drew on prevailing assumptions about the importance of physical allure. "The mores of society decree that girls should not excel in physical skill after the early adolescent period," stated the authors of an article in the Chapel Hill–based *High School Journal*, championing programs that would accommodate rather than challenge such concerns. A half-century before, physical educators had forcefully stressed health over fashion, as when Mary Coleman brushed off complaints that wearing gym shoes would enlarge a young woman's feet, or when one of her predecessors, New Orleans's legendary Clara Baer, forced students to "sweat off" their corsets. The *High School Journal* promoted a far different approach, at one point describing an effective gym teacher as someone who "will not insist on swimming which would ruin a $1.50 hairdress."[58]

As the *High School Journal* articles suggested, postwar physical education classes often became a forum not for the development of skills but for the display of what was seen as charming awkwardness. At Charlotte's Central High, which had eliminated varsity competition in the 1930s, this tendency was clear as early as the 1940s. In 1946 Mickie Bradley scored 1,300 points on the physical-education-inspired state point system, a considerable achievement (a mere 400 points were needed to win the state equivalent of a varsity letter). But in the school annual her feat was submerged in a comic depiction of physical

The basketball efforts of this 1954 Harding High School physical education class were more amusing than impressive. From *The Acorn*; photograph courtesy of the Robinson-Spangler Carolina Room, Public Library of Charlotte and Mecklenburg County.

education classes, which juxtaposed photographs of young women in ungainly poses with humorously condescending comments such as "Check those gams!" "Maybe she can't get down," and "Why would anyone want to do this?" Early in the century, members of one enthusiastic Charlotte team had dubbed themselves The Amazons. The description of the Central High School classes was titled "Our Glamazons."[59]

The triumph of cheerleading over both varsity sports and physical education underscored the risks inherent in the strategy physical educators had adopted when they turned their backs on varsity athletics in favor of more privately focused character-building efforts. In their campaign against varsity sports, North Carolina's physical educators had set themselves a bold and ambitious task. Rather than meshing their athletic philosophy with the society taking shape around them, they sought to fashion games and sports that challenged some of the central components of twentieth-century society: competition, financial success, popularity, and female sexual appeal. In turn they calculated that the young women shaped by their efforts would help to guide society in the direction of an alternate social vision. As an essay in a 1948 basketball guide put it, "We women are different from boys so that everything that is good for a boy is not necessarily good for a girl. We must not lose those innately feminine qualities which men respect, for it is through those qualities that we, as women, can help raise the living standards of society."[60]

As the quotation suggests, however, physical educators carved out their space largely by playing on prevailing assumptions about differences between men and women. Physical educators had fashioned what was in many ways a powerful critique of modern society, posing fundamental questions about intensive competition, passive spectatorship, and the superficiality of many of the values embodied in commercial popular culture. In theory these ideas applied to young men as well as to young women. Mary Coleman directed some of her most pointed comments at college football programs. The state education officials who banned the girls' state basketball championship would have liked to eliminate the boys' event as well. But by the early twentieth century, popular support for organized male sports was strong enough to deflect most attempts to curb young men's competition. Physical educators thus gained outside support not through their more substantive critique of U.S. society, but rather by working to refute assertions that what was good for boys was also good for girls, thus creating a separate realm for women's sports.

In adopting such a strategy physical educators stood in a distinguished line of female reformers who had cloaked pioneering social efforts in the white gloves, impeccable manners, and domestic imagery of feminine convention, effectively deflecting attention from the substantive social changes they were pursuing. As in the past, the assertion of distinctive female nature could serve several ends, bolstering claims to female authority, masking activities that otherwise might threaten male status or identity, and defending the autonomy of women's institutions. But the triumph of cheerleading over both varsity sports and physical education revealed the growing drawbacks of this approach. In a world where image and mass communication were gaining greater sway over U.S. society, abandoning the highly public realm of competitive athletics held particular perils. Limiting the role that women played in such a significant cultural activity to that of attractive cheerleaders posed little challenge to popularly prevailing concepts of competition, sexuality, or commercialism. Rather, it relegated women to a tightly restricted position within that larger cultural complex.

The implications of this development could perhaps be most clearly seen at African American colleges. The athletic model that developed at black schools after World War II, in which men competed while women cheered or sat enthroned on the sidelines, formed a stark contrast to the roles filled by men and women in academic matters, student organizations, and almost every other college activity. On one level this disparity might seem of limited importance. Many parents and educators would certainly have applauded Burrell Brown's decision to end his daughter's basketball career in favor of academic work. But it was athletics that garnered by far the greatest public notice, becoming a major advertisement of the "realities" of college life. Early in the twentieth century black colleges had built their public images largely around their famed choral ensembles, coeducational groups that toured the nation to give concerts and raise funds. By midcentury, however, athletics had assumed much of that function, serving as the focus not only for most media coverage of school activities but for large, emotional gatherings of students and alumni.

Throughout much of the country, visions of virile male athletes cheered on by alluring female cheerleaders became a key component of a postwar culture in which increasing numbers of women were held to narrowing standards of conduct and appearance, called upon to be cooperative, supportive and sexually attractive. Such images would provide ammunition for opponents of women's attempts to transcend conventional female roles and would often impose significant strains on women who openly challenged this sharply gendered order. The compelling rituals that sports events created—the large, public gatherings; the dramatic displays of male strength and daring; and the roars of approval for highly feminine and often sexually suggestive cheering squads—could have profound psychological as well as intellectual repercussions and may well have played a particularly significant role in reinforcing such assumptions.[61]

These narrowing horizons offer a sharp contrast to the narrative of postwar progress that became a staple of North Carolina public and athletic life. In this story the remarkable postwar development of men's college basketball meshes neatly with visions of a state where growing ties to national institutions and priorities sparked a range of modernizing benefits, including economic expansion, educational advancement, and a growing racial liberalism. The concurrent demise of women's basketball raises a host of questions about this story, about the temptation to see history through the rosy lens of progress, and about the significance of the middle-class culture that had come to dominate state as well as national institutions. Women's basketball had flourished in precisely those areas that lay at the margins of this dominant public culture: rural regions, working-class communities, the South itself. Such patterns challenge widespread assumptions that cast urban areas in general and the Northeast in particular as the vanguard of cultural progress or modern thought—particularly since it was precisely the expanding reach of urban, middle-class influences that undermined such a significant, thoroughly modern women's institution.

Such questions, however, garnered little public notice in the late 1950s. Instead, as North Carolina's leaders worked to expand the state's economic appeal, and as a rising tide of African American protest brought a new urgency to questions of race, women's basketball slipped quietly away, taking with it a particularly significant realm of development and self-discovery. While cheerleading offered a mirror of commercial culture, and physical education sought to promote a more private set of ethics, competitive basketball had allowed young women to mediate between these various realms, moving between their own interests, the priorities of their communities, and those of the world outside. The expansive sense of possibility that basketball offered its participants had produced enormous strength and satisfaction as well as joyous enthusiasm. The closing of such opportunities had equally profound effects.

The rueful recollections of West Charlotte player Mary Alyce Clemmons, who like many other young women found her basketball career cut short in the early 1950s, hints at both the expansive possibilities that varsity sports could offer and the pain involved in the decline of such a significant institution. Clemmons loved athletics and idolized Babe Didrikson. While she was in high school, reveling in her own sporting accomplishments, Clemmons was able to look past the condescension that frequently marked reports of Didrikson's athletic feats, as well as racial difference, to find inspiration in the realities of her heroine's accomplishments. But her confidence was shaken when her own athletic ambitions were thwarted by local institutions, specifically Johnson C. Smith University, which by the time Clemmons enrolled, offered only intramural women's play. "I could see it coming," she explained. "I felt as if I were being betrayed. But what can you do? There weren't the organizations that could go speak. [We were] all black and had no voice. Nothing that could be said. I thought of myself as another Babe Didrikson Zaharias. I thought I could do anything athletically that I had the opportunity to do. But that was the missing thing, the opportunity. . . . I thought I would play basketball until I couldn't move anymore. But it didn't work out like that. Didn't work out that way at all."[62]

## CHAPTER NINE

# The Seat of the Trouble

## Athletes, Cheerleaders, and Civil Rights, 1938–1971

In early February 1968 the starting fives for the North Carolina State Wolfpack and the University of North Carolina Tar Heels trotted out onto the Reynolds Coliseum floor, prepared for yet another episode in a long and heated rivalry. Despite a freezing storm that had closed the public schools and turned roads into treacherous sheets of ice, Reynolds, as always, was packed full with loyal Wolfpack fans. The lights of Everett Case's applause meter flickered up and down to the rhythm of their cheers, and as the players readied themselves for the opening jump ball, the air tingled with a familiar anticipation. But there was a major difference on the floor that night, a difference obvious to everyone in the arena. For the first time in the schools' half-century of basketball rivalry, the players ringed around the center line were not all white. UNC sophomore Charlie Scott, a slender, 6′6″ African American forward, would be the focus of attention for much of the night, in part for his great skill and in part for his race. The game was a dogged battle that, in the estimation of the *Daily Tar Heel*, "looked more like the roller derby than it did a basketball game," and which the Tar Heels won by the close and relatively low score of 68-66. Amid the shoving and shouting, Scott found himself the target not only of State players' elbows but of some State fans' insults. As the *Daily Tar Heel* discreetly put it, "'Hey Leroy, show us your stuff,' was one of the nicer things yelled at Scott."[1]

Charlie Scott's much-publicized Tar Heel career marked a turning point in North Carolina, the beginning of a transformation in the way many state residents thought about their flagship university and its most venerated team. The Reynolds Coliseum game, in which one group of North Carolinians rallied behind a black player while a handful of others sought refuge in racial epithets, spotlighted the uneven movements of a society in uneasy transition. Scott's breach of a long-held color line outraged some North Carolinians. UNC coach

Charlie Scott takes a shot against North Carolina State. Courtesy of Hugh Morton.

Dean Smith would carefully preserve the angry letters he received after announcing that he had signed the state's most talented high school player, a young man who, according to official statements, only happened to be black. North Carolina State supporters would not be the only ones to shout insults, and in 1969, a year during which Scott dominated ACC play, five voters for league honors would omit him from their first-team ballots. But other white fans focused on the skills that Scott so obviously possessed. A few days before the game in Reynolds Coliseum, *Charlotte News* sportswriter Ronald Green had described him as the talk of the state, and "only incidentally because he is the first Negro to become a genuine star" in North Carolina. "His feats have been heralded, his talents weighed where ever basketball is talked in this area," Green continued. "It is generally agreed that he is destined to become one of the outstanding players the league has ever produced."[2]

For the state's African Americans, Scott's career meant even more, providing a welcome sign that racial barriers could indeed be breached. The postwar excitement sparked by ACC teams had attracted black as well as white fans. In 1959, when Stanley Johnson arrived at Fayetteville State Teachers' College from Washington, D.C., he was surprised to find so many fellow students avidly rooting for ACC teams, even though the schools enrolled only token numbers of African Americans. Scott was also a familiar figure to black North Carolinians— the New York native had spent a portion of his high school career at Laurinburg Institute, a private black academy in Laurinburg, North Carolina. During his high school years, basketball enthusiasts had crowded black school gymnasiums from Raleigh to Charlotte just to see him play. "When they would play West Charlotte here, you're talking about a game that would draw anywhere from three thousand maybe to six thousand people," recalled Rudolph Torrence. At many of those contests, the white coaches in the stands indicated Scott might well be the player who became the first black ACC star. "All of the white coaches, they were coming, because they were courting Charlie," Torrence continued, "because this was the time when they could take him on board."[3]

As well as delighting in his on-court skills, Scott's African American supporters noted his off-court achievements. By the time Scott signed with the University of North Carolina, black athletes had reason to be wary of majority white schools, some of which had developed a reputation for disregarding the education of black athletic stars as well as mismanaging their talents. Concern about such images was clearly evident at UNC; in the *Daily Tar Heel* article that heralded Scott's signing, coach Dean Smith emphasized that Scott wanted to be part of the regular student body and "not just a gladiator."[4] Scott's multiple successes—he played brilliantly on the court, became an academic All-American, and after graduation pursued successful careers in both professional basketball and business—offered an encouraging example.

In the age of Jim Crow segregation, North Carolina's African Americans had contended with a social structure that set them rigidly apart from mainstream society and that they, in turn, defined themselves against. "At least in my family there was a very clear delineation between me and segregation," Charlotte resident James Ross recalled of his 1930s childhood. "That while these are the laws and these are the rules that operate, there's nothing wrong with you.

There's something wrong with the rules, but there's nothing wrong with you." The demise of legal segregation heralded the recasting of this racial paradigm, pushing questions of race onto less absolute ground and giving African Americans a wary optimism about society's new arrangements, which seemed to promise a more universal set of standards. "Made me change my mind," Second Ward High basketball star Scoopie Joplin recalled of Charlie Scott's college successes. "It didn't matter what color you were, or none of that. If you're good enough, the door's open for you. And if you're good enough, you can open the door. And I believed that. I always did believe that, because they proved it to me. I seen one of the greatest players I had seen come through North Carolina, and still play good and finish. And do the right thing in going to the pros. So I knew it could be done. . . . Do the right thing, and follow the rules, and you might be the one too."[5]

The multiple successes logged by Charlie Scott and other black athletes of his generation resonated with long-held hopes among African American leaders. For almost a century black leaders around the country had looked to sports as one path toward black advancement and racial reconciliation. By succeeding at such a widely admired endeavor, they reasoned, African American athletes could work meaningful changes on white Americans, gaining respect for their race as a whole and helping to combat the prejudice that stereotype, segregation, and political conflict had rooted in so many hearts. In 1942 columnist and educator Gordon Hancock, writing in admiration of the acclaim boxer Joe Louis had achieved throughout U.S. society, had argued in the *Carolina Times* that combating individual prejudice was the major challenge African Americans faced. "Even our gains before the courts of the land do not reach the seat of the trouble," Hancock wrote. "What Joe Louis has done does reach the seat of the trouble." Many years later John McLendon offered a similar assessment. "If you can get the sports thing going, that's the best way to go," he explained. "Because everybody pulls for their team. They don't pull for part of their team. . . . You can't divide up your loyalty. And then you begin to think—you might start admiring [someone]. And then you want your son to play like he does. . . . Pretty soon race is not the most important thing."[6]

During the 1960s North Carolinians would begin to put such ideas to the test, as growing numbers of African Americans moved into the state athletic spotlight. Charlie Scott, who followed in the footsteps of national stars such as Joe Louis, Jesse Owens, and Jackie Robinson, would be the first of dozens of black stars plying the courts and gridirons of the state's major colleges. In small towns across the state, in the near-sacred rituals of Friday nights, multiracial high school teams would perform before communities that only a few years before had stuck strictly to the laws of segregation. Black athletes would help give a new, assertive confidence to mainstream images of black men. The successes of these talented individuals would indeed play a meaningful role in state life, as North Carolinians negotiated the long, difficult road out of a segregated world.

At the same time, however, the experiences of both black athletes and integrated teams would harbor multifaceted meanings. Stories of athletic integration frequently assume a near-miraculous aura, as with the legendary day in 1970 that Sam Cunningham, black fullback for the University of Southern California, almost single-handedly destroyed the University of Alabama's celebrated, all-white football squad. In the frequently echoed view of Alabama coach Bear Bryant, Cunningham "did more for integration in the South in sixty minutes than Martin Luther King did in twenty years."[7] In contrast, for athletes, coaches, and communities in North Carolina, the realities of athletic integration involved an often lengthy period of adjustment and determined effort, which produced significant but usually far less dramatic results.


By the time North Carolina institutions began to desegregate in earnest, North Carolinians had known about black athletes for decades. Beginning with the 1930s achievements of Jesse Owens and Joe Louis and accelerated by the dramatic debut of Jackie Robinson with the Brooklyn Dodgers in 1946, a steadily growing stream of African Americans had made their mark on U.S. athletics, becoming an indispensable part of the national athletic scene. From basketball great Bill Russell, who had joined the 1956 Olympic basketball team after a personal appeal from President Dwight Eisenhower, to football star Jim Brown, who was on his way to becoming the greatest rushing threat in the rapidly expanding National Football League, black players were inspiring admiration in many sections of the country.[8]

North Carolinians had also seen the prospect of integrated competition brought closer to home, as the growing prominence of African American athletes at nonsouthern colleges had put pressure on the state's white college teams. Early in the twentieth century, southern college teams had almost unanimously refused to play against black athletes, requiring integrated opposing teams to leave African American players on the bench during the game. As early as the 1920s, however, as colleges around the country became more concerned about their national athletic reputations, such demands met more resistance. In some states, most notably Mississippi, public officials steadfastly refused to put athletic success above the principles of segregation. Mississippi's white state colleges were forced to decline berths at integrated national tournaments until

1963, the year the Mississippi State basketball squad evaded injunction-wielding officials and sneaked out of the state to take part in that year's NCAA tournament. But in North Carolina, an Upper South state where racial arrangements were somewhat less rigidly policed, teams who aspired to a measure of national status began to change their policies far earlier.[9]

The 1938 contest played by the legendary "Iron Duke" football squad against Syracuse University, which boasted a star black quarterback named Wilmeth Sidat-Singh, offered a particularly telling example of this openness to integrated competition. When Duke and Syracuse drew up their schedules, Syracuse signed a standard contract agreeing not to use black players during the game. The week before the contest, however, the situation changed. As the *Durham Morning Herald* explained, "Sidat-Singh, great Negro passer for Syracuse is free to play in the game, if Syracuse wants to use him. The contract for the game calls for Syracuse not to use the Negro, but Coach Wallace Wade made a scrap of paper out of the document, in order that Syracuse might put its strongest team on the field against Duke." Syracuse was understandably reluctant to take the field without its starting quarterback. But Sidat-Singh's presence also mattered to Duke. The game was part of a decade-long campaign designed by Wallace Wade to win a coveted Rose Bowl invitation and the chance to play for a symbolic national championship. Sidat-Singh was essential to Duke's aspirations—defeating a Syracuse team that had benched its finest player would have done little to help Duke build the respect required for a Rose Bowl bid.[10]

After World War II, as North Carolina's college basketball teams sought their own measure of national renown, and as increasing numbers of African Americans joined teams outside the South, such changes offered a powerful incentive not only to play integrated teams but to do so on southern soil. In 1950 North Carolina State athletic director Roy B. Clogston was still defending in-state segregation, politely explaining to coach Leo Harris, whose University of Oregon team had been invited to that year's Dixie Classic, "I seriously doubt if it would be wise for us to be the first to play a colored athlete." But shifting postwar attitudes toward the rights of black Americans as well as the intensifying competition in national college sports made nonsouthern teams increasingly unwilling to travel south without their African American players. In 1949 Penn State had agreed not to bring its lone black player to the Dixie Classic. But Harris refused to make the same concession and declined the invitation.[11]

Three years later, integrated college basketball came to Reynolds Coliseum along with the NCAA tournament. North Carolina State had won the chance to host the initial Eastern Division matchups—a major advantage for the Wolfpack, who could then play their first two rounds at home. But obtaining the tournament meant agreeing to host NCAA-nominated teams regardless of their racial makeup, and in 1953 Eastern Division contender Penn State brought black freshman star Jesse Arnell to Raleigh. Arnell's debut was met by relative equanimity, and in subsequent years, as North Carolina cities clamored to host the nation's top squads, state residents consistently pointed to the generally courteous reception of visiting black players as an important indication of North Carolina's fitness to be included in national affairs. In 1954 Clogston assured Temple University's Josh Cody that "your colored boys would be treated just the same as anyone else," adding that "Arnell of Penn State played here in our Coliseum, and he received the greatest ovation I have ever seen given any athlete in the William Neal Reynolds Coliseum." The Dixie Classic was integrated in grand style in 1958 when the nation's two top-ranked teams—the University of Cincinnati and Michigan State—accepted invitations. Michigan State boasted black star Johnny Green. The University of Cincinnati was led by Oscar Robertson, unquestionably the finest basketball player in the country.[12]

North Carolinians' growing interest in accommodating integrated teams showed particularly clearly in Charlotte in 1958. The first groups of black players to visit North Carolina had played with their teammates on the court but had usually stayed in segregated hotels and eaten in segregated restaurants. Just before the Charlotte tournament, however, Temple athletic director Josh Cody announced that top-ranked Temple would not play in Charlotte if its integrated team—which included black All-American Guy Rodgers—could not room and eat together. The announcement posed a serious threat to both local and regional aspirations. "If Temple spurns the almost-assured invitation, it means no NCAA tournament can receive spontaneous success in the South," lamented *Charlotte News* sports editor Josh Quincy. Davidson College athletic director Tom Scott, who was spearheading tournament plans, later recalled that civic leaders "got busy right away." The coliseum manager, the city's mayor, and members of the local NCAA committee began to negotiate with hotel and restaurant owners, trying to work out a solution. Eventually the Coliseum Inn, along with its adjoining Stork Club restaurant, agreed to house and feed the entire Temple team.[13]

Such changes seem to have caused limited public stir, perhaps in part because everyone involved sought to downplay their significance. The state's major papers generally supported decisions to play integrated games and adopted a variety of largely self-righteous rhetorical strategies in an attempt to portray state teams as above the petty details of race. The *Durham Morning Herald* cast Duke's 1938 decision to play against Sidat-Singh as a gesture of sportsmanship: "The incident of the Negro created quite a stir for a while, among the Syracuse contingent. They insisted upon bringing up the subject of a Negro playing against a southern team until officials of Duke University finally wired them to go ahead and play the Negro. Nothing happened from playing the black boy, and as it turned out Syracuse made a mountain out of a molehill." The *Charlotte News* insisted that Josh Cody's concerns about his players' Charlotte accommodations were unfounded, based on a "false impression" of southern life. After the 1958 Dixie Classic the *Raleigh News and Observer* staunchly defended southern honor by announcing, "Certainly . . . any charges of Southern discrimination were effectively answered when the 71 newsmen, most of them Southern, covering the tournament, gave most votes for the All-Classic first team to Oscar Robertson of Cincinnati and John Green of Michigan State, both Negroes. It will be hard to find discrimination against Negroes in that vote." Such pronouncements generally overlooked the very real discrimination black players faced. Charlotte officials, for example, had no plans for desegregated accommodations until Cody's complaints, and Oscar Robertson and Johnny Green had been housed on the North Carolina State campus to avoid Raleigh's still-segregated hotels. Still, the newspapers' statements also held out an alternative ethic, offering readers a picture of fair play that could transcend race.[14]

African American athletes who competed against North Carolina teams were generally described in respectful tones, treatment similar to that accorded national stars such as Joe Louis and Bill Russell. When the *Durham Morning Herald* sized up the Syracuse team in 1938, the paper's reporter noted that Wilmeth Sidat-Singh "rates as a tosser deluxe and will be the most feared player on the field." In 1953 the *Raleigh News and Observer* reported that Jesse Arnell was "the talk of the tournament." As the 1958 Dixie Classic approached, descriptions of Oscar Robertson dominated state sports pages. The Sunday before the tournament began, the *Raleigh News and Observer* printed a compelling picture on the front of its sports section, one that departed sharply from conventional stereotypes of African American men. In the picture Robertson stood sideways, knees bent, a look of focused determination on his face. He held one hand out toward the camera, and the other, holding a basketball, was drawn back, taut, as though he were preparing to slam the ball forward into the lens. Throughout the tournament *News and Observer* writers sang Robertson's praises. His play, writers assured their readers, was "as great as advertised," and they admired his leadership, rebounding, passing, and team play as well as his formidable scoring ability. "He did all anyone could ask of him," Dick Herbert wrote after Cincinnati's defeat of Wake Forest, and at the end of the tournament another writer summed up Robertson's accomplishments by asserting, "Oscar Robertson came into the Classic rated as the best player in the country and turned in a superlative job."[15]

The growing number of games with integrated college teams set athletic precedents in North Carolina, opening cracks in absolutist notions of racial separa-

Oscar Robertson, the greatest college player in the country in 1958, thrilled North Carolina fans at that year's Dixie Classic. Reprinted with permission of the *News and Observer* of Raleigh, North Carolina.

tion. The most significant test of athletic desegregation in North Carolina,
however, would come not at the lofty levels of college play but at the grass roots,
as communities throughout the state struggled with a mandate that black and
white young people attend school together. In 1954, the year after Jesse Arnell
came to Raleigh, the U.S. Supreme Court sent a jolt through southern school
systems, ruling in *Brown v. the Board of Education of Topeka, Kansas*, that segregated schooling was unconstitutional. Although southern resistance would
prop up dual systems for more than a decade, by the mid-1960s such strategies
were becoming less effective. At a time when the state's major colleges had
recruited only a handful of black players, high schools were enrolling large
numbers of both black and white athletes.

High school athletic integration took place against a backdrop of extraordinary tension, as civil rights activities as well as white resistance built in intensity.

Like other southern states, North Carolina saw a revival of the Ku Klux Klan after the *Brown* decision, and Klan activity intensified in the mid-1960s. Many whites who disapproved of Klan violence still resented African American demands for wholesale social change. By the end of the decade anger had also begun to mount within black communities, as African Americans became frustrated with both the slow pace of change and the direction it was taking. Schools became a particular focus of black resentment. In the late 1960s, when it had become abundantly clear that southern school boards were avoiding all but token efforts at desegregation, a combination of legal action and federal mandates compelled school districts to adopt immediate, full-scale desegregation plans. Many white-dominated school boards responded by closing black schools that had sat at the heart of communities for generations and assigning black students to previously all-white institutions. As communities watched beloved schools close and as large numbers of black teachers and administrators began to lose their jobs as a result, tensions built in cities around the state.[16]

In the city of Burlington a race-based dispute over a student election at Walter Williams High School flared into a full-scale disturbance in the spring of 1969. The school board had already announced its plans to close historically black Jordan Sellers High at the end of the school year and to reassign the majority of Sellers students to Walter Williams, a historically white school that enrolled a token handful of black students. That spring at Walter Williams, black cheerleading candidates were booed by a small group of white students at the public tryouts. After the majority white student body had elected an all-white squad, fights began to break out at the school. The day after the election, protesting students occupied the school's front lawn and confronted the school superintendent. That night conflict erupted in the streets of black Burlington. In scenes reminiscent of the highly publicized riots that had plagued northern cities, buildings were burned, shops were looted, and the sound of gunshots filled the air. One young man, fifteen-year-old Leon Mebane, was shot to death, and the entire city was shaken. Burlington was far from alone. As the 1960s came to an end, race-related violence erupted in numerous North Carolina cities, and no community could be confident it would escape.[17]

Such conflicts did not bode well for high school sports. While the emotional action of sports could help bond players and communities, it could just as easily exacerbate divisions. Arthur Griffin Jr., who attended Charlotte's Second Ward High School in the 1960s, recalled the smoldering anger that he and his companions felt toward the entire white world and how they saw sports as a possible release. "Growing up in Second Ward, we'd say 'Let's go beat the white boy's ass,'" he explained. "We'd say, 'Why won't they let us go play Myers Park?' Not for sheer competitiveness, but there was a sense of anger and hostility. We wanted to play white schools so we could beat them up and bloody them. Not to just play them." As black athletes began to filter onto white teams, they became the target of the resentments that ran the other way. Steve Cherry, who coached basketball and football at East Lincoln High, recalled the extent to which his black players suffered at the hands of white opponents who frequently turned racism into strategy. "I had players . . . that the opposing team tried to get thrown out of the game. They called them everything but holy and pinched them and pulled their jerseys. I had a black center one time that came to the bench crying, begging me to let him hit their center. Said, 'He's called me everything, he's talked about my mama, he's done everything in this world to me,' and said, 'I know I can't swing and hit him because you'll kill me. Just please let me hit him one time.' Cried tears running down out of his eyes."[18]

Concerns about sports lay not simply with players but with sporting contests themselves. The emotional intensity that had developed around athletic events could be as dangerous as it was useful. As in the nineteenth century, when African American educators were keenly aware of the extent to which sporting events could inflame racial tensions, administrators and communities were frequently wary of athletic encounters. William Hamlin, a graduate of West Charlotte High, recalled that such concerns had a dramatic effect on football game attendance in the early years of full desegregation in Charlotte. "During that period of time the participation dropped off," he explained. "I think that there was a general fear in the community that 'We don't want to be in an environment that's going to put the races together in masses and may cause something.'" At East Lincoln High, Steve Cherry faced this danger directly when two fathers—one black and one white—chose a Friday night football game to carry on a dispute that their sons had begun at school. "I stood between a man that I know that was president of the Klan in Lincoln County," Cherry recalled. "I knew that he had a pistol in his boot. I knew that and I stood belly to belly with him and another man directly behind me with a baseball bat in his hands telling me that he was going to kill him and the other guy said 'Let me at him,' and all I'm saying is 'You don't want to cause trouble here where there are four thousand people here at this football game.'" The men's sons had argued at school the previous week, and "everything's going to happen at the crowd at the football game on Friday night. 'I'll get you at the game,' you know."[19]

The status athletics had gained as a symbol of white manly prowess also made it a particularly charged arena. The Confederate symbolism adopted by southern college teams at the turn of the century still ran strong at many schools and had gained added force with the revival of Confederate imagery that accompanied white resistance to civil rights demands. Such imagery had also spread to high schools, many of which had adopted rebel mascots and made playing "Dixie" a sacred ritual. "You had to stand up for 'Dixie,'" Brenda Tapia recalled of the white high school, where she was transferred in the late 1960s. "You could sit down for the national anthem, but you had to stand for 'Dixie.'"[20]

Admitting African Americans to this realm indeed challenged long-held associations between athletic prowess and white supremacy, and attempts at athletic integration, like other efforts to modify Jim Crow, provoked resistance in a variety of forms. University of North Carolina system president William Friday saw the intense identification some North Carolinians attached to race and sports in the critical letters and comments he received after the Tar Heels signed Charlie Scott. "The intensity of hate in some of these experiences told me how hard it was for that individual to accept anything," he recalled. "Sometimes they don't even understand what they're transmitting. It's a blind thing with them, a rageful kind of thing." East Lincoln coach Steve Cherry experienced a particularly direct form of attempted intimidation when a team booster came into his office "and told me that he wanted—since he had known me for so long— that he wanted to make me aware of something. And I said, 'What's that?' He said, 'There's a man that's going to blow your head off if you keep playing all them niggers on your basketball team.'" Henry Barkley, East Lincoln's girls' basketball coach faced a possible boycott from some of his team members when the first black player went out for the team. "I had two or three of my starters come up to me at some point in time and said, 'Coach, we can't play with her,'" he recalled. "'We've never played with a black, and we ain't going to play with one now. If she's going to make the team, then we can't play.'"[21]

Even where resistance was less overt, pressure from communities could narrow black players' opportunities, pointing up the myriad layers of history and tradition that complicated integration efforts. At Myers Park High School, in Charlotte's wealthiest neighborhood, no one threatened to shoot coaches for playing too many "niggers." But as football player James Dawkins learned, pressure could come in other ways. "There's no tension on the field when you're playing," he explained. "But there is tension with family and coaches and a family who wants—they want to see their kid out there playing. Because, you know, 'I went there, my grandfather went there, so-and-so went there.' . . . You could hear it in the stands. 'Play so-and-so.' 'Put so-and-so in the game.' 'Put so-and-so in the game.' 'This person in the game.' You would hear that from the crowd." The result, as Dawkins saw it, was a lot of black players on the bench. "There was one time that we actually boycotted a couple of practices," Dawkins noted. "And we went in and talked to the coach and said, 'We have some guys that we know that can play. And they don't have to be starting, they can be on a specialty team, the kickoff team, the punting team, because we're gassing out out there, trying to hold it. He did that for one game . . . and we played West Mecklenburg, I think, and we blew them off the field by thirty-something. But slowly and surely it went back to the way it was and those guys were back on the bench."[22]

As Dawkins's experience made clear, the obstacles black high school students faced at their new schools went well beyond open hostility. Like many of her peers, Brenda Tapia found the shift to a majority white school profoundly disheartening. "Imagine coming from a school setting where everyone knew you, everyone liked you, you were very involved in all the extracurricular activities, where you were always late for class because people were stopping and talking to you, asking you about this meeting or these class notes or something," she explained. "To walk into a school where you suddenly become invisible. Nobody sees you. Nobody knows you. Nobody says anything to you. People could bump into you, walk all over you, and never crack their lips because you're not there. To raise your hand in class and be the last one called on, if you're called on. And then when you are called on, everybody stops and they are staring down your throat." Tapia's frustration extended to the more intimate realm of schoolwork. "To get A papers back with Cs on them and no correction marks," she continued. "To up and ask the teacher, 'Well, can you tell me what I got wrong? . . . Where's my error? I want to do better. I want to make As.' To be told, 'Take your seat. Are you questioning my grade? How dare you? Do you want to go to the office?' "[23]

Even when white students and teachers were not obviously hostile, Garfield Carr recalled, black students had a difficult time deciding how to interact with them. "If you had a problem with homework, you didn't want to appear to be dumb because in some cases, that's what some of them may have thought about you," he explained. "You didn't want to give the appearance that you were. You didn't know whether to ask another student to help you because again you didn't know what they were going to think about you. Or whether they would or not. Or what they told you was even the truth. So most of the time, when you had a break you would all tend to get with your friends—somebody we could really associate with."[24]

The uncertainty and alienation that many black students experienced had a definite effect on their interest in athletics. Becoming a high school athlete required considerable sacrifice and commitment, a dedication that was sometimes hard to muster in such uncertain circumstances. Black athletes at times worried about their own safety. John Costner, who played on the first integrated basketball team at Gastonia's Ashley High School, remembered an away game where the opposing team dimmed the lights for the national anthem, prompting sudden fears of racial violence. "That was frightening, it really was," he later recalled. "I never will forget that game. I was a wreck the first half." When black players had concerns about team policy, such as the amount of playing time given to African Americans, they were often reluctant to challenge the authority of well-established white coaches. "These coaches, they were big people," Scoopie Joplin explained. "They was known to be good coaches, and know what they were talking about. So if you said something about it, you would look like the ignorant one."[25]

A considerable number of players, faced with the new situation, apparently felt that joining unfamiliar teams was not worth the effort. In 1966, Gastonia's black Highland High School was made a junior high, and its students trans-ferred to previously white Ashley High. That fall, the Ashley football coach expected fifty Highland football players to arrive at summer tryouts and was sorely disappointed when only twenty showed up. At Lincolnton High School, during the first year of full integration, both the football and basketball teams had high rates of black attrition. "Every practice there would be less and less," recalled basketball coach Clyde Smith. Smith's account of the events underlined the dilemma black athletes faced; during a tense and uncertain time many were asked to fit into new situations in which few adjustments were made for them. "I just have to be honest, in my stance they couldn't adapt to our ways," Smith explained, adding in retrospection, "Whether our ways were right, I don't know."[26]

The difficulties of an unfamiliar, often racially tense situation, Bighouse Gaines noted, could cut both ways. At times the atmosphere was poisoned by a coach's attitude. One of Gaines's All-American players fought constant battles with his high school coach "because the coach was seemingly always talking down to them. In other words, there was still this white superiority." The coach took the player's anger as a personal affront and acted accordingly, Gaines explained. "The coach didn't even recommend him—he wouldn't even recom-mend this kid to go to college, said he was a bad actor. But he had used this language, talking down to these kids as if they were third-class citizens. And this boy reacted." On the other hand, Gaines continued, some white coaches who were reluctant to discipline their new black players "found out if you give a kid an inch he takes a yard."[27]

A final sticking point could involve playing and practice style, an issue with particular resonance for basketball. Black basketball players around the state had been heavily influenced by the fluid, energetic, fast-break style pioneered in the state by John McLendon and his dominating North Carolina College Ea-gles. White coaches, on the other hand, tended to favor a slower, more defense-oriented approach. When players and coaches came together, these and other differences could be difficult to negotiate, even as the normal challenges of disciplining energetic young men were compounded by the unfamiliar situation.[28]

Willard Isley, the white basketball coach at Walter Williams, had eagerly anticipated integration, specifically because the Jordan Sellers students who had been assigned to Williams included one young man whose black skin paled before his almost seven feet of height. Isley later recounted the moment when school superintendent Brank Proffitt, seeking to open a head coaching slot for a former Sellers coach, asked him if he would trade his job for the better-paid position of athletic director. "I immediately panicked and started talking a blue streak," he explained. "I told him I didn't want to leave Williams, that for years I had been only a mediocre coach and that now I had a 6-11 boy, Jeff Crompton, who was gonna make someone a tremendous coach and I was just selfish enough—damn it, I admitted it—to want that someone to be me." After integration, however, Isley had considerable trouble dealing with his new black players. By the end of the season only Crompton, whose college scholarship prospects gave him particular incentive to keep playing, remained on the team. Isley accounted for the attrition in stylistic terms, explaining, "The blacks liked to fast break and I wanted to play a more deliberate game."[29]

Even as coaches, players, and communities struggled with the difficulties and dilemmas posed by integration, however, athletics also held a number of advantages that made it a potentially promising realm for racial interaction. The dramatic achievements of athletes such as Jim Brown or Jackie Robinson meant that North Carolina's black high school athletes arrived at their schools with a measure of respect that was rare in other areas of school life. Even in lower grades, black athletes often found themselves welcomed with far greater warmth than many of their peers. When Scoopie Joplin became one of the first black students at Sedgefield Junior High, he recalled, many of his fellow students had a hard time even finding someone to talk to. He did not have that problem. While most of the black students headed straight back to their neighborhood after school, he stayed around and played pickup basketball on the school playground and in a nearby park. "My ball game got me over, a little bit," he surmised. "Because I could play ball, they accepted me. Even before basketball came around, the season, I had done played ball in the park with so many of the young blokes, and they would tell their families and uncles about me. They would come to see me play on the park, even before I even made the school team. So I had kind of been accepted, from playing park basketball." Joplin's white teammates invited him to their homes, and parents frequently offered to drive him back to his center-city neighborhood after games or practice. "They seemed as though they liked me," he recalled.[30]

As Scoopie Joplin's memories suggest, black and white athletes could also draw on a long history of informal contact. While official competition between black and white men was discouraged for the first half of the century, unofficial play had frequently flourished. In the 1930s, William Friday recalled, any time his community baseball team came up short of players, he would recruit a young black neighbor who "could throw harder than anybody I played with." In the years just after World War II, interracial basketball became an accepted part of daily life in the small town of Wade, North Carolina. Such contests, recalled participant Melton McLaurin, were ruled by a relatively untainted athletic democracy. "Teams composed of boys of only one race rarely played one an-other, because teams were selected by team captains who took turns choosing one player at a time," McLaurin wrote. "Since both captains wanted winning teams and since from years of playground experience they knew the individual skills of each participant, they selected the best players first, regardless of race." Similar conditions prevailed throughout the contests. "Although race was not completely ignored on the courts, it rarely influenced the conduct of a game," McLaurin continued. "In all the years I played in such integrated contests, I never saw a fight provoked for racial reasons, though disputes over fouls, out-of-bounds plays, and other technicalities occurred with monotonous regularity during practically every game." When Lincolnton High integrated, two of the school's new football teammates—Alan "Zeke" Stoudemire and Boyce Blake—had been friends for much of their lives, a friendship cemented in part by their common interest in athletics.[31]

The structure that athletics provided also helped players and coaches learn how to negotiate the complexities of their new situation. In classroom work students struggled individually to master material, and the measure of achieve-ment, as Brenda Tapia learned, could frequently seem mysterious or unfair. Athletics, on the other hand, was a realm where students had to work together, and where skills and accomplishments had more public and frequently more clearly measurable results. Team coaches, who frequently came to their tasks with lengthy histories of working closely with students, could also be especially well suited to the task of bringing a disparate group of individuals together. Good coaching required careful attention to individual and team emotions, and coaches often developed particularly intimate relationships with young people, inspiring them to sacrifice, motivating them to achieve, and consoling them after losses.

While some white coaches subscribed to prevailing racial ideologies, talking down to black athletes or seeing them only as potentially useful "nigger horses," others were more open to change. During segregation some North Carolina whites had come to identify so completely with the ideology of white su-premacy that they were ready to use threats and violence to defend it. Others had accepted the system and the privileges it brought them in a far less explicit manner, as suggested by East Lincoln basketball coach Henry Barkley's memories of his childhood. Barkley, who lived in a rural area, recalled how he unthinkingly accepted the inequities he saw between his experience and that of one of his black neighbors. "When we'd see him walking to school and us riding the bus to school, we didn't think anything about it. We thought, 'That's the way it's supposed to be. That's the way it is.' . . . We didn't know any different. You know, that's just the way we thought it was. We were supposed to be on a nice bus and he's supposed to be walking. That's sad, but that's the way we saw it."[32]

When high schools integrated, coaches who had accepted but not identified with segregation frequently approached their teams with a relatively open mind, particularly if sticking to discrimination—such as keeping a talented black player on the bench—would have forced them to compromise other long-held principles, such as a commitment to fairness, to winning, or a little bit of both. At the same time, most coaches had considerable experience with community pressure—years of booster advice and critique over everything from playing time to offensive strategy—and the best of them had learned to stand up for themselves and their decisions.

When the East Lincoln fan appeared in Steve Cherry's office to warn him about "playing all them niggers," Cherry's reaction was not fear but anger. "Inside, I was furious," he recalled. "I was mad. Because at the time I had the best five players playing that I could possibly find, and I was in P.E., and I was going through every gym class hunting basketball players, because we were trying to build a tradition at East Lincoln that eventually took us to the state. Got beat in the state championship game before I quit coaching. And I searched every gym class so I knew that I had the best five players at East Lincoln High School playing basketball. I knew that. . . . If they weren't, I'd have gotten them out of that gym class and put a uniform on them." Larry Rhodes, who coached basketball at Gastonia's Ashley High School, followed a similar philosophy. "The way I looked at it in my coaching, and what I'd always been taught, you play the best guys," he explained. "You play what's going to win for you. You can't let politics or anything like that enter in. You can't say because you've got a good friend, that I'm going to play his son a little bit more. Those guys, they've got to understand it. And if they don't, you've just got to let that rub off."[33]

While some teams fell apart under the strains of interracial contact, many coaches also found ways to deal with the new situation. After unrest spread from Walter Williams High School into the Burlington community in the spring of 1969, the Burlington school superintendent sought to calm community tensions by taking the unprecedented step of appointing the black head football coach from Jordan Sellers High, Jerome Evans, to head the newly integrated Williams squad. After decades of coaching, Evans understood the delicate balance that athletic discipline entailed, and he was particularly careful about dealing with his team members. When a group of white players tested his authority by showing up for practice with their hair down to their shoulders, he refrained from simply ordering them to cut it, as he would have with an all-black team. Instead, he formed a student committee to set rules for hair length, reasoning that "if I just made a strict rule some of them might have quit on me and before you know it you have race problems."[34]

Finally, the status that came with playing on a school athletic team and with backing a successful effort gave coaches considerable leverage over both players and communities. White players initially leery of playing with African Americans learned they had no choice but to put aside their prejudices if they wanted to stay on school teams. When Henry Barkley was confronted with the prospect of white players quitting if a black player made the East Lincoln High women's basketball squad, he replied, " 'Well, girls, she just made the ball club. So y'all make up your mind what you want to do, because she's made the ball club.' And she had. And the girls didn't quit. They didn't like it. But they didn't quit." For African American players facing hostile opponents, the desire to keep playing encouraged them to handle slurs and insults with dignified rationality, as when Steve Cherry's beleaguered center held back the anger such assaults provoked and listened to his coach's advice. "I just patted him on the back and said, 'No, Joe, you don't need to do that,' " Cherry replied to the student's pleas to let him lash out at his tormentors. "I said, 'We need you in this ballgame and we need you against him.' I said, 'He's not going to hurt you with words. You just keep playing. The best way you can hurt him is to get thirty-five, and every ball that goes on the boards is yours.' "[35]

An interest in playing could also spur athletes and coaches to break past communication barriers. At Lincolnton High School a number of black players dropped silently off the football squad. Leroy Diamond did not. Diamond had been a stellar player at black Newbold High School, and the town's black leaders had promised coach Von Ray Harris that he would shine at Lincolnton as well. Harris, however, had been unimpressed with Diamond's performance in practice and did not give him much playing time in the first game of the season. Diamond did not directly confront Harris about the issue. But he did speak to Bobby Joe Easter, a black player who had enrolled at Lincolnton shortly before full integration and who had developed a closer relationship with the Lincolnton coaches. Easter spoke to Harris. "Bobby Joe came to coach after the game and said, 'Coach, I don't know whether you know this, but Leroy is a Friday night ballplayer,' " Clyde Smith recalled, adding that Harris was ready to respond. "He looked at Bobby Joe and he said, 'Look Bobby Joe, I'm going to tell you something. You need to get word to Leroy that I'm a Monday, Tuesday, Wednesday, and Thursday coach. If he wants to play for me on Friday night, he needs to come out here on Monday, Tuesday, Wednesday, and Thursday in practice and give what it takes to play on Friday night.' And Bobby Joe said 'okay.' So Bobby Joe evidently got the message to him because come Monday evening, Leroy was a different participant in practice. And that Friday night, Leroy Diamond scored five touchdowns. In fact, we finally had to take him out of the ballgame to keep him from scoring."[36]

As coaches and players across the state worked on their new teams, a few such combinations stepped beyond simply maintaining racial calm and became dramatic illustrations of the gains that could be made when whites and African Americans pooled their talents. Such results shone with particular clarity at Gastonia's Ashley High School in 1967. The decision to transform black Highland High into a junior high school and to transfer Highland students to previously white Ashley both angered members of Gastonia's black community and threatened a long-held goal of Highland's senior basketball players. Five years earlier, Highland High basketball coach Joseph Robinson had noticed that year's seventh grade held a particularly talented group of young basketball players. In a long-established tradition within African American communities, he had begun grooming them for his team, aiming at the state title of the black North Carolina Athletic Conference.

"We were in the seventh grade," John Costner recalled. "He had invited us to the Highland gym. And we would play each night from about five-thirty to about seven-thirty. And I can remember one of his friends came into the gym one night and asked him, he said, 'Joe, what are you doing?' And he said, 'In 1967, I'm going to win the championship with these boys.'" In 1967, when Highland High School had become Highland Junior High, and when Joseph Robinson had ceded the head basketball position to Larry Rhodes, the players did not give up their goal. The team members worried about their safety at away games and about whether their new coach would give them the chance to play to their potential. But they were determined to persist. Early in the season they met and decided to pursue their state championship ambitions. Players who usually competed in both football and basketball even chose to give up football so that they could concentrate on basketball.[37]

Like other black athletes, the Highland players arrived at Ashley with advantages that other black students did not necessarily have. Highland High was renowned for basketball, and the team's reputation had preceded it. Tommy

Bryant, one of the Ashley players, recalled anticipating the year with a mix of trepidation and excitement. "Man, you're going to have to work your fanny off, just to make the team," he told himself. But he was also eager to be part of the new season. "They had a great team at Highland," he explained. "I was tickled to death to be able to be associated with them."[38] In many other areas of school life, black and white students were able to pass each other at a distance; white students who resented desegregation often ignored their new black colleagues, and black students focused on their goals of learning and graduation. In sports, like it or not, they had to work together to succeed.

The Highland players quickly determined that concerns about their new coach were unfounded. "Coach Rhodes proved to be a very fair and competent coach," John Costner recalled. Once those initial fears had been overcome, the Highland players threw themselves into practice and into play. Their dedication to their goal also kept them going during the low moments that were a part of every athletic season. Costner recalled one day when Rhodes got angry at what he saw as lackluster practice and punished players by making them run large numbers of laps. "And there was a suggestion from one of the guys, I don't know who it was now, 'Hey, let's quit,'" Costner recalled. "And I think someone said, 'No. You know what we said in our meeting. We've come a little too far; we've done too much. Quitting is not right.' So we didn't quit." As practices progressed and the team began to win, the Highland players' determination proved catching. "The guys that came from Highland came with a cause," Larry Rhodes explained. "I think those guys were dedicated to it. And then when the whole team saw what we had, it meshed together—I think they realized it. And they worked hard at it. On and off the court."[39]

The team's concentration on winning also led to an exchange of strategies. The Highland players had come to Ashley playing the pressing, high-scoring offensive ball that had become so popular in black high schools. "When we played, when I was in high school if you scored sixty-something points, that was a lot of points," Larry Rhodes recalled. "Then with them, we were hitting in the eighties. And then some nights even a little bit higher than that." But Rhodes was a defensive specialist, a student of the intricacies of man-to-man defense, who considered the infamous defensive war waged in the 1966 ACC finals, in which Duke defeated Chapel Hill by the score of 21-20, as one of his all-time favorite games. At Walter Williams this difference in approach split the basketball team apart. At Ashley, players and coach learned from each other. "I would say probably my biggest coaching problem was to get them to play the skills of man-to-man defense," Rhodes explained. "And then again it goes back to what they wanted to accomplish, and it was easier for me to teach them that. Usually it takes you a couple of years or more. You like to start on that with the

Former Highland High School student Ronnie Lee Phillips soars for Ashley High School in 1967. Courtesy of Larry Rhodes.

J.V. team and then the juniors. . . . [But] these guys worked at it so hard. They could do a lot of things defensively, eventually."[40]

Early in the season the Ashley team stumbled, losing two games in a row. But then the players hit their stride and remained undefeated through the rest of the season and the district tournament. A few games into the season, Larry Rhodes determined that his most productive strategy was to start all five Highland players—a highly controversial move in those racially uneasy days. The decision did not go unnoticed, and Rhodes began to receive threatening calls at his home. "We would get phone calls," he recalled. "My girls were little at that time. And they would call here. We'd win every game, and they'd call and say, 'Well you so-and-so's won again.' You know. Referring to the black guys. And it was sort of tough, I think, for my girls, because a lot of times they would answer the phone." Some longtime Ashley fans also had trouble identifying with such a transformed team. "People would say that had followed us, and that had had sons, would say 'Larry, I hope you win, but it's sort of hard for me to pull for you.' " But the players' successes helped pull members of Gastonia's black community into the new school. "I think it definitely gave a lot of people encouragement not only to want to go, but to be a part of the school," John Costner recalled. Whites rallied to their side as well. As the players prepared for the state championship tournament held in Chapel Hill, the business community mustered its customary support. "We played on a Wednesday night, and one of the boys that played with me, his mother, Mrs. Ruby Bryant, went out into the business world and said, 'Hey, we need some money, we need to get some people up there,' " Rhodes recalled. "And they took nine busloads of kids. On a Wednesday night."[41]

The busloads of supporters were not disappointed, as Ashley beat Winston-Salem Reynolds in a thrilling, overtime semifinal. Then, in a game that demonstrated the players' mastery of Rhodes's defensive system, they defeated Wilmington—New Hanover 51-44 to win the NCHSAA state championship. The finals were televised across North Carolina, giving particular satisfaction to the Highland players, who relished the chance to demonstrate their capabilities to an entire state. After the victory the *Gaston Gazette* praised the team in language that could easily have been applied to a team of any race. "There were no special 'stars' on this team," the editors wrote. "It was five players working as one. They thought as one. They passed off many times when it would have been as easy to take a shot for glory themselves. We congratulate this fine team, its coach, and the entire school."[42]

Team members were elated. "They were just great days," Tommy Bryant recalled. "You can't speak it until you've been there. You see these kids win NCAA championships. I know they've got a great feeling, but I don't know that

The state champion Ashley High School team, 1967. John Costner is number 30; Tommy Bryant is number 12. Courtesy of Larry Rhodes.

they've got any better feeling than we had that day." Players were also aware of the way their efforts had helped pull a divided community together, at least in this one instance. "The fact that there are people from the same community, same city, gathered together and cheering for the same common cause in itself is togetherness," John Costner said. "Traveling together, rooting for the same team—that in itself creates a bond." In Larry Rhodes's estimation, the team had a significant impact on Ashley integration as a whole. "A lot of people can look at that year and say, 'Well, it went off without too many hitches,'" he explained. "But that was a tough situation, and you have to give everybody credit. The whites, you've got to give them credit, you've got to give the blacks credit for coming in that year. And I just think that having a good basketball team that year went a long way. I know the preacher of my church, Dr. Douglas Aldrich, was on the city committee, and he'd always say that people in Gastonia didn't realize how important the 1967 basketball team was."[43]

Integrating school athletic teams did not, of course, completely transform North Carolina society. Black and white students might attend school together, might work jointly on the details of offensive and defensive strategy, but after school let out, and after the gymnasium lights had been turned off, students still went home to different neighborhoods, different churches, different worlds. Athletics did contribute to a number of fast friendships around the state. Frequently, however, when players and coaches discussed team relationships, they focused more on the development of mutual respect than on intimate friendship. Although Scoopie Joplin felt comfortable playing at Sedgefield Junior High—"It seemed as though they liked me"—he was cautious not to draw overly grand conclusions from his acceptance. "If you're really good, a coach who don't even like blacks is going to let you play," he explained. "But when I came there, they had respect for me. I started. And the players, I don't know if they liked me. I didn't care about that. They respected me. Whether they liked me, it didn't matter. I respect you, you respect me. That's all I require." Henry Barkley noted similar relationships in his first integrated team. "Marcella did not start but she came off the bench and did a super job," he said of the team's first game. "And after that she started the rest of the season—didn't miss a ballgame. Made all-conference. The two girls that come to mind in particular . . . by the time the year was out, would fight for her. Their attitude had totally changed to the point that no they didn't date together and run around together or do anything like that, but as far as athletics, they would defend her and she would defend them and they were as close, I mean, as close to teammates as you could be."[44]

The tone of team encounters also differed from community to community, depending on a shifting mix of individuals and circumstances. At Ashley, where the basketball season went so well, learning to work together brought an exhilarating feeling heightened by a realization of the magnitude of the team's off-court accomplishments. "It was a happy time," Rhodes recalled. "I think a lot of things entered into the picture that year because of our integration. That the white members of the team and the black members got along so well. On and off the court. And you would think that there would have been a lot of resentment maybe there—'well if these guys weren't here we'd be playing a lot more.' But they made the integration work." John Costner concurred, explaining, "We were a team in every sense of the word."[45]

At Walter Williams, where the previous spring's riot had raised the stakes for athletic integration, and where the appointment of Jerome Evans as head football coach marked a far more dramatic change than at most schools around the state, the close of the season left participants more exhausted than exhilarated. Evans and his team had avoided major racial blowups and had finished a respectable 8-2, the team's best record in a decade. But at the end of the season, a visiting reporter sensed fatigue, particularly among the team's white players, whom he concluded were "tired of being conscious of their every word and act, tired of liking blacks, of liking their coach, tired, in fact, of all the pressures that had been heaped upon them since the first moment Jerome Evans appeared." For his part, Evans had fulfilled virtually all the expectations of both black and white communities, and like most of North Carolina's African Americans, he was far more practiced in the self-conscious action that weighed so heavily on his white players. Still, the satisfaction he took from such achievements was tinged with little joy, and he looked back at his coaching at Jordan Sellers and at the small, rural school of Farmville with considerable nostalgia. "The more I make it in the white world, the less I enjoy life," he said after the season finished. "I enjoyed myself a lot at Sellers, and even more at Farmville. I didn't enjoy myself much at Williams at all. Isn't that strange?"[46]

Despite such complications, however, high school athletics often brought blacks and whites closer than almost any other newly integrated endeavor. In order to succeed, black and white players had to work closely together and to trust one another to some degree. They persevered through triumphs, losses, and not infrequently, racial hostility. "I had tri-captains that year," Larry Rhodes recalled. "And two blacks and a white, they'd go out to center court and find that maybe some of the players that we played against wouldn't shake hands with our black players. And Doug Lanham was the white co-captain. And he used to get so infuriated with those people that would do that. And, you know, we talked about those things."[47] In many schools around the state, athletics became by far the most prominent example of interracial cooperation and a major symbol of the transformations North Carolina was undergoing.


The growing recognition accorded African American athletes helped influence a shift in the images of black manhood circulating through North Carolina society. During the first half of the century, white perceptions of black men were dominated by deep-rooted stereotypes of African Americans as shiftless, undisciplined, overly emotional, and potentially dangerous, as well as by misleading impressions created by the well-mannered deference with which most black North Carolinians approached employers and other whites. In the 1950s and 1960s, however, North Carolina's African Americans began to show themselves in public in new ways, mounting a widespread challenge to habitual assumptions for the first time in decades. The male presence in the growing civil rights movement was particularly charged; as elsewhere in the country, North Carolina women provided the backbone of protest and organization, but male leaders drew most of the public notice. North Carolina's activists ran a wide gamut, from open advocates of armed self-defense to well-dressed students who sat calmly at lunch counters to promoters of black power, who talked forcefully about building a separate black society. The black athletes who plied the state's courts and gridirons added their own twist to these changing public images, offering prominent displays of speed, dexterity, determination and confident, assertive action.[48]

Athletics, however, proved no panacea for stereotype or discrimination. Even as black athletes challenged prevailing white views of black manhood, the image they presented held some definite attractions for whites uneasy with the era's social shifts—attractions that could both facilitate athletic integration and limit its long-term significance. Acceptance of black athletes could be smoothed by the complex nature of athletic achievement, which allowed some white fans to focus on African Americans' physical abilities, rather than on either mental or moral worth. As early as 1905, Talladega College professor William Pickens had suggested that whites "would accept from a Negro physical and athletic superiority but . . . stand aloof when one approaches with moral or intellectual superiority." As black athletes scored dramatic successes in national and international athletic arenas, such achievements indeed prompted widespread discussions of black physicality. Scientists and nonscientists alike speculated on topics such as the proportions of blacks' skeletons, a supposedly higher tolerance for pain, and the strength that enslaved Africans had required to survive the harsh conditions of the Middle Passage.[49]

The difficulties black athletes faced in overcoming a broad range of stereotypes came clear in reactions to the thrashing the UNC Tar Heels suffered at the hands of Purdue in the semifinals of the 1969 NCAA tournament. Charlie Scott had a lackluster game, and a *New York Times* reporter noted that while many white fans had cheered Scott on, a number of them assessed his poor performance by falling back on long-held stereotypes that depicted African Americans as overly emotional and lacking in determination or persistence. One Chapel Hill student who had cried out "Charlie for God" when Scott hit a last-second basket to win the East Regional Final in the preceding game glumly observed that the Purdue loss "just proves 'niggers' choke in the clutch." At a Winston-Salem barbershop, another fan offered a less pointed but equally telling assessment, advising the *Times* reporter, "You can pretty well tell how a colored boy is going to play by what he does in the first few minutes."[50]

At the same time, even as black athletes forced whites to at least partially change their ideas about black men, most athletes posed a relatively limited challenge to the larger workings of North Carolina and U.S. society—a welcome development in a world that by the mid-1960s seemed to many to be spinning out of control. The 1960s were a time of extraordinary turbulence and uncertainty, encompassing ongoing Cold War tensions, intensified conflicts over the Vietnam War, heightened civil rights–related violence, a series of prominent assassinations, and many other disturbing events. The month before the first Highland students arrived at Ashley High, *Gaston Gazette* editorial writers expressed their concerns about the future of the country in near-apocalyptic prose. The preceding week's news had been especially troubling—the paper had reported on a violent clash between the Ku Klux Klan and workers in the Southern Christian Leadership Conference's Chicago-based Open Housing movement as well as on Charles Whitman, who had climbed the highest build-ing at the University of Texas and murdered sixteen people with well-aimed sniper fire. "There is currently creeping across the face of this land a dangerous lawlessness that threatens to make life miserable for every law-abiding citizen who resides within our borders," the *Gazette* proclaimed. "Within the past few years, it has picked up a momentum that now will be difficult to stop. It is a boulder going downhill. It is a flash-flood that grows in its monstrosity. It is an evil, growing thing that makes one realize that it is not the people in prison whom we have to worry about—but those who aren't."[51]

As in past eras of wrenching social change, organized athletics offered a reassuring alternative to seeming chaos, presenting a realm where differences could be contained and resolved within an ordered set of rules. Incorporating African Americans into existing sports programs reaffirmed that order, even as it challenged long-held assumptions about who deserved to be included in it. Some people in Burlington resented the appointment of Jerome Evans to the most prominent position at historically white Walter Williams High. But for the school administration, and probably for most town residents, a black head football coach was clearly preferable to the social unrest the cheerleading dis-pute had provoked. And in an era in which a growing number of African American leaders had begun to publicly reject many aspects of U.S. life, espous-ing instead the controversial rhetoric of separatism and black power, evidence that many of North Carolina's African Americans shared the goals and values of the state's white population could be as comforting as it was disturbing.

Seen from a broader perspective, however, precisely those aspects of black athletic success that gained black athletes broad acceptance also limited the value of athletics as a model for other kinds of civil rights efforts. Critics of the prominence black athletes gained during this and subsequent eras frequently focus on the effect such widely publicized achievements have had on young African Americans, encouraging them to set their sights on the elusive goal of professional athletic careers and to neglect their studies in the process. But this was not the only limitation athletics posed. The circumstances of most athletic integration, where individual African Americans made their mark on pre-viously all-white teams or institutions, offered yet another layer of support to conceptions of the United States as a land of equality where talented individuals rose or fell according to their own merits. The major moral symbol sports encompassed—the level playing field—invoked just such an idea, holding out the expectation that, given a fair chance, African Americans could prove themselves to be as worthy, competent, and deserving as anyone else. Pioneering black athletes such as Jackie Robinson, Joe Louis, or Charlie Scott lived up to such ideals, breaking through the customs that barred African Americans from the nation's most prominent athletic fields. They rarely challenged other aspects of the games they played so well. The lessons Scoopie Joplin drew from Charlie Scott's success emphasized the effects of such achievements. "Do the right thing, and follow the rules, and you might be the one too," Joplin told himself.

But as the civil rights movement began to reach its initial goals, eliminating legal segregation and achieving greater access to the voting booth, activists were forced to confront more recalcitrant obstacles, often rooted not in overt racial barriers, but in the hard rock of majority rule and structural economic inequality. In cities such as Greensboro and Charlotte, civil rights workers began to confront the difficulties of electing African Americans in contests where black voters were in the minority but city officials were elected at large. In impoverished black neighborhoods around the state, organizers faced long-entrenched patterns of shabby, overpriced rental housing, limited community investment, and low-wage jobs—problems that individual achievement could do little to dislodge. As African Americans approached these and other challenges, the symbol of the level playing field offered them only limited guidance.[52]

Within North Carolina schools, one such dilemma surfaced on the sidelines of school athletic fields, in the cheering squads and homecoming courts that had become such significant arenas of young women's status. While athletic teams frequently integrated with apparent ease, the selection of cheerleading squads caused far greater stir, as dramatically emphasized by the riot that rocked the town of Burlington. "The football season got under way and things went pretty well," Clyde Smith recalled of his experience at Lincolnton High. But away from the field, tensions were building. "Just little things, undercurrent things that we didn't sense," Smith explained. "The blacks began to be left out. Like in the homecoming court, no black girls were selected. Then with cheerleading . . . things were voted on, and obviously the procedure in place was probably a majority vote. For boys, they earned their position on the athletic teams, but then all of a sudden when it became voting issues. . . ." The selection of cheerleading squads would, in fact, become one of the most volatile school desegregation issues around the South as students at numerous schools staged walkouts and protests over the issue.[53]

In the 1960s, cheerleading offered by far the highest status available to young women at many North Carolina high schools. "It was just a big deal," recalled Susan Shakelford, a graduate of Wake County's Millbrook High. "If you were a cheerleader you could get the best guys to go out with, you got invited to the best parties, you were more likely to win a class office, you were more likely to be on the homecoming court. It was just an avenue to so many things." At Lincolnton High School, Alan Stoudemire explained, "grooming of the cheerleaders . . . generally started in junior high. The younger girls would curry favor with the more senior cheerleaders, who helped them learn and practice the cheers and the various gymnastic routines involved. Some degree of politicking occurred, with ambitious cheerleader candidates going out of their way to 'suck up' to the teachers known to be on the selection committee. Becoming a cheerleader ensured celebrity social status, instant popularity, and dating success."[54]

At newly desegregated schools, the high stakes involved in cheerleader selection were complicated by the diverse cheering styles that had developed at black and white schools. The fluid improvisations of African American cheering, with its emphasis on strong rhythms, verbal eloquence, and crowd participation, stood in sharp contrast to white cheerleading styles, which relied more on straight-armed, almost military precision as well as elaborate gymnastic routines. The difference between the two could hardly have been more pronounced. When Steve Cherry took a junior high school team to a black school for the first time, he recalled, he and his players found the atmosphere profoundly disconcerting. "We had not been used to that type cheering," he explained. "Not actually loud but more of a chanting type. Everybody involved kind of cheering as opposed to the white cheerleaders going out and saying a cheer and then everybody calming down and maybe yelling occasionally at a referee or something of that nature. This was almost constant throughout the game, the singing and chanting, and it was very intimidating."[55]

Such distinctions placed black cheerleaders at an enormous disadvantage in the performance-based tryouts that were customary at white schools. As so frequently happened in the early years of desegregation, the changing situation prompted few adjustments on the part of white administrators, and black cheerleaders were expected to conform to the standards of majority white student bodies or of judges who had been evaluating white cheerleaders for years. In many cases the result was an all-white squad. Attempts to justify the outcome could carry a tone of condescension that only increased black students' frustration. At Lincolnton High School, Alan Stoudemire recalled, "The all white selection committee of female teachers insisted that the process was 'perfectly fair,' that it was simply a matter of the black girls' lack of familiarity with the traditional LHS cheers and the accompanying drills and gymnastics required. They just needed a year or two to 'catch up.' " After Lincolnton judges picked an all-white squad, previously muted frictions between black and white students escalated. Similarly, when judges chose an all-white squad at Mill-brook High, Susan Shakelford began to sense "a huge amount of tension—an amount of tension I had not felt, really, since the first week of school."[56]

At schools across the state, all-white cheerleading squads became a symbol of the broader frustrations black students felt over the adjustments they were expected to make to their new situation—frustrations that were heightened by the countervailing celebration of African American cultural strength embodied in the growing black power movement. At Asheville High School, following a racially charged melee that led city officials to impose a curfew and put several black "militants" on trial, black students drew up a list of grievances that mixed concerns about uneven discipline and inadequate bus service with potent cultural issues. According to the first complaint on the list, "The majority of majorettes or cheer leaders at AHS were white girls." Students also protested that "in cosmetology class, the instructor had said she couldn't do Negroes' hair," and that "Negro history is taught by a white teacher, and the history textbook's author is a white man, and neither is competent to teach Negro history."[57]

Cheerleading disputes were intensified by their multiple implications. Cheerleader selection, students knew, involved more gymnastics or drills. Cheerleaders were expected not simply to master routines but to project a "look," a combination of clothing, hairstyle, figure, and enthusiastic charm considered to embody the ideals of youthful womanhood. Shutting black women out of this highly charged arena could thus symbolize rejection not just of their performance but also of themselves. At Lincolnton, Alan Stoudemire sensed, the rejected candidates were not simply angry; they also felt "humiliated." In such circumstances it was easy to suspect that many whites remained unwilling to consider black women worthy of the multifaceted status that cheerleading conferred, a suspicion that only heightened student anger.[58]

Homecoming queen contests, which embodied similar issues of womanly status, also came under dispute. The apparent reluctance of white school officials to crown a black homecoming queen became a subject of discussion among black students at Ashley High School in the fall of 1966, the year the integrated basketball team achieved such great success. That year, John Costner recalled, a single black student competed with several white candidates for homecoming queen. Although African Americans formed a distinct minority at the school—a disadvantage that would plague black students across the state in areas of school life settled by election—the multiple contestants gave the black candidate a chance. After the votes were counted, however, school officials announced plans for a runoff election between the black candidate and

Millbrook High School cheerleading squad, 1971. Cheerleading squads proved more difficult to integrate than sports teams. From *The Laurel*; photograph courtesy of Susan Shakelford.

one of the white women. Black students smelled a rat. "There was a runoff between the most popular white girl and the most popular black girl," Costner explained. "Now you have to ask yourself, 'How does that happen when you have one black person running and five or six white people running?' So we felt that Andrea won, no doubt about it. But no way she's going to win, and there's just two people running. No way she's going to win now."[59]

The obstacles that confronted potential black cheerleaders and homecoming queens underscored the difficulties that African Americans faced as they sought to make places for themselves within previously white institutions. Battles for respect and equal treatment would frequently have to be fought one by one, often on varying terrain. The sexual dynamics that had developed around athletic contests—dramatized by the athletes on the field and the cheerleaders on the sidelines—should have meant that integrating one piece of that puzzle would prompt wholesale reconsideration. One issue raised by integrated sports, in fact, involved the explosive possibility of contact between white women and black men. When Oscar Robertson and Johnny Green integrated the Dixie Classic, organizers had worried less about their play than about their interactions with the Dixie Classic Queen—the contest for queen remained thoroughly unintegrated, and the winner traditionally crowned the tournament's champion, frequently bestowing a kiss along with the trophy. But although black cheerleaders or homecoming queens would clearly have helped mute such concerns, the status such positions had attained among white women complicated efforts to abandon or modify existing systems of selection.[60]

Schools eventually adopted a variety of strategies for achieving integrated squads. At many schools, including Lincolnton High School and Hyde County's Mattamuskeet School, student committees formed to work through issues of racial balance. The Lincolnton committee proposed that at least three of the twelve cheerleading positions be reserved for blacks, while the Mattamuskeet students decided initially to have both black and white homecoming queens and graduation speakers. Some schools held separate contests for black and white cheerleaders. In Mecklenburg County the Charlotte-Mecklenburg Board of Education instituted systemwide quotas designed to "guarantee that at least one-third of the students elected to offices such as student government representative, cheerleader or lettergirl must be black and at least one-third white."[61]

Still, while such solutions helped ease tensions at many schools, neither integrated cheering squads nor the strategies by which they were achieved gained nearly the acclaim accorded to integrated sports. In fact, the prominence athletics was assuming as a model for African American success had the potential to heighten dissatisfaction with alternate methods of integration, which by comparison could seem manipulative and unfair. When black student protests prompted Millbrook administrators to add black members to the cheerleading squad, Susan Shakelford recalled, many white students supported the move. Others, however, "were mad about it. They felt like that the system was a meritocracy, and if the squad was all black, well, all black kids made it. If it was all white, all white, or mixed or whatever. And that's just the way they felt." A proposal to add a black cheerleader to the Walter Williams squad prompted one resident to write the local paper, using language that echoed the criticism of efforts to reform college basketball. "Our national elections are not held this way, so why must we force our students to vote this way?" the writer asked. "In my opinion, it borders on communism."[62]

Many African Americans themselves seemed uneasy with the process, anticipating a day when a more universal standard could once again reign. Looking back at the early years of integration at West Charlotte High School, graduate Tim Gibbs recalled, "We went through a thing where there was a white queen and a black queen, and you were trying to divide the cheerleaders based on the percentage of blacks to whites at the school. And I think most folks sort of understood that this was something that needed to happen. There needed to be some breaking of the ice, if you will." Jerome Evans voiced similar sentiments. "For the first few years of integration we'll need ratios," he speculated. "In a few years we'll have our own blue chips who can earn their way. But that's still a few years off."[63]

The limits on the role that athletics could play in African American struggles also showed at the college level, as the politics of the civil rights movement continued to shift. In the mid-1960s, as the philosophy of black power gained growing numbers of adherents, a group of activists began to change their thinking about the role African American athletes should play in the broader civil rights movement. Rather than simply serving as symbols of African American achievement, this analysis ran, black athletes should use the prominence they had won to lead battles against other, more entrenched problems. Boxer Muhammad Ali had set the stage for this development in 1966 when he cited racial injustice as one reason for his refusal to be inducted for service in the Vietnam War. Inspired by his example, a group of activists based in California had launched an effort to make the 1968 Olympics a showcase for broader African American grievances, seeking both to shame their country's leadership and to galvanize ordinary African Americans. The movement, which began with a boycott effort, culminated in spectacular style when sprinters Tommie Smith and John Carlos, who had finished first and third in the 200-yard dash, climbed the victory podium, bowed their heads, and in one of the most memorable moments in sporting history, raised their fists in a black power salute.[64]

Within North Carolina there were hints that the state's black athletes might try to use their status to take similar stands. In the fall of 1968, for example, a group of the University of North Carolina's black food service workers, with the assistance of the newly formed Black Student Movement (BSM), began to put pressure on the university, demanding both better wages and better treatment. As talks dragged on into 1969, Charlie Scott and freshman basketball player Bill Chamberlain put in an appearance at one of the negotiating sessions, drawing immediate attention. "Black Cagers May Join BSM Unless Group Demands Met," ran the headline in the *Daily Tar Heel*. The *Durham Sun*, which headed its report of the meeting with "Basketball Stars At Conference As 'Mediators,'" quoted coach Dean Smith as saying that he and the players "had discussed the black student demands on many occasions" and that he had encouraged them to go to the meeting.[65]

At the *Daily Tar Heel*, editors responded eagerly to the basketball players' appearance, urging them on in words that echoed the newly militant political language being heard around the country. Sports editor Owen Davis lauded the players for being "prepared to take an open stand on racial problems" and anticipated further action. "What Scott and Chamberlain are now doing in connection with BSM will be unpopular in many quarters," Owen continued. "They will be branded as troublemakers, as have others in the civil rights movement for years. Carolina alumni, who like to identify with the winning basketball team, will sit uneasily while Scott and Chamberlain emerge as spokesmen for a cause [of] which most in the state disapprove. But there are few heroes in history who have not been vilified by the public in their time." The masthead editorial that ran the day after the event used even stronger terms. "The two athletes imply that they are going to use their positions as basketball stars as a club to force the Administration to act, and this probably will gall a lot of people. We, however, see nothing wrong with it. Blacks lack power in our society, and in order to get that which they should have had long ago, it is only proper that they use whatever power they can get their hands on, whether it be vote power, economic power, or athletic power."[66]

Despite the *Daily Tar Heel*'s forceful rhetoric, however, the power of such gestures would prove hard to employ in local efforts like the food service workers' struggle. Athletes such as Muhammad Ali had achieved their greatest effect when they used their own experience to dramatically crystallize the great contradictions in U.S. democratic rhetoric. The vision of Tommie Smith and John Carlos, who had reached the pinnacle of their sport but still faced widespread discrimination in the country they represented, gained its power from precisely this tension, as did Ali's oft-quoted phrase, "No Viet Cong ever called me nigger." But attempts to move from broad symbolic gestures into the details of individual struggles frequently met with the same complications faced by other efforts to put symbol into practice. Although the *Daily Tar Heel* spoke confidently of "athletic power," the actual power that college athletes wielded was limited indeed.

The complications of an athlete's involvement in other African American struggles quickly became evident in events at Chapel Hill. Three days after Scott and Chamberlain appeared at the negotiation meeting, the food service workers went on strike. Shortly afterward, clashes between supporters and opponents of the effort led Chapel Hill police to intervene with riot gear. North Carolina governor Robert Scott, a North Carolina State alumnus, was already impatient with the racial tensions that had been developing at the school and in the state. He quickly turned the strike into a symbolic demonstration of his refusal to tolerate social unrest, sending state police to Chapel Hill and ordering nearby national guard units to be ready to move onto the campus. Only after a month of tense negotiations that involved demonstrations, threats of faculty strikes, and the state-directed eviction of students who had established a "Soul Food" cafeteria in a university building did the governor agree to raise the state minimum wage, giving the food workers their victory and defusing the conflict.[67]

In such a situation, with statewide political stakes so dramatically raised, athletes such as Charlie Scott and Bill Chamberlain wielded little power. Whether or not a sports team won was of limited import at a campus occupied by state police. Like Ali, Carlos, and Smith, athletes could prove an inspiration to protesters, urging them on and giving them a sense of pride and confidence in African American abilities. But the circumstances of the food workers' strike complicated efforts to draw the rhetorical connections to fair play that made athletics such a potent metaphor in other situations. The conflict between Governor Scott and the cafeteria workers bore little resemblance to an athletic event, with evenly matched teams competing under an accepted set of rules. Rather, it was a struggle over the rules themselves—over the fundamental relationship between workers and employers. While paying low wages for jobs that had historically been filled by African Americans was indeed a pernicious form of discrimination, that issue also did not lend itself to the metaphor of the level playing field.[68]

While the effectiveness of athletes' contributions to struggles such as the food service workers' strike remained in question, the short-term consequences were clear. In the polarized racial climate of the later 1960s, black athletes who became overtly militant drew enormous criticism from mainstream white society. *Raleigh News and Observer* sportswriter Dick Herbert had penned dozens of glowing reports of African American athletes such as Oscar Robertson and Charlie Scott. But he reacted angrily to Carlos and Smith's Olympic demonstration. He blasted bronze-medalist Carlos for having "loafed" during the race, suggesting that his supposedly unpatriotic attitude had been reflected in his performance, and asserted that the two runners had broken one of the cardinal rules of athletics: "When [Carlos] and Smith accepted places on the team, they tacitly accepted the rules, regulations and policies of that team. That's the way it is in sports." Scott and Chamberlain's status as pioneering black athletes at a southern school, where acceptance was frequently tenuous in even the best circumstances, further complicated the situation. Even the suggestion that Scott might put politics above performance was enough to turn some Carolina fans against him. As a *New York Times* reporter sat in a Winston-Salem barbershop watching the Tar Heels go down to humiliating defeat against Purdue, one observer noted that he had heard a rumor that Scott might have planned to play badly on purpose, in solidarity with student and striker grievances. "I don't doubt it a bit," another responded. "Damned nigger."[69]

In the end Charlie Scott, along with most African American athletes around the country, pursued the older strategy, placing his faith in the long-term benefits of individual African American achievement. As one of the nation's top college players, he had faced not only the struggles in Chapel Hill but also the issue of the Olympic boycott. "Somebody asked me recently how I felt about some of the Negro athletes' plans to boycott the Olympics," he told the *Daily Tar Heel* in February 1968. "I really couldn't answer that. I couldn't say on the spur of the moment that because some other Negro says he's going to do something, I'm going to do it. I would have to have a really strong reason." In the end he joined the Olympic team and performed with distinction in Mexico City, helping the United States win the gold medal. Whatever he thought of John Carlos and Tommie Smith, he apparently did not express it to reporters. In a brief article written on his return, the *Daily Tar Heel* noted simply that he was pleased to have won a gold medal and found the Olympics "a great challenge."[70]

Scott briefly dropped his guard in the spring of 1969 when, at the end of a stellar season, ACC voters failed to name him unanimously to the all-conference squad. For the first time since he had come to Chapel Hill, he complained bitterly to reporters about racial discrimination in the conference and hinted at a waning faith in the path he had taken. "This is a frustrating thing when you go to the Olympics and represent your state, your country, your conference," he added. "It really makes you think. It makes you wonder."[71] But aside from that brief statement, he let his performance speak for him. He played splendidly throughout his career, was a first-team All-America selection his senior year, and maintained warm ties with his alma mater after graduation. Black leaders committed to such a strategy of integration could have asked for no more. Within North Carolina the story of Scott's career took much the same shape as that of Jackie Robinson. He was remembered as a young man who shouldered a difficult burden, passed through the fire of threat and insult, and emerged victorious, having won an honored place in the pantheon of beloved state heroes.

Such stories would, in fact, be the major legacy of the widespread success black athletes achieved in the 1960s, as well as in subsequent decades. In 1971, the year after Charlie Scott played his last college game, North Carolina State emerged victorious from a hard-fought recruiting battle to sign Boiling Springs native David Thompson, one of the top prospects in the nation. The soft-spoken, gloriously talented Thompson would lead State to its first national championship, helping fulfill Everett Case's never-realized dream and, in the process, expanding the hold that Charlie Scott had laid on the state's sporting affections. But neither Thompson nor many of the other African American athletes who plied the state's courts and gridirons would venture far into the turbulent waves of racial politics. Players would join in a number of campus protests, especially in efforts to eliminate Civil War–related symbols such as Confederate flags and the playing of "Dixie." They would work remarkable stylistic transformations on the games they played—most notably basketball—through the fluid effort and dramatic flair that had become such an integral part of African American sporting aesthetics. But the main message of their play would be one of acceptance, once again offering the hope that by proving their ability and following the rules, African Americans could indeed grasp the benefits of mainstream U.S. society. "One way to protest is to defeat your adversary," John McLendon explained in 1997, still committed to the strategy that he had first pursued almost sixty years earlier. "It's a back way to go. But . . . racial problems disappear more quickly when you earn the respect of people. You may not earn rights, but you can earn their respect—I think that athletics gives you a chance to do that."[72]

# Sports and Social Change

he NCAA championship game had wound down to its final moments as the UNC Tar Heels, trailing, set up for one last play. The spectators that packed the large arena, exhausted but exhilarated by the contest they had witnessed, leaned forward in anticipation, and in homes across the country eager viewers fixed their eyes on television screens. The defenders ranged themselves around the basket, the ball came into bounds, and as countless Tar Heel supporters held their breath, it rested for an instant in the hands of player number 23, who then sent it arching toward the goal. The net shook briefly as the ball fell through the center of the rim. Charlotte Smith, who had just won the Lady Tar Heels their first national championship, fell to the floor in joy.

Charlotte Smith's winning basket, along with the statewide celebration that ensued, offered one example of the many changes that North Carolina sports had undergone during the previous century. During the 1950s, North Carolina women's basketball had been swept out of the public eye, pressed by shifts in popular culture and state society that devastated women's sports, even as they raised male athletes to new heights of prestige and popularity. But in the 1970s, as a broad-based women's movement built up around the country, women's athletics took on renewed significance. Like their predecessors early in the century, female activists saw sports as a way for women to throw off physical and emotional restrictions, developing skills, pride, and confidence. They also launched a long and hard-fought battle for a place in the public spotlight, amid the high school and college teams that commanded such widespread attention and respect. The resulting transformations, highlighted by the Lady Tar Heels' 1994 national title, underscored the connections between athletics and the dynamic process by which North Carolinians—and Americans in general—have made and remade their social institutions and themselves. A century of athletic endeavor charts a complex web of interactions, illuminating the many ways that sports have both reflected and influenced the society surrounding them. Today, when sports have gained unprecedented prominence in American culture, this long, revealing history offers fuel for celebration and for caution, recounting stories not only of courage and achievement but of tensions and contradictions that are with us to this day.

In the late nineteenth century, when today's athletic institutions began to take shape in North Carolina, the state's residents were contending with a society in which political and economic affairs increasingly seemed to embody the competitive forces that Charles Darwin had depicted as driving the natural world. The crumbling of the antebellum social order and the expansion of a commercially driven economy laid new stress on the merits of individuals, on the ability to make one's own way amid changing, competitive circumstances. At the same time, a group of powerful white men used a different set of arguments about nature and heredity to limit participation in the state's affairs, excluding women, African Americans, and most of the state's new corps of industrial workers from political and economic power. The athletic programs sponsored by North Carolina's most prominent universities closely paralleled such developments. A new emphasis on organized team sports—primarily college football—reflected a society seen in competitive terms, where institutions ranging from graded schools to textile mill YMCAs sought to train the state's citizens in the corresponding virtues of discipline, teamwork, and determined effort. The young players who plied the state's newly laid gridirons—educated, ambitious, male, and white—represented an emerging elite, the pinnacle of the state's new social hierarchy. The games that they so eagerly organized thus became multifaceted metaphors for North Carolina society, embodying social and economic arrangements that the era's social Darwinists portrayed as reflecting the natural order of the world.

In ensuing decades, however, athletics took on far more expansive meanings, as a broad range of citizens—women, African Americans, textile mill workers—made athletic games their own, transforming fields and courts into arenas for pursuing their own ends. The many changes state society was undergoing required residents from every walk of life to refashion lives and identities, responding to the demands of industrial labor, urban life, and the ideas and images spread through the expanding institutions of national mass culture. Athletics became one way for North Carolinians to engage this new society, an arena where residents could school themselves in the discipline and coordinated effort that were becoming hallmarks of American achievement, experiment with the pleasures of self-expression and public performance, and negotiate the boundaries between local cultures and national ideals. The teams that sprang up at schools around the state became a focus for community life, drawing residentes together around events that dramatized a new set of increasingly shared values. Athletics also created spaces in which those who had been excluded from political and economic power could conduct a distant dialogue with those worlds, using athletic achievement to build their own confidence, while laying symbolic claim to broader roles in state affairs.

This multifaceted appeal helped build school sports into an institution that stretched across the many boundaries that marked North Carolina society, giving it enormous influence. From the state's major universities to its smallest textile mill towns, from rural pastures to big-city gymnasiums, from white women's colleges to African American institutions, sports grew into a cherished ritual, the rounds of games and seasons becoming an integral component of community life. The widespread admiration that athletic ability inspired would help transform athletic fields from grounds of symbolic play to forces for social change, places where a wide range of citizens could publicly and at times effectively challenge the assumptions that cast them as unworthy of full participation in U.S. society. While athletic successes would not rid society of prejudice or stereotype—black athletes would continue to confront racial slurs, and sports would remain for many a cornerstone of a specifically masculine identity—the well-publicized achievements of athletes such as Charlie Scott, Michael Jordan, Charlotte Smith, and Mia Hamm lent meaningful support to the idea that women or African Americans or a wide range of other individuals possessed the discipline, intelligence, and poise to contend for position or influence in every arena of national life.

Still, even as athletics became a powerful arena for challenging deep-seated assumptions about race or gender, it also provided significant support to other components of twentieth-century American society—most notably to the theory that competitive individualism should form the basis of social and economic life, sorting those who deserved society's rewards from those who fell behind. The meaning of competitive endeavor had been a source of controversy since the nineteenth century, when shifting social and economic currents turned competition into a metaphor that seemed to govern much of human action. Uneasy observers such as Emory University's Warren Candler had fretted over the lack of larger purpose such contests seemed to entail, denouncing a scramble for profits and status that transformed individuals into little more than "money-making or business machines." Other participants in the emerging social order, however, cast their competitive efforts in a different light, claiming to pursue far nobler ends. As Darwinism worked its way into American social thought, adherents blended the theory with firmly held beliefs in progress and religious destiny, producing a vision of human advancement that made competition into a potent moral force and gave the victors of such struggles, whether political, athletic, or economic, special worth. At the turn of the century, textile executive D. A. Tompkins drew on such a vision to portray competition as both inevitable and desirable, justifying imperial expansion, white supremacy and ruthless business tactics by arguing not only that "the fittest survive" but that "it must be so, else there is no life, no progress."[1]

The athletic programs taking shape at precisely the time that D. A. Tompkins offered his pronouncements took such ideas and turned them into compelling dramas, investing theory with emotional force. Athletics joined a panoply of institutions—graded schools, business enterprises, political campaigns—that were making competition an accepted, seemingly immutable component of American life. But athletic contests enacted these principles with unusual clarity, overlaid with a powerful blend of community identity, educational imperative, and individual heroism. Athletics also offered its supporters a vivid, appealing language with which to discuss other competitive affairs. Even as sports took on the language of industry, with coaches speaking of "well-oiled machines" or of "clicking on all cylinders," politicians and business leaders began to describe their endeavors in terms of home runs, of fast breaks, and of hitting the line hard—frequently blurring distinctions between athletics and society. The tight connections that developed between sports and educational institutions extended such associations, as supporters cast their games as useful preparation for the challenges of life. Perhaps most significant, athletics wove the structures and rhythms of competition into everyday routines, profoundly affecting even those citizens not engaged in the day-to-day workings of commerce or political affairs. Through practice and example, through effort and experience, myriad young Americans learned how to win. Through the charged rituals of games, tournaments, statistics, college scholarships, awards ceremonies, and community celebrations, they also learned how much winning seemed to matter.

Like the proponents of white supremacy, advocates of all-out competition did not go unchallenged. While men such as D. A. Tompkins had imbued competition with a strong sense of moral purpose, many others, including Charles Darwin himself, offered far less reassuring views. The Darwinian studies from which advocates of competition drew much of their language portrayed struggles structured by environment and circumstance, in which victors emerged from the evolutionary fray not according to purpose or design, but simply because they happened to possess traits that suited the particular conditions under which they lived. Athletics offered ample support for this perspective, tempering ideal with practical effect. Enormous efforts were poured into making athletes into larger-than-life heroes, linking sporting success not simply with discipline and ambition, but also with a range of other virtues such as honesty and compassion. But while many athletes did indeed possess these valued qualities, the fortunes of numerous teams and individuals made clear that athletic competition more consistently rewarded other, less morally charged traits such as physical agility, single-minded focus, or ruthless determination. As the stakes for victory grew higher, especially in college sports, it also became clear that when winning became the main gauge of success, those qualities most likely to foster victory frequently took precedence over those with more redeeming social value. The battles that developed over talented college recruits showed yet another face of competition: not only did the fierce struggle do little to foster honesty or fair play; it in fact became a force that those who sought to uphold such virtues had to fight against.

Contradictions between the aims and the realities of school sports produced numerous challenges of their own, inspiring nineteenth-century religious critiques of college football, physical educators' endeavors to build cooperation-centered athletic programs, and a series of attempts to downplay big-time college sports. But none of these efforts achieved lasting success. Measures to reform college sports met especially sharp resistance, opposition that underscored the symbolic weight that sports had gained as a model for a conservative view of the American social and economic order. Even as university officials sought to curb athletic programs, opponents—frequently invoking business experience—adopted the Darwinian stance that cast all-out competition as an inevitable, generally admirable fact of life. "Whether you accept this reasoning or not, life is one victory after another," wrote one staunch proponent of the Dixie Classic.[2]

Efforts to question the value of athletic competition were further complicated by the deep-seated, almost mythical appeal that sporting ideals held for many Americans, attractions that frequently swamped consideration of sports' less savory realities. The scandals that plagued athletic history, ranging from recruiting violations to point-shaving schemes to athletes jailed for robbery or assault, were consistently pressed into near-obscurity by the celebratory rhetoric that filled conventional athletic histories. College sports fans regularly lamented the way that cutthroat recruiting and rising infusions of cash tainted the purity of the games they loved so well. But they watched anyway, in greater and greater numbers, setting aside such concerns to revel in the magic of well-executed tackles and last-second, three-point plays. The legends that sprang up around outstanding athletes followed similar patterns. David Thompson,

North Carolina State's great star, had his college career disrupted by recruiting violations, and his talents did not insulate him from either the temptations of cocaine or the stubborn, persistent press of racial prejudice. But the tales told by North Carolinians, as well as sports fans around the country, more often conjured the vision of a red clay backyard, lit into the night by the headlights of a battered car, narrating the equally true story about the way that hard work and dazzling skill carried a deserving young man from poverty to national renown, as well as how a talented and engaging African American won the hearts of a racially divided state's white fans.[3]

Athletics has thus proved at once radical and conservative, challenging some aspects of American society while underpinning others. In part, this dual function can be linked to social context. The most effective efforts to employ athletics in the service of social change have generally been linked with broader social shifts; young women started playing varsity basketball during the heady atmosphere of the woman suffrage campaigns, while African American athletes made their greatest national strides amid the liberalizing racial attitudes of the post–World War II era. The revival of women's sports in the 1970s was closely linked to the developing women's movement. Those who have sought to curb or refashion competitive endeavors have rarely had such favorable times in which to work.

Still, athletics' multiple effects can also be related to the structure of sports itself. Sports offer human beings an arena within which to test themselves—the structure of a game matters far less than the efforts and emotions that participants expend while playing it. The depth of this engagement and the deeply human efforts it draws forth give sports much of their great appeal, for both players and spectators. It also makes athletics a powerful realm for demonstrating individual potential—the reason that outstanding female, African American, and other athletes have been able to make meaningful impressions on both fans and doubters. But sports offer far less room for questioning the rules under which athletes compete, let alone the larger meaning of competition itself.[4]

Athletics would thus serve as a near-perfect model for the civil-rights-inspired push to open American institutions to a broader range of citizens—the process so brilliantly demonstrated by Charlie Scott and other African American athletes of his era. It would also lend metaphorical support to conservative thinkers who sought to uphold other aspects of the social and economic status quo, to arguments that once overt racial barriers were dropped, individual African Americans should follow in the footsteps of Scott or Jackie Robinson, pursuing individual success within existing institutions. Sports would prove less useful to efforts to transform such institutions, to students promoting a broader understanding of what made a good cheerleader, or to union members seeking to recast the balance of power between workers and employers. Athletic success could promote the kind of pride that gave individuals the confidence to challenge the status quo, and the solidarity of team play could offer an inspiring example for collective endeavor. But when it came to the details of forging plans for a more just, diverse society, the model of competition and individual effort embodied in athletic games offered limited guidance and could even prove an obstacle.[5]

Over a century of play, athletics has proved a powerful force in countless American lives, exerting an influence that can seem almost timeless. In school programs throughout the country, the pleasures and challenges of sport have encouraged young people to develop discipline and determination, to pull from themselves often-remarkable reserves of energy and creativity. While the demands of competition often fall short of inspiring the full range of virtues so frequently linked to school athletics, uncounted coaches and educators have taken a broad view of their mission, laboring to combine instruction in strategy and technique with lessons in honesty, dignity, and mutual respect. Athletics has become a means by which communities have drawn together, frequently over great distances, to celebrate the ways that human beings rise to challenges through individual and collective efforts. The concept of the level playing field remains a potent symbol for the best promise of U.S. society as a place where individuals depend on their own merits, are judged by what they do, not who they are.

A century of sporting history, however, offers a far more complex tale, rife not with the clarity of legend but with the entanglements of time and circumstance. As such, it has far more to teach. The games Americans have played highlight the numerous connections that link this nation's diverse communities, as well as the forces that have divided them. The many debates athletics has provoked shed light on the deep-seated assumptions that guide social affairs, conceptions about manhood and womanhood, race and competition, progress and achievement. The symbolic role that sports and athletes have assumed within popular culture, the play of images that proves both troubling and exhilarating, points to key cultural dilemmas of modern life. Lastly, the changing nature of athletic institutions and the battles that have been waged over their shape and purpose make it possible to understand the extent to which the institutions that surround us, the rituals we follow, are not timeless but contingent, freighted with the circumstances and assumptions that influenced their making. Such history recommends considerable caution, warning us not to take the shape of sports—or any other cultural institution—too easily for granted. It should also be a source of inspiration. Amid the complexities of the modern world, it is easy to take a Darwinian view, to see social and economic institutions as impossible to influence, and to turn to a more individualized perspective, focusing on the quality of play rather than the nature of the game. The creative efforts of generations of North Carolinians, the many issues that they faced, and the changes they wrought in both their lives and their society should instead spur us to probe deeper and work harder, learning not only how to win, but when to leave the game behind.

# NOTES

## INTRODUCTION

1. Grundy, *Most Democratic Sport*, 4.

2. For an account of David Thompson's career, see Herakovich, *Pack Pride*, 88–89. Thompson was also national player of the year in 1975. In 1999 *Sports Illustrated* editors placed Thompson on their Team of the Ages, anointing him as one of the best five college players of the twentieth century.

3. Private conversation; Ivory interview, 6.

4. Some of the dynamic connections between play, sport, and society are analyzed in Huizinga, *Homo Ludens*, and Geertz, *Interpretation of Cultures*, 412–53. For a classic account that sets a particular sport in the context of its society, see James, *Beyond a Boundary*. Numerous works in the growing field of sports history have also begun to draw insightful links between sports and society in the United States. Some of the best are Cahn, *Coming on Strong*; Festle, *Playing Nice*; Oriard, *Reading Football*; Gorn, *Manly Art*; and Sperber, *Onward to Victory*.

5. For accounts of post–Civil War transformations in North Carolina, see Hall et al., *Like a Family*; Escott, *Many Excellent People*; Leloudis, *Schooling the New South*; Hanchett, *Sorting Out the New South City*; Tullos, *Habits of Industry*; Greenwood, *Bittersweet Legacy*; and Gilmore, *Gender and Jim Crow*. For descriptions of transformations in character and culture that accompanied industrialization elsewhere in the country, see Ryan, *Cradle of the Middle Class*; Paul E. Johnson, *Shopkeeper's Millennium*; Kasson, *Rudeness and Civility*; and Lawrence Levine, *Highbrow/Lowbrow*.

6. A detailed, insightful account of the cultural and psychological ramifications of the shift from antebellum schooling to a graded system, as well as the significance that schooling came to assume in postbellum North Carolina, can be found in Leloudis, *Schooling the New South*; quotes are from ibid., 20, 23. The classic text exploring the ways that schooling shapes character as well as ideas is Durkheim, *Moral Education*. For an account of the early development of graded school philosophy, see Tyack, *One Best System*. For the significance that education held for southern African Americans in the postbellum era, see Anderson, *Education of Blacks in the South*.

7. The affinities between sports and North Carolina's emerging social and educational institutions fit effectively into Antonio Gramsci's theories of hegemony; they helped weave assumptions about competition, success, and individual achievement so tightly into American culture that they would become almost invisible to many Americans. For a discussion of Gramsci's usefulness for cultural history, see Lears, "Concept of Cultural Hegemony." For descriptions of the transformation of sports in the modern era as well as arguments about its educational worth, see Huizinga, *Homo Ludens*, 195–213; Gorn, *Manly Art*, 179–206; Oriard, *Reading Football*, 23–56; and Gorn and Goldstein, *Brief History of American Sports*, 153–82.

8. A particularly thoughtful treatment of sports and identity among women can be found in Cahn, *Coming on Strong*, 223–45. My concepts of identity-building as a fluid process influenced by shifting combinations of a variety of images and ideas are influenced by Claude Lévi-Strauss's theory of bricolage, as recounted in his *Savage Mind*, 16–33. The growing significance of leisure and recreation as arenas where nineteenth- and twentieth-century Americans located and played with central aspects of their identity is considered in, for example, Hunter, *To 'Joy My Freedom*; Kasson, *Amusing the Million*; Rosenzweig, *Eight Hours for What We Will*; and Peiss, *Cheap Amusements*.

9. The significance vigorous sports assumed among white college men is considered in Doyle, "Turning the Tide," and Patrick B. Miller, "The Manly, the Moral, and the Proficient." Meanings of North Carolina's women's sports are explored in Dean, " 'Dear Sisters' and 'Hated Rivals.' " An interpretation of sporting activities at African American schools can be found in Patrick B. Miller, " 'To Bring the Race along Rapidly.' "

10. For a nuanced and compelling account of the multiple interpretations attached to the sport of football, see Oriard, *Reading Football*, 1–20. As Oriard notes, the multiple meanings sports assume also make it difficult to theorize effectively about them. Pierre Bourdieu also acknowledges the difficulties of such a task; see Bourdieu, *Distinction*, 217. For treatments of the ways that multiple meanings have been attached to other mass culture institutions in the twentieth century, see Grundy, " 'We Always Tried to Be Good People,' " and Lawrence Levine, "Folklore of Industrial Society." Theories of play are elucidated with enduring elegance in Huizinga, *Homo Ludens*. While the play aspects of sports remained a significant source of appeal within North Carolina, this work will concentrate largely on those aspects of North Carolina that seem to throw the greatest light on state and national society. Huizinga himself questioned the extent to which U.S. school athletics embodied the play instincts he delineated; see *Homo Ludens*, 197–98.

11. A broad and growing literature on the practice of oral history emphasizes the powerful role that personal and historical memories play in the actions and decisions of daily life. Rather than focusing on whether such memories accurately reflect historical reality, I consider the process by which they are formed and the uses to which they are put, examining both the patterns of thinking they reflect and the subsequent influence they wield. A useful overview of this literature, including an extensive bibliography, is Thomson, "Fifty Years On." For other examples of both theory and practice, see Thompson, *Voice of the Past*; Frisch, *Shared Authority*; Hall, " 'You Must Remember This' "; Terkel, *Hard Times*; and the articles in the special issue "Memory and American History," *Journal of American History* 75 (March 1989). Because I was particularly interested in the meanings of direct experience with school sports, I interviewed mostly players and coaches. My decisions about whom to interview were directed toward engaging the sporting experiences of a broad variety of individuals, rather than a systematic effort to obtain a representative sample. Since much of the interviewing was done in conjunction with museum projects covering the several counties that surround Charlotte, there is a definite bias toward that part of the state.

12. For a discussion of this dialogue-centered approach to writing history, see Lu Ann Jones, "Voices of Southern Agricultural History." The writings of many scholars, both in North Carolina and elsewhere, have influenced this work, but I have drawn particularly often on Anderson, *Education of Blacks in the South*; Cahn, *Coming on Strong*; Chafe, *Civilities and Civil Rights*; Dean, "Covert Curriculum"; George, *Elevating the Game*; Gilmore, *Gender and Jim Crow*; Hall et al., *Like a Family*; Kasson, *Rudeness and Civility*; Kelley, " 'We Are Not What We Seem' "; Leloudis, *Schooling the New South*; Liberti, " 'We Were Ladies' "; Oriard, *Reading Football*; and Tullos, *Habits of Industry*.

13. Perhaps the most significant decision I made was to place my major treatments of black women's sports in chapters focusing on women rather than on race, thus emphasizing the gendered over the racial aspects of these women's experiences. I made this choice in large part because I was particularly intrigued by the way that patterns of athletic development among different groups of North Carolina women complicated assumptions about categories of womanhood that tend to be defined along the lines of race and class. Still, a greater emphasis on the racial components of black women's experiences would likely have proved equally, if not more, illuminating of other issues. Despite considerable thought and struggle, I could not come up with a satisfactory narrative structure that allowed me to pursue both directions to a greater extent than I have here.

14. For an insightful argument regarding the significance of the "everyday," especially in popular conceptions of race, see Thomas C. Holt, "Marking."

15. Particularly intriguing treatments of immigrants and sports can be found in Gorn, *Manly Art*; Peter Levine, *Ellis Island to Ebbets Field*; Barth, *City People*, 149–91; and Sperber, *Onward to Victory*, 3–14. The power of modern athletics, I argue, lies partly in how athletic events are able to exercise cultural authority on many levels, both intellectual (in their reliance on widespread concepts of the value of competitive endeavor) and emotional (in the powerful, direct effect they have on observers). In this way they meet Max Weber's criteria of both affectual and value-rational legitimacy. For Weber's outline of forms of legitimacy, see his *Economy and Society*, 31–40.

CHAPTER ONE

1. *Living Stone*, April 1891, 120–21.

2. Ibid.

3. A thoughtful account of baseball's ties to modern U.S. life can be found in Barth, *City People*, 148–91. For other accounts of early baseball, see Goldstein, *Playing for Keeps*; Peter Levine, *A. G. Spalding*; Riess, *Touching Base*; Adelman, *Sporting Time*; and Peterson, *Only the Ball Was White*, 16–51.

4. Kratt, *Charlotte*, 50.

5. For a detailed description of this transformation in the city of Charlotte, see Hanchett, *Sorting Out the New South City*, 31–45.

6. *Star of Zion*, May 27, July 15, 1897; *Davidson Monthly*, March 1896, 213–14. The *Star of Zion* did not use page numbers until June 1898.

7. The founding of African American schools is recounted in Gilmore, *Gender and Jim Crow*, 37–38. Teacher training schools are described in Leloudis, *Schooling the New South*, 74–76. The white agricultural college eventually became North Carolina State University, and the black college became North Carolina Agricultural and Technical University.

8. Leloudis, *Schooling the New South*, 55; Griffin, *Black Theology As the Foundation of Three Methodist Colleges*, 92. A description of debates over the direction of black college education can be found in Anderson, *Education of Blacks in the South*, 31–78.

9. Sumner, "John Franklin Crowell," 9–11.

10. Fonvielle, *Reminiscences of College Days*, 73.

11. Lingle, *Memories of Davidson College*, 21–23, 46.

12. The Livingstone banner is described in Fonvielle, *Reminiscences of College Days*, 83. Examples of student exhortations can be found in *Living Stone*, April 1891, 119–20, and *Davidson Monthly*, October 1891, 18–19, and October 1894, 58–65. Accounts of the

relationship between a developing industrial economy and shifting ideas of character development among the northeastern middle class can be found in Ryan, *Cradle of the Middle Class*, and Paul E. Johnson, *Shopkeeper's Millennium*.

13. Horace Williams, *Education of Horace Williams*, 10; *State Normal Magazine*, December 1898, 353; *Davidson College Magazine*, November 1897, 73. A more comprehensive discussion of changes at North Carolina colleges can be found in Leloudis, *Schooling the New South*, 37–72.

14. *Davidson Monthly*, March 1896, 213–16.

15. Barrier, *On Carolina's Gridiron*, 19. The interest in balancing academic work with physical endeavors showed clearly in a wide range of student publications, which regularly condemned overstudious pupils and praised those who pursued a wider variety of activities, among them sports.

16. *Living Stone*, October 1890, 60; *Charlotte Observer*, May 14, 1893, 5.

17. *University of North Carolina Alumni Quarterly*, October 1894, 35.

18. Fonvielle, *Reminiscences of College Days*, 67. Ayers, *Promise of the New South*, 313–16.

19. The most comprehensive and insightful account of the symbolic significance college football acquired in national circles is Oriard, *Reading Football*. Excellent accounts of some of the early meanings of southern football are Doyle, "Foolish and Useless Sport," and Miller, "The Manly, the Moral, and the Proficient." See also Ayers, *Promise of the New South*, 313–15.

20. Gorn and Goldstein, *Brief History of American Sports*, 158–59; Crowell, *Personal Recollections*, 231; *University of North Carolina Alumni Quarterly*, October 1894, 28.

21. *University Record*, November 1907, 7.

22. *Charlotte Observer*, May 14, 1893, 5.

23. *North Carolina Teacher*, December 1892, 158, and January 1893, 204–5; *Davidson Monthly*, December 1892, 218.

24. Lingle, *Memories of Davidson College*, 50.

25. For an account of football strategy, see Oriard, *Reading Football*, 25–35. In his study of nineteenth-century prizefighting, Elliot Gorn concluded that "scientific" regulations heightened violence as well; when players switched from bare knuckles to gloves, blows to competitors' heads increased markedly (while hitting someone in the head with bare hands was more likely to injure the hand than the head, gloves gave hands more protection, prompting the change in strategy). See Gorn, *Manly Art*, 204–5. Even the most carefully written rules often did little to restrain such competitive fervor. In 1891, when YMCA instructor James Naismith drew up basketball's first thirteen rules, he was specifically seeking to avert the violent contact that characterized games such as football. Early contests, however, belied these efforts. With characteristic calm, Naismith described the first contest at the Springfield, Massachusetts, college where he taught: "There was no team work, but each man did his best. The forwards tried to make goals and the backs tried to keep the opponents from making them. The team was large, and the floor was small. Any man on the field was close enough to the basket to throw for goal, and most of them were anxious to score" (Naismith, *Basketball*, 57).

26. *Raleigh News and Observer*, December 1, 1888, 1; Crowell, *Personal Recollections*, 46.

27. *Davidson College Magazine*, December 1899, 145.

28. Lingle, *Memories of Davidson College*, 44. For an account of game-related unruliness in the Northeast, see Oriard, *Reading Football*, 100–101. In general, early-nineteenth-century entertainment had blurred the lines between performance and spec-

tator in a variety of venues until a series of efforts, driven largely by an interest in establishing middle-class cultural authority, hardened those boundaries. For accounts of this process, see Kasson, *Rudeness and Civility*, 215–56, and Lawrence Levine, *Highbrow/Lowbrow*.

29. Lingle, *Memories of Davidson College*, 44.

30. Sumner, "John Franklin Crowell," 11; Pugh, "History of Men's Intercollegiate Athletics at Johnson C. Smith University," 11.

31. Crowell, *Personal Recollections*, 231.

32. *Davidson Monthly*, June 1894, 357. For a description of religious metaphors of sport, see Oriard, *Sporting with the Gods*, 152–59. A discussion of nineteenth-century manhood can be found in Bederman, *Manliness and Civilization*, 10–13.

33. A detailed and thoughtful discussion of the arguments southern evangelicals raised against football can be found in Doyle, "Foolish and Useless Sport"; quotations from 314, 322, 327.

34. Porter, *Trinity and Duke*, 38, 49–50.

35. Gorn and Goldstein, *Brief History of American Sports*, 82; Gorn, *Manly Art*, 191–93.

36. Bederman, *Manliness and Civilization*, discusses at length the growing celebration of "primitive" masculine energy among middle-class white men, as well as the connections between such celebrations and claims to gender and racial dominance during the late nineteenth and early twentieth centuries. The Roosevelt quote is on p. 186.

37. Doyle, "Foolish and Useless Sport," 331; Gorn, *Manly Art*, 191.

38. See Gilmore, *Gender and Jim Crow*, 61–68.

39. Winston, *Builder of the New South*, 303, 265; Tullos, *Habits of Industry*, 159. For an account of struggles over mill work and mill village conditions, see Hall et al., *Like a Family*, 58–60, 119–39.

40. Winston, *Builder of the New South*, 299, 304. For descriptions of the broad hold such ideas had over North Carolina's industrial leaders, see Hanchett, *Sorting Out the New South City*, 48–88, and Escott, *Many Excellent People*, 196–219.

41. For other public challenges that individual African Americans mounted to assumptions of white supremacy, see Gilmore, *Gender and Jim Crow*, 102–5.

42. For shifts in the North Carolina farming economy, see Escott, *Many Excellent People*, 171–79. Between 1880 and 1900, Escott notes, the number of tenants working North Carolina farms increased from 53,000 to 93,000. For accounts of the complexities of regionwide economic change, the hardships it worked on once-independent farmers, and the resulting political discontents, see Hahn, *Roots of Southern Populism*; Durrill, "Producing Poverty"; and Goodwyn, *Democratic Promise*. For discussions of Fusion philosophies and achievements, see Gilmore, *Gender and Jim Crow*, 77–78, and Escott, *Many Excellent People*, 245–54.

43. *Raleigh News and Observer*, July 5, 1898, 3. For details about Fusion politics and about Democratic Party leaders, see Greenwood, *Bittersweet Legacy*, 186–213, and Hanchett, *Sorting Out the New South City*, 70–88. Acts of intimidation during the election ranged from the breaking up of opposition political meetings to the violence that broke out in the city of Wilmington just after the election, in which a group of Democrats forcibly ousted the city's elected government after sparking a riot in which a number of black citizens were injured. Cecelski and Tyson, *Democracy Betrayed*, offers a multifaceted assessment of the riot. For an account of similar bloodshed in a South Carolina community, as well as its aftermath, see Gavins, *Perils and Prospects of Southern Black Leadership*, 6–7. For a description of the way Theodore Roosevelt promoted his wartime heroics as evidence of racial revival, see Bederman, *Manliness and Civilization*, 190–92.

North Carolina's African Americans themselves would look on the conflict as a way to assert their own patriotic manhood, joining volunteer militias and eagerly anticipating a chance at combat. But while black North Carolinians drew great pride from their actions, racial tensions within the military hampered their efforts to reach the front, and racial propaganda diminished the impact of their efforts within the state. See Gilmore, *Gender and Jim Crow*, 78–82. A fascinating contemporary interpretation of black wartime participation is Edward A. Johnson, *Negro Soldiers in the Spanish-American War*.

44. Escott, *Many Excellent People*, 258–61; Gilmore, *Gender and Jim Crow*, 111–13.

45. *Davidson College Magazine*, March 1899, 296.

46. Gorn and Goldstein, *Brief History of American Sports*, 147–48; *Davidson College Magazine*, October 1899, 47.

47. Ayers, *Promise of the New South*, 315. For Confederate-related developments in one arena of southern football, see Doyle, "Turning the Tide." The growth of Confederate nostalgia in the late nineteenth century is analyzed perceptively in Wilson, *Baptized in Blood*, and Foster, *Ghosts of the Confederacy*.

48. Gilmore, *Gender and Jim Crow*, 14–25.

49. Fonvielle, *Reminiscences of College Days*, 21.

50. Washington, *Up from Slavery*, 265–66; Jowers, "History of Men's Intercollegiate Athletics at Shaw University," 17–18.

51. Washington, *Up from Slavery*, 266; Fonvielle, *Reminiscences of College Days*, 257.

52. Fonvielle, *Reminiscences of College Days*, 64; *Living Stone*, February 1892, 165, and March 1901, 35. A description of early baseball at Biddle can be found in Parker, *Biddle–Johnson C. Smith University Story*, 14. Details of the national development of African American baseball in the nineteenth century can be found in Peterson, *Only the Ball Was White*, 16–51.

53. Article reprinted in Fonvielle, *Reminiscences of College Days*, 67.

54. *Star of Zion*, November 16, 1893. Descriptions of the game can also be found in Chalk, *Black College Sport*, 197–99; Pugh, "History of Men's Intercollegiate Athletics at Johnson C. Smith University," 11; and Rountree, *Blue Bear Trax*, 5. A survey of nineteenth- and early-twentieth-century black college football games can be found in Chalk, *Black College Sport*, 197–207.

55. *Living Stone*, January 1892, 138; Pugh, "History of Men's Intercollegiate Athletics at Johnson C. Smith University," 11.

56. Walls, *Joseph Charles Price*, 319. A description of debates over the direction of black college education can be found in Anderson, *Education of Blacks in the South*, 31–78.

57. For an account of Shaler's work, see Williamson, *Crucible of Race*, 86–88.

58. *Raleigh News and Observer*, July 18, 1898, 6; Williamson, *Crucible of Race*, 121. For a thoughtful analysis of the civilization arguments adopted by African American leaders, and the pitfalls they held, see Gaines, *Uplifting the Race*, 67–99. Bederman, *Manliness and Civilization*, offers an intriguing analysis of the discourses that developed around concepts of civilization, particularly Ida B. Wells's skillful use of the idea in her campaign against lynching. The *Caucasian's* editor Marion Butler, interestingly, would later become a high-ranking Populist, serve as chairman of the national executive committee of the Populist Party, and become a Fusion senator from North Carolina, a career that hints at the fluidity of political positions and alliances that characterized the 1890s.

59. Price, "Education and the Race Problem," 76; *Star of Zion*, March 17, 1898. See also Greenwood, *Bittersweet Legacy*, 83–86, and Gaines, *Uplifting the Race*, 34–37. Greenwood notes that alcohol formed a particular image-linked concern for black leaders because "uneducated" black votes had been loudly blamed for defeating statewide pro-

hibition in 1882. For descriptions of the public physical presence fashioned by many African Americans following Emancipation, see White and White, *Stylin'*, 85–179, and Gilmore, *Gender and Jim Crow*, 73–77, 102–5.

60. *Star of Zion*, April 29, 1897. Discussion of the optimistic outlook of North Carolina's African Americans up to the eve of disfranchisement can be found in Greenwood, *Bittersweet Legacy*, 172–86.

61. For a discussion of competing nineteenth-century theories about the relative physical capacities of different races, see Hoberman, *Mortal Engines*, 33–55. While most of North Carolina's black schools were governed largely by whites throughout the nineteenth century—Livingstone College, founded by the AME Zion Church, was the exception—the era's most prominent institutions were church related and drew on missionary philosophies that resonated closely with the ideals of educated black leaders. The best of the white leaders not only labored to educate black students for full participation in American life, but they also sought to use their positions to combat racial stereotypes and other forms of discrimination. For an account of the philosophies that governed church-related education as well as relations between white and African Americans leaders at such schools, see Anderson, *Education of Blacks in the South*, 238–45.

62. *New York Times*, November 26, 1897, 1. The article has been reprinted in its entirety. Other information on the game can be found in Chalk, *Black College Sport*, 201.

63. Black readers of the *New York Times* article probably drew little consolation from its placement below another football-related piece, "A FIGHT AT ANNAPOLIS," which described a prolonged and bloody struggle waged by naval cadets over team flags. Details about Fred Staples come from Chalk, *Black College Sport*, 201. A better-publicized struggle with the possibilities and pitfalls of using football to gain racial recognition was waged by the team representing Carlisle Indian Industrial School in Carlisle, Pennsylvania. Carlisle head R. H. Pratt saw the sport as a way to build respect for his students, and he allowed them to form a team after offering a warning and exacting a promise:

> You will never, under any circumstances, slug. . . . You will play fair straight through, and if the other fellows slug you will in no case return it. Can't you see that if you slug, people who are looking on will say, "There, that's the Indian of it. Just see them. They are savages and you can't get it out of them." Our white fellows may do a lot of slugging and it causes little or no remark, but you have to make a record for your race. If the other fellows slug and you do not return it, very soon you will be the most famous football team in the country. If you can set an example of that kind for the white race, you will do a work in the highest interests of your people.

The Carlisle players' own remarks suggest that many read their own achievements in terms of self-discipline and intelligence, often inverting conventional distinctions between "civilized" whites and "savage" Indians. Renowned Carlisle coach Glen "Pop" Warner recalled one player who responded to an illegal hit by asking his opponent, "Who's the savage now?" Another wrote home after a victory that while white men might be "better with cannon and guns," Indians were "just as good in brains." Accounts of Carlisle's games in white newspapers, however, often painted a different portrait. In 1896, for example, the *New York World* described a Carlisle-Brown match in thoroughly stereotypical terms: "There was fought yesterday the bloodiest, the most savage contest between brawn and brain that modern athletic days have seen. The contestants were eleven young football players from Brown University, at Providence, R.I., representing the highest type of New England culture, and eleven young Indians from the Government school at Carlisle, Pa., drawn from the uncivilized sections of the far West and trained into the ways of the white man." When the game ended in a Brown victory, the reporter drew a predictable conclusion: "Brains won in the contest, as they always do in the long run. Science triumphed with her mysterious tricks and ways that are dark and puzzling to the untutored mind." See Pratt, *Battlefield and Classroom*, 317–18; David Wallace Adams, *Education for Extinction*, 181–90; and Oriard, *Reading Football*, 237. For an illuminating account of the Carlisle team's experiences, see Oriard, *Reading Football*, 233–47.

64. Another hint of the tantalizing possibilities athletics held for promoting racial respect could be found in a brief article in the *Star of Zion* in 1898 that recounted the international cycling record set by Marshall "Major" Taylor, a young black man from Indianapolis. "Marshall Taylor, colored, better known as 'Major,' is the fastest cyclist in the world," the editors wrote. "This was proven at the Woodside Park track in Phila-delphia in October and November. He is a young chap, slim built, and bending his chest down until it touches his low handle bars, riding faster than any wheelman has ever ridden before, he speeds with vengeance like a cyclone, smashing the world's record by making a mile in 1:31 ⅘. He believes he can outrun the fastest engine. White and colored wheelmen all over the country are sending him congratulatory telegrams." The article concluded simply but pointedly: "Give the Negro an equal chance and he will get there" (*Star of Zion*, December 1, 1898, 4). Taylor was also invoked as a counter to theories of African American physical decline in Edward A. Johnson, *Negro Soldiers in the Spanish-American War*, 178–79.

65. *AME Zion Quarterly Review*, October–December 1900, 64–65. For an account of the career of another pioneering African American college football player, see Carroll, *Fritz Pollard*.

CHAPTER TWO

1. *Charlotte Observer*, April 9, 1907, 4.

2. Ibid.

3. Accounts of early women's basketball activities can be found in Hult and Trekell, *Century of Women's Basketball*, 3–154.

4. Lojko, "Effects of Societal and Cultural Changes," 13; *Salisbury Daily Sun*, quoted in *Living Stone*, March 1901, 6. Detailed and thoughtful examinations of the development of "new women" at the State Normal and Industrial College in Greensboro, the largest women's school in the state, can be found in Dean, "Covert Curriculum," and Leloudis, *Schooling the New South*, 73–106. College education among North Carolina's African American women is covered in Gilmore, *Gender and Jim Crow*, 31–46. The classic analysis of nineteenth-century images of southern women is Scott, *Southern Lady*.

5. An account of the demands of urban life, particularly regarding the images urban dwellers created for themselves, can be found in Kasson, *Rudeness and Civility*, 70–146.

6. *Catalog and Circular of the Institute for Young Ladies, Charlotte, N.C., 1875–76* (Charlotte, 1876), 6, folder 4, and *Circular of the Institute for Young Ladies, Charlotte, N.C., 1878–79* (Raleigh, 1878), 6, folder 5, both in box C89-5, Queens College Collections, Charlotte. For a general account of attitudes toward women's sport in the nineteenth and early twentieth centuries, along with a dissection of several theories about women and exercise, see Cahn, *Coming on Strong*, 7–30, esp. 13. A typical expression of such theories appeared in a 1907 *Charlotte Observer* article headlined, "WOMEN HAVE SMALL BRAINS!" The article described the work of a German doctor who had studied brain sizes and had drawn the typically sweeping conclusion that "the difference in the sexes is due to the fact that the principal duty of women is motherhood, and nature cannot afford to

waste on her either physical or mental powers which are not essential to that function" (*Charlotte Observer*, April 7, 1907, sec. 2, p. 23).

7. *Catalog of the Presbyterian College for Women, Charlotte, N.C., 1899–1900* (Charlotte, 1899), 27, folder 14, box C89-5, Queens College Collections, Charlotte; Lojko, "Effects of Societal and Cultural Changes," 29. A description of the role the Boston Normal School played in spreading the gospel of women's exercise can be found in Hult and Trekell, *Century of Women's Basketball*, 21.

8. Leloudis, *Schooling the New South*, 101; Bloomer, *Life and Writings of Amelia Bloomer*, 65–81.

9. Larrabee, "Women and Cycling," 90.

10. *Catalog and Circular of the Charlotte Female Institute* (Charlotte, 1886), 35, folder 9, box C89-5, Queens College Collections, Charlotte; Paul, "Clara Gregory Baer," 47.

11. *State Normal Magazine*, April 1899, 483.

12. Ibid., June 1900, 173.

13. *Living Stone*, March 1901, 35; Lojko, "Effects of Societal and Cultural Changes," 46, 35.

14. Dean, "Covert Curriculum," 150.

15. *Living Stone*, February–March 1891, 112.

16. *State Normal Magazine*, April 1902, 293–94. For a description of Lady Principal Kirkland, see Nettie Allen Deans to J. I Foust, October 18, 1934, folder 4, box 3, Foust Papers, University of North Carolina, Greensboro.

17. *State Normal Magazine*, January 1908, 59.

18. Ibid., October 1903, 13.

19. *Charlotte Observer*, April 14, 1907, 2. A handful of the words were cut off when the papers were microfilmed. At Newcomb College in New Orleans, where basketball got an early start under the direction of Clara Baer, it was said that the noise made by alumnae at the annual class tournament rivaled any heard at the football games between Tulane and Louisiana State. See Paul, "Clara Gregory Baer," 47.

20. *Carolinian*, 1911, 66.

21. *Elizabethan*, 1905, 128, folder 7, box C89-4, Queens College Collections, Charlotte. The selection of "Amazons" was particularly striking, since the term had often been employed to chide politically active women, branding their activities as unnatural. See Varon, "Tippecanoe and the Ladies," 510, 520.

22. *North Carolina State Normal and Industrial College Decennial*, 1902, 128.

23. Ibid., 132; Berta Albright Moore to J. I. Foust, March 1935, folder 4, box 3, Foust Papers, University of North Carolina, Greensboro.

24. *North Carolina State Normal and Industrial College Decennial*, 1902, 76. The parenthetical question mark is in the original. That this "quiet, unpretentious class" won the school tournament, while the confident sophomores had been upset the year before, may have been a lesson in itself.

25. *Carolinian*, 1910, 152.

26. *Edelweiss*, 1915, 25; 1907, 77; 1908, 125, all in box C89-4, Queens College Collections, Charlotte.

27. Hult and Trekell, *Century of Women's Basketball*, 25.

28. Lebsock, "Woman Suffrage and White Supremacy," 81; *Elizabethan*, 1913, n.p., folder 9, box C89-4, Queens College Collections, Charlotte. There do seem to have been some definite connections between athletics and interest in political rights at Elizabeth. Three of the four officers of that year's Suffragists club, including Jessica Britt, played basketball, as did one of the other four club members.

29. *Carolinian*, 1910, 156.

30. Ibid., 163.

31. *State Normal Magazine*, May 1910, 203–4.

32. For a consideration of the many ambiguities with which young women at the State Normal College wrestled, including in their relationships to men, see Dean, "Learning to be New Women."

33. *Living Stone*, January 1913, 14; Gilmore, *Gender and Jim Crow*, 36–39.

34. *Living Stone*, March 1901, 35. Livingstone's records of this early period are more complete than those at other schools, but histories of other sports programs chart a growing interest in sports after the turn of the century. See Pugh, "History of Men's Intercollegiate Athletics at Johnson C. Smith University," and Jowers, "History of Men's Intercollegiate Athletics at Shaw University." More general descriptions of early-twentieth-century athletic programs at black schools can be found in Ashe, *Hard Road to Glory*, 1:77–81, 94–98, and Chalk, *Black College Sport*, 37–69, 197–241.

35. George, *Elevating the Game*, 23–24. In the kind of error of detail common to this book, George misstates the CIAA founding date as 1916. See Ashe, *Hard Road to Glory*, 1:80. The switch from "Colored" to "Central" was common for black organizations once the description "colored" fell out of general use.

36. *Living Stone*, March 1913, 16. Only scattered issues of the magazine are preserved in the college archives, but almost every issue provides a great deal of information about men's sports, in contrast to their silence on women's activities. For the Shaw photograph, see *Thirty-sixth Annual Catalog of the Officers and Students of Shaw University, 1909–10* (1910), University Archives, Shaw University, Raleigh.

37. *Living Stone*, March 1901, 35. For a discussion of southern femininity, see Sims, *Power of Femininity in the New South*, 1–3.

38. Leloudis, *Schooling the New South*, 105. For a description of the politics surrounding white women's education, see ibid., 94–106. Accounts of debates over black women's education and activities can be found in Gilmore, *Gender and Jim Crow*, 37–45, 153–54.

39. Stephanie Shaw, *What a Woman Ought to Be and to Do*, 14.

40. Throughout the country, for example, critics of women's athletics referred to possible sexual ramifications in veiled but easily interpreted terms, warning, for example, that the rush of competition gave rise to troublingly "powerful impulses." See Cahn, *Coming on Strong*, 21–23.

41. Fonvielle, *Taint of the Bicycle*, 10–11. Copy located in the College Archives, Livingstone College, Salisbury, N.C.

42. Ibid., 21.

43. Dean, " 'Dear Sisters' and 'Hated Rivals,' " 348–49.

44. Delany and Delany, *Having Our Say*, 128.

45. *Charlotte Observer*, April 9, 1907, 4. Although the writer mentions "abbreviated skirts," photographs and illustrations make clear that the players were wearing bloomers.

46. Ibid., April 9, 1907, 4, and April 7, 1907, 6; *Charlotte News*, April 9, 1907, 5.

47. *Charlotte Observer*, April 9, 1907, 6. The illustration can be found in *Charlotte News*, April 12, 1907, 1.

48. *Charlotte News*, April 9, 1907, 5.

49. *Charlotte Observer*, April 9, 1907, 4.

50. *Edelweiss*, 1908, 125, box C89-4, Queens College Collections, Charlotte.

51. Ibid., 133, and 1910, 127.

52. For a description of early-twentieth-century debates about southern black education, see Anderson, *Education of Blacks in the South*, 79–109. The quotation, from North Carolina educator George T. Winston, is on p. 85.

53. *Shaw University, Raleigh, North Carolina*, and *An Appeal for the Girls' New Building*, n.p., both in North Carolina Collection, University of North Carolina, Chapel Hill. A year after Shaw's pamphlet was issued, an inspector for the General Education Board faulted the school for emphasizing "classical training." See Anderson, *Education of Blacks in the South*, 132. For other examples of such efforts, see Gilmore, *Gender and Jim Crow*, 138–41.

54. *State Normal Magazine*, April 1902, 304.

55. See Leloudis, *Schooling the New South*, 102–6.

56. An examination of this rhetorical style among white women and a thorough consideration of the new roles women were taking in public education, can be found in ibid., 73–106. For an account of black women's activities and rhetorical strategies, see Gilmore, *Gender and Jim Crow*, 147–57.

57. Marion Stevens Hood to J. I. Foust, March 15, 1935, folder 4, box 3, Foust Papers, University of North Carolina, Greensboro.

58. "38th Annual Report to the Trustees of Shaw University and the Secretary of the American Baptist Home Mission Society," folder "1903," box "Correspondence, 1895–1904," Meserve Papers, Shaw University, Raleigh.

59. Delany and Delany, *Having Our Say*, 62. Also *Forty-second Annual Catalog of the Officers and Students of Shaw University, 1916–17* (1916), 27; *Forty-third Annual Catalog of the Officers and Students of Shaw University, 1917–18* (1917), 11; *Forty-sixth Annual Catalog of the Officers and Students of Shaw University, 1921–22* (1920), 15, all in University Archives, Shaw University, Raleigh.

60. *Forty-second Annual Catalog of the Officers and Students of Shaw University, 1916–17* (1916), 27, and *Forty-third Annual Catalog of the Officers and Students of Shaw University, 1917–18* (1917), 11 (italics in original), in University Archives, Shaw University, Raleigh. Photographs suggest that players at white schools had started wearing bloomers without skirts as much as a decade earlier. For work done by slave women, see Jacquelyn Jones, *Labor of Love, Labor of Sorrow*, 1–29. For black women's labor after Emancipation, see Hunter, *To 'Joy My Freedom*.

61. A list of basketball's original rules, as well as a fascinating description of the development of the game, can be found in Naismith, *Basketball*, 53–55, 61–99. For a description of perceptions of basketball as a women's sport, see Pharr and Pharr interview, 1, and Cahn, *Coming on Strong*, 85–86. Basketball quickly became popular among men at YMCAs, but the religious orientation of those institutions contributed to the game's less than manly reputation in some circles.

62. Dean, " 'Dear Sisters' and 'Hated Rivals,' " 350.

63. The literature on the Progressive movement is extensive, but the classic account of its philosophy remains Wiebe, *Search for Order*. For an account that pays particular attention to Progressivism in North Carolina, see Link, *Paradox of Southern Progressivism*. A useful discussion of the complications of defining southern Progressivism, along with a historiographical accounting, can be found in Gilmore, *Gender and Jim Crow*, 147–50.

64. *Living Stone*, February–March 1891, 4. For examples of activities among African American women, see Gilmore, *Gender and Jim Crow*, 147–75. For reform efforts among white schoolteachers, see Leloudis, *Schooling the New South*, 155–66. Descriptions of the political styles developed by North Carolina women can be found in Nasstrom, " 'More Was Expected of Us,' " and Wilkerson-Freeman, "From Clubs to Parties." This analysis, of course, did not extend to all southern women. Class elections at the State Normal College were often hard-fought battles, intense enough to produce a 1910 denunciation of the "girl who wants a definite office and is willing to do definite things to gain the

office" (*State Normal Magazine*, March 1910, 155). Hall, *Revolt against Chivalry*, provides a vivid portrait of a woman who relished political conflict.

65. Concerns about maintaining moral authority came clear in the state's early campaigns for woman suffrage, when a number of the state's most prominent female reformers initially joined the antisuffragist camp. Part of this reluctance could be linked to the racial dynamics that suffused every facet of North Carolina politics. Some black women were cool toward suffrage because they doubted white female voters would prove any less dedicated to white supremacy than their male counterparts. In contrast, a common white antisuffragist position argued that any tampering with voting legislation would bring black women, and thus eventually black men, into the sacred space of the voting booth. But still other women demurred because they questioned whether the power of the vote would make up for the loss of the moral "higher ground" that they had worked so diligently to capture and exploit. See Gilmore, *Gender and Jim Crow*, 211–12, and Sims, *Power of Femininity in the New South*, 158. For a detailed discussion of the suffrage battles, see Sims, *Power of Femininity in the New South*, 155–88.

66. For a more detailed description of the developing philosophy of physical education, see Cahn, *Coming on Strong*, 23–29. The philosophy would initially attain its greatest influence in schools for white women, but a number of influential black colleges, including Howard, Spelman, and Fisk, would adopt it as well. See Gissendanner, "African-American Women and Competitive Sport," 86–88.

67. *Carolinian*, 1913, 312; Umstead, "Mary Channing Coleman," 149.

68. *Carolinian*, 1913, 359.

69. Ibid., 1914, 173; Mary Channing Coleman, "Wentworth," graduation talk delivered at Wentworth High School, 1937, n.p., in folder "Selected Writings of Coleman," box I, Coleman Papers, University of North Carolina, Greensboro. As Susan Cahn makes clear, it is often difficult to sort through the varying influences that shaped physical education philosophy. Physical educators were concerned about professional, social, and sexual respectability as well as about the potential "excesses" of competitive endeavor. They were more likely to support competition in the sport of field hockey, an upper-class, exclusively female sport, than in basketball. Cahn's focus on issues of gender and sexuality leads her to concentrate on those threads of influence. Because this work gives more emphasis to questions of social and political organization, I have emphasized strains of physical education philosophy that speak to those issues. See Cahn, *Coming on Strong*, 83–109.

70. *Charlotte Observer*, April 9, 1907, 4.

## CHAPTER THREE

1. *Pine Burr* (Lincolnton High School annual), 1927, 59.

2. For participation figures, see "High School Athletic Association of North Carolina," 5, copy in North Carolina Collection, University of North Carolina, Chapel Hill.

3. *Dixie Doings*, January 28, 1916, 3; Ardrey and Kell interview, 4. Copies of *Dixie Doings* are in folder "A Game for Everyone," "Most Democratic Sport" collection, Museum of the New South, Charlotte. The impression of the Dixie High School students is backed by state surveys, which consistently list basketball as the high school sport with greatest participation. See, for example, "High School Principal's Reports," box 20, Division of Instructional Services, Department of Public Instruction, North Carolina State Archives, Raleigh. Regarding Lavinia Kell's name, one of the complications of writing a history that centers in part on women's recollections of their youth involves

deciding whether to use maiden or married names. Where possible, and with an occasional exception required for style or clarity, I have used both names on first reference and married name afterward.

4. Gorn and Goldstein, *Brief History of American Sports*, 188–97.

5. *Charlotte Observer*, February 11, 1910, 3; *Second Ward Herald*, 1928, 1; Grundy, *Most Democratic Sport*, 35. Issues of the *Second Ward Herald* are in the archives of the Second Ward High School National Alumni Foundation, Charlotte.

6. For a comprehensive treatment of the transformation of North Carolina schools, see Leloudis, *Schooling the New South*.

7. A detailed account of these efforts can be found in Link, *Paradox of Southern Progressivism*. For the hookworm campaign in particular, see Link, " 'Harvest Is Ripe.' "

8. For a description of this transformation, see Tullos, *Habits of Industry*, 134–71. The industrial transformation of the southern Piedmont, along with the many social and cultural tensions that it caused, has been examined in numerous fine works. Those with the most influence over this study are Tullos, *Habits of Industry*; Hall et al., *Like a Family*; Carlton, *Mill and Town in South Carolina*; Leloudis, *Schooling the New South*; Hanchett, *Sorting Out the New South City*; and Pope, *Millhands and Preachers*.

9. Hall et al., *Like a Family*, 137.

10. Ibid., 130–39. For comparisons between southern and New England textile industries, see Tindall, *Emergence of the New South*, 75–78.

11. A comprehensive and insightful description of this shift can be found in Leloudis, *Schooling the New South*, 20–35.

12. David Tyack notes that "in the theory accepted by many of the administrative progressives, the school system sorted out students by ability and probably careers and educated them accordingly. This presupposed an economic order that would be open to talented recruits from the lower ranks of society; indeed, the notion of a school-filtered meritocracy was becoming the twentieth-century version of the earlier self-made man ideology" (Tyack, *One Best System*, 221). For a description of the ideas that guided the development of American graded school education, see ibid., 39–54.

13. The actual high school attendance figures were 61 percent of eligible whites and 26 percent of eligible African Americans; see Anderson, *Education of Blacks in the South*, 236. For a general description of barriers to schooling, see Hall et al., *Like a Family*, 128–29. North Carolina officials did not begin to build public high schools for blacks until the 1920s, when it became clear that without such opportunities even more black citizens would join the northward migration that threatened to deprive the state of a large part of its labor force. See Anderson, *Education of Blacks in the South*, 202–3.

14. *Hickory Daily Record*, March 21, 1926, 8; *Second Ward Herald*, March 1932, 1.

15. Miller and Parker, *Physical Education in the High School*, 5, copy in North Carolina Collection, University of North Carolina, Chapel Hill. For a summary of the nationwide development and spread of play theories, see Gorn and Goldstein, *Brief History of American Sports*, 174–82.

16. Miller and Parker, *Physical Education in the High School*, 6; *Biddle Outlook*, May 1917, 1.

17. *North Carolina Education*, February 1923, 13. This publication was generally aimed at the state's white teachers. For Helen Shipman's experiences, see Liberti, " 'We Were Ladies,' " 186. The appeal of sports also helped keep some students in school, an added boon for educators attempting to meet ambitious attendance goals (and obtain attendance-based funding) in institutions where attendance was not yet compulsory. Sometimes, though, this appeal seems to have gotten out of hand, as in the community

of Newell, where former student Frances Freeman recalled that "a lot of the boys would not do well in school just to get to play ball about five or six years" (Austin, Cochran, Freeman, Faulk, and Kimbrell interview, 6).

18. Escott, *Many Excellent People*, 144–46, 247–51; Leloudis, *Schooling the New South*, 136–41.

19. *North Carolina Education*, December 1914, 7.

20. Ardrey and Kell interview, 4; Hewins, Hewins, and Edwards interview, 5.

21. Davis, *History of Mary Potter School*, 15. For the story of the Newell gymnasium, see Austin, Cochran, Freeman, Faulk, and Kimbrell interview, 2.

22. Grundy, *Most Democratic Sport*, 35.

23. Participation figures come from "High School Athletic Association of North Carolina," 4. Comprehensive information on African American school sports is difficult to gather for these early years, but brief accounts in newspapers and school publications note a variety of leagues and competitions.

24. An excellent account of the history of this debate in the nineteenth and early twentieth centuries can be found in Oriard, *Reading Football*, 142–88.

25. Naismith, *Basketball*, 84. Johan Huizinga marks a similar distinction between serious "sport" and the more pleasure-centered enjoyments of "play" in *Homo Ludens*, 196–97.

26. Written memoir by Jane Kuykendall, Mocksville, N.C., basketball player, 1927–28, fall 1993, folder "A Game for Everyone," "Most Democratic Sport" collection, Museum of the New South, Charlotte.

27. Ardrey and Kell interview, 3; Callaway interview, 5. Interestingly, the coach of Pineville's girls' team at the time was apparently far more serious than the boys' coach.

28. Thompson interview, tape 1, side A.

29. *Raleigh News and Observer*, February 5, 1933, 10.

30. Ibid., January 22, 1921, 8; January 14, 1921, 2; February 8, 1921, 7; February 9, 1921, 2.

31. *Southern Textile Bulletin*, May 19, 1921, 1. A description of changes in the textile industry can be found in Hall et al., *Like a Family*, 195–212.

32. Ward, *Baseball*, 143–44.

33. *Charlotte News*, January 12, 1922, 4; *Hickory Daily Record*, March 17, 1926, 1; *Raleigh News and Observer*, February 6, 1921, 16. "Indighted" is the *Hickory Daily Record*'s spelling.

34. Avery, *Idle Comments*, 23–24; *Journal of Proceedings of 11th Annual State Convention of the Y-M-C-A-*. Copy in the North Carolina Collection, University of North Carolina, Chapel Hill.

35. *Hickory Daily Record*, March 5, 1926, 2. This interest in schools as centers for moral education was a common theme in industrializing societies throughout the world, most famously analyzed by educational sociologist Emile Durkheim. See Durkheim, *Moral Education*, and Fenton, Reiner, and Hamnet, *Durkheim and Modern Sociology*, 143–74.

36. *Hickory Daily Record*, March 5, 1926, 2; *Charlotte News*, February 7, 1929, 17, and February 10, 1929, sec. A, p. 3. Although such attention might seem an advantage in to-day's publicity-oriented atmosphere, the statement was clearly meant as a chastisement.

37. "High School Athletic Association of North Carolina," 5.

38. *Southern Textile Bulletin*, February 23, 1922, 26.

39. *Carolina Times*, February 4, 1950, 4.

40. Naismith, *Basketball*, 74; *Raleigh News and Observer*, January 23, 1921, 2.

41. Naismith, *Basketball*, 94. For accounts of the dynamics of cultural authority employed to "discipline" spectators in the late nineteenth century, when a mixture of

regulation and admonition was used to compel audiences who had once noisily participated in plays and musical events to sit in quiet admiration and accept the authority of
the performers on the stage, see Kasson, *Rudeness and Civility*, 215–56, and Lawrence
Levine, *Highbrow/Lowbrow*.

42. Newitt interview, 2.

43. Ibid.

44. *North Carolina Education*, October 1922, 9.

45. Descriptions of the development of some of these postwar divisions can be found
in Escott, *Many Excellent People*; Cash, *Mind of the South*; Pope, *Millhands and Preachers*; and Grundy "From *Il Trovatore* to the Crazy Mountaineers." A perceptive account
from neighboring South Carolina is Carlton, *Mill and Town in South Carolina*.

46. Cunningham interview, 2. The ability of athletics to dramatize larger social conflicts was, of course, one of its major appeals. Particularly acute accounts of this phenomenon in other sporting arenas are Elliot Gorn's analysis of boxing and ethnic
tensions in nineteenth-century America in *Manly Art* and C. L. R. James's account of
color and ethnicity in West Indian cricket, analyzed in *Beyond a Boundary*.

47. *North Carolina Education*, March 1920, 1. For a thoughtful account of home front
experience during World War I, including a description of wartime patriotic rhetoric,
see Kennedy, *Over Here*.

48. *North Carolina Teachers Record*, October 1931, 70, 77.

49. *School Life*, September 1921, 4–5.

50. For the postwar aspirations and experiences of African Americans, see Lewis,
*When Harlem Was in Vogue*, 3–24. For the coal mining conflicts, see Corbin, *Life, Work,
and Rebellion in the Coal Fields*.

51. Hall et al., *Like a Family*, 186–90; quotes are on 187, 189.

52. Miller and Parker, *Physical Education in the High School*, 7; Naismith, *Basketball*,
184–89. In order, the qualities listed by Miller and Parker were leadership, self-control,
cooperation, fairness, truthfulness, self-confidence, obedience, courage, loyalty, determination, quickness of perception, and quickness of action. Traits chosen by Naismith
were initiative, agility, accuracy, alertness, cooperation, skill, reflex judgment, speed,
self-confidence, self-sacrifice, self-control, and sportsmanship.

53. *North Carolina Teachers Record*, May 1932, 32–33, and January 1932, 8.

54. Ibid., May 1931, 55, 42–43 (italics in original).

55. For a discussion of the multiple meanings in depression era popular culture, see
Lawrence Levine, "Folklore of Industrial Society." For an account of reactions to Amos
'n' Andy, see Ely, *Adventures of Amos 'n' Andy*. For hillbilly music, see Grundy, " 'We
Always Tried to Be Good People.' "

CHAPTER FOUR

1. Ashe interview, tape index. Background information on the strike can be found in
Carol Shaw, "City in Conflict," 1–9.

2. *Charlotte News*, August 10, 1919, 18; Cloniger interview, tape 1, side A. Cloniger was a
union member, but the membership had voted that he could continue supervising the
car barn during the strike. Southern Public Utilities, in fact, appeared somewhat willing
to negotiate on wages and on recognition of a local union, but they balked at the
workers' insistence that they be allowed to affiliate with the Chicago-based Amalga-
mated Association of Street and Electrical Railways Employees of America, a move that
would have greatly strengthened the local drivers' ability to negotiate and strike.

3. *Charlotte News*, September 8, 1919, 2; for a description of the committee, see September 7, 1919, 11.

4. The McCáchrens and their achievements were regularly featured in newspaper articles and historical accounts, as well as in other contexts. See, for example, Rappoport, *Tar Heel North Carolina Basketball*, 48–53; Quincy, *They Made the Bell Tower Chime*, 46–47; Grundy, *Most Democratic Sport*, 20; and Tom Bost interview, 34–35.

5. As the acute racial tensions of the late nineteenth century were replaced by a social order in which white men were firmly in control, and as the dictates of racial segregation meant that blacks and whites lived much of their lives in separate worlds, struggles over white identity that had once been focused on drawing sharp lines between whites and African Americans frequently became debates conducted exclusively among whites, with little sense of racial contingency. For discussions of these developments, see Hale, *Making Whiteness*, 242–44, 264–68. Like many institutions, sports had its racially permeable edges—informal, integrated games were common in the state, and in the 1930s both Duke and the University of North Carolina played a small number of football contests against racially integrated teams outside the region (see Chapter 9). But such events apparently had little long-term effect on white public consciousness, and the major public discussions that took place around white university and industrial sports in the 1930s were carried on almost exclusively among whites. For an account of early integrated sports, see Martin, "Rise and Fall of Jim Crow," 256–59.

6. *Charlotte Observer*, September 11, 1922, reprinted in Dunnagan, *Red Strings Baseball Team*, 47; Webster interview, 22. Despite his second-tier status among young boys, William Jennings Bryan was a well-known figure in Yadkin County; Dunnagan related the story of an Elkin nine who styled themselves the "Bryan Baseball Team," complete with silver caps and uniforms, and of the day the Red Strings carried out a plan to beat them by the Free Silver score of 16-1 (see Dunnagan, *Red Strings Baseball Team*, 14).

7. Slaughter, *Country Hardball*, 6–8.

8. In the urban Northeast in the late nineteenth century, big-city papers began to establish sports departments and publish sports pages, supplementing specialized sports publications such as the *Spirit of the Times*, the *New York Clipper*, and the *Police Gazette*. In North Carolina, however, most newspapers mixed sports with news until well after the turn of the century. See Barth, *City People*, 83.

9. T. H. Higdon to Editor, *Alumni Review*, March 5, 1932, folder "Athletics, Intercollegiate Basketball, 1932," subgroup 1, series 4, Graham Records, University of North Carolina, Chapel Hill (hereafter cited as Graham Series). For accounts of Merriwell and his creator, see Cutler, *Gilbert Patten*.

10. Sumner, *History of Sports*, 48–52.

11. *Alumni Review*, October 15, 1930, 1. In 1930 *Alumni Review* editors added dated biweekly football editions to their customary monthly publishing schedule.

12. David O. Levine, *American College*, 38–44, 59; Tullos, *Habits of Industry*, 290–91.

13. *Alumni Review*, February 1928, 136.

14. Ibid., October 1927, 14, and May 1931, 207. For a historical account of business skepticism toward higher education, see David O. Levine, *American College*, 53–57.

15. W. B. Truitt to Frank Porter Graham, January 25, 1936, folder "1936: January 16–26," subgroup 1, series 1, subseries 4, Graham Series.

16. Marvin L. Ritch to Frank Porter Graham, February 1, 1932, folder "Athletics, Intercollegiate Basketball, 1932," subgroup 1, series 4, Graham Series. For descriptions of games that raised the above issues, see T. H. Higdon to Editor *Alumni Review*, March 5, 1932, ibid., and *Alumni Review*, October 1927, 16. More than half a century after football

coach Chuck Collins came to Chapel Hill from Notre Dame's renowned program, two longtime university supporters described him with a vividness that suggested he was a focus for debates about culture as well as athletics. In a series of oral history interviews conducted in the 1980s, J. Maryon "Spike" Saunders, one of the school's staunchest alumni boosters, recalled Collins's six-year career with enthusiasm, exclaiming, "He hit Chapel Hill fresh and vigorous, with that Notre Dame spunk and spirit." Longtime university administrator Robert Burton House described the coach in less emotive terms: "And we had a man who came here from Notre Dame and wore an old green uniform and walked up and down the sidelines cussing. That was his contribution. We got rid of him." See Saunders interview, 24, and House interview, 18.

17. "Athletic Manifesto," forwarded to Frank Porter Graham by Davidson College president Walter Lingle, November 28, 1936, folder "December 1936," subgroup 1, series 1, subseries 4, Graham Series; *Alumni Review*, March 1928, 173.

18. The most comprehensive account of the North Carolina textile industry is Hall et al., *Like a Family*. For a specific discussion of textile industry economics in the 1920s, see ibid., 183–212.

19. Frank Porter Graham to James Rowland Angell, January 25, 1936, in folder "1936: January 16–26," subgroup 1, series 1, subseries 4, Graham Series. For an account of Graham's life, see Ashby, *Frank Porter Graham*.

20. For a synopsis of the differences between these two forms of interaction, see Lévi-Strauss, *Savage Mind*, 30–33.

21. Dunnagan, *Red Strings*, 51; Tom Bost interview, 3.

22. Frank Porter Graham to John Tunis, December 1, 1936, folder "December 1936," subgroup 1, series 1, subseries 4, Graham Series.

23. Savage, *American College Athletics*, vii, 265.

24. Stone, "Graham Plan," 279.

25. *Alumni Review*, October 1930, 6.

26. See K. P. Lewis to Frank Porter Graham, December 13, 1935, in folder "1935—December"; W. George Thomas to Frank Porter Graham, January 1936, in folder "1936: January 16–26"; and J. Will Pless Jr. to Frank Porter Graham, March 22, 1936, in folder "1936: March 16–31," all in subgroup 1, series 1, subseries 4, Graham Series.

27. "Copy of Resolution adopted by the University of North Carolina Alumni of New Hanover County, Wilmington, N.C."; "Resolution of the Davidson County Chapter of the Alumni Association of the University of North Carolina Alumni"; "Copy of Resolution adopted by the University of North Carolina Alumni of Durham County, Durham, N.C.," all January 1936, in folder "1936: January 1–15"; W. George Thomas to Frank Porter Graham, January 24, 1936, in folder "1936: January 16–26," all in subgroup 1, series 1, subseries 4, Graham Series. For an example of "Practical Discussions," see *Southern Textile Bulletin*, December 27, 1923, 14.

28. K. P. Lewis to Frank Porter Graham, January 1, 1936, in folder "1936: January 1–15," subgroup 1, series 1, subseries 4, Graham Series.

29. John Small Jr. to Frank Porter Graham, January 24, 1936; W. A. Blount to Frank Porter Graham, January 21, 1936, both in folder "1936: January 16–26," and K. P. Lewis to Frank Porter Graham, January 1, 1936, 2, in folder "1936: January 1–15," all in subgroup 1, series 1, subseries 4, Graham Series.

30. *Southern Textile Bulletin*, November 28, 1929, 22–23, and December 19, 1929, 23.

31. Link, *William Friday*, 22.

32. Daniels also added a questioning postscript that hinted at his skepticism about potential violations by other schools: "Do you think Maryland is going to stick up to this

agreement?" See Frank Daniels to Frank Porter Graham, January 20, 1936, and Frank Porter Graham to Frank Daniels, January 24, 1936, both in folder "1936: January 16–26," subgroup 1, series 1, subseries 4, Graham Series.

33. J. Will Pless Jr. to Frank Porter Graham, March 22, 1936, in folder "1936: March 16–31," in ibid.

34. *Charlotte Observer*, February 29, 1936, 1. The ongoing university consolidation had created considerable consternation among some alumni who disagreed both with the idea of centralizing university operations and with some of the specific decisions about program distribution.

35. T. E. Wagg Jr. to Frank Porter Graham, January 25, 1936, in folder "1936: January 16–26," and Nat Henry to Frank Porter Graham, March 1, 1936, in folder "1936: March 1–15," both in subgroup 1, series 1, subseries 4, Graham Series.

36. *Alumni Review*, January 1928, 104.

37. For a description of Graham's early years, see Ashby, *Frank Porter Graham*, 3–81. For a southern version of the Social Gospel, see Ayers, *Promise of the New South*, 169–71.

38. *Southern Textile Bulletin*, December 26, 1929, 22. Clark's role in industrial and educational affairs is described in Hall et al., *Like a Family*, 59–60, and Tullos, *Habits of Industry*, 294. The child labor lawsuits, along with Clark's involvement, are discussed in Wood, *Constitutional Politics in the Progressive Era*, and in Simmons, "Child Labor in North Carolina's Textile Industry."

39. *Southern Textile Bulletin*, February 6, 1930, 15, 23. Clark also reprinted Graham's letter.

40. Thomas C. Guthrie Jr. to Frank Porter Graham, March 23, 1936, in folder "1936: March 16–31," subgroup 1, series 1, subseries 4, Graham Series.

41. For an analysis of university relations with industry, see Tullos, *Habits of Industry*, 285–302.

42. C. W. Tillett Jr. to Frank Porter Graham, April 18, 1936, 5–6, in folder "1936: April 16–30," subgroup 1, series 1, subseries 4, Graham Series.

43. Stone, "Graham Plan," 279–90.

44. T. E. Wagg Jr. to Frank Porter Graham, January 25, 1936, in folder "1936: January 16–26," subgroup 1, series 1, subseries 4, Graham Series; Stone, "Graham Plan," 290–91; Sumner, *History of Sports*, 50.

45. The suggestion of callous disregard for young men of modest background implied by these arguments particularly angered Frank Porter Graham, who often went out of his way to help students who were struggling to pay their bills. See Frank Porter Graham to W. C. Jackson, December 18, 1935, in folder "1935—December," subgroup 1, series 1, subseries 4, Graham Series.

46. Herring, *Welfare Work*, 135.

47. Eula and Vernon Durham interview, 50–52.

48. Webster interview, 3–5. Future University of North Carolina president Bill Friday also experienced the benefits of baseball skill during a summer job where he spent almost half his working hours playing on the company team. See Link, *William Friday*, 17.

49. Slaughter, *Country Hardball*, 10, 13.

50. Austin interview, index. For a description of textile workers' accounts of relationships with town, see Hall et al., *Like a Family*, 222–23.

51. *Southern Textile Bulletin*, February 9, 1922, 18.

52. For a description of the Highland Park confrontation, see Hall et al., *Like a Family*, 183–95.

53. *Southern Textile Bulletin*, February 23, 1922, 26.

54. For a description of the culture that developed within mill villages, see Hall et al., *Like a Family*, 114–80, 237–88.

55. Hoyle and Mamie McCorkle interview, 19.

56. In southern textile communities, the balance between protest and accommodation could be extremely delicate. For a particularly thoughtful analysis of these dynamics, see Waldrep, *Southern Workers and the Search for Community*.

57. Faucette interview, 63; Herring, *Welfare Work*, 138–39.

58. *Southern Textile Bulletin*, November 21, 1935, 31.

59. Ashe interview, tape 1, side A. For the Loray team switch, see Hall et al., *Like a Family*, 220.

60. Hoyle and Mamie McCorkle interview, 29; Herring, *Welfare Work*, 135.

61. Webster interview, 7–8. Unionization efforts in the South continued, particularly as the Congress of Industrial Organizations began to take an interest in the region. But the area would not see another uprising on the scale of the 1934 action.

62. James Rowland Angell to Frank Porter Graham, January 29, 1936, in folder "1936: January 27–31"; *Norfolk Virginian-Pilot*, November 24, 1935, clipping in folder "1935— November"; Walter Lingle to Frank Porter Graham, March 5, 1936, in folder "1936: March 1–15"; and Wiley Hurie to Frank Porter Graham, January 22, 1936, in folder "1936: January 16–26," all in subgroup 1, series 1, subseries 4, Graham Series.

63. C. W. Tillett Jr. to Frank Porter Graham, April 18, 1936, 5–6, in folder "1936: April 16–30," in ibid.

64. Ibid. T. E. Wagg offered a critique that resembled Tillett's, writing to Graham that "the effort to prevent football's becoming a piece of commercialism—as admirable as it may be—can in my poor estimation be best approached in a gradual manner and without attendant fanfare and screaming sports headlines" (Wagg to Graham, January 25, 1936, in folder "1936: January 16–26," in ibid.). Regarding athletics and union activity, it is interesting to note that Marvin Ritch, who had so bitterly informed Graham that the university's dismal athletic performance contradicted North Carolina's image as "the most progressive and forward looking State of the South," first made his statewide reputation by representing several different unions (among them the Charlotte streetcar workers) in a variety of highly confrontational situations. See, for example, reports of an altercation related to a textile strike in Albemarle, in which the Stanly County sheriff was shot and Ritch was charged with inciting a riot; see *Charlotte News*, September 18, 1919.

## CHAPTER FIVE

1. Worthy interview, 1–2, 5.

2. Ibid., 6.

3. Ibid., 4.

4. Bauguess interview, 4.

5. For descriptions of changing female careers, see Hall, *Revolt against Chivalry*, 169–71. For an account of North Carolina's hosiery industry, see Hall et al., *Like a Family*, 255–57. Descriptions of shifts in popular culture regarding young women's appearance can be found in Brumberg, *Body Project*, 97–107, and Banner, *American Beauty*, 201–18. See also Ryan, *Womanhood in America*, 220–27. For descriptions of changing images of African American women, see Giddings, *When and Where I Enter*, 183–90. An account of the effects of the cosmetics industry on portrayals of women in popular culture can be found in Peiss, *Hope in a Jar*.

6. Dalton and McMillan interview, 1; *Snips and Cuts* (Central High School annual), 1921, n.p.

7. *Pine Burr*, 1925, 59, 73, and 1926, 77.

8. Grundy, *Most Democratic Sport*, 34. For descriptions of women's different public activities, see Hall et al., *Like a Family*, 212–36; Chafe, *Civilities and Civil Rights*, 20–21; and Korstad, "Those Who Were Not Afraid."

9. Newitt interview, 5. A more detailed analysis of shifting meanings in basketball uniforms can be found in Grundy, "Bloomers and Beyond," 52–67.

10. Concepts of male and female nature had political implications, but in the case of basketball these tended to center on women's role in public life, as opposed to the questions of economic organization so evident in the controversy over men's college sports.

11. Hewins, Hewins, and Edwards interview, 3; Frances Bullard to editor, *Charlotte Observer*, August 30, 1993, sec. A, p. 8. Helen Shipman's experiences are recounted in Liberti, " 'We Were Ladies,' " 186.

12. Hewins, Hewins, and Edwards interview, 3. For descriptions of family labor and women's roles in textile strikes, see Hall et al., *Like a Family*, 51–77, 225–31, and Hall, "Disorderly Women."

13. *Barber-Scotia Index*, October 27, 1933, 3.

14. Baker interview, 21.

15. For the "beauty industry," see Peiss, *Hope in a Jar*, 97–133. For beauty pageants, see Banner, *American Beauty*, 255–70.

16. White and White, *Stylin'*, 209, 199. For a fascinating account of debates among African Americans over female beauty and the use of cosmetics during this era, see Peiss, *Hope in a Jar*, 201–37.

17. Kirkpatrick and Perry, *Southern Textile Basketball Tournament*, 11.

18. *Charlotte Observer*, February 20, 1929, sec. 2, p, 1; Hewins, Hewins, and Edwards interview, 3; Williams interview, 4.

19. *Shaw University Journal*, January 1925, 11; Liberti, " 'We Were Ladies,' " 142.

20. *Register*, May 1938, 1, and February 1937, 3. Accounts of wartime unrest can be found in Lewis, *When Harlem Was in Vogue*, 3–24. For an assessment of the implications coeducation held for black college students, as well as an account of Charlotte Hawkins Brown's North Carolina career, see Gilmore, *Gender and Jim Crow*, 37–45, 178–90. Scotia Seminary, Mary McLeod Bethune's Concord, N.C., alma mater, later merged with Barber College to form Barber-Scotia College.

21. Gilmore, *Gender and Jim Crow*, 185, 199–201.

22. *Carolina Times*, January 15, 1938, 4; Chafe, *Civilities and Civil Rights*, 20–21.

23. Throughout the 1920s, for example, Shaw University maintained the same rules for young women it had adopted in 1881, including a strict dress code, a ban on talking to male students between classes, and assertion of the administration's right to open female students' private mail. See Carter, *Shaw's Universe*, 141, 147. The 1881 rules remained in place until 1931. For a more comprehensive account of black college revolts, see Wolters, *New Negro on Campus*.

24. Wolters, *New Negro on Campus*, 37; Baker interview, 30.

25. Cozart, *Venture of Faith*, 42–44. For another assessment of black women's education that focuses on the significance of developing ambition and independence, see Slowe, "College Woman and Her Community."

26. Rackham Holt, *Mary McLeod Bethune*, 34–35; *Barber-Scotia Index*, February 1, 1933, 3.

27. *Barber-Scotia Index*, February 11, 1938, 1; March 23, 1934, 1; March 26, 1937, 1; April 13, 1935, 1; April 10, 1933, 3.

28. *Blue Bear*, 1930, 78; Liberti, " 'We Were Ladies,' " 131–32; 93.

29. Cozart, *Venture of Faith*, 45.

30. Information on numerous tournaments can be found in Shayle Edwards, *Basketball Championship Scores of Catawba County*. In the region around Hickory, for example, the town of Barium Springs inaugurated a long-running tournament in 1932, the Landis American Legion began to sponsor competitions in 1935, and the community of Valdese opened its Gold Medal competition in 1939.

31. Boulware, Carter, Hinkle, and Martin interview, 1.

32. Ibid.

33. *Hickory Daily Record*, February 22, 1928, 2.

34. *Wilmington Morning Star*, March 31, 1928, 6; *Baltimore Afro-American*, February 28, 1942, quoted in Liberti, " 'We Were Ladies,' " 165.

35. *Greensboro Daily News*, March 9, 1934, 12, quoted in Liberti, " 'We Were Ladies,' " 91.

36. Powell and Rotan interview, 9.

37. *Greensboro Daily News*, March 9, 1952, sports section, 6; Boulware, Carter, Hinkle, and Martin interview, 5; Bill Bost interview, 4.

38. *Barber-Scotia Index*, November 5, 1934, 3; Ardrey and Kell interview, 4. For an account of the ways in which black communities nurtured young women's confidence, see Stephanie Shaw, *What A Woman Ought to Be and to Do*, 13–16.

39. Blake interview, 1; *Barber-Scotia Index*, December 20, 1935, 3. A fascinating account of debates over girls' rules among African American sports enthusiasts can be found in Liberti, " 'We Were Ladies,' " 118–25.

40. Clemmons interview, 2; Boulware, Carter, Hinkle, and Martin interview, 1.

41. Clemmons interview, 3.

42. Cloyd, "Study of Girls' Interscholastic Basketball," 17. In the *Winston-Salem Journal-Sentinel* tournament, for example, before World War II the winning team generally scored in the 10s or 20s in the championship game. From 1946 to 1951 the winning scores were generally in the 40s, at a time when the winning boys' team generally scored in the 30s. See Shayle Edwards, *Championship Basketball Scores of Catawba County*, 47. For an account of Nancy Isenhour's High Point College career, see Bishop, "Amateur Athletic Union Women's Basketball," 13.

43. Southern Textile Basketball Tournament program, 1966, 35–36, in accession 95-34, Monagham Baptist Church, Special Collections, Clemson University Libraries. Typically, the tournament included three divisions for men's competition and two for women's. Teams traveled to Greenville, S.C., the tournament's host city, from North Carolina, South Carolina, Tennessee, Georgia, and Alabama. Southern women's basketball prowess was most sharply illustrated at the national championship held by the Amateur Athletic Union, where every contest from 1950 to 1971 was won by either Hanes Hosiery, the team representing the secretarial-oriented Nashville Business College, or the Wayland Flying Queens of Wayland Baptist College in Plainview, Texas (so named because a Plainview businessman was so enamored of the team that he regularly provided it with private air transportation). See Bishop, "Amateur Athletic Union Women's Basketball." For an account of the Wayland college team, see Redin, *Queens Fly High*. The AAU would not admit its first African American team until the mid-1950s.

44. Bauguess, Futch, Jordan, and Phillips interview, tape 1, side A; Bishop and Fulton, "Shooting Stars," 51; Jordan interview.

45. Bishop, "Amateur Athletic Union Women's Basketball," 12; Bauguess, Futch, Jordan, and Phillips interview, tape 1, side A.

46. Bishop and Fulton, "Shooting Stars," 51; Bauguess, Futch, Jordan, and Phillips interview, tape 1, side A.

47. *Winston-Salem Journal-Sentinel*, April 12, 1953, sec. B, p. 14; Bishop, "Amateur Athletic Union Women's Basketball," 19–20.

48. Bishop and Fulton, "Shooting Stars," 53.

49. Williams interview, 10; Futch and Jordan interview, 16; Gleaves interview, 7–8.

50. Wall, " 'We Always Loved to Play Basketball,' " 20; Grundy, *Most Democratic Sport*, 38. For a description of Chatham dress regulations, see Wall, " 'We Always Loved to Play Basketball,' " 32–33. Many young women experienced the transition from youthful tomboy behavior, an accepted role in many U.S. communities, to more stringent expectations of ladylike demeanor as they grew older. For a thoughtful discussion of this phenomenon, see Cahn, *Coming on Strong*, 228–32.

51. Boulware, Carter, Hinkle, and Martin interview, 8.

52. Liberti, " 'We Were Ladies,' " 98; Bauguess interview, 6.

53. Peiss, *Hope in a Jar*, 97–166.

54. *Charlotte Observer*, February 20, 1929, sec. 2, p. 1.

55. *Barber-Scotia Index*, October 27, 1933, 4. For an account of working-class black women who transformed themselves at night, see Hunter, *To 'Joy My Freedom*, 179–83. The *Barber-Scotia Index* reported with detailed enthusiasm on the cakes students and teachers baked, describing, for example, a creation that depicted "a miniature circus menagerie" made of "animal crackers, grated chocolate, green sugar, stick candy and a tiny umbrella" as well as "browned cocoanut for hay" (*Barber-Scotia Index*, October 27, 1933, 4).

56. Wall, " 'We Always Loved to Play Basketball,' " 22.

57. Tate, "Justification of a Women's College," 24. For a description of women's interwar politics, see Filene, *Him/Her/Self*, 123–44. For an analysis of Jesse Daniel Ames's postsuffrage activism, see Hall, *Revolt against Chivalry*, 52–58.

58. Boulware, Carter, Hinkle, and Martin interview, 2–3. Hazel Smith probably knew what they were doing; it seems unlikely that she would not have noticed the convenient timing of the players' cycles. The American Medical Association officially discouraged vigorous women's competition until the 1960s. See Hult and Trekell, *Century of Women's Basketball*, 214–15.

59. Baker interview, 45. For a thoughtful analysis of the strengths young women drew from sports, particularly regarding their relationships to prevailing feminine norms and to criticisms of women's sport, see Cahn, *Coming on Strong*, 232–45.

60. Williams interview, 11.

61. Boulware, Carter, Hinkle, and Martin interview, 5; Hewins, Hewins, and Edwards interview, 2.

62. Liberti, " 'We Were Ladies,' " 98. Arledge's comments are part of Bishop, *Women's Basketball*. For a description of Arledge's high school career, see *Carolina Times*, March 21, 1953, 5.

63. Liberti, " 'We Were Ladies,' " 167.

64. Boulware, Carter, Hinkle, and Martin interview, 9.

CHAPTER SIX

1. McLendon interview, tape 1, side A.

2. Ibid.

3. Ibid.

4. Ibid.

5. Gaines interview, tape 1, side B. The literature on black schools in North Carolina

and the South has grown enormously in recent years. Particularly useful works include Chafe, *Civilities and Civil Rights*; Anderson, *Education of Blacks in the South*; Gilmore, *Gender and Jim Crow*; Leloudis, *Schooling the New South*; Cecelski, *Along Freedom Road*; and Walker, *Their Highest Potential*. Following in the footsteps of authors such as Walker, I attempt not to single out those aspects of African American schools or athletic programs that differed from white schools but, rather, to depict the educational world within which black students moved. Many of the themes and ideas in this chapter would be familiar to graduates of white schools as well. For an account of a black professional team's relationships with its Pittsburgh community, see Ruck, *Sandlot Seasons*.

6. For discussions of some of the many levels of significance in the leisure activities pursued by working-class black southerners, see Hunter, *To 'Joy My Freedom*, 145–86; Kelley, *Race Rebels*, 35–53, 161–81; White and White, *Stylin'*; and Lawrence Levine, *Black Culture and Black Consciousness*. For a portrait of a black middle-class community in North Carolina, see Weare, *Black Business in the New South*.

7. For a thoughtful account of the complexities, dilemmas, and opportunities found in the day-to-day operation of Jim Crow segregation, see Hale, *Making Whiteness*, 121–97. For a discussion of strategies of resistance pursued within the segregated space of city buses, see Kelley, *Race Rebels*, 55–75.

8. Murray, *Proud Shoes*, 269; Jesse Daniel Ames to N.C. Newbold, January 30, 1947, folder A, section July 1946–June 1947, box 15, General Correspondence of Director, Division of Negro Education Records, Department of Public Instruction, North Carolina State Archives, Raleigh. The building and funding of black schools is covered in Anderson, *Education of Blacks in the South*, 202–4; Rodgers, *Black High School*, 112; and Hanchett, "Rosenwald Schools." In 1932 white schools received over three times more money per pupil than black schools did, with a ratio of $3.11 to $1.00; see Hanchett, "Rosenwald Schools," 423. Funding differentials are clearly apparent in the school budgets filed with the state Department of Public Instruction. In Mecklenburg County, for example, capital outlays in the school year 1929–30 came to $22,281 at the county's white schools, including money for athletic fields and equipment, while they totaled $375 at black schools. The same year, Iredell County spent $159,450 on white schools, mostly on buildings, and $920 on black schools, $500 of which was supplied by the Rosenwald Fund. See folders Mecklenburg County and Iredell County, box 53, Division of Professional Services, Department of Public Instruction, North Carolina State Archives, Raleigh.

9. Brown interview, 4; Griffin interview, tape 1, side A; Camp interview, tape 1, side A. For accounts of the roles black teachers played in their students' lives, see Chafe, *Civilities and Civil Rights*, 20–24; Cecelski, *Along Freedom Road*, 57–68; and Walker, *Their Highest Potential*.

10. William Stuart Nelson to Frank Porter Graham, February 13, 1936, in folder "1936: February 1–15," subgroup 1, series 1, subseries 4, Graham Series; *Carolina Times*, March 30, 1940, 2. A detailed treatment of debates over athletics at black colleges can be found in Patrick B. Miller, "To 'Bring the Race along Rapidly,' " 121–31. See also *North Carolina Teachers Record*, March 1930, 4, 6, and January 1933, 18.

11. Finger, "Just Another Ball Game," 75.

12. *1986 Panther*, 16, a commemorative edition of the Ridgeview High School annual, produced for the 1986 alumni reunion. Copy in the North Carolina Collection, University of North Carolina, Chapel Hill.

13. Torrence interview, tape 1, side B; Brown interview, 4.

14. *Second Ward Herald*, January 1934, 4, and January 1936. A description of similar

pride in resourcefulness at black colleges can be found in Patrick B. Miller, "To 'Bring the Race along Rapidly,' " 118–19.

15. Rodgers, *Black High School*, 54; *North Carolina Teachers Record*, January 1933, 18. For a description of black high school organizations around the South, see George, *Elevating the Game*, 26–30.

16. Ramsey, *Enduring Rivalry*.

17. Torrence interview, tape 1, side A.

18. Finger, "Just Another Ball Game," 75; Grier interview, tape 1, side A; Ivory interview, 4. George, *Elevating the Game*, offers an extended analysis of the development of a distinctive African American street basketball style. Another description can be found in Rose, *Black American Street Life*, 1–3.

19. Ramsey, *Enduring Rivalry*; Ivory interview, 3.

20. Ivory interview, 11; Grundy, *Most Democratic Sport*, 40–41.

21. For a brief description of the urban "hipster" side of masculine identity, seen in the context of conflicts with authority on Birmingham city buses, see Kelley, *Race Rebels*, 65–67.

22. Mebane, *Mary*, 137–38.

23. Joplin interview, tape 1, side A.

24. Ely and Diamond interview, tape 1, side A.

25. Gaines interview, tape 1, side A; George, *Elevating the Game*, 90.

26. Ivory interview, 11; *Coaching Clinic*, August 1963, 22.

27. *Carolina Times*, January 22, 1938, 4; Grundy, *Most Democratic Sport*, 40–41.

28. *Carolina Times*, June 11, 1938, 4. Austin made this comment while discussing the achievements of nationally known black athletes. For a description of the dozens and related forms of black folk culture, see Lawrence Levine, *Black Culture and Black Consciousness*, 344–68.

29. *Carolina Times*, January 22, 1938, 7. A thoughtful discussion of Kipling's significance for white North Carolinians during the period can be found in Gilmore, *Gender and Jim Crow*, 61–64.

30. Kipling, *Ruyard Kipling's Verse*, 648.

31. McLendon interview, tape 1, side A; Cunningham interview, 3.

32. Torrence interview, tape 1, side A.

33. Brown interview, 9; Gaines interview, tape 1, side B.

34. Grundy, *Most Democratic Sport*, 41.

35. Torrence interview, tape 1, side A; Grundy, *Most Democratic Sport*, 41. H. B. Thompson used a similar approach when trying to convince players who had little experience of the college world to join his teams at academically challenging Fisk, saying, "I don't have a lot of money. But I promise you you'll get a good education and a pretty wife." See George, *Elevating the Game*, 72–76, 93. Black aspirants to even blue-collar jobs often found themselves competing with college graduates, and while North Carolina's textile mills boasted a healthy range of white industrial teams, the tobacco industry, where most black industrial work was concentrated, rarely sponsored such teams.

36. *1986 Panther*, 42.

37. Brown interview, 7, 3. For a broader discussion of the parental nature of relationships between black teachers and their students during this period, see Walker, *Their Highest Potential*, 65–139.

38. Ross interview, tape 1, side B.

39. Ibid.

40. Ibid. "You couldn't hit a bull in the ass with a lumberyard" was one of Ross's

favorite baseball jabs. Conversely, he noted, a good hitter could connect "in the moon-light with a walking stick."

41. Blake interview, 4; Brown interview, 5.

42. The statement, by University of Southern California coach Sam Barry, is quoted in McCallum, *College Basketball*, 62. For a discussion of African American versions of the new game, see George, *Elevating the Game*, 58–63.

43. *Carolina Times*, March 4, 1939, 7, and January 14, 1950, 1. A description of northern players moving South can be found in George, *Elevating the Game*, 24–26. For Wilt Chamberlain's summer visits, see *Raleigh News and Observer*, March 24, 1957, sec. II, p. 2. Out-of-state stars had an effect on North Carolina high school play, an attitude that allowed Person County coach J. Royal "Skinks" Browning to play havoc with the psyches of some of his opponents in 1953. When the team traveled to Statesville, where Morn-ingside High School fielded a far more talented squad, Browning was warned that players "Paul Ostenburg," "Johnny Caine," and "Phil Onslow" could not step on the floor because they were not from Person County. While Person County could boast of no such ringers, "the team had three 'home grown' ninth graders on the squad who were making their first western swing and who were telescopic answers to the descriptions of the rumored 'out of state' players." "Although the freshmen did not play," Browning wrote, "the very sight of them kept the Statesville boys on edge to the extent that they merely shaved Person County by two points." When the Statesville team came to Person County's home court, where two of the young men in question spent some time in the game, Person County romped to victory, an outcome that was doubly enjoyable because of the ongoing deception. "Actually these rumored 'stars' could hardly hold the ball," Browning chortled. See *Carolina Times*, February 23, 1953, 5.

44. *Carolina Times*, March 4, 1939, 7.

45. Ibid., March 15, 1952, 5.

46. Ibid., February 11, 1950, 4. The drawbacks of adopting a swashbuckling ethic that shunned the "freeze" technique could be seen at A&T in the spring of 1951, when the Aggies, "scorning to 'freeze' the ball had it stolen from them by Tom Ramey . . . who slid in under the basket and put the game on ice with a lay-up shot" (*Register*, February–March 1951, 5). Participants in the infamous 1950 game between the National Basketball Association's Minneapolis Lakers and Fort Wayne Pistons, whose 19-18 score helped inspire the creation of the shot clock, recalled negative fan reactions with considerable sympathy. "The fans hated it," Slater Martin explained. "They booed for a while. Then they gave up and started reading newspapers." A little later, Fred Schaus noted, "they started throwing the newspapers and other garbage on the floor." Martin concluded, "After the game the fans wanted their money back and I didn't blame them" (Pluto, *Tall Tales*, 25–26). North Carolina would have its own infamously low scoring game in 1966, before the institution of the college shot clock, when Duke beat Chapel Hill in the Atlantic Coast Conference tournament 21-20. See Chansky, *Dean's List*, 28–29.

47. *Carolina Times*, January 21, 1950, 4.

48. Brown interview, 10. Both Holtzclaw and Truesdell appear in Ramsey, *Enduring Rivalry*.

49. For a description of some of these social and cultural rifts within black commu-nities, see Kelley, " 'We Are Not What We Seem.' "

50. For issues relating to the constructions of such communities, see Kelley, *Race Rebels*, 51–53. For the dilemmas of black intellectuals, see Wolters, *New Negro on Cam-pus*, 341–43.

51. Ross interview, tape 1, side B; Griffin interview, tape 1, side A.

52. Chafe, *Civilities and Civil Rights*, 18, 62.

53. Cunningham interview, 2.

54. George, *Elevating the Game*, 87.

55. McLendon, *Fast Break Basketball*, ix, 11.

56. *Carolina Times*, January 28, 1950, 4; December 20, 1952, 2; January 3, 1953, 5; February 28, 1953, 2; Gaines interview, tape 1, side B. By 1954, scoring at black schools was so high that Winston-Salem State was averaging ninety-four points a game. See *Carolina Times*, January 6, 1954, 5.

57. McLendon, *First CIAA Championship*, 27; copy in the North Carolina Collection, University of North Carolina, Chapel Hill.

58. Ibid., 38–39, 46.

59. *Carolina Times*, February 19, 1955, 3, and March 12, 1955, 5.

60. McLendon, *First CIAA Championship*, 24, 13.

61. *The 1945 Bulletin of the CIAA* (Norfolk, Va.: Guide Quality Press, 1945), 13, folder 1, box 9, Gaines Papers, Winston-Salem State University Archives, Winston-Salem, N.C.

62. Ibid.

63. Patrick B. Miller, "To 'Bring the Race along Rapidly,'" offers a detailed discussion of the varying positions in black athletic controversies, particularly those that erupted at Howard and Fisk. The Du Bois quote is in ibid., 128–29.

64. Brown interview, 7–8. The *North Carolina Teachers Record* is replete with discussions of the importance of cooperative endeavor. See, for example, January 1932, 8; October 1932, 74–75; and May 1934, 43.

65. *North Carolina Teachers Record*, May 1950, 14, and October 1957, 8.

66. Brown interview, 4–5. Although Brown and Johnson were from other states, many native North Carolinians also intensified their demands for better treatment in this period. For a description of postwar shifts in attitude toward state funding in one North Carolina community, see Walker, *Their Highest Potential*, 57–59. See also Chafe, *Civilities and Civil Rights*, 24–28. J. C. Johnson later became coach of LeMoyne-Owen College in Memphis, Tennessee, where his accomplishments included winning an NCAA championship in 1975 and being named national coach of the year. See *1986 Panther*, 6.

67. McLendon interview, tape 1, side B. Informal integrated games were in fact relatively commonplace within the state, but most such matches were carefully concealed from public attention.

68. Ibid.

69. *Carolina Times*, March 18, 1950, 8.

70. Katz and McLendon, *Breaking Through*, 7, 37. When black coaches first presented their petition, the NAIA was known as the National Association of Intercollegiate Basketball (NAIB), but the organization changed its name soon afterward. The NCAA justified its exclusion of black colleges in part by relegating them to small-college status at a time when the organization did not sponsor a small-college tournament. See ibid., 13. For an account of Earl Monroe's Winston-Salem State career, see George, *Elevating the Game*, 165–71.

71. *Register*, March 1952.

CHAPTER SEVEN

1. Bill Bost interview, 5.

2. Athletic department archives at North Carolina State are full of letters from Clark on subjects such as promising players he thought coaches should see, football players'

grades, game strategy, suggestions for portraying the school's athletic history, and critiques of the design of various athletic facilities. Clark played a major role in raising funds for Reynolds Coliseum, and when the facility was opened, he had first choice of seats. He has his own folders in the N.C. State athletic archives; see folders "David Clark, 1948–53" and "David Clark, 1954–1960," box 1, Athletics Department General Correspondence, University Archives, North Carolina State University, Raleigh (hereafter cited as Athletics Department General Correspondence).

3. Link, *William Friday*, 79. For Case's recruitment, see Herakovich, *Pack Pride*, 20–23. Three years later, however, the University of North Carolina would hire Tatum, reflecting either rising postwar pressures for winning teams or a double standard on the part of university administrators, depending on the point of view. The consolidated university was organized with a chancellor at the head of each institution and a president who oversaw the entire system.

4. The frustration black schools felt at their lack of statewide notice was invoked in 1952 when Johnson C. Smith scored a stunning CIAA upset of powerhouse West Virginia State, and a *Carolina Times* columnist noted that the victory, along with its impressive "101 to something score," was "carried lightly and loosely and in all instances grudgingly by the white press which knew vaguely that the 'Central' Intercollegiate AA was having a tournament." See *Carolina Times*, March 15, 1952, 5.

5. Herakovich, *Pack Pride*, 19.

6. Ibid., 24–34. The prestige of the NIT tournament would not be eclipsed by the NCAA contest until the mid-1950s.

7. Sumner, "Everett Case Conquers Dixie," 11; Link, *William Friday*, 108.

8. Herakovich, *Pack Pride*, 22.

9. Undated press release, folder "Second Day—Dixie Classic December 30, 1960," box "Dixie Classic," Athletics Department Records, North Carolina State University, Raleigh. The alumnus reminiscence is described in Herakovich, *Pack Pride*, 132.

10. *Raleigh News and Observer*, December 29, 1956, 4.

11. Ibid., December 27, 1959, sec. IV, p. 2, and December 28, 1958, 1. See also December 30, 1958, 11.

12. For a detailed account of the 1951 scandals, see Sperber, *Onward to Victory*, 301–15.

13. *Sports Illustrated*, February 4, 1957, 9.

14. Roy B. Clogston to Smith Barrier, March 8, 1955, folder "ACC-Service Bureau 1954–60," box 1, Athletics Department General Correspondence. For details of the postwar growth in North Carolina basketball, see Barrier, *On Tobacco Road*, 92–114.

15. *Raleigh News and Observer*, March 11, 1957, 13; March 21, 1957, 25; March 25, 1957, 1, 4, 13.

16. Roy B. Clogston to David Clark, November 4, 1954, folder "David Clark, 1948–53," box 1, Athletics Department General Correspondence; *Raleigh News and Observer*, March 25, 1957, 4.

17. *Raleigh News and Observer*, March 24, 1957, sec. II, p. 2, and March 25, 1957, 13.

18. These developments are discussed in fascinating and insightful fashion in Sperber, *Onward to Victory*, 3–136. Given the emotional complications of many men's lives in the 1950s, when wartime heroism had been replaced by corporate life and an interest in financial and emotional security, the ability of idealized athletes to combine the drama of individual heroism with emotional commitments to family members, coaches, and teammates no doubt held particular appeal. See Filene, *Him/Her/Self*, 169–76, and May, *Homeward Bound*, 27–30, 87–91.

19. Sperber, *Onward to Victory*, 3–136. The stories behind the making of *Knute Rockne*

and *Pride of the Yankees* are fascinating. *Knute Rockne*, along with the genre of sports films from which it sprang, is covered in Sperber, *Onward to Victory*, 29–55. An account of *Pride of the Yankees* can be found in Robinson, *Iron Horse*, 275–76.

20. *Raleigh News and Observer*, December 1, 1956, 9.

21. Lefler and Newsome, *North Carolina*, 637, 648–49.

22. Letter to William C. Friday, June 1, 1961, folder "Athletics, Dixie Classic Controversy, 1961," II (There are two folders with this title. The first, which I have designated "I," holds letters in support of Friday; the second, designated "II," includes disagreements.); and letter to William Friday, January 20, 1964, folder "Athletics, Dixie Classic Controversy, 1964," both in subgroup 1, series 1, William C. Friday Records, University Archives, University of North Carolina, Chapel Hill (hereafter cited as Friday Records). In the interests of privacy, I have not included the names of letter writers unless their identity is essential to interpreting their comments.

23. Herakovich, *Pack Pride*, 134; *Raleigh News and Observer*, December 16, 1950, 11.

24. *Raleigh News and Observer*, February 8, 1961, 13, and December 20, 1956, 14.

25. Ibid., December 20, 1956, 17, and December 28, 1956, 14.

26. For an account of the Moreland scandal, see Herakovich, *Pack Pride*, 47–48. Rhea later repeated her accusations in a newspaper interview. See *Raleigh News and Observer*, December 28, 1956, 14.

27. For background on the NCAA, see Smith, *Sports and Freedom*, 198–208, and Fleisher, Goff, and Tollison, *National Collegiate Athletic Association*, 46–50.

28. Roy B. Clogston to R. T. Burkman, April 22, 1949, folder "Athletics Department, Roy B. Clogston, 1948–50," box 1, and Roy B. Clogston to David Clark, February 1, 1950, folder "David Clark, 1948–53," box 2, Athletics Department General Correspondence. For Hines's travails, see, for example, David Clark to Carey H. Bostian, August 19, 1954, folder "David Clark 1954–60," and Roy B. Clogston to David Clark, February 1, 1950, folder "David Clark, 1948–53," both in box 2, and Thomas Hines to W. N. Wood, July 18, 1950, and to Dick Peacock, November 3, 1950, both in folder "Roy B. Clogston, Athletic Director, 1950–52," box 1, Athletics Department General Correspondence. Over the years the major carried several different titles, including Industrial Recreation, Industrial and Rural Recreation, and Recreation and Parks Administration.

29. Taylor interview, tape 3, side 2, 2–3. Taylor also noted that despite these generous offers, the player decided to enroll at Duke instead.

30. *Sports Illustrated*, February 4, 1957, 43–44.

31. Chansky, *Dean's List*, 12–14.

32. *Raleigh News and Observer*, December 13, 1956, 21; Chansky, *Dean's List*, 11; Link, *William Friday*, 99–103. For an example of similar attitudes toward NCAA regulations at the University of Maryland, see Sperber, *Onward to Victory*, 239–42.

33. Reprinted in *Raleigh News and Observer*, March 15, 1957, 9. See also the observations of the *Winston-Salem Journal-Sentinel*, reprinted in the same issue.

34. "Observations, recommendations, and conclusions by Commissioner James H. Weaver in connection with the disturbance which occurred shortly before the end of the University of North Carolina–Wake Forest basketball game played at Winston-Salem, North Carolina, Thursday, February 12, 1959," February 23, 1959, p. 2, folder "Correspondence with Atlantic Coast Conference, 1959–1961," box 10, Aycock Series, Chancellor's Records, University Archives, University of North Carolina, Chapel Hill (hereafter cited as Aycock Series).

35. James H. Weaver, "Observations," n.d., folder "Correspondence with Atlantic Coast Conference, 1959–1961," box 10, Aycock Series; *Raleigh News and Observer*, February 6, 1961, 9.

36. *Raleigh News and Observer*, February 13, 1959, 19, and February 8, 1961, 4.

37. Link, *William Friday*, 102–4. For an account of the devastating effect the scandal had on Hawkins in particular, see George, *Elevating the Game*, 126–31.

38. *Report to the House of Representatives by Chancellor John T. Caldwell and President William Friday*, n.d., folder "Dixie Classic, 1959–63," box 9, Aycock Series.

39. Letter to Jack Horner, March 3, 1958, folder "Athletics, Jan.–Aug. 1958," box 9, Aycock Series; *Raleigh News and Observer*, April 20, 1963, 11, and March 25, 1957, 1; Herakovich, *Pack Pride*, 54.

40. Jesse Helms, WRAL Viewpoint #780, January 27, 1964, folder "WRAL Television Editorials, 1961–1971," subgroup 1, series 8, Friday Records; *Durham Morning Herald*, May 21, 1961, sec. B, p. 1.

41. Herakovich, *Pack Pride*, 54; *Look*, February 13, 1962, 86.

42. *Raleigh News and Observer*, May 28, 1961, sec, II, p. 1.

43. *Charlotte Observer*, May 24, 1961, sec. B, p. 2; *Raleigh News and Observer*, May 15, 1961, sec. A, p. 4.

44. *Charlotte Observer*, May 24, 1961, sec. B, p. 2; letter to William B. Aycock, June 15, 1961, folder "Public Response, April–August 1961," box 10, Aycock Series.

45. *Look*, February 27, 1962, 77, and February 13, 1962, 89.

46. *Daily Tar Heel*, May 12, 1961, 2; *Raleigh News and Observer*, May 20, 1961, sec. A, p. 4. For more general material about the quiz show scandals, see Oakley, *God's Country*, 408–14.

47. Link, *William Friday*, 106.

48. *Charlotte Observer*, March 7, 1962, sec. B, p. 2; *Charlotte News*, undated clipping, folder "Athletics, Oct. 18–31 1962," box 9, Aycock Series.

49. *Charlotte Observer*, June 11, 1961, sec. E, p. 2.

50. *Saturday Evening Post*, November 2, 1957, 90; anonymous to Friday, May 22, 1961, folder "Athletics: Dixie Classic Controversy, 1961," II, subgroup 1, series 1, Friday Records; letter to William C. Aycock, December 14, 1962, folder "Dixie Classic, 1959–63," box 9, Aycock Series; *Charlotte News*, October 20, 1962, sec. B, p. 2. For a description of the nationwide shift in sporting rhetoric that highlights Tatum's remarks, see Sperber, *Onward to Victory*, xix–xxv. The anonymous nature of a number of the protesting letters might be seen as further support for the idea that many protesters viewed the world in Darwinian terms; the writers apparently suspected that openly expressing disagreement would expose them to reprisals on the part of university officials. Such strategies, however, clashed with many university officials' own concepts of courage—Friday wrote "Coward" at the top of one such missive. See anonymous to Friday, May 22, 1961, folder "Athletics: Dixie Classic Controversy, 1961," II, subgroup 1, series 1, Friday Records.

51. *Greensboro Daily News*, May 15, 1961, sec. A, p. 6.

52. Letters to Friday, May 23, 29, 1961, both in folder "Dixie Classic Controversy, 1961," II, subgroup 1, series 1, Friday Records. Disputes over academic requirements were often rooted in these differing perspectives on university education. When, for example, David Clark sought to keep the North Carolina State recreation department from requiring "extra hours or subjects which will be of no benefit to the graduates," he was probably expressing not only an interest in competing for players but also a skepticism about the worth of too much classroom education. See David Clark to Carey H. Bostian, August 19, 1954, folder "David Clark 1954–60," box 2, Athletics Department General Correspondence. Disputes over the contours of a university education would become a major point of statewide dispute in the 1960s and 1970s, as communities and politicians around the state sought to extend university status to a variety of state educational institutions, even as consolidated university officials worried that many of the aspiring

institutions lacked the resources to develop top-quality programs. For a lengthy description of these disputes, see Link, *William Friday*, 221–46. Interestingly, Roy Jenkins, the head of East Carolina College and one of the leading proponents of an expansion of university status, stated his staunch support for competitive athletics during the controversy, hinting at a vision of a less hierarchically organized curriculum by stating, "We are definitely emphasizing athletics and make no apology for it. We emphasize music, art and everything we do." The undated clipping quoting Jenkins's statements was enclosed in a protest letter to William Aycock, which addressed Aycock as "Caesar"; see anonymous to "Caesar," 1962, folder "Dixie Classic, 1959–63," box 9, Aycock Series.

53. *Durham Morning Herald*, April 21, 1963, sec. C, p. 1; letters to Friday, May 23, 26, 1961, both in folder "Dixie Classic Controversy, 1961," II, subgroup 1, series 1, Friday Records; *Charlotte News*, October 20, 1962, sec. B, p. 2; H. L. Ferguson to editor, undated clipping, folder "Dixie Classic 1959–63," box 9, Aycock Series.

54. Undated clipping in folder "Athletics, April 1963," box 10, Aycock Series; N. P Hayes to Friday, May 26, 1961, folder "Dixie Classic Controversy, 1961," I, subgroup 1, series 1, Friday Records.

55. Jesse Helms, WRAL Viewpoint #780, January 27, 1964, folder "WRAL Television Editorials, 1961–1971," subgroup 1, series 8, and letter to Friday, May 1961, folder "Dixie Classic Controversy, 1961," II, subgroup 1, series 1, Friday Records.

56. Letter to William C. Aycock, December 14, 1962, folder "Athletics, Nov.–Dec. 1962," box 9, Aycock Series.

57. Ibid.

58. Jesse Helms, WRAL Viewpoint #780, January 27, 1964, folder "WRAL Television Editorials, 1961–1971," subgroup 1, series 8, Friday Records.

59. Examples of this debate are legion, ranging from religious arguments over the question of whether to improve society by focusing on individual conversion or on political and social action, to debates over child labor, which turned on whether the practice resulted from the laziness of parents or the inadequacy of textile mill wages, to the contention that racial discrimination reflected not unjust exclusion but the failure of individual African Americans to prove themselves worthy of full citizenship. For an account of political maneuverings over the Dixie Classic, see Link, *William Friday*, 108–27. For an overview of this political division, see Luebke, *Tar Heel Politics*, esp. "Jesse Helms," 124–36.

60. Anonymous to "Caesar," 1962, folder "Athletics, Jan.–March 1962," box 9, Aycock Series; *Charlotte News*, October 20, 1962, sec. B, p. 2; W. C. Harris Jr. to Friday, May 23, 1961, folder "Athletics: Dixie Classic Controversy, 1961," II, subgroup 1, series 1, Friday Records. See also letter to Friday, June 1, 1961, same folder.

61. Friday to W. C. Harris Jr., February 3, 1964, folder "Athletics: Dixie Classic Controversy, 1964," subgroup 1, series 1, Friday Records. Friday and other university officials also worried that repeated scandals would lead to a heavier regulatory hand on the part of the NCAA, further circumscribing the university's authority over its own activities. See Link, *William Friday*, 101–2.

62. This process was, of course, only an intensification of a much longer term shift away from the dynamics of face-to-face communities and direct experience. Concerns about judgment and appearance in nineteenth-century cities are covered in Kasson, *Rudeness and Civility*, 70–111. A suggestion of the growing willingness of citizens to accept this process can be seen in the gradual ebbing of concerns about having North Carolina schools represented by players from other states, a shift that suggests not only a growing tolerance of outsiders but also a greater willingness to see sports in largely symbolic terms.

63. Jesse Helms, WRAL Viewpoint #994, December 11, 1964, folder "WRAL Television Editorials, 1961–1971," subgroup 1, series 8, Friday Records.

64. W. C. Harris Jr. to Friday, January 20, 1964, folder "Athletics: Dixie Classic Controversy, 1964," subgroup 1, series 1, Friday Records. See also Friday to Harris, February 3, 1964, same folder.

65. *Look*, February 27, 1962, 82.

66. Herakovich, *Pack Pride*, 23. For McGuire's comments, see "Special NCAA Questionnaire," [June 2, 1961], n.p., folder "N.Y. Basketball Scandal 1961," box 10, Aycock Series.

## CHAPTER EIGHT

1. Boulware, Carter, Hinkle, and Martin interview, 10.

2. *Greensboro Daily News*, March 12, 1952, sec. 2, p. 3; Ramsey, *Women's Rules*. A tournament draw can be found in Gary B. Adams, "Girls' Invitational State Basketball Tournament," 86.

3. *Greensboro Daily News*, March 15, 1952, sec. 2, p. 3, and March 18, 1951, 7. The NCHSAA had held state championship games since 1915, but not until 1948 did it sponsor a full-fledged tournament.

4. *Greensboro Daily News*, April 11, 1952, sec. 4, p. 4.

5. Umstead, "Mary Channing Coleman," 82–83. The Gold Medal Tournament was held in the furniture manufacturing center of High Point, N.C.

6. Ibid.

7. An account of the development and aspirations of the national physical education establishment can be found in Cahn, *Coming on Strong*, 55–82.

8. Ibid. For a description of the North Carolina point system, see Coleman and Phillips, "Athletics for High School Girls," 56–58.

9. Mary Channing Coleman, "Athletics for High School Girls," typescript, n.d., p. 4, folder "Speeches—Coleman Radio Talks file," box 1, School of Health, Physical Education, Recreation, and Dance Collection, University Archives, Jackson Library, University of North Carolina, Greensboro (hereafter cited as School of Health Collection); "The Constitution of the Women's Sports Day Association," n.d., n.p., folder 27, box 160-10, Allen Papers, Moorland-Spingarn Research Center, Howard University, Washington, D.C. (hereafter cited as Allen Papers).

10. Mary Channing Coleman, "Athletics for High School Girls," typescript, n.d., p. 2, folder "Organizations: Girls High School Athletic Association, 1922–1938," box 2, School of Health Collection.

11. Brumberg, *Body Project*, 97–107; Banner, *American Beauty*, 201–18; Giddings, *When and Where I Enter*, 183–90.

12. Maryrose Reeves Allen to Mr. Goodman, February 6, 1957, p. 5, folder 5, box 160-9, Allen Papers; Mary Channing Coleman, "Education and the Sports Business," n.d., p. 2, folder "Selected Writings of Coleman," box 1, School of Health Collection. For a detailed description of the way Allen applied her philosophy to Howard's physical education program, see "The Deeper Meaning of The Department of Physical Education for Women," n.d., folder 17, box 160-8, Allen Papers.

13. Umstead, "Mary Channing Coleman," 88–101. Figures for the North Carolina High School Girls' Athletic Association come from Gary B. Adams, "Girls' Invitational State Basketball Tournament," 8.

14. *Hickory Daily Record*, February 22, 1928, 2; *Charlotte Observer*, February 20, 1929, 15; *Charlotte News*, February 17, 1929, 13. Coverage of women's basketball in big-city

newspapers such as the *Observer* dropped precipitously in the 1930s. See Cloyd, "Study of Girls' Interscholastic Basketball," 8.

15. *Snips and Cuts*, 1921, n.p.; 1930, 110; 1933, 127.

16. For a discussion of black physical educators, see Gissendanner, "African-American Women and Competitive Sport," 86–88.

17. Slowe, "Education of Negro Women and Girls," 15, folder 148, box 90-7, Slowe Papers, Moorland-Spingarn Research Center, Howard University, Washington, D.C.; "What Shall We Teach Our Youth," delivered to Baltimore YMCA, February 1, 1925, folder 150, box 90-6, ibid.; "The College Woman and Her Community," 10–11, folder 148, box 90-7, ibid.

18. Tate, "Justification of a Women's College," 22–26. For figures on black women's enrollment and employment as well as an assessment of tensions that sometimes accompanied those achievements, see Giddings, *When and Where I Enter*, 196, 245–48.

19. Tate, "Justification of a Women's College," 24; "Proceedings of the Eleventh Annual Meeting of the Association of Women and Advisors to Girls," 233.

20. "Proceedings of the Eleventh Annual Meeting of the Association of Women and Advisors to Girls," 238. The matter had been discussed but not acted on in earlier years.

21. Maryrose Reeves Allen to Dr. Charles H. Thompson, October 14, 1939, p. 3, file 9, box 160-8, Allen Papers.

22. *The Palmer Memorial Institute, 1931–32*, n.p.; *Bulletin—The Palmer Memorial Institute, 1936–37*, 4; and *Bulletin—The Palmer Memorial Institute, 1937–38*, 7, all on reel 4, Brown Collection, Radcliffe College, Cambridge, Mass. While Palmer Memorial Institute was primarily a secondary school, it included a college division in the 1930s. For a description of the relationship between changing state teacher requirements and course offerings in black colleges, see Ellis, "Status of Health and Physical Education for Women in Negro Colleges and Universities," 62.

23. *Bulletin of the Agricultural and Technical College of North Carolina* 30 (July 1939): 13, 113–15; *Register*, December 1938, 5; May 1940, 1; March 1938, 6. Copies of the *Register* are in the University Archives, Bluford Library, North Carolina Agricultural and Technical University, Greensboro.

24. "Handbook: Women's Sports Day Association" [1960s], n.p., in folder 27, box 160-10, Allen Papers; Liberti, " 'We Were Ladies,' " 157–60; *Register*, April 1942, 1.

The demise of Shaw University's program was announced in a 1942 athletic report. "For the first time our girls did not represent the University in Basketball," the school's athletic committee wrote.

> This was not due that the young ladies did not represent the University as a team, as Coach Cook worked faithfully with them in preparation for a team. Only three of the schools of the Association for Young Women would have a team and because of this lack of opposition Coach Cook decided to cancel activities for the young ladies. The Committee was sorry that the young ladies did not have a chance to carry on successfully as in the past. It appears that this state of affairs will continue there-fore not giving the young ladies an opportunity of representation. The Committee hopes that a strong Physical Education activity will be started next year in which all the young ladies will be benefited. Several Colleges have this program where during the year an intramural day for the young ladies is observed.

"Athletic Committee Report for 1941–42," 2–3, folder "Annual Reports," box "Sports," University Archives, Shaw University, Raleigh.

25. Cloyd, "Study of Girls' Interscholastic Basketball," 2, 10–12. The survey asked

whether women's teams should be allowed to play in contests beyond the level of a county tournament. It was sent to 700 schools and received 441 responses, a rate of 63 percent.

26. A comprehensive account of postwar development efforts in states around the South can be found in Cobb, *Selling of the South.*

27. *Greensboro Daily News*, March 26, 1952, sec. 2, p. 4; Gary B. Adams, "Girls' Invitational State Basketball Tournament," 76.

28. Gary B. Adams, "Girls' Invitational State Basketball Tournament," 77.

29. *Greensboro Daily News*, April 11, 1952, sec. 4, p. 4; Gary B. Adams, "Girls' Invitational State Basketball Tournament," 48.

30. *Greensboro Daily News*, February 21, 1953, sec. 2, p. 3.

31. Gary B. Adams, "Girls' Invitational State Basketball Tournament," 48.

32. Wall, " 'We Always Loved to Play Basketball,' " 39. The demise of women's industrial programs is examined in ibid., 36–40. Prior to the 1950s, industrial teams had dominated national AAU competition. They gave way to teams from business schools and small colleges, some of which maintained commitments to the sport. See Bishop, "Amateur Athletic Union Women's Basketball," 19–20.

33. Although the All American Girls Baseball League, the first major attempt at a women's professional sports league, developed strong followings in team cities, the national press generally treated players as attractive novelties, usually focusing on the provocative contrast between the intensity of their play and their carefully cultivated feminine images. See Cahn, *Coming on Strong*, 147–60. For the decline of minor league baseball in North Carolina, see Sumner, *History of Sports*, 61–63.

34. Herakovich, *Pack Pride*, 22.

35. *The 4th Annual North Carolina AAA-AA-A High School Championship Basketball Tournaments* (Chapel Hill: North Carolina High School Athletic Association, 1951), n.p. Copy in the North Carolina High School Athletic Association Archives, Chapel Hill.

36. Herakovich, *Pack Pride*, 23.

37. *Greensboro Daily News*, March 18, 1951, 7.

38. Bill Bost interview, 4. Support for women's basketball, perhaps not surprisingly, seems to have remained particularly strong in states that did not develop prominent men's basketball programs, such as Iowa, Texas, Arkansas, and South Carolina. In contrast, in the basketball hotbeds of Indiana and Kentucky, most women's high school play met an early demise. See Herb Schwomeyer, *Hoosier HERsteria*, 71–73; Peggy Stanaland, "Early Years of Basketball in Kentucky," 167–80; and Beran, "Iowa, the Longtime 'Hot Bed' of Girls Basketball," 181–204.

39. Wall, " 'We Always Loved to Play Basketball,' " 21.

40. Brown interview, 6; *Greensboro Daily News*, March 18, 1951, 7; Bill Bost interview, 4.

41. Bauguess interview, 5. Several former Lincolnton players expressed similar dismay over their daughters' lack of interest in the game. See Boulware, Carter, Hinkle, and Martin interview, 10.

42. Gary B. Adams, "Girls' Invitational State Basketball Tournament," 96.

43. *Greensboro Daily News*, March 9, 1952, 6.

44. *Register*, December 1931, 1, and April 1942, 2. North Carolina A&T had been founded in the 1890s as a coeducational institution, but it admitted only male students from the turn of the century until the late 1920s.

45. Hanson, *Go! Fight! Win!*, 21–22. Successful management of a crowd's emotions was, in fact, quite a demanding task, but it was one that the most effective individuals accomplished without seeming to try very hard.

46. *1959 North Carolina Basketball Preview* (Greensboro: Pyramid Pub. Co., 1959), 4;

*Register*, October 1950, 6. A copy of *1959 North Carolina Basketball Preview* is in the North Carolina Collection, University of North Carolina, Chapel Hill.

47. For a thoughtful account of the new postwar interest in marriage and sexuality, see May, *Homeward Bound*. For an account of the changing images of women promoted by cosmetics companies during and after World War II, as well as a description of the segmentation of the booming postwar cosmetics market, see Peiss, *Hope in a Jar*, 238–58.

48. *Register*, March 1950, 10. For information on marketing to teenagers, see Palladino, *Teenagers*, 52–57, 97–115. The *Register* noted this trend in 1953 when editors optimistically announced, "With the closing of world markets to American manufacturers, resulting from the influence of Communism, many institutions now are taking a second look at the Negro market which never has been developed to its fullest potential. . . . Almost every big national concern is searching for intelligent and trained young Negro men and women to represent their products and concerns" (*Register*, January 1953, 1).

49. *Register*, July 6, 1934, 3, and March 1950, 3, 10.

50. Harry James to Willis Casey, November 31, 1956, folder "Dixie Classic, 1953–54," box 4, Athletics Department General Correspondence.

51. Herakovich, *Pack Pride*, 35. For one analysis of the postwar public emphasis on sexuality, see May, *Homeward Bound*, 101–13.

52. *Greensboro Daily News*, March 11, 1952, sec. 2, p. 3.

53. "Department of Physical Education for Women, 1955–56," 3, folder 17, box 160-8, Allen Papers.

54. Boulware, Carter, Hinkle, and Martin interview, 6.

55. *Register*, November 1947, 2, and October 1950, 1.

56. *Snips and Cuts*, 1939, n.p.

57. For reports of disparaging accounts of Soviet male and female athletes, see Cahn, *Coming on Strong*, 210, and Festle, *Playing Nice*, 86–93. For an assessment of associations between athletics and lesbianism, see Cahn, *Coming on Strong*, 164–84. The Cold War would eventually offer women's sports some benefits, as the political symbolism given to Olympic success eventually prompted the federal government to launch a campaign to encourage U.S. women's sports, seeking to counter Soviet women's domination of women's events. See Festle, *Playing Nice*, 89–101. A comprehensive analysis of Babe Didrikson's career can be found in Cayleff, *Babe*.

58. Bridgeman and Steitz, "Needs and Problems of Adolescents in the Area of Physical Development," 39–40; Paul, "Clara Gregory Baer," 47; Corrubia, "Provisions for the Physical Health of High School Students," 46. Descriptions of postwar thinking about gender and sexuality and of the accusatory atmosphere with which female physical educators had to contend during the period can be found in Festle, *Playing Nice*, 1–7, 22–27.

59. *Snips and Cuts*, 1946, n.p.

60. Gary B. Adams, "Girls' Invitational State Basketball Tournament," 37.

61. The psychological pressures such assumptions placed on athletic-minded women in particular is thoughtfully discussed in Festle, *Playing Nice*, 21–27. The added expectations and struggles faced by African American women during this era are analyzed in Giddings, *When and Where I Enter*, 241–58, 311–24.

62. Clemmons interview, 2–3.

## CHAPTER NINE

1. *Daily Tar Heel*, February 11, 1968, 5.

2. Ibid., February 4, 1968, 4; Chansky, *Dean's Domain*, 62–65, and *Dean's List*, 49–53.

3. Torrence interview, tape 1, side B; Stanley Johnson to Pamela Grundy, e-mail, March 13, 2000. When Johnson arrived in Fayetteville, he recalled, "My roommates were for UNC and Duke. They felt it odd at the time that racial/political matters influenced my attitude toward sports. . . . Some were very disappointed when integrated teams with Black stars defeated the segregated ACC teams." Johnson credited the 1963 national championship run by Loyola of Chicago, a team that boasted four black starters, with sparking more racially oriented athletic thinking at Fayetteville State. Loyola received national notice not only because of its championship season but also because the Mississippi State team it faced in the first round had gone to the tournament in defiance of regulations that prevented Mississippi teams from taking the court against integrated squads. For a description of Loyola, see Finger, "Just Another Ball Game," 74. For descriptions of the Mississippi State team, see Finger, "Just Another Ball Game," 78–79, and Henderson, "1963 Mississippi State University Basketball Controversy."

4. *Daily Tar Heel*, May 5, 1966, 5. For an account of the concerns that developed among African Americans about majority white colleges, see George, *Elevating the Game*, 132–39. One particularly prominent example was Texas Western University, which had made history by winning the 1965 NCAA championship with an all-black starting five but where, it was subsequently charged, none of the black basketball players was succeeding academically.

5. Ross interview, tape 1, side A; Joplin interview, tape 1, side A.

6. *Carolina Times*, January 31, 1942, 2; McLendon interview, tape 1, side B.

7. Bryant and Underwood, *Bear*, 322.

8. For an account of Robinson's storied career, along with an assessment of his effect on the country, see Tygiel, *Baseball's Great Experiment*. A thoughtful consideration of Joe Louis's career can be found in Lawrence Levine, *Black Culture and Black Consciousness*, 420–40.

9. Henderson, "1963 Mississippi State University Basketball Controversy."

10. *Durham Morning Herald*, November 8, 1938, 8; Martin, "Rise and Fall of Jim Crow," 256–58. See also Sumner, *History of Sports*, 50. As Martin explains, under the leadership of Frank Porter Graham the University of North Carolina team played a handful of symbolic games with integrated teams in the 1930s, but the gesture had little long-term effect. In the absence of a national playoff, college football championships were garnered through a complex mix of victories, strategic scheduling, and political maneuvers. Duke's decision paid off, as the Iron Duke squad defeated Syracuse and won a Rose Bowl bid, although they lost that contest to the University of Southern California.

11. Roy B. Clogston to Leo A. Harris, July 18, 1952, folder "Basketball—Varsity—1948–51," box 2, Athletics Department General Correspondence. In a fairly typical defense of segregation, Clogston argued to Harris that such decisions largely served the interests of black players, explaining that in the case of Penn State, "When we told them that [it] would be impossible for a colored boy to live in a Southern hotel with the whites and that he might not be very well received by some of the spectators, they decided it would be best not for him to make the trip. I think it is tougher on the negro boy than it is on the whites."

12. Roy B. Clogston to Josh Cody, November 23, 1954, folder "Roy B. Clogston, 1952–54," box 1, Athletics Department General Correspondence. Clogston's description of Arnell's reception was apparently not hyperbolic; years later the Penn State coach spoke admiringly of the way his player had been applauded. See Herakovich, *Pack Pride*, 39.

13. *Charlotte News*, September 20, 1958, sec. B, p. 6; Scott interview.

14. *Durham Morning Herald*, November 14, 1938, 6; *Charlotte News*, September 20, 1958, sec. B, p. 6; *Raleigh News and Observer*, January 3, 1959, 4. For an account of

Robertson and Green's experience in Raleigh, see Martin, "Rise and Fall of Jim Crow," 262–63.

15. *Durham Morning Herald*, November 8, 1938, 8; *Raleigh News and Observer*, March 25, 1953, 13; December 28, 1958, sec. II, p. 1; December 30, 1958, 11–12; January 2, 1959, 16.

16. For an account of Klan activities, see Chafe, *Civilities and Civil Rights*, 161–63. For an overview of the desegregation process and the unrest it sparked in black communities, see Cecelski, *Along Freedom Road*, 7–10, 171–72.

17. Jordan, *Black Coach*, 73–79. For an account of a school dispute that escalated into an armed standoff in Greensboro, see Chafe, *Civilities and Civil Rights*, 185–200.

18. Griffin interview, tape 1, side B; Cherry interview, tape 1, side B.

19. Hamlin interview, tape 1, side A; Cherry interview, tape 1, side A.

20. Tapia interview, tape 1, side A.

21. Friday interview, tape 1, side A; Cherry interview, tape 1, side B; Barkley interview, tape 1, side A.

22. Dawkins interview, tape 1, side A.

23. Tapia interview, tape 1, side A.

24. Carr interview, tape 1, side A.

25. Bryant and Costner interview, tape 1, side A; Joplin interview, tape 1, side B.

26. *Gaston Gazette*, August 14, 1966, sec. B, p. 2, and August 16, 1966, sec. D, p. 8; Smith interview, tape 1, side A.

27. Gaines interview, tape 1, side B.

28. The style of the North Carolina Eagles was widely admired by North Carolina high school coaches. Burrell Brown studied John McLendon's fast-break treatise, and in the late 1940s he and fellow coach J. C. Johnson traveled to Durham, where a former player was competing for McLendon, to learn about fast-break techniques in person. See Brown interview, 2.

29. Jordan, *Black Coach*, 98–99, 192.

30. Joplin interview, tape 1, side B.

31. Friday interview, tape 1, side A; McLaurin, *Separate Pasts*, 34–36. White players did often hold definite advantages in interracial play, McLaurin noted, describing in particular a game that involved another white boy named Howard Lee. "Although we played on a black playground, the white kids controlled the situation because we controlled the ball," McLaurin wrote. "None of the black players had a ball, so without us there was no game. Under the circumstances it made little difference which team won. However, had the black players challenged what Howard and I perceived as our rights on the court, we probably would have taken the ball and left the game." For a detailed account of Stoudemire and Blake's friendship, along with a description of desegregation at Lincolnton High, see Stoudemire, *Place at the Table*.

32. Jordan, *Black Coach*, 99; Barkley interview, tape 1, side A.

33. Cherry interview, tape 1, side B; Rhodes interview, tape 1, side A.

34. Jordan, *Black Coach*, 120.

35. Barkley interview, tape 1, side A; Cherry interview, tape 1, side B.

36. Smith interview, tape 1, side A. See also Harris interview, tape 1, side A.

37. Bryant and Costner interview, tape 1, side A.

38. Ibid.

39. Ibid.; Rhodes interview, tape 1, side A.

40. Rhodes interview, tape 1, side A.

41. Ibid.

42. *Gaston Gazette*, March 7, 1967, 4.

43. Bryant and Costner interview, tape 1, side A; Rhodes interview, tape 1, side A.

44. Joplin interview, tape 1, side B; Barkley interview, tape 1, side A.

45. Rhodes interview, tape 1, side A; Bryant and Costner interview, tape 1, side A.

46. Jordan, *Black Coach*, 229, 129. A further description of team dynamics can be found on 122–25.

47. Rhodes interview, tape 1, side A.

48. For descriptions of both sit-ins and black power activities, see Chafe, *Civilities and Civil Rights*. Tyson, *Radio Free Dixie*, offers a compelling portrait of Monroe, N.C., native Robert F. Williams, a nationally renowned advocate of armed self-defense.

49. Hoberman, *Darwin's Athletes*, 13, 187–93.

50. *New York Times*, March 22, 1969, 20.

51. *Gaston Gazette*, August 5, 1966, sec. A, p. 3; August 1, 1966, sec. A, p. 1; August 2, 1966, sec. A, p. 1.

52. For a thoughtful description of the political challenges black activists faced in Greensboro, see Chafe, *Civilities and Civil Rights*, 157–78.

53. Smith interview, tape 1, side A. Jerome Evans called cheerleading "the major racial issue throughout the state." See Jordan, *Black Coach*, 75. Integrating cheerleading squads posed difficulties throughout the South, as evidenced in part by a number of federal appeals court cases that dealt with the issue in states from Mississippi to Muncie, Indiana. See, for example, *Banks v. Muncie Community SCHS*, 433 F.2d 292, 1970 U.S. App. LEXIS 8274; *Dunn v. Tyler Independent School District*, 460 F.2d 137, 1972 U.S. App. LEXIS 13096; *Goss v. Board of Education of Knoxville*, 482 F.2d 1044, 1973 U.S. App. LEXIS 8726; *Boykins v. Fairfield Board of Education*, 492 F.2d 697, 1974 U.S. App. LEXIS 9183; *Callahan v. Price*, 505 F.2d 83, 1974 U.S. App. LEXIS 5653; and *Augustus v. School Board of Escambia City*, 507 F.2d 152, 1975 U.S. App. LEXIS 16423.

54. Shakelford interview, tape 1, side A; Stoudemire, *Place at the Table*, 172.

55. Cherry interview, tape 1, side A. For a detailed account of perceived differences between black and white cheerleading from the point of view of two white cheerleaders, see Jordan, *Black Coach*, 130–35.

56. Stoudemire, *Place at the Table*, 173.

57. *Asheville Citizen*, September 30, 1969, sec. 2, p. 1.

58. Stoudemire, *Place at the Table*, 173. Cheerleading criteria are described in Shakelford interview, tape 1, side A.

59. Bryant and Costner interview, tape 1, side A. Runoff elections, of course, became a prime method by which black candidates were kept out of office throughout the South for many years after blacks won the right to vote.

60. Friday interview, tape 1, side A.

61. Stoudemire, *Place at the Table*, 195; Cecelski, *Along Freedom Road*, 160–61; *Charlotte Observer*, February 12, 1975, sec. B, p. 1.

62. Shakelford interview, tape 1, side A; Jordan, *Black Coach*, 73–74.

63. Gibbs interview, tape 1, side A; Jordan, *Black Coach*, 126.

64. For a brief description of black athletic activism, see Rader, *American Sports*, 299–303. The Olympic boycott effort is described in more detail in Harry Edwards, *Revolt of the Black Athlete*.

65. *Daily Tar Heel*, February 19, 1969, 1; *Durham Sun*, February 19, 1969, sec. A, p. 1; Link, *William Friday*, 144. For an account of the Black Student Movement and the food workers' strike, see J. Derek Williams, " 'It Wasn't Slavery Time Anymore.' "

66. *Daily Tar Heel*, February 21, 1969, 5, and February 19, 1969, 2.

67. Link, *William Friday*, 145–56.

68. *Durham Sun*, February 19, 1969. sec. A, p. 1.

69. *Raleigh News and Observer*, October 19, 1968, 4; *New York Times*, March 22, 1969, 20.

70. *Daily Tar Heel*, February 4, 1968, 4, and October 30, 1968, 4. Leon Coleman, an Olympic hurdler from Winston-Salem State, was more outspoken, protesting the expulsion of Carlos and Smith from the Olympic Village to a Raleigh reporter; see *Raleigh News and Observer*, October 19, 1968, 4. Johnson C. Smith sprinter Vincent Matthews described his contacts with boycott supporters in Matthews, *My Race Be Won*, 161–62.

71. *Durham Morning Herald*, March 16, 1969, sec. C, p. 2.

72. McLendon interview, tape 1, side B; Martin, "Rise and Fall of Jim Crow," 280–84; Rader, *American Sports*, 302–3.

EPILOGUE

1. Winston, *Builder of the New South*, 304; Doyle, "Foolish and Useless Sport," 327. For a discussion of this transformation of Darwinian theory, see Bederman, *Manliness and Civilization*, 25–31. A comprehensive account of early-nineteenth-century concerns about the economic and social changes the country was undergoing can be found in Watts, *Republic Reborn*.

2. Anonymous to Friday, May 22, 1961, folder "Dixie Classic Controversy, 1961," II, series 1, subgroup 1, Friday Records.

3. For examples of portrayals of Thompson's career, see Herakovich, *Pack Pride*, 88–89; Wolff, *100 Years of Hoops*, 108; *Sports Illustrated*, November 15, 1999, 73. For an account of criticism Thompson received after he married a white woman, see Lapchick, *Broken Promises*, 193–94.

4. For a description of the structure and function of athletic games and the interplay between rules and individual effort, see Huizinga, *Homo Ludens*, 10–11.

5. For a fascinating account of the conservative embrace of Jackie Robinson, and on the critique of Robinson's highly publicized achievements by activists facing the challenges of the later civil rights movement—challenges that included combating structural economic inequalities, devising plans for minority political representation, and preserving distinctive African American institutions—see Tygiel, *Baseball's Great Experiment*, 345–51.

# BIBLIOGRAPHY

## INTERVIEWS

Ardrey, Sam, and Lavinia Ardrey Kell. Interview by Peter Felkner. Pineville, N.C., December 10, 1992. Museum of the New South, Charlotte, N.C.

Ashe, Jesse. Interview by Allen Tullos. Charlotte, N.C., June 13, 1980. Southern Historical Collection, Wilson Library, University of North Carolina, Chapel Hill.

Austin, Ernest B., Lloyd Cochran, Frances Freeman, Russell G. Faulk, and Vera Kimbrell. Interview by Peter Felkner. Newell, N.C., January 16, 1993. Museum of the New South, Charlotte, N.C.

Austin, Ralph. Interview by James Leloudis. Charlotte, N.C., June 14, 1979. Southern Historical Collection, Wilson Library, University of North Carolina, Chapel Hill.

Baker, Ella. Interview by Sue Thrasher and Casey Hayden. New York, N.Y., April 19, 1977. Southern Historical Collection, Wilson Library, University of North Carolina, Chapel Hill.

Barkley, Henry. Interview by Mark Jones. Denver, N.C., May 4, 1999. In Jones's possession.

Bauguess, Mildred Little. Interview by Pamela Grundy. Claremont, N.C., May 14, 1993. Museum of the New South, Charlotte, N.C.

Bauguess, Mildred, Eunies Futch, Eckie Jordan, and Hazel Phillips. Interview by Pamela Grundy. Charlotte, N.C., March 30, 1996. Museum of the New South, Charlotte, N.C.

Blake, Alma. Interview by Pamela Grundy. Charlotte, N.C., October 14, 1993. Museum of the New South, Charlotte, N.C.

Bost, Bill. Interview by Pamela Grundy. Catawba, N.C., March 15, 1993. Museum of the New South, Charlotte, N.C.

Bost, William Thomas "Tom." Interview by Clarence E. Whitefield. Chapel Hill, N.C., June 2, 1983. Southern Historical Collection, Wilson Library, University of North Carolina, Chapel Hill.

Boulware, Nancy, Betty Carter, Ramona Hinkle, and Billie Martin. Interview by Pamela Grundy. Lincolnton, N.C., September 28, 1993. Museum of the New South, Charlotte, N.C.

Brown, Burrell. Interview by Pamela Grundy. Hickory, N.C., March 31, 1993. Museum of the New South, Charlotte, N.C.

Bryant, Thomas, and John Costner Jr. Interview by Pamela Grundy. Gastonia, N.C., September 29, 1993. Museum of the New South, Charlotte, N.C.

Callaway, Elizabeth. Interview by Pamela Grundy. Denver, N.C., March 11, 1993. Museum of the New South, Charlotte, N.C.

Camp, Patsy Rice. Interview by Pamela Grundy. Charlotte, N.C., March 23, 1999. Southern Historical Collection, Wilson Library, University of North Carolina, Chapel Hill.

Carr, Garfield. Interview by Laura Hajar. Davidson, N.C., March 16, 1999. Southern
Historical Collection, Wilson Library, University of North Carolina, Chapel Hill.

Cherry, Steve. Interview by Mark Jones. Denver, N.C., February 19, 1999. Southern
Historical Collection, Wilson Library, University of North Carolina, Chapel Hill.

Clemmons, Mary Alyce. Interview by Pamela Grundy. Charlotte, N.C., September 2,
1993. Museum of the New South, Charlotte, N.C.

Cloniger, Loy. Interview by Allen Tullos. Charlotte, N.C., June 18, 1980. Southern
Historical Collection, Wilson Library, University of North Carolina, Chapel Hill.

Cunningham, Herman. Interview by Pamela Grundy. Monroe, N.C., September 7, 1993.
Museum of the New South, Charlotte, N.C.

Dalton, Mary, and Mildred McMillan. Interview by Peter Felkner and Pamela Grundy.
Charlotte, N.C., December 7, 1992. Museum of the New South, Charlotte, N.C.

Davis, Dan. Interview by Pamela Grundy. Monroe, N.C., October 12, 1993. Museum of
the New South, Charlotte, N.C.

Dawkins, James. Interview by Kate Feldmeier. Charlotte, N.C., April 16, 1999. Southern
Historical Collection, Wilson Library, University of North Carolina, Chapel Hill.

Durham, Eula, and Vernon Durham. Interview by James Leloudis. Bynum, N.C.,
November 29, 1978. Southern Historical Collection, Wilson Library, University of
North Carolina, Chapel Hill.

Ely, Vermelle, and Kenneth Diamond Jr. Interview by Pamela Grundy. Charlotte, N.C.,
March 10, 1993. In Grundy's possession.

Faucette, Ethel. Interviews by Allen Tullos. Burlington, N.C., November 16, 1978, and
January 4, 1979 (combined transcript). Southern Historical Collection, Wilson
Library, University of North Carolina, Chapel Hill.

Friday, William. Interview by Pamela Grundy. Chapel Hill, N.C., September 7, 1999.
Southern Historical Collection, Wilson Library, University of North Carolina,
Chapel Hill.

Futch, Eunies, and Eckie Jordan. Interview by Susan Cahn. Winston-Salem, N.C., July
18, 1988. In Cahn's possession.

Gaines, Clarence "Bighouse." Interview by Pamela Grundy. Winston-Salem, N.C.,
March 8, 2000. In Grundy's possession.

Gibbs, Timothy. Interview by Pamela Grundy. Charlotte, N.C., May 27, 1998. Southern
Historical Collection, Wilson Library, University of North Carolina, Chapel Hill.

Gleaves, Margaret Sexton. Interview by Susan Cahn. Nashville, Tenn., July 6, 1988. In
Cahn's possession.

Grier, Paul, Sr. Interview by Peter Felkner. Charlotte, N.C., July 1993. Museum of the
New South, Charlotte, N.C.

Griffin, Arthur, Jr. Interview by Pamela Grundy. Charlotte, N.C., May 7, 1999. Southern
Historical Collection, Wilson Library, University of North Carolina, Chapel Hill.

Hamlin, William. Interview by Pamela Grundy. Charlotte, N.C., May 29, 1998.
Southern Historical Collection, Wilson Library, University of North Carolina,
Chapel Hill.

Harris, Von Ray. Interview by Reid McGlamery. Lincolnton, N.C., April 7, 1999.
Southern Historical Collection, Wilson Library, University of North Carolina,
Chapel Hill.

Hewins, Vada Setzer, Romer Hewins, and John Shayle Edwards. Interview by Pamela
Grundy. Catawba, N.C., March 15, 1993. Museum of the New South, Charlotte, N.C.

Holtzclaw, Walter. Video interview by David Ramsey. Charlotte, N.C., January 1994.
Museum of the New South, Charlotte, N.C.

House, Robert Burton, and Lee Roy Wells Armstrong. Interviews by Clarence E. Whitefield. Chapel Hill, N.C., April 5 and 26, 1983 (combined transcript). Southern Historical Collection, Wilson Library, University of North Carolina, Chapel Hill.

Ivory, Titus. Interview by Pamela Grundy. Charlotte, N.C., March 24, 1993. Museum of the New South, Charlotte, N.C.

Joplin, Willie L. "Scoopie." Interview by Pamela Grundy. Charlotte, N.C., April 2, 1999. Southern Historical Collection, Charlotte, N.C.

Jordan, Eckie. Telephone interview by Pamela Grundy. April 8, 2000.

McCorkle, Hoyle, and Mamie McCorkle. Interview by James Leloudis. Charlotte, N.C., July 11, 1979. Southern Historical Collection, Wilson Library, University of North Carolina, Chapel Hill.

McCullough, Charles. Interview by Pamela Grundy. Charlotte, N.C., August 30, 1993. Museum of the New South, Charlotte, N.C.

McLendon, John. Interview by Pamela Grundy. Winston-Salem, N.C., February 26, 1998. Southern Historical Collection, Wilson Library, University of North Carolina, Chapel Hill.

Newitt, Elizabeth. Interview by Peter Felkner and Pamela Grundy. Charlotte, N.C., December 7, 1992. Museum of the New South, Charlotte, N.C.

Pharr, Frederic "Chuck," and Sarah Pharr. Interview by Joy Pharr Smith. Charlotte, N.C., January 2, 1993. Museum of the New South, Charlotte, N.C.

Powell, George, and Lib Sifford Rotan. Interview by Peter Felkner. Charlotte, N.C., March 8, 1993. Museum of the New South, Charlotte, N.C.

Rhodes, Larry. Interview by Pamela Grundy. Gastonia, N.C., September 23, 1993. In Grundy's possession.

Ross, James. Interview by Pamela Grundy and Thomas Hanchett. Charlotte, N.C., February 10, 2000. Southern Historical Collection, Wilson Library, University of North Carolina, Chapel Hill.

Saunders, J. Maryon "Spike." Interview by Clarence E. Whitefield. Chapel Hill, N.C., September 8, 1982. Southern Historical Collection, Wilson Library, University of North Carolina, Chapel Hill.

Scott, Tom. Interview by Peter Felkner. Davidson, N.C., July 21, 1993. Museum of the New South, Charlotte, N.C.

Shakelford, Susan. Interview by Pamela Grundy. Charlotte, N.C., November 19, 1999. Southern Historical Collection, Wilson Library, University of North Carolina, Chapel Hill.

Skipper, Otis. Interview by Peter Felkner. Mint Hill, N.C., January 6, 1993. Museum of the New South, Charlotte, N.C.

Smith, Clyde. Interview by Reid McGlamery. Lincolnton, N.C., March 17, 1999. Southern Historical Collection, University of North Carolina, Chapel Hill.

Tapia, Brenda. Interview by Laura Hajar. Davidson, N.C., April 28, 1999. Southern Historical Collection, Wilson Library, University of North Carolina, Chapel Hill.

Taylor, H. W. "Pop." Interview by Maurice Toler. Raleigh, N.C., November 11, 1975. University Archives, North Carolina State University, Raleigh, N.C.

Thompson, John. Interview by Joy S. Burton. Charlotte, N.C., March 1993. Museum of the New South, Charlotte, N.C.

Torrence, Rudolph. Interview by Pamela Grundy. Charlotte, N.C., May 27, 1998. Southern Historical Collection, Wilson Library, University of North Carolina, Chapel Hill.

Vinroot, Richard. Interview by Peter Felkner. Charlotte, N.C., April 19, 1993. Museum of the New South, Charlotte, N.C.

Webster, Frank. Interview by Allen Tullos. Burlington, N.C., January 30, 1979. Southern Historical Collection, Wilson Library, University of North Carolina, Chapel Hill.

Williams, Maxine Vaughn. Interview by Susan Cahn. Winston-Salem, N.C., July 16, 1988. In Cahn's possession.

Worthy, Gladys Thompson. Interview by Pamela Grundy. Gastonia, N.C., May 6, 1993. Museum of the New South, Charlotte, N.C.


## MANUSCRIPT COLLECTIONS

Cambridge, Mass.
 Radcliffe College, Arthur and Elizabeth Schlesinger Library on the History of Women in America
  Charlotte Eugenia Hawkins Brown Collection
Chapel Hill, N.C.
 North Carolina High School Athletic Association
  NCHSAA Archives
 University of North Carolina, Wilson Library
  North Carolina Collection
  Southern Historical Collection
   William C. Friday Papers
  University Archives
   Athletic Department Records
   Chancellor's Records, Aycock Series
   Frank Porter Graham Presidential Records
Charlotte, N.C.
 Johnson C. Smith University
  University Archives
 Museum of the New South
  "The Most Democratic Sport" Collection
 Public Library of Charlotte and Mecklenburg County, Robinson-Spangler Carolina Room
  African American Photography Collection
 Queens College, Everett Library
  Queens College Collections
 Second Ward High School National Alumni Foundation Archives
Clemson, S.C.
 Clemson University Libraries, Special Collections
  Monagham Baptist Church Records
  Textile Hall Records
Concord, N.C.
 Barber-Scotia College, Sage Memorial Library
Davidson, N.C.
 Davidson College
  Davidsoniana Room
Greensboro, N.C.
 North Carolina Agricultural and Technical University, Ferdinand D. Bluford Library
 University of North Carolina at Greensboro, Walter Clinton Jackson Library
  Special Collections
   School of Health, Physical Education, Recreation, and Dance Collection

       Mary Channing Coleman Papers
       Julius Isaac Foust Papers
Lincolnton, N.C.
  Lincolnton Public Library
Raleigh, N.C.
  North Carolina State Archives
    Department of Public Instruction
      Division of Negro Education Records
      Division of Professional Services Records
  Shaw University
    University Archives
      Charles Francis Meserve Presidential Papers
  North Carolina State University
    University Archives
      Athletics Department General Correspondence
      Athletics Department Records
Salisbury, N.C.
  Livingstone College, Carnegie Library
    College Archives
Washington, D.C.
  Howard University
    Moorland-Spingarn Research Center
      Maryrose Reeves Allen Papers
      Lucy Diggs Slowe Papers
Winston-Salem, N.C.
  Winston-Salem State University, C. G. O'Kelley Library
      Clarence "Bighouse" Gaines Papers


## NEWSPAPERS AND JOURNALS

*AME Zion Quarterly Review*
*Asheville Citizen*
*Carolina Times*
*Charlotte News*
*Charlotte Observer*
*Cleveland Plain Dealer*
*Coaching Clinic*
*Durham Morning Herald*
*Durham Sun*
*Greensboro Daily News*
*Greensboro News and Record*
*Hickory Daily Record*
*High School Journal*
*Look*
*New York Times*
*North Carolina Basketball Preview*
*North Carolina Education*
*North Carolina Teacher*
*Raleigh News and Observer*

*Salisbury Daily Sun*
*School Life*
*Southern Textile Bulletin*
*Sports Illustrated*
*Star of Zion*
*Wilmington Morning Star*
*Winston-Salem Journal-Sentinel*


### HIGH SCHOOL, COLLEGE, AND UNIVERSITY PUBLICATIONS

Barber-Scotia College, Concord, N.C.
  *Barber-Scotia Index*
Central High School, Charlotte, N.C.
  *Lace and Pig Iron*
  *Snips and Cuts*
Charlotte Female Institute, Charlotte, N.C.
  *Catalog and Circular of the Charlotte Female Institute*
Davidson College, Davidson, N.C.
  *Davidson College Magazine*
  *Davidson Monthly*
Dixie High School, Mecklenburg County, N.C.
  *Dixie Doings*
Elizabeth College, Charlotte, N.C.
  *Elizabethan*
Harding High School, Charlotte, N.C.
  *The Acorn*
Institute for Young Ladies, Charlotte, N.C.
  *Catalog and Circular of the Institute for Young Ladies*
  *Circular of the Institute for Young Ladies*
Lincolnton High School, Lincolnton, N.C.
  *Pine Burr*
Livingstone College, Salisbury, N.C.
  *Blue Bear*
  *Living Stone*
Millbrook High School, Raleigh, N.C.
  *The Laurel*
North Carolina Agricultural and Technical University, Greensboro, N.C.
  *Register*
Presbyterian College, Charlotte, N.C.
  *Catalog of the Presbyterian College for Women*
  *Edelweiss*
Queens College, Charlotte, N.C.
  *Caps and Belles*
Ridgeview High School, Hickory, N.C.
  *Panther*
Second Ward High School, Charlotte, N.C.
  *Second Ward Herald*
Shaw University, Raleigh, N.C.
  *Annual Catalog of the Officers and Students of Shaw University*
  *Shaw University Journal*

Shelby High School, Shelby, N.C.
  *The Legend*
Johnson C. Smith University, Charlotte, N.C.
  *Biddle Outlook*
University of North Carolina, Chapel Hill
  *Alumni Review*
  *Daily Tar Heel*
  *University of North Carolina Alumni Quarterly*
  *University Record*
  *Yackety-Yack*
University of North Carolina, Greensboro
  *Carolinian*
  *North Carolina State Normal and Industrial College Decennial*
  *State Normal Magazine*


## BOOKS, ARTICLES, PAMPHLETS, AND VIDEOS

Abrahams, Roger D. *Singing the Master: The Emergence of African-American Culture in the Plantation South*. New York: Penguin, 1993.

Adams, David Wallace. *Education for Extinction: American Indians and the Boarding School Experience, 1875–1928*. Lawrence: University Press of Kansas, 1995.

Adelman, Melvin L. *A Sporting Time: New York City and the Rise of Modern Athletics, 1820–70*. Urbana: University of Illinois Press, 1986.

Alexander, John Brevard. *Reminiscences of the Past Sixty Years*. Charlotte, N.C.: Ray Printing, 1908.

Anderson, James D. *The Education of Blacks in the South, 1860–1935*. Chapel Hill: University of North Carolina Press, 1988.

*An Appeal for the Girls' New Building, Livingstone College and Industrial School*. N.p., 1910.

Ashby, Warren. *Frank Porter Graham: A Southern Liberal*. Winston-Salem, N.C.: John F. Blair, 1980.

Ashe, Arthur R., Jr. *A Hard Road to Glory: A History of the African-American Athlete*. 3 vols. New York: Amistead Press, 1993.

Avery, Isaac Ervin. *Idle Comments*. Charlotte, N.C.: Publishers' Printing, 1905.

Axthelm, Pete. *The City Game: Basketball in New York from the World Champion Knicks to the World of the Playgrounds*. New York: Harper's Magazine, 1970.

Ayers, Edward L. *The Promise of the New South: Life after Reconstruction*. Oxford: Oxford University Press, 1992.

Banner, Lois W. *American Beauty*. New York: Knopf, 1983.

Barrier, Smith. *On Carolina's Gridiron, 1888–1936: A History of Football at the University of North Carolina*. Durham, N.C.: Seaman Printery, 1937.

——. *On Tobacco Road: Basketball in North Carolina*. New York: Leisure Press, 1983.

Barth, Gunther. *City People: The Rise of Modern City Culture in Nineteenth-Century America*. Oxford: Oxford University Press, 1980.

Bederman, Gail. *Manliness and Civilization: A Cultural History of Gender and Race in the United States, 1880–1917*. Chicago: University of Chicago Press, 1995.

Ben, Philip L., ed. *Tar Heel Tradition: One Hundred Years of Sports at Carolina*. Chapel Hill: Jonashmark Publishers, 1988.

Beran, Janice A. "Iowa, the Longtime 'Hot Bed' of Girls Basketball." In *A Century of Women's Basketball: From Frailty to Final Four*, edited by Joan S. Hult and Marianna

Trekell, 181–204. Reston, Va.: American Alliance for Health, Physical Education, Recreation and Dance, 1991.

Bishop, Elva E., prod. *Women's Basketball: The Road to Respect*. Chapel Hill: University of North Carolina Public Television, 1997.

Bishop, Elva E., and Katherine Fulton. "Shooting Stars: The Heyday of Industrial Women's Basketball." *Southern Exposure* 7 (fall 1979): 50–54.

Bloomer, D. C. *Life and Writings of Amelia Bloomer*. Boston: Arena Pub. Co., 1895.

Bourdieu, Pierre. *Distinction: A Social Critique of the Judgement of Taste*. Cambridge, Mass.: Harvard University Press, 1984.

Bridgeman, Donald F., and Edward S. Steitz. "Needs and Problems of Adolescents in the Area of Physical Development." *High School Journal* 35 (November 1951): 34–40.

Brumberg, Joan Jacobs. *The Body Project: An Intimate History of American Girls*. New York: Random House, 1997.

Bryant, Paul W., and John Underwood. *Bear: The Hard Life and Good Times of Alabama's Coach Bryant*. New York: Bantam, 1974.

Cahn, Susan. *Coming on Strong: Gender and Sexuality in Twentieth-Century Women's Sport*. New York: Free Press, 1994.

Carlton, David. *Mill and Town in South Carolina, 1880–1920*. Baton Rouge: Louisiana State University Press, 1982.

Carroll, John M. *Fritz Pollard: Pioneer in Racial Advancement*. Urbana: University of Illinois Press, 1992.

Carter, Wilmoth A. *Shaw's Universe: A Monument to Educational Innovation*. Raleigh, N.C.: Shaw University, 1973.

Cash, W. J. *The Mind of the South*. New York: Knopf, 1941.

Cayleff, Susan E. *Babe: The Life and Legend of Babe Didrikson Zaharias*. Urbana: University of Illinois Press, 1995.

Cecelski, David S. *Along Freedom Road: Hyde County, North Carolina, and the Fate of Black Schools in the South*. Chapel Hill: University of North Carolina Press, 1994.

Cecelski, David S., and Timothy E. Tyson, eds. *Democracy Betrayed: The Wilmington Race Riot of 1898 and Its Legacy*. Chapel Hill: University of North Carolina Press, 1998.

Chafe, William H. *Civilities and Civil Rights: Greensboro, North Carolina, and the Black Struggle for Freedom*. Oxford: Oxford University Press, 1980.

Chalk, Ocania. *Black College Sport*. New York: Dodd, Mead, 1976.

Chansky, Art. *Dean's Domain: The Inside Story of Dean Smith and His College Basketball Empire*. Atlanta: Longstreet, 1999.

———. *The Dean's List: A Celebration of Tar Heel Basketball and Dean Smith*. New York: Warner, 1996.

Cobb, James. *The Selling of the South: The Southern Crusade for Industrial Development, 1936–1980*. Baton Rouge: Louisiana State University Press, 1982.

Coleman, Mary C., and Guy B. Phillips. "Athletics for High School Girls." *North Carolina College for Women Extension Bulletin* 3 (November 1925).

Corbin, David. *Life, Work, and Rebellion in the Coal Fields: The Southern West Virginia Miners, 1880–1922*. Urbana: University of Illinois Press, 1981.

Corrubia, Helen. "Provisions for the Physical Health of High School Students." *High School Journal* 35 (November 1951): 40–57.

Cott, Nancy. *The Grounding of Modern Feminism*. New Haven: Yale University Press, 1987.

Cozart, L. S. *A Venture of Faith: Barber-Scotia College, 1867–1967*. Charlotte, N.C.: Heritage Printers, 1976.

Crosby, Emilye. "The Most Democratic Sport: Basketball and Culture in the Central Piedmont, 1893–1994." Exhibition review. *Journal of American History* 83 (June 1996): 155–60.

Crowell, John Franklin. *Personal Recollections of Trinity College, North Carolina, 1887–1894.* Durham, N.C.: Duke University Press, 1939.

Cutler, John Levi. *Gilbert Patten and His Frank Merriwell Sage: A Study in Sub-literary Fiction, 1896–1913.* Orono, Maine: University Press, 1934.

Davis, Owena Hunter. *A History of Mary Potter School, Oxford, North Carolina.* Privately printed, 1942.

Dean, Pamela. " 'Dear Sisters' and 'Hated Rivals': Athletics and Gender at Two New South Women's Colleges, 1893–1920." *Journal of Sport History* 24 (fall 1997): 341–57.

——. "Learning to Be New Women: Campus Culture at the North Carolina Normal and Industrial College." *North Carolina Historical Review* 68 (July 1991): 286–306.

Delany, Sarah L., and A. Elizabeth Delany, with Amy Hill Hearth. *Having Our Say: The Delany Sisters' First One Hundred Years.* New York: Dell, 1994.

Doyle, Andrew. "Foolish and Useless Sport: The Southern Evangelical Crusade against Intercollegiate Football." *Journal of Sport History* 24 (fall 1997): 317–40.

——. "Turning the Tide: College Football and Southern Progressivism." *Southern Cultures* 3 (fall 1997): 28–51.

Dunnagan, M. R. *The Red Strings Baseball Team of Yadkin County, N.C., 1896–1902.* New Bern, N.C.: Owen G. Dunn, 1956.

Durkheim, Emile. *Moral Education: A Study in the Theory and Application of the Sociology of Education.* Edited by Everett K. Wilson. New York: Free Press of Glenco, 1961.

Durrill, Wayne K. "Producing Poverty: Local Government and Economic Development in a New South County, 1874–1884." *Journal of American History* 71 (March 1985): 764–81.

Edwards, Harry. "The Olympic Project for Human Rights: An Assessment Ten Years Later." In *American Sport: A Documentary History*, edited by Peter Levine, 136–143. Englewood Cliffs, N.J.: Prentice Hall, 1989.

——. *The Revolt of the Black Athlete.* New York: Free Press, 1969.

——. *The Struggle That Must Be: An Autobiography.* New York: Macmillan, 1980.

Edwards, Shayle. *Basketball Championship Scores of Catawba County High Schools, 1926–1990.* Privately printed, 1990.

Ellis, A. W. "The Status of Health and Physical Education for Women in Negro Colleges and Universities." *Journal of Negro Education* 8 (1939): 58–63.

Ely, Melvin Patrick. *The Adventures of Amos 'n' Andy: A Social History of an American Phenomenon.* New York: Free Press, 1991.

Escott, Paul D. *Many Excellent People: Power and Privilege in North Carolina, 1850–1900.* Chapel Hill: University of North Carolina Press, 1985.

Fenton, Steve, Robert Reiner, and Ian Hamnet. *Durkheim and Modern Sociology.* Cambridge: Cambridge University Press, 1984.

Festle, Mary Jo. *Playing Nice: Politics and Apologies in Women's Sports.* New York: Columbia University Press, 1996.

Filene, Peter G. *Him/Her/Self: Gender Identities in Modern America.* Baltimore: Johns Hopkins University Press, 1998.

Finger, Bill. "Just Another Ball Game." *Southern Exposure* 7 (fall 1979): 74–81.

Fleisher, Arthur A., III, Brian L. Goff, and Robert D. Tollison. *The National Collegiate Athletic Association: A Study in Cartel Behavior.* Chicago: University of Chicago Press, 1988.

Flowers, Linda. *Throwed Away: Failures of Progress in Eastern North Carolina*. Knoxville: University of Tennessee Press, 1990.

Fonvielle, William F. *Reminiscences of College Days*. Raleigh, N.C.: privately printed, 1904.

——. *The Taint of the Bicycle*. Goldsboro, N.C.: privately printed, 1902.

Foster, Gaines M. *Ghosts of the Confederacy: Defeat, the Lost Cause, and the Emergence of the New South, 1865–1913*. New York: Oxford University Press, 1987.

Frisch, Michael. *A Shared Authority: Essays on the Craft and Meaning of Oral and Public History*. Albany: State University of New York Press, 1990.

Gaines, Kevin K. *Uplifting the Race: Black Leadership, Politics, and Culture in the Twentieth Century*. Chapel Hill: University of North Carolina Press, 1996.

Gavins, Raymond. *The Perils and Prospects of Southern Black Leadership: Gordon Blaine Hancock, 1884–1970*. Durham, N.C.: Duke University Press, 1977.

Geertz, Clifford. *The Interpretation of Cultures*. New York: Basic Books, 1973.

George, Nelson. *Elevating the Game: The History and Aesthetics of Black Men in Basketball*. New York: Simon and Schuster, 1992.

Giddings, Paula. *When and Where I Enter: The Impact of Black Women on Race and Sex in America*. New York: William Morrow, 1984.

Gilmore, Glenda. "Gender and Jim Crow: Sarah Dudley Pettey's Vision of the New South." *North Carolina Historical Review* 68 (July 1991): 261–85.

——. *Gender and Jim Crow: Women and the Politics of White Supremacy in North Carolina, 1896–1920*. Chapel Hill: University of North Carolina Press, 1996.

Gissendanner, Cindy Himes. "African-American Women and Competitive Sport." In *Women, Sport, and Culture*, edited by Susan Birrell and Cheryl Cole, 81–92. Champaign, Ill.: Human Kinetics, 1994.

Goldstein, Warren Jay. *Playing for Keeps: A History of Early Baseball*. Ithaca, N.Y.: Cornell University Press, 1989.

Goodwyn, Lawrence. *Democratic Promise: The Populist Moment in America*. New York: Oxford University Press, 1976.

Gorn, Elliot. *The Manly Art: Bare Knuckle Prize Fighting in America*. Ithaca, N.Y.: Cornell University Press, 1986.

Gorn, Elliot, and Warren Goldstein. *A Brief History of American Sports*. New York: Hill and Wang, 1993.

Greenwood, Janette Thomas. *Bittersweet Legacy: The Black and White "Better Classes" in Charlotte, 1850–1910*. Chapel Hill: University of North Carolina Press, 1994.

Griffin, Paul R. *Black Theology As the Foundation of Three Methodist Colleges: The Educational Views and Labors of Daniel Payne, Joseph Price, Isaac Lane*. Lanham, Md.: University Press of America, 1984.

Grundy, Pamela. "Bloomers and Beyond: North Carolina Women's Basketball Uniforms, 1901–1997." *Southern Cultures* 3 (fall 1997): 52–67.

——. *The Most Democratic Sport: Basketball and Culture in the Central Piedmont, 1893–1994*. Charlotte, N.C.: Museum of the New South, 1994.

——. " 'We Always Tried to Be Good People:' Respectability, Crazy Water Crystals, and Hillbilly Music on the Air, 1933–1935." *Journal of American History* 81 (March 1995): 1591–1620.

Hahn, Steven. *The Roots of Southern Populism: Yeoman Farmers and the Transformation of the Georgia Upcountry, 1850–1890*. New York: Oxford University Press, 1983.

Hale, Grace Elizabeth. *Making Whiteness: The Culture of Segregation in the South, 1890–1940*. New York: Pantheon, 1998.

Hall, Jacquelyn Dowd. "Disorderly Women: Gender and Labor Militancy in the Appalachian South." *Journal of American History* 73 (September 1986): 354–82.

——. *Revolt against Chivalry: Jessie Daniel Ames and the Women's Campaign against Lynching.* New York: Columbia University Press, 1974.

——. " 'You Must Remember This': Autobiography as Social Critique." *Journal of American History* 85 (September 1998): 439–65.

Hall, Jacquelyn Dowd, James Leloudis, Robert Korstad, Mary Murphy, Lu Ann Jones, and Christopher B. Daly. *Like a Family: The Making of a Southern Cotton Mill World.* Chapel Hill: University of North Carolina Press, 1987.

Hanchett, Thomas W. "The Rosenwald Schools and Black Education in North Carolina." *North Carolina Historical Review* 65 (October 1988): 387–444.

——. *Sorting Out the New South City: Race, Class, and Urban Development in Charlotte, 1875–1975.* Chapel Hill: University of North Carolina Press, 1998.

Hanson, Mary Ellen. *Go! Fight! Win! Cheerleading in American Culture.* Bowling Green, Ky.: Bowling Green State University Popular Press, 1995.

Henderson, Russell J. "The 1963 Mississippi State University Basketball Controversy and the Repeal of the Unwritten Law: 'Something More Than the Game Will Be Lost.' " *Journal of Southern History* 63 (November 1997): 827–54.

Henson, Josiah. *Father Henson's Story of His Own Life.* Boston: John P. Jewett, 1858.

Herakovich, Douglas. *Pack Pride: The History of N.C. State Basketball.* Cary, N.C.: Yesterday's Future, 1994.

Herring, Harriet L. *Welfare Work in Mill Villages: The Story of Extra-Mill Activities in North Carolina.* Chapel Hill: University of North Carolina Press, 1929.

Hewitt, Nancy A., and Suzanne Lebsock, eds. *Visible Women: New Essays on American Activism.* Urbana: University of Illinois Press, 1993.

"The High School Athletic Association of North Carolina." *University of North Carolina Extension Bulletin* 4 (October 16, 1924).

Hoberman, John M. *Mortal Engines: The Science of Performance and the Dehumanization of Sport.* New York: Free Press, 1992.

Holt, Rackham. *Mary McLeod Bethune: A Biography.* Garden City, N.Y.: Doubleday, 1964.

Holt, Thomas C. "Marking: Race, Race-making, and the Writing of History." *American Historical Review* 100 (February 1995): 1–20.

Huizinga, Johan. *Homo Ludens: A Study of the Play Element in Culture.* Boston: Beacon Press, 1955.

Hult, Joan S., and Marianna Trekell, eds. *A Century of Women's Basketball: From Frailty to Final Four.* Reston, Va.: American Alliance for Health, Physical Education, Recreation, and Dance, 1991.

Hunter, Tera W. *To 'Joy My Freedom: Southern Black Women's Lives and Labors after the Civil War.* Cambridge, Mass.: Harvard University Press, 1997.

James, C. L. R. *Beyond a Boundary.* Durham, N.C.: Duke University Press, 1993.

Johnson, Edward A. *A History of Negro Soldiers in the Spanish-American War and Other Items of Interest.* Cincinnati: W. H. Ferguson, 1899.

Johnson, Paul E. *A Shopkeeper's Millennium: Society and Revivals in Rochester, New York, 1815–1837.* New York: Hill and Wang, 1978.

Jones, Jacquelyn. *Labor of Love, Labor of Sorrow: Black Women, Work, and the Family, from Slavery to the Present.* New York: Vintage, 1985.

Jones, Lu Ann. "Voices of Southern Agricultural History." In *International Annual of Oral History, 1990: Subjectivity and Multiculturalism in Oral History*, edited by Ronald J. Grele, 135–44. New York: Greenwood, 1992.

Jordan, Pat. *Black Coach*. New York: Dodd, Mead, 1971.

*Journal of Proceedings of 11th Annual State Convention of the Y-M-C-A-, Associations of North Carolina, Raleigh, 1–3 April 1887*. Raleigh, N.C.: Edwards and Broughton, 1887.

Kasson, John F. *Amusing the Million: Coney Island at the Turn of the Century*. New York: Hill and Wang, 1978.

———. *Rudeness and Civility: Manners in Nineteenth-Century Urban America*. New York: Hill and Wang, 1990.

Katz, Milton S., and John B. McLendon Jr. *Breaking Through: The NAIA and the Integration of Intercollegiate Athletics in Post World War II America*. Privately printed, 1988. Copy in the North Carolina Collection, University of North Carolina, Chapel Hill.

Kelley, Robin D. G. *Race Rebels: Culture, Politics, and the Black Working Class*. New York: Free Press, 1996.

———. " 'We Are Not What We Seem': Rethinking Black Working-Class Opposition in the Jim Crow South." *Journal of American History* 80 (June 1993): 75–112.

Kennedy, David M. *Over Here: The First World War and American Society*. New York: Oxford University Press, 1980.

Kipling, Rudyard. *Rudyard Kipling's Verse, Inclusive Edition, 1885–1926*. Garden City, N.Y.: Doubleday, Doran, 1941.

Kirkpatrick, Mac C., and Thomas K. Perry. *The Southern Textile Basketball Tournament*. Jefferson, N.C.: McFarland Co., 1997.

Korstad, Bob. "Those Who Were Not Afraid: Winston-Salem, 1943." In *Working Lives: The Southern Exposure History of Labor in the South*, edited by Marc S. Miller, 184–99. New York: Pantheon, 1980.

Kratt, Mary Norton. *Charlotte: Spirit of the New South*. Winston-Salem, N.C.: John F. Blair, 1992.

Lapchick, Richard Edward. *Broken Promises: Racism in American Sports*. New York: St. Martin's/Marek, 1984.

Larrabee, Lisa. "Women and Cycling: The Early Years." In *How I Learned to Ride the Bicycle: Reflections of an Influential Nineteenth-Century Woman*, by Frances Willard, edited by Carol O'Hare, 81–97. Sunnyvale, Calif.: Fair Oaks, 1991.

Lears, T. J. Jackson. "The Concept of Cultural Hegemony." *American Historical Review* 90 (June 1985): 567–93.

Lebsock, Suzanne. "Woman Suffrage and White Supremacy: A Virginia Case Study." In *Visible Women: New Essays on American Activism*, edited by Nancy A. Hewitt and Suzanne Lebsock, 62–100. Urbana: University of Illinois Press, 1993.

Lefler, Hugh Talmage, and Albert Ray Newsome. *North Carolina: The History of a Southern State*. Rev. ed. Chapel Hill: University of North Carolina Press, 1963.

Leloudis, James L. *Schooling the New South: Pedagogy, Self, and Society in North Carolina, 1880–1920*. Chapel Hill: University of North Carolina Press, 1996.

Levine, David O. *The American College and the Culture of Aspiration, 1915–1940*. Ithaca, N.Y.: Cornell University Press, 1986.

Levine, Lawrence. *Black Culture and Black Consciousness: Afro-American Folk Thought from Slavery to Freedom*. New York: Oxford University Press, 1977.

———. "The Folklore of Industrial Society." *American Historical Review* 97 (December 1992): 1369–99.

———. *Highbrow/Lowbrow: The Emergence of Cultural Hierarchy in America*. Cambridge, Mass.: Harvard University Press, 1988.

Levine, Peter. *A. G. Spalding and the Rise of Baseball: The Promise of American Sport*. New York: Oxford University Press, 1985.

———. *Ellis Island to Ebbets Field: Sport and the American Jewish Experience*. New York: Oxford University Press, 1992.

———, ed. *American Sport: A Documentary History*. Englewood Cliffs, N.J.: Prentice Hall, 1989.

Lévi-Strauss, Claude. *The Savage Mind*. Chicago: University of Chicago Press, 1966.

Lewis, David Levering. *When Harlem Was in Vogue*. New York: Oxford University Press, 1981.

Lingle, Walter L. *Memories of Davidson College*. Richmond, Va.: John Knox Press, 1947.

Link, William A. " 'The Harvest Is Ripe, but the Laborers Are Few': The Hookworm Crusade in North Carolina, 1909–1915." *North Carolina Historical Review* 67 (January 1990): 1–27.

———. *The Paradox of Southern Progressivism, 1880–1930*. Chapel Hill: University of North Carolina Press, 1993.

———. *William Friday: Power, Purpose, and American Higher Education*. Chapel Hill: University of North Carolina Press, 1995.

Love, Rose Leary. *Plum Thickets and Field Daisies*. Charlotte, N.C.: Public Library of Charlotte and Mecklenburg County, 1996.

Luebke, Paul. *Tar Heel Politics: Myths and Realities*. Chapel Hill: University of North Carolina Press, 1990.

McCallum, John D. *College Basketball, U.S.A., since 1892*. New York: Stein and Day, 1980.

McLaurin, Melton A. *Separate Pasts: Growing Up White in the Segregated South*. Athens: University of Georgia Press, 1987.

McLendon, John B., Jr. *Fast Break Basketball: Fundamentals and Fine Points*. West Nyack, N.Y.: Parker Pub. Co., 1965.

———, ed. *The First CIAA Championship Basketball Tournament*. Westmont, Ill.: Scotpress, 1988.

Marchand, Roland. *Advertising the American Dream: Making Way for Modernity, 1920–1940*. Berkeley: University of California Press, 1985.

Martin, Charles H. "The Rise and Fall of Jim Crow in Southern College Sports: The Case of the Atlantic Coast Conference." *North Carolina Historical Review* 76 (July 1999): 253–84.

Matthews, Vincent, with Neil Amdur. *My Race Be Won*. New York: Charterhouse, 1974.

May, Elaine Tyler. *Homeward Bound: American Families in the Cold War Era*. New York: Basic Books, 1988.

Mebane, Mary Elizabeth. *Mary*. New York: Viking, 1981.

Miller, J. F., and W. C. Parker. *Physical Education in the High School*. Educational Publication 104. Raleigh, N.C.: State Superintendent of Public Instruction, 1926.

Miller, Marc S., ed. *Working Lives: The Southern Exposure History of Labor in the South*. New York: Pantheon, 1980.

Miller, Patrick B. "The Manly, the Moral, and the Proficient: College Sport in the New South." *Journal of Sport History* 24 (fall 1997): 285–316.

———. "To 'Bring the Race along Rapidly': Sport, Student Culture, and Educational Mission at Historically Black Colleges during the Interwar Years." *History of Education Quarterly* 35 (summer 1995): 111–33.

Mumau, Thad. *Dean Smith: A Biography*. Winston-Salem, N.C.: John F. Blair, 1990.

Murray, Pauli. *Proud Shoes: The Story of An American Family*. New York: Harper and Row, 1978.

Naismith, James. *Basketball: Its Origin and Development*. New York: Association Press, 1941.

Nasstrom, Kathryn. " 'More Was Expected of Us': The North Carolina League of

Women Voters and the Feminist Movement in the 1920s." *North Carolina Historical Review* 68 (July 1991): 307–19.

Oakley, J. Ronald. *God's Country: America in the Fifties*. New York: Debner, 1986.

Oriard, Michael. *Reading Football: How the Popular Press Created an American Spectacle*. Chapel Hill: University of North Carolina Press, 1993.

———. *Sporting with the Gods: The Rhetoric of Play and Game in American Culture*. Cambridge: Cambridge University Press, 1991.

Palladino, Grace. *Teenagers: An American History*. New York: Basic Books, 1996.

Parker, Inez Moore. *The Biddle–Johnson C. Smith University Story (A Historical Narrative)*. Charlotte, N.C.: Charlotte Press, 1975.

Paul, Joan. "Clara Gregory Baer: Catalyst for Women's Basketball." In *A Century of Women's Basketball: From Frailty to Final Four*, edited by Joan S. Hult and Marianna Trekell, 37–52. Reston, Va.: American Alliance for Health, Physical Education, Recreation, and Dance, 1991.

Peiss, Kathy Lee. *Cheap Amusements: Working Women and Leisure in Turn-of-the-Century New York*. Philadelphia: Temple University Press, 1986.

———. *Hope in a Jar: The Making of America's Beauty Culture*. New York: Metropolitan Books, 1998.

Perry, Thomas K. *Textile League Baseball: South Carolina's Mill Teams, 1880–1955*. Jefferson, N.C.: McFarland, 1993.

Peterson, Robert. *Cages to Jump Shots: Pro Basketball's Early Years*. New York: Oxford University Press, 1990.

———. *Only the Ball Was White: A History of Legendary Black Players and All-Black Professional Teams*. New York: Oxford University Press, 1992.

Pluto, Terry. *Tall Tales: The Glory Years of the NBA, in the Words of the Men Who Played, Coached, and Built Pro Basketball*. New York: Fireside Books, 1994.

Pope, Liston. *Millhands and Preachers: A Study of Gastonia*. New Haven: Yale University Press, 1942.

Porter, Earl W. *Trinity and Duke, 1892–1924: Foundations of Duke University*. Durham, N.C.: Duke University Press, 1964.

Pratt, Richard Henry. *Battlefield and Classroom: Four Decades with the American Indian, 1867–1904*. New Haven: Yale University Press, 1964.

Price, Joseph. "Education and the Race Problem." In *He Spoke Now They Speak: A Collection of Speeches and Writings of and on the Life and Works of J. C. Price*, edited by Walter L. Yates, 73–87. Salisbury, N.C.: Rowan Printing Co., 1952.

"Proceedings of the Eleventh Annual Meeting of the Association of Women and Advisors to Girls." *Quarterly Review of Higher Education among Negroes* 8 (October 1940): 288–39.

Quincy, Bob. *They Made the Bell Tower Chime*. Chapel Hill, N.C.: Campbell, 1973.

Rader, Benjamin G. *American Sports: From the Age of Folk Games to the Age of Televised Sports*. 4th ed. Upper Saddle River, N.J.: Prentice Hall, 1998.

Ramsey, David, prod. *Enduring Rivalry*. Charlotte, N.C.: Museum of the New South, 1994.

———. *Women's Rules*. Charlotte, N.C.: Museum of the New South, 1994.

Rappoport, Ken. *Tar Heel North Carolina Basketball*. Huntsville, Ala.: Strode Publishers, 1976.

Redin, Harley J. *The Queens Fly High*. Edited by J. P. Woodward. Privately printed, 1958.

Riess, Steven A. *City Games: The Evolution of American Urban Society and the Rise of Sports*. Urbana: University of Illinois Press, 1989.

——. *Touching Base: Professional Baseball and American Culture in the Progressive Era.* Westport, Conn.: Greenwood, 1980.

Robinson, Ray. *Iron Horse: Lou Gehrig in His Time.* New York: Harper Perennial, 1991.

Rodgers, Frederick A. *The Black High School and Its Community.* Lexington, Mass.: D. C. Heath, 1975.

Rose, Dan. *Black American Street Life: South Philadelphia, 1969–1971.* Philadelphia: University of Pennsylvania Press, 1987.

Rosenzweig, Roy. *Eight Hours for What We Will: Workers and Leisure in an Industrial City, 1870–1920.* New York: Cambridge University Press, 1983.

Rountree, Louise Marie. *Blue Bear Trax: Highlights of the Livingstone College Blue Bear Football Record and Gridiron Greats.* Salisbury, N.C.: Livingstone College, 1967.

Ruck, Rob. *Sandlot Seasons: Sport in Black Pittsburgh.* Urbana: University of Illinois Press, 1987.

Ryan, Mary P. *The Cradle of the Middle Class: The Family in Oneida County, New York, 1790–1865.* Cambridge: Cambridge University Press, 1981.

——. *Womanhood in America from Colonial Times to the Present.* New York: New Viewpoints, 1983.

Savage, Howard J., Harold W. Bently, John T. McGovern, and Dean F. Smiley. *American College Athletics.* New York: Carnegie Foundation, 1929.

Schwomeyer, Herb. *Hoosier HERsteria: A History of Indiana High School Girls Basketball.* Greenfield, Ind.: Mitchell-Fleming Printing, 1985.

Scott, Anne Firor. *The Southern Lady: From Pedestal to Politics, 1830–1930.* Chicago: University of Chicago Press, 1970.

Shaw, Stephanie. *What a Woman Ought to Be and to Do: Black Professional Women Workers during the Jim Crow Era.* Chicago: University of Chicago Press, 1996.

*Shaw University, Raleigh, North Carolina.* Boston: Frank Wood, 1902.

Sims, Anastatia. *The Power of Femininity in the New South: Women's Organizations and Politics in North Carolina, 1880–1930.* Columbia: University of South Carolina Press, 1997.

Slaughter, Enos, with Kevin Reid. *Country Hardball: The Autobiography of Enos "Country" Slaughter.* Greensboro, N.C.: Tudor Publishers, 1991.

Slowe, Lucy Diggs. "The College Woman and Her Community." *Journal of the Washington College Alumnae Club: L. D. Slowe Memorial Issue* (1939): 11–17.

——. "The Education of Negro Women and Girls." *Journal of the Washington College Alumnae Club: L. D. Slowe Memorial Issue* (1939): 8–11.

Smith, Ronald A. *Sports and Freedom: The Rise of Big-Time College Athletics.* Oxford: Oxford University Press, 1988.

Snider, William D. *Light on the Hill: A History of the University of North Carolina at Chapel Hill.* Chapel Hill: University of North Carolina Press, 1992.

Sperber, Murray. *Onward to Victory: The Crises That Shaped College Sports.* New York: Henry Holt, 1998.

Stanaland, Peggy. "The Early Years of Basketball in Kentucky." In *A Century of Women's Basketball: From Frailty to Final Four*, edited by Joan S. Hult and Marianna Trekell, 167–80. Reston, Va.: American Alliance for Health, Physical Education, Recreation, and Dance, 1991.

Stevens, Tim, and Rick Strunk, eds. *North Carolina High School Record Book.* Raleigh, N.C.: News and Observer Pub. Co., 1991.

Stone, Richard. "The Graham Plan of 1935: An Aborted Crusade to De-emphasize College Athletics." *North Carolina Historical Review* 64 (July 1987): 275–93.

Stoudemire, Alan. *A Place at the Table: The True Story of Two Men—Best Friends in Their Youth, Reunited in Adversity*. Atlanta: Cherokee Pub. Co., 2000.

Sumner, Jim L. "Everett Case Conquers Dixie: Hoosier Basketball in North Carolina." *Traces of Indiana and Midwestern History* 5 (fall 1993): 4–13.

———. *A History of Sports in North Carolina*. Raleigh: Division of Archives and History, North Carolina Department of Cultural Resources, 1990.

———. "John Franklin Crowell, Methodism, and the Football Controversy at Trinity College, 1887–1894." *Journal of Sport History* 17 (spring 1990): 5–20.

Tate, Merze. "The Justification of a Women's College." *Journal of the National Association of College Women* 14 (1937): 22–26.

Terkel, Studs. *Hard Times: An Oral History of the Great Depression*. New York: Pantheon, 1970.

Thompson, Paul. *The Voice of the Past: Oral History*. New York: Oxford University Press, 1988.

Thomson, Alistair. "Fifty Years On: An International Perspective on Oral History." *Journal of American History* 85 (September 1998): 581–95.

Tindall, George Brown. *The Emergence of the New South, 1913–1945*. Baton Rouge: Louisiana State University Press, 1967.

Tullos, Allen. *Habits of Industry: White Culture and the Transformation of the Carolina Piedmont*. Chapel Hill: University of North Carolina Press, 1989.

Tyack, David B. *The One Best System: A History of American Urban Education*. Cambridge, Mass.: Harvard University Press, 1974.

Tygiel, Jules. *Baseball's Great Experiment: Jackie Robinson and His Legacy*. Expanded ed. Oxford: Oxford University Press, 1997.

Tyson, Timothy. *Radio Free Dixie: Robert F. Williams and the Roots of Black Power*. Chapel Hill: University of North Carolina Press, 1999.

Valenti, John, with Ron Naclerio. *Swee'pea and Other Playground Legends: Tales of Drugs, Violence, and Basketball*. New York: Michael Kesend, 1990.

Varon, Elizabeth R. "Tippecanoe and the Ladies, Too: White Women and Party Politics in Antebellum Virginia." *Journal of American History* 82 (September 1995): 494–521.

Vennum, Thomas, Jr. *American Indian Lacrosse: Little Brother of War*. Washington, D.C.: Smithsonian Institution Press, 1994.

Waldrep, G. C., III. *Southern Workers and the Search for Community: Spartanburg, S.C.* Urbana: University of Illinois Press, 2000.

Walker, Vanessa Siddle. *Their Highest Potential: An African American School Community in the Segregated South*. Chapel Hill: University of North Carolina Press, 1996.

Walls, William Jacob. *Joseph Charles Price: Educator and Race Leader*. Boston: Christopher Publishing House, 1943.

Ward, Geoffrey C. *Baseball: An Illustrated History*. New York: Knopf, 1994.

Washington, Booker T. *Up from Slavery*. Williamstown, Mass.: Corner House Publishers, 1989.

Watts, Steven. *The Republic Reborn: War and the Making of Liberal America, 1790–1820*. Baltimore: Johns Hopkins University Press, 1987.

Weare, Walter B. *Black Business in the New South: A Social History of the North Carolina Mutual Life Insurance Company*. Urbana: University of Illinois Press, 1973.

Weber, Max. *Economy and Society*. Edited by Guenther Roth and Claus Wittich. Berkeley: University of California Press, 1978.

White, Shane, and Graham White. *Stylin': African American Expressive Culture from Its Beginnings to the Zoot Suit*. Ithaca, N.Y.: Cornell University Press, 1998.

Wiebe, Robert H. *The Search for Order, 1877–1920*. New York: Hill and Wang, 1967.

Wilkerson-Freeman, Sarah. "From Clubs to Parties: North Carolina Women in the Advancement of the New Deal." *North Carolina Historical Review* 68 (July 1991): 320–39.

Willard, Frances E. *How I Learned to Ride the Bicycle: Reflections of an Influential Nineteenth Century Woman*. Edited by Carol O'Hare. Sunnyvale, Calif.: Fair Oaks, 1991.

Williams, Horace. *The Education of Horace Williams*. Chapel Hill: H. H. Williams, 1936.

Williamson, Joel. *The Crucible of Race: Black-White Relations in the American South since Emancipation*. New York: Oxford University Press, 1984.

Wilson, Charles Reagan. *Baptized in Blood: The Religion of the Lost Cause, 1865–1920*. Athens: University of Georgia Press, 1980.

Winston, George Tayloe. *A Builder of the New South: Being the Story of the Life Work of Daniel Augustus Tompkins*. Garden City, N.Y.: Doubleday, Page, 1920.

Wolff, Alexander. *100 Years of Hoops: A Fond Look Back at the Sport of Basketball*. Birmingham, Ala.: Oxmoor House, 1991.

Wolters, Raymond. *The New Negro on Campus: Black College Rebellions of the 1920s*. Princeton, N.J.: Princeton University Press, 1975.

Wood, Stephen B. *Constitutional Politics in the Progressive Era: Child Labor and the Law*. Chicago: University of Chicago Press, 1968.

Wyatt-Brown, Bertram. *Southern Honor: Ethics and Behavior in the Old South*. Oxford: Oxford University Press, 1982.

## PAPERS, THESES, AND DISSERTATIONS

Adams, Gary B. "The Girls' Invitational State Basketball Tournament, 1950–1953, and Why and by Whom It Was Stopped." M.A. thesis, University of North Carolina, Chapel Hill, 1978.

Bishop, Elva E. "Amateur Athletic Union Women's Basketball, 1950–1971: The Contributions of Hanes Hosiery, Nashville Business College, and Wayland Baptist College." M.A. thesis, University of North Carolina, Chapel Hill, 1984.

Cloyd, Edward Lamar, Jr. "A Study of Girls' Interscholastic Basketball in North Carolina." M.A. thesis, University of North Carolina, Chapel Hill, 1951.

Dean, Pamela. "Covert Curriculum: Class, Gender, and Student Culture at a New South Woman's College, 1892–1910." Ph.D. diss., University of North Carolina, Chapel Hill, 1994.

Grundy, Pamela. "From *Il Trovatore* to the Crazy Mountaineers: WBT-Charlotte and Changing Musical Culture in the Carolina Piedmont, 1922–1935." M.A. thesis, University of North Carolina, Chapel Hill, 1991.

Jowers, Johnnie Edward. "A History of Men's Intercollegiate Athletics at Shaw University." M.A. thesis, North Carolina Central University, 1958.

Liberti, Rita. " 'We Were Ladies, We Just Played Basketball Like Boys': A Study of Women's Basketball at Historically Black Colleges and Universities in North Carolina, 1925–1945." Ph.D. diss., University of Iowa, 1998.

Lojko, Gloria Jean. "The Effects of Societal and Cultural Changes on the Historical Development of the Athletic Association at the State Normal and Industrial School in Greensboro, North Carolina, from 1900 to 1920." M.A. thesis, Appalachian State University, 1983.

Medwin, Jule Alfred. "A Study of Varsity Letter-Winners Who Graduated from the University of North Carolina from 1935 through 1951." Ph.D. diss., University of North Carolina, Chapel Hill, 1953.

Pugh, David Lee. "History of Men's Intercollegiate Athletics at Johnson C. Smith University." M.A. thesis, North Carolina Central University, 1960.

Shaw, Carol. "A City in Conflict: The 1919 Charlotte Streetcar Strike." Honors essay, American Studies, University of North Carolina, Chapel Hill, 1980.

Simmons, Sharon P. "Child Labor in North Carolina's Textile Industry: Its Genesis and Abolition." M.A. thesis, University of North Carolina, Charlotte, 1991.

Umstead, Elizabeth Claire. "Mary Channing Coleman: Her Life and Contributions to Health, Physical Education, and Recreation." M.A. thesis, University of North Carolina, Chapel Hill, 1967.

Waldrep, George C., III. "Politics of Hope and Fear: The Struggle for Community in the Industrial South." Ph.D. diss., Duke University, 1996.

Wall, Kathryn L. " 'We Always Loved to Play Basketball': A Window of Opportunity for Working-Class Women's Sports, Winston-Salem and Elkin, North Carolina, 1934–1949." M.A. thesis, University of North Carolina, Chapel Hill, 1994.

Williams, J. Derek. " 'It Wasn't Slavery Time Anymore': The Foodworkers' Strike at Chapel Hill, Spring 1969." M.A. thesis, University of North Carolina, Chapel Hill, 1980.

# ACKNOWLEDGMENTS

Any work that aims at synthesis first and foremost owes a debt to those who have gone before. While working on this project I had the great good fortune to be surrounded by stellar efforts, not simply in the books that I read but in a group of fellow scholars with an abiding commitment to history, to the South, and to the many ordinary citizens whose lives and labors have made this country what it is.

John Kasson's work helped me to see how the smallest details of everyday life, manners, and mannerisms come freighted with meaning. As my dissertation advisor, he was both challenging and encouraging, cheerfully enduring endless drafts and consistently pointing me toward the larger ideas and trends my stories illuminated. He never told me the project was too large—that a century was too much time to cover in a dissertation—or that I could hardly hope to move effectively between so many communities and perspectives. Neither did he suggest it was too small—that a single, southern state was not significant enough to warrant such attention. For this and for his constant, gentle support I am enormously grateful.

Jacquelyn Hall also encouraged this work throughout the many years between its inception and this final version. *Like a Family*, the multiauthor study of textile mill life that she directed, and one of the first works of academic oral history I encountered, remains a model for me to this day. Her thoughtful comments and her insistence on good writing echo through these pages, I hope not too faintly. Over our many years of friendship and association, I have only grown more impressed by the volume of work she does, by the guidance she provides her many students, and by her commitment to the significance of history for the present day.

As a teaching assistant in Jim Leloudis's undergraduate survey of North Carolina history I learned as much as I did in any graduate seminar. The vision of North Carolina's past I gained from that experience, as well as Jim's own work on southern schooling, have profoundly shaped my approach to this project. Both he and Lu An Jones, another fine scholar and North Carolina native, have also helped me learn how to simultaneously celebrate and ask hard questions, and to let affection for a state or region become a spur to a more searching examination of the points at which it has failed to live up to its ideals.

Studying with Glenn Hinson opened windows onto many worlds—most notably those of African American music—and taught me never to be surprised by the insight and ingenuity of ordinary people. He and his wife, Sally Peterson, have been both friends and inspirations, models for an approach to research that rests on thoughtful collaboration with the communities and individuals with which they work, demanding rigorous responsibility and self-evaluation of both themselves and their students. These are high standards to meet, but aiming at them has helped make this a better work.

Susan Cahn's writing opened up to me the world of women's sports at a time when this project was a museum exhibit rather than a book. In person she has been consistently and effectively encouraging, and she took time out of a busy schedule to give the manuscript a detailed and thoughtful critique, which helped me enormously in my final round of revisions. My understanding of women's sport draws heavily on her analysis as well as on the thoughtful interpretations—conveyed in conversation and in writing—of Mary Jo Festle and Rita Liberti.

Soon after leaving graduate school, at a time when many young scholars feel intellectually adrift, I was fortunate to meet the members of my writing group, Jerma Jackson and William Dargan. Over the past two years our meetings have offered one of the most rewarding intellectual experiences that I have ever had, as we have torn each other's work almost limb from limb but, in the process, developed a close and lasting friendship. This book—and my life—are far richer as a result.

Countless other friends and colleagues have contributed as well. During my years of dissertation writing, Peter Coclanis was always quick to read chapters, offer support, and make sure that I avoided an overly romantic view of any subject that I covered. Tom Hanchett, himself a skilled scholar of cultural endeavors, introduced me to the city of Charlotte, where I first began my study of North Carolina. Over many years he and his wife, Carol Sawyer, have proved both good colleagues and great friends. David Cecelski's work on Hyde County schools helped me chart the dynamics of state school desegregation, and he also was generous enough to read the entire manuscript, offering buoyant enthusiasm at a time when I greatly needed such encouragement. Molly Rozum also read the entire work, only adding to the enormous debt I owe her for her generosity with both her Chapel Hill apartment and her marvelous library. David Thelen, Donald Matthews, Peter Wood, Glenda Gilmore, Pamela Dean, Peter Filene, David Whisnant, Joel Williamson, Harry Watson, and numerous other colleagues have influenced my thinking about sports, culture, and history. I have also had the support of a wide range of fellow students, among them Lisa Aldred, Jen Ritterhouse, Barbara Lau, Erin Kellen, and Alicia Rouverol, who have helped keep me going through the years.

This project began as a museum exhibit called *The Most Democratic Sport* and sponsored by Charlotte's Museum of the New South. In this and other projects, museum staff and associates Robert Weis, Amy Swisher, Emily Zimmern, Cathy Grybush, Sally Robinson, and especially Jean Johnson have offered a wide range of comments, advice, and support, and I greatly value my association with them. Museum research associate Peter Felkner, a fine oral history interviewer, did a good portion of the research that became *The Most Democratic Sport*, and then this book.

I am also grateful to David Goldfield, who encouraged me to teach my first class on sports history, and particularly to Earl Edmondson and Sally McMillen, for making it possible for me to spend a pleasant and productive year in the history department at Davidson College. One class in particular— the oral history seminar I taught in the spring of 1999—contributed enormously to the final chapter of this book. Thanks to my students—Jill Williams, Brian Campbell, Laura Hajar, Kate Feldmeir, Amanda Covington, Michelle Markey, and particularly Mark Jones and Reid McGlamery—for helping me with both interviews and ideas.

Any historian also owes a great debt to the archivists and librarians who cheerfully search for materials, suggest sources, and help make sense of badly written reference notes. Among the many archivists who have helped me, I am particularly graceful to Jeff Hicks, Harry McKown, Alice Cotten, Jerry Cotten, and Bob Anthony at the North Carolina Collection; John White of the Southern Historical Collection; Sheila Bumgarner and Chris Bates of the Public Library of Charlotte and Mecklenburg County; Elizabeth Mosby of Livingstone College; Betty Carter of the University of North Carolina at Greensboro; Reginald Douglas of Johnson C. Smith University; Rosemary Arneson of Queens College; Carter Cue of Winston-Salem State University; Jan Blodgett of Davidson College; Stephen Massengill of the North Carolina Department of Archives and History; and James Cross of Clemson University. Rick Strunk of the North Carolina High School Athletic Association shared both his archives and his network of connections across the state. Perhaps most significant, he introduced me to the work of Catawba County sports historian Shayle Edwards, whose expansive view of high school sports has been both source and inspiration.

This project would have been far more daunting without generous support from several organizations. During my first three years at Chapel Hill, I was funded by a William R. Kenan Jr. fellowship, which spared me from many of the economic stresses history graduate students endure. I owe special thanks to the

Spencer Foundation, which has supported this work with both a dissertation fellowship and a National Academy of Education postdoctoral fellowship. A Spencer Foundation fellowship offers far more than monetary aid; the diverse range of fellow scholars I have met and talked with at Spencer-sponsored meetings have offered much stimulating food for thought. Throughout both experiences, the gentle presence of program officer Catherine Lacey has been comfort and inspiration. Several of the Charlotte interviews were funded by the Z. Smith Reynolds Foundation as part of an interviewing project conducted by the Southern Oral History Program. Thanks also to the University of North Carolina Press, to Ron Maner, Stephanie Wenzel, and especially to my editor, David Perry, for his strong advocacy of the work, his thoughtful and encouraging comments, and his patience.

The heart of this book, of course, lies in the generosity of the many North Carolinians who unselfishly took the time to share their sporting experiences and ideas, as well as the photographs that enliven these pages. Oral history is for me a constant source of intellectual and emotional renewal. The eloquence with which so many people relate their pasts, the life that flows so strongly through their words, and the insights they offer into their own experiences never fail to amaze and inspire me. I have done my best to convey that energy and grace and hope that it echoes, however remotely, in these pages.

Lastly, I owe endless thanks to my parents, Scott and Lois Grundy, who have given me all the support that any child could want, and especially to my husband, Peter Wong, who designed the breathtaking house in which I did most of my writing, and whose presence has made it an enduring joy to live there.

# INDEX